BIRDSCAPING IN THE MIDWEST

photo above: White-breasted Nuthatch

front cover top: Baltimore Oriole   bottom: Butterfly Weed

back cover top: House Wren   bottom: American Redstart

One of the most important things bird lovers can do is create bird habitats in their own backyards. —David Allen Sibley

photo: Cedar Waxwings

BIRDSCAPING IN THE MIDWEST

*A Guide to Gardening
with Native Plants to Attract Birds*

Mariette Nowak

Bird Photography by Jack Bartholmai

THE UNIVERSITY OF WISCONSIN PRESS

The University of Wisconsin Press
1930 Monroe Street, 3rd Floor
Madison, Wisconsin 53711-2059
uwpress.wisc.edu

3 Henrietta Street
London WC2E 8LU, England
eurospanbookstore.com

Library of Congress Cataloging-in-Publication Data

Birdscaping in the Midwest : a guide to gardening with native plants to attract birds / Mariette Nowak.
    p. cm.
Originally published by Itchy Cat Press in 2007.
Includes bibliographical references and index.
ISBN 978-0-299-29154-9 (pbk. : alk. paper) — ISBN 978-0-299-29153-2 (e-book)
1. Gardening to attract birds–Middle West. 2. Native plant gardening–Middle West. I. Title.
QL676.56.M53N69 2012
635'.04–dc23

2012020846

Designed by Flying Fish Graphics,
Blue Mounds, Wisconsin
Printed in Canada

photo: Sneezeweed

For my grandsons, Max and Wolfie, with the hope that they'll discover many wild things, not only in books but also in their own backyards.

CONTENTS

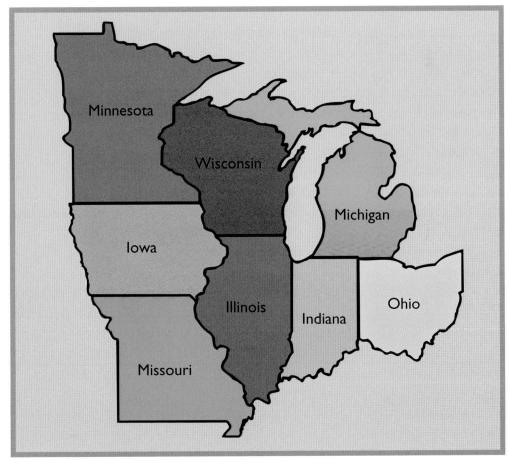

The region covered by this book includes these eight midwestern states.

ACKNOWLEDGMENTS

This book could not have been written without the able and loving assistance of my husband, Dave. His computer savvy helped me through numerous computer glitches and, in the final months of preparation, a complete computer breakdown and replacement. In addition, he made computer images of the garden designs and numerous other illustrations in this book, took many of the photos and edited several drafts of each and every chapter of this book.

I would also like to extend a special thanks to Jack Bartholmai for the many outstanding photographs of birds he so generously provided for this book. Anyone who has attempted to take photographs of birds knows the time, patience and dedication needed to achieve results of this quality.

My thanks as well to the many gardeners who shared their homes, yards, photos, expertise and philosophy with me: Patricia Armstrong, Pat and Carl Brust, Robert Cashman, Kitty L. Clasing, Susan and Paul Damon, Delene Hanson, Marion Lopina, Christine McCullough, Elizabeth Mueller, James B. and Mary Norton, Nathan Pate, Mandy Ploch, Tom and Nancy Small, Tom Ueberroth, Donna VanBuecken and Kim Lowman Vollmer. These dedicated environmentalists and their beautiful gardens have inspired me and will likewise, I believe, inspire the readers of this book.

Lorrie Otto, native landscaping pioneer, deserves special mention. She introduced me to the joys of landscaping with native plants and I have been grateful ever since. I would also like to thank Neil A.Harriman, curator emeritus of the University of Wisconsin–Oshkosh Herbarium, who gave guidance on plant nomenclature and reviewed the scientific names of the plants used in this book. The review of portions of this book by Sheryl De Vore and Steven D. Bailey was also much appreciated.

The Wisconsin Metro Audubon Society and the Milwaukee Southwest-Wehr Chapter of Wild Ones: Native Plants, Natural Landscapes deserve special mention for their generous contributions toward the color production of this book.

Finally, I'd like to thank my publishers, Caroline Beckett and Frank Sandner, for the beautiful design of this book, their meticulous devotion to detail, and all their efforts to insure superior quality in the production of this book.

I am most grateful that the University of Wisconsin Press has reprinted my book. They put my book on the fast track earlier this year and helped immensely with updates. Matthew Cosby in acquisitions did an exceptional job in coordinating the project. Editor Sheila McMahon was painstakingly thorough in proofreading my revisions, including the many websites listed as resources for readers. Many thanks to both of them.

FOREWORD

Earth is the only place in the universe with birds, plants and a great array of other species, including us humans. Yet many of the organisms around us—and not just the tigers of the world—are facing extinction. With the destruction of habitats, the spread of invasive species, the selective gathering of plants and animals in nature for food and medicine, and global climate change, it is likely that a majority of all the kinds of plants and animals in the world will become extinct during the course of this century. This book, with its emphasis on habitat restoration, shows how individuals, in their own yards, on their own properties, large or small, can begin the important steps toward reversing the destruction.

I firmly believe that individuals can and must play an essential role in preventing the loss of species. Like it or not, we're in the position of Noah just before the flood, looking at ongoing and worsening rates of extinction, and realizing that we alone are responsible for saving as many creatures as we can. And these creatures must be kept alive and well in many places to insure their survival in an unpredictable world, where small isolated populations can so easily be wiped out and lost forever. Unless we do so in our gardens, parks and other urban and suburban spaces, the level of extinction will be much greater—nature cannot be preserved in protected areas alone. And it is mainly in our gardens, city parks, and other such spaces that children will come into contact with nature, another deeply significant contribution to the future.

Gardeners can play a vital role by restoring and preserving many small patches of native communities with their associated plants, birds and other wildlife. As gardeners everywhere take up this enterprise, the various species will indeed have multiple chances for survival in many yards and neighborhoods and rural back forties. Ideally, these patches will, in time, become enlarged into corridors and broader expanses of native plant and animal communities interwoven within the fabric of human affairs. And the native species of every neighborhood and community will survive and thrive.

In *Birdscaping in the Midwest* Mariette Nowak takes the reader step by step along the path toward habitat restoration. While the focus is on bird habitat, other animals and plants will benefit from these restorations. Indeed, birds are considered barometers of the health of an ecosystem, and as birds increase or decrease, so also do all other species within that ecosystem.

In part 1, Nowak describes the complexities of coevolutionary relationships between birds and native plants. She defines the particular geography of a plant implied in the descriptive term "native" and explains the indispensable role that native plants play in providing habitat and resources for birds and animals. The threat posed by invasive exotic plants, especially as they affect birds, is appropriately highlighted.

In part 2, the stories behind natural habitat gardens in eight midwestern states are presented—gardens created on small city lots, in suburban subdivisions and on old farm fields. The gardeners share their motivations and methods, their challenges and rewards.

The rest of the book provides in-depth coverage of the nuts and bolts of habitat restoration. Part 3 outlines the basics of habitat restoration, with practical hands-on information on planning, design, site preparation, planting and seeding.

Part 4 sets this book apart from other treatments of landscaping for birds, with its specific plans and instructions for creating nine different habitat gardens for birds—the hummingbird garden, prairie bird garden, bluebird savanna garden, woodland bird garden, wetland bird garden, migratory bird garden, shrubland bird garden, winter bird garden, and water bird garden. While hummingbird gardens have long been popular, little has been written on the creation of these other distinctive and important bird habitats.

Part 5 provides details on the physical characteristics and cultivation of recommended plant species, along with their native ranges in the midwestern states. No other book on landscaping for birds provides as extensive coverage of the native plants of the Midwest.

Part 6 covers the maintenance of a habitat garden and its enhancement with feeders and birdhouses. Nowak also gives abundant practical advice on the problems gardeners may encounter, from plant-devouring deer and predatory cats to window collisions and bird diseases.

Many sources of further information are provided—books, pamphlets, websites, organizations, and native plant nurseries and consultants—all of which will be invaluable for readers.

Throughout the book, Nowak uses case histories and personal stories to illustrate her themes. And in the conclusion, she describes how the gardeners featured earlier have gone beyond their own garden gates to work for the protection and restoration of habitat on a larger scale in their neighborhoods and communities.

As I have often pointed out, ordinary people in the United States must think carefully about their own surroundings and how to preserve the biodiversity that occurs around them. The world that results will be a patchwork with bright spots, richer places and more beautiful areas. And that will happen because individuals took responsibility and acted.

We have relatively short lives, and yet by preserving the world in a condition that is worthy of us, we win a kind of immortality. We become stewards of the earth and our work lives on, generation after generation.

This readable and richly detailed book will serve as an indispensable reference for midwestern gardeners wishing to leave such a legacy. Unlike books that are national in scope, this one presents valuable information specific to the Midwest. Every region of our country needs its own guide of this kind.

—Peter H. Raven, President
Missouri Botanical Garden
St. Louis

•

INTRODUCTION

Like most folks, my husband and I once had lots of lawn and virtually all nonnative plants in our quarter-acre suburban Milwaukee yard. But gradually, over the years, we rescued native plants from sites under development and purchased many more from native plant nurseries. In time, we created a small prairie favored by finches, a mini woodland that drew migrant warblers and year-round woodpeckers, a shrubby corner visited by fall migrants, a hummingbird haven with a few of their favorite flowers and a small marshy spot where our sump pump discharged that was visited by Mallards and even by an American Woodcock.

These small pockets of habitat, lush with the beautiful native plant species of the Midwest, became a magnet for birds. Where once we had only a few common birds, we eventually had a bird species count of 78, not bad for a small lot in the most populated county in Wisconsin. When we moved not long ago, we sold the house in a week to a family that was thrilled with the natural landscaping, birds and other wildlife. The elderly mother, confined to a wheelchair, could enjoy lovely window views and a natural setting right outside the door.

We have since moved to a rural area and are again enhancing our yard—two acres—with the native shrubs, wildflowers and grasses it lacks. Much of the lawn will be replaced, and we removed most of the invasive nonnative shrubs last summer. Our orders are in to native plant nurseries, and in the coming spring our restoration efforts will begin anew.

The developers' adage "Build it and they will come" unfortunately has resulted in the loss of much habitat for birds, but we can help reverse this trend by building habitat. Birds will come and our properties will be enlivened with their color, beauty and music.

Beyond the Bird Feeder

There are 53 million backyard bird watchers in the United States and they spend over three billion dollars a year for bird food. But birds need more than sunflower seeds, suet and sugar water. They need a place to raise their young, hide from predators, rest, drink and bathe. They need a place that offers the native plants and animals upon which they depend for the majority of their food. In short, they need their natural habitats in order to thrive, far more than they need feeder food.

Many birds seldom or never eat at feeders, preferring natural foods—berries, insects, worms, seeds of native plants, small mammals, even other birds. Of the 78 species of birds we attracted to our suburban yard, only a third (26) ever visited our feeders and some of these only rarely, preferring natural foods. Craig Tufts, chief naturalist for the National Wildlife Federation, reports that of the 99 birds that he's found on his one-acre property, only 21 are feeder visitors.

The natural foods provided by native plants and animals are foods with which birds have evolved over long years of coexistence. A flock of several dozen Cedar Waxwings comes to our yard in spring not for the feeder food but for our serviceberries. They feast on the fruit, often passing the berries back and forth between mates before eating, then splash in the birdbath for a while. The

Cedar Waxwings bathe in the author's yard.

warblers come to scan the leaves and twigs of our pesticide-free trees and bushes for the bugs of their choice. Hawks come to feed on the songbirds, to the dismay of some bird lovers, but not to others who recognize hawks as a vital part of a healthy ecosystem, as well as creatures of beauty and brawn.

Even the regulars at bird feeders get only a portion of their nutrition from feeder food. A study by Margaret Brittingham and Stanley Temple from the University of Wisconsin found that chickadees depended on feeders for only 21% of their food. When they're not at your feeder, chickadees are gleaning the twigs and branches of trees for insect eggs, grubs and other critters. Goldfinches and Pine Siskins gorge on the seeds of native sunflowers and coneflowers, as well as on the niger seed you put out in a tube feeder. Sparrows, likewise, devour the seeds of prairie forbs. Hummingbirds imbibe the nectar of Orange Jewelweed, Michigan Lily and Oswego Tea, in addition to the sugar water in your feeder. Birds grew fat on all these natural foods for millions of years before feeders made the scene. Feeder food should be considered only as a supplement to the natural foods you provide in your yard by landscaping with native plants. Those plants will provide berries, nuts and seeds of choice throughout the year.

Birds also need nesting sites. Bird boxes and nesting platforms are invaluable, as bird lovers know. But snags and hollow trees with natural cavities are even better. Some birds are ground nesters that need unmowed grasses and low vegetation for their nest sites. Many feeder birds, like cardinals and jays, build nests on the limbs of shrubs and trees. Again native plants are better as nest sites—one study has shown that predation is significantly higher in nonnative shrubs than in natives, apparently due to a difference in branch structure.

Water is essential, too, and can be provided by birdbaths, ponds and other water features. A water garden surrounded with native plants can offer both food and cover.

In summary, then, you will want to provide your backyard birds with the best of the basics: food, cover, nesting sites, space and water. In supplying all these things, you'll create natural habitats for the birds you love. By landscaping with a diversity of native plants, you'll offer a year-round smorgasbord of insects, seeds and berries—in effect making your entire yard a supersized bird feeder. Standard bird feeders will merely supplement this natural fare. You'll offer evergreens and dense shrubbery for cover and for nest sites. You'll preserve snags and old trees with plenty of cavities, adding nest boxes as needed. And finally, you'll supply the birds with water for drinking and bathing, as they feed from the cornucopia in your yard.

Your Yard Can Bring Surprises

Best of all, you will love your new landscaping and the birds it brings. A naturally land-scaped yard is a constant surprise—you never know what you'll get. Several years ago in fall, we were thrilled and amazed to discover a Green-tailed Towhee, a western bird seldom seen in Wisconsin, scratching for seed below our feeders. My husband took digital photos, which helped document the bird for the Wisconsin Society for Ornithology. It was only the tenth record of this species in our state, and it was first time the bird had ever been seen in the fall of the year (it is a rare winter visitor). The Green-tailed Towhee prefers dense brush and chaparral, so perhaps the shrubby edges of our yard, thick with native dogwoods and viburnums, looked a bit like home to the towhee, who stayed for several days.

Another year, seventeen Christmas guests watched through our sunroom windows as our roosting Eastern Screech Owl woke and peered out its own "window"—the hole in a nest box. Then it perched on a snag, did some 270-degree head swiveling as only owls can and swooped off into the night. For most of our visitors, it was the first wild owl they'd ever seen. On another day, guests were captivated by a Cooper's Hawk perched on a shrub near the rear of our lot. It sat long and silently, as we all enjoyed wonderfully detailed views through our scope.

Birds of all kinds—mostly common, sometimes rare—will bring their aerial antics and beauty to your naturalized yard, too. And our outstanding native midwestern flora will encircle your home with ever-changing seasonal color, form and texture. In your new landscape, you will reestablish your link with nature on a daily basis. No need to wait for a vacation in a national park—a beautiful and intriguing world will beckon just beyond your doorstep.

The aim of this book is to inspire every bird lover to go beyond the bird feeder, dig up some lawn and begin planting some of our midwestern native plants. Whether you're transforming a small city lot, a suburban spread or a larger rural property, you'll be rewarded with a bounty of birds, the beauty of a natural landscape and the satisfaction of helping to heal the Earth around your home.

Plant Names

The common names of plants used in this book are, in most cases, those given in *Plants of the Chicago Region* by Floyd Swink and Gerould Wilhelm (4th ed., 1994). The Chicago region, as defined in that book, encompasses portions of four midwestern states and is located at the heart of the eight-state region covered in this book. *Plants of the Chicago Region* includes a substantial number of the plants common to all of the Midwest, many of which are of great value to birds, and provides extensive information on the ecology, habitats and companion species of these plants.

Common names, however, are not standardized and may vary from place to place. As a result, there may be numerous common names for a single species of plant. For example, Serviceberry (*Amelanchier* species) has also been called Juneberry, Saskatoon, Shadblow and Shadbush. In addition, there are more specific common names like Smooth Serviceberry, Running Serviceberry, Round-leaved Serviceberry, Inland Shadblow, Low Shadblow, Allegheny Shadblow and others, with little agreement as to which particular species each name refers to. For this reason I have included Latin names. Latin names are more consistent and standardized (although occasionally taxonomists change them).

In this book, the Latin names generally follow the *Manual of Vascular Plants of Northeastern United States and Adjacent Canada* by Henry A. Gleason and Arthur Cronquist (2nd ed., 1991), the most widely used reference in the Midwest. Although Latin names are usually standardized within a region, taxonomists sometimes disagree about how to classify and name a plant. In cases where taxonomists commonly use an alternate Latin name, I give this alternate name in parentheses after the name given in the Gleason and Cronquist manual.

When purchasing seeds or plants for your native plant garden, you will need Latin names to indicate exactly which species you want so you can be sure that the species you buy are native to the Midwest and not to another part of our country or even another country. And don't be afraid of mispronouncing them. I've heard all sorts of variations in the pronunciation, even by professional botanists and native plant growers.

The Latin names for species of plants are binomials; that is, they consist of two words. (They are italicized in print, except in a caption that's already italicized. Then they are roman type, to differentiate them.) The first part of the Latin name is the genus, and the second part is the species. For example, all true sunflowers have the genus name, *Helianthus*; Prairie Sunflower is named *Helianthus pauciflorus*. Large groups of related plants are called families. Sunflowers are in the aster family, along with asters, goldenrods and other similar plants.

Bird Names

Fortunately, the common names of birds are standardized by the American Ornithologists' Union (AOU). Those used in this book follow the seventh edition (1998) of the AOU's *Check-list of North American Birds* and the 45th supplement (2004) to the *Check-list*.

1 BIRDS & PLANTS

A Black-capped Chickadee probes for insects in a cluster of sumac berries.

If homeowners used native plants in their yards—which would enable them to control pests without using pesticides—it would represent the largest habitat-restoration program for birds ever undertaken.

—John Flicker, President, National Audubon Society

As background for your efforts in planning and creating bird habitats, part 1 describes the complex coevolution of plants and birds. This ancient collaboration has resulted in mutually beneficial relationships between birds and plants and attests to the value of using native plant species in creating bird habitats. You'll also learn fascinating details about research on the importance of native plants for birds, as well as data on the deleterious effects of some invasive exotic (nonnative) plant species on birds.

(previous page) A Hermit Thrush sits in a crabapple tree.

CHAPTER 1
An Ancient Collaboration

There is no finer animal to disperse a
seed than a migratory bird.
　　　　—John C. Kricher, *A Field Guide to Eastern Forests*

Cedar Waxwings gorge on the berries of Eastern Red Cedar and spread their seeds far and wide, reforesting cedar glades. Each fall, migrating thrushes fatten up on newly ripe berries, dispersing the seeds en route to wintering grounds. Hummingbirds sip on the nectar of Oswego Tea and, in so doing, carry its pollen from flower to flower, aiding in the pollination and subsequent seed production of these dazzling red flowers. Each spring, migrating warblers arrive just in time to feast on the emerging leaf-eating caterpillars, thus helping keep insects under control until the leaves build up their defenses. Such complex interrelationships between birds and native plants have been perfected over thousands of years of coevolution

The very names of birds, such as the Cedar Waxwing, often indicate the plants with which they've developed intimate associations. The Spruce Grouse thrives on the needles and buds of spruce trees. The Pinyon Jay devours pinyon pine seeds. The Acorn Woodpecker hoards acorns, and the Pine Grosbeak favors the seeds of northern pines. Three-fourths of the diet of Sage Grouse consists of the leaves and flower clusters of various species of sage.

Other names refer to the plants among which the birds court and nest and spend their lives—the Willow Flycatcher and Willow Ptarmigan, the Cactus Wren, the Alder Flycatcher, the Sedge Wren, the Sage Sparrow and Sage Thrasher. Then there are names associated with habitat, such as the birds of sunny, open spaces—Prairie Falcons, Prairie Chickens and the Eastern and Western Meadowlarks. And those of woodlands, like the Wood Duck, Eastern Wood-Peewee and Wood Thrush, and those in the northernmost forests, like the Boreal Chickadee. The Mangrove Cuckoo, similarly, inhabits coastal mangroves, and the Swamp Sparrow inhabits lowland swamps. All such names suggest the long and comingled evolution of birds and plants.

Birds help to pollinate plants, eat the insects that can ravage them and disperse their seeds. To entice birds and other animals to do these things, plants have evolved colorful, nectar-filled flowers and luscious, nutrient-packed fruits and seeds to nourish them. In addition, their limbs and leaves offer nesting sites and cover. It's been a long-standing and, literally, fruitful interrelationship for both.

photo: Frosty berries

Worldwide Service

Birds have had a profound influence on plant distribution throughout the world, says Henry F. Howe, an ecologist at the University of Illinois at Chicago. The Madder plant family (Rubiaceae), for example, is extremely widespread and its dispersal is largely attributed to birds. This family includes such midwestern representatives as Buttonbush, which ducks eat, and Partridge Berry, a low-growing ground cover. Turkeys, grouse and quail eat its bright red fruit.

Unable to move from place to place, fruiting plants depend on birds and other animals to disperse their seeds. Colorful, juicy fruits containing seeds are the bait plants have evolved to lure wildlife to do this work for them. If the seeds simply fell beneath the shrubs and trees, few would survive under the heavy competition from their parents and siblings for light, water, space and minerals. In addition, the masses of fallen seeds would likely attract seed "predators"—insects, rodents and other animals—who would destroy the seeds instead of dispersing them.

In contrast, when birds eat fruits, they digest the pulp and either regurgitate or excrete the seeds some distance from the parent plant. Cedar Waxwings, for example, defecate all the seeds they ingest, while thrushes regurgitate most seeds. Many fruit seeds cannot germinate without the removal of the pulp, which attracts molds within days. This is particularly true of fruits that are high in fat. Some seeds avoid this problem by germinating quickly, in less than a week.

For many fruit-bearing plants, the birds are as important for removing pulp as for dispersing seeds. I discovered this when we tried to restore an understory of herbaceous plants in a woodland at the nature center where I worked. We had removed the invasive buckthorn and honeysuckle. We planned to collect fruits of woodland plants like Jack-in-the-Pulpit and Blue Cohosh to plant in the restoration site. In researching the subject, we learned we had to remove the pulp. But how would we do that? It turned out to be a ridiculously messy and difficult job. We tried a blender, but separating the seeds from the slippery, macerated pulp was quite a chore. Nurseries work on a large scale and use machines like harvest mills, feed grinders and even concrete mixers to prepare seeds. Birds accomplish this job—a major undertaking for us—efficiently and economically.

In the past, it was also thought that scarification, or scraping of the seed coat as it passes through the guts of the birds, was important to the seed's germination. In reality, only a few birds actually scarify seeds, says Howe (in D. R. Murray, ed., *Seed Dispersal* 1986, Academic Press). Furthermore, damage to the seed coat could actually harm the seed and prevent germination. It was thought that the feces surrounding defecated seeds act as fertilizer and enhance germination. While this may be true in some cases, a few studies, including one by Gretchen A. Meyer of Williams College and Mark C. Witmer of Cornell University, have shown that regurgitated seeds germinate better than those "planted" with feces. The feces may reduce germination by attracting bacterial or fungal growths on the seeds. Nonetheless, seeds passed by birds either through regurgitation or excretion have been found to germinate better than seeds simply taken from trees. We have much to learn about the details, but there's no question that birds do an outstanding job in dispersing and "planting" seeds.

They do such a great job, in fact, that birds have sometimes frustrated human whims. In the eighteenth century, the Dutch wanted to maintain a monopoly in the nutmeg trade, but to their dismay, fruit pigeons carried the seeds to other islands. Even islands thousands of miles from the continents, like the Hawaiian Islands, have many plants with fleshy fruits which have evolved from species carried, as seeds, by birds from the mainland.

In the Midwest, Blue Jays were important in establishing the oaks as the weather became too warm and dry to support the conifer forests that came in after the Ice Age. The jays brought acorns from the south and, like squirrels, sometimes buried them but failed to retrieve them. The oaks began to thrive at a rate far faster than could be accomplished by ground-bound squirrels, who generally hide acorns only about 150 feet away from the oaks on which they feed. Blue Jays, in contrast, carry acorns one to two miles before stashing them, making this winged dispersal over 35 times faster.

This dispersion of plants is still going on today in our midwestern landscape. In a study at the Argonne National Laboratory in Illinois, researcher Albert Smith found that birds spread 13 different fruiting species in a plantation of Jack Pines. While Jack Pines are nonnative to that area, the species the birds introduced were largely native and included cherries, grapes, raspberries, mulberries, sumac, roses, elderberries and Virginia Creeper. Unfortunately, some species introduced by the jays were the troublesome invasives, buckthorns and honeysuckles.

Birds are so important as dispersers and pollinators of

SOME OTHER FRUIT-EATING BIRDS

Finch Family
Northern Cardinal
Rose-breasted Grosbeak
Pine Grosbeak
Evening Grosbeak
Purple Finch
House Finch

Swallow Family
Tree Swallow

Flycatcher Family
Great Crested Flycatcher
Eastern Kingbird

Vireo Family
Red-eyed Vireo
Warbling Vireo

Titmouse Family
Tufted Titmouse

Wood Warbler Family
Yellow-rumped Warbler
Yellow-breasted Chat

Kinglet Family
Golden-crowned Kinglet
Ruby-crowned Kinglet

Tanager Family
Summer Tanager

Blackbird Family
Orchard Oriole
Baltimore Oriole

Sparrow Family
Fox Sparrow
Harris's Sparrow
White-crowned Sparrow
Eastern Towhee

flowering plants that the "ecological balance in nature would be seriously disturbed without them," wrote the late Wisconsin ornithologist Joel Welty, in *The Life of Birds* (1975, W.B. Saunders Company). In the eastern deciduous forests alone, says Audubon ornithologist Stephen Kress, over 300 species of trees, shrubs and vines depend on birds to spread their seeds. And that doesn't even take into account the many herbaceous plants, like Jack-in-the-Pulpit, Solomon's Seal and baneberries, whose fruits are eaten and dispersed by birds.

Billboards for Birds

Like living billboards, plants advertise their wares to avian fly-bys. And like ad artists, they use color as a come-on. Most birds, with the exception of such night birds as owls and Whip-poor-wills, see the full palette of colors that we do. Plants have evolved using color to entice birds to stop for a taste. Bright red is an all-time favorite among birds. That's why so many plants have red fruits—from raspberries and strawberries to sumac berries and rose hips. Darker colors, like deep blue and violet to black, also are popular with birds. In an Illinois study by ecologists Mary F. Willson of the University of Illinois and John N. Thompson of Washington State University, these darker hues were found to be the most common fruit colors in trees (54% of 13 species) and shrubs and vines (60% of 101 species).

The combination of red and dark colors can be even more irresistible than either alone to avian gourmets. Sometimes two colors occur simultaneously in the fruit of the plant—the unripe fruit is red and the ripe fruit is dark blue or black. Usually, however, unripe fruit is green, not red.

Seeking to discover why some fruits are red when they are "green" (that is, unripe), ecologists Willson and Michael N. Melampy of the University of Puerto Rico experimented with various color displays of the fruits of Black Cherry and Pokeweed in an Illinois woodland. Black Cherries often show a natural color contrast, with immature red fruits displayed at the same time as the ripe dark fruit. Pokeweed has bright pinkish red stems, reddish immature fruit and ripe black fruit. The researchers offered the birds the mature fruit with and without the red contrasts and found that the birds ate much more of the fruit presented in the black and red displays.

What's in it for the plants? Why should they bother displaying several colors of fruit at once? By catering to the birds' preferences, the plants increase the likelihood that the birds will feed on them. But more than that, by offering only a limited number of ripe fruits at any one time, chances are that more of them will be dispersed and also that they will be eaten quickly, before they rot.

Other biologists, including John C. Kricher, suggest that the duller colors characteristic of most unripe fruits—orange, yellow, and green—are used as "pre-ripening flags." For example, a typical berry is often green at first, then turns pink or red, and finally, blue or purple. This is particularly true of summer-ripening fruits like blueberries, blackberries and mulberries, as well as black cherries. The pale and subtly changing colors may help alert resident birds to the fact that ripe fruit will soon be available and encourage them to remain in the area until they can eat the ripe fruit. And this, of course, maximizes the successful dispersal of the fruit.

There are other benefits to these pre-ripening flags. Some birds begin to leave their nesting territories to forage on fruits in midsummer. Woodpeckers of several species, for example, have been observed feeding on black cherries in areas where they don't nest. In addition, the young of some species, such as thrushes, robins and towhees, are often fed fruit by their parents. Once independent, juvenile birds are likely to continue to eat fruit. Since they're still discovering what's good to eat, the various fruit flags may entice them to sample and disperse these fruits.

In early autumn, plants frequently use two-color displays to hawk their wares. Although their fruits are not always red, the presence of bright stems, bracts or colorful leaves helps to bring in the birds. Gray dogwood, for example, has white fruit on ruby red stems, making a great show.

Other plants lose the green chlorophyll in their leaves at the same time their fruit is ripening in fall. The bright underlying orange and gold pigments in the leaves make their debut; after further chemical action, the famous reds of the season appear. All these bedazzling colors provide a brilliant backdrop for berries. The creamy white berries of poison ivy and the deep blue fruits of wild grapes and Virginia Creeper are irresistible when framed in fall foliage and are especially conspicuous as they entwine around tree trunks. Even we humans can be enticed by the beauty of these berries. Several acquaintances of mine have unknowingly picked poison ivy berries for fall decorations. One was a botany student who added the vine branches loaded with berries to a fall bouquet of dried wildflowers; the other, a neighbor, had a beautiful wreath of poison ivy berries on her door! Although the berries are poisonous to so many of us, birds eat them and suffer no ill effects.

Other species with an early flush of fall color include Black Gum, Sassafras, Spicebush, sumacs and dogwoods. Biologists suggest that such "foliar fruit flags," as they're called, may serve as long-distance signals to help migrating birds quickly locate food supplies as they wing their way to their wintering grounds. Many plant species with foliar fruit flags are widely scattered, so they need a big splash of color to help birds find them. In addition, many have a high fat content causing them to rot readily—all the more important that birds find and eat them as quickly as possible.

Willson and Thompson found that about 30% of woody plants, including trees, shrubs and vines, produce two-color displays in Illinois and this is likely to be true for much of the Midwest. These two-tone displays tend to occur before and after peak migration, in both Illinois and the Carolinas. Birds are fewer then, mostly resident birds, and the plants apparently "work" harder to attract birds and increase the probability that the birds will find and eat their fruits.

Could all the wonderful fruit colors and visual displays have occurred simply by chance, instead of through natural selection spurred by the coevolution of plants and birds? Willson and Thompson don't think so. Such a large variety of plant groups has developed bicolor fruit displays that it seems unlikely to be accidental. They also point out that the green-red-black sequence of some species, like cherries, is not a physiological necessity. The fruits of many other species turn from green to black without the intermediate red color, including Carrion Flower which is found in the Midwest. Some genera, in fact, contain species both with and without bicolor displays, including sarsaparilla, buckthorn and hawthorn.

In contrast to the "off-season" gala displays of two-color fruits and foliage, one-color fruit displays are more likely to be offered during peak migration. Willson and Thompson found this to be true, again, in both Illinois and the Carolinas. There's less need for a big splash of color when there are hungry masses of migrating birds eager to feed on all the fruits they can find.

How amazing are all these evolution-guided intricacies in the relationships between birds and plants! Furthermore, plants offer various nutritional packages of perfect size, precisely timed for the birds' requirements. It seems that plants are not only advertising wizards, but also marketing specialists to boot.

A Smorgasbord to Please

Fruits & Seeds. Besides color, bird-distributed plants have adapted the size of their fruits to attract birds. Although size varies from the very small fruits of elderberry to the larger cherries, most "bird" fruits are about 3/5 inch in diameter, making them the perfect size. Birds, in turn, especially those who eat only fruit, have adapted by evolving bills with wider gapes, so they can swallow the fruit whole.

Some fruits, of course, attract both mammals and birds. These include the berries that ripen in mid to late summer—blueberries, blackberries, huckleberries, strawberries, mulberries, plums and cherries. Most of these berries are displayed within six feet of the ground, in easy reach of both mammals (who don't climb much) and birds. The fruits are also very tasty and fragrant, making them especially appealing to mammals. Birds generally have poor senses of smell and taste, so these attractants have likely evolved to appeal to mammals, not birds. Mice, squirrels, fox, raccoons and bears are some of the mammals that feed on these berries, not to mention we humans who grow and cultivate many of these delicious fruits.

The berries on this crabapple are the perfect size for a robin's beak.

The plums and wild cherries, all in the *Prunus* genus, are among the most abundant fruiting plants of northern forests. The cherries, in particular, have outstanding value for wildlife. They usually display their fruits above six feet, with the mammals generally eating those that fall to the ground. While small rodents like mice and chipmunks usually gnaw on and destroy the seeds in these fruits as they eat, the larger mammals and birds leave the seeds intact, dispersing them through regurgitation or excretion. Forty-nine different species of birds have been documented feeding on these species (primarily the cherries), as well as skunks, opossums, raccoons and fox.

It is also interesting to note that the fruits of summer attract both resident mammals and birds. Not so with fall fruits. These appear to be "designed" almost exclusively for birds, at a time when resident populations of birds swell with migrants. The dogwoods, viburnums and other fall-fruiting species are devoured by birds, but lack the taste and aroma needed to entice mammals. There was no need, no evolutionary mandate, to attract mammals, given the bounty of birds in autumn. Another intriguing piece of the coevolutionary puzzle!

Seasonal Menus. The berries of summer are timed not only to supply supplementary food as the early flush of insects is diminishing, but also to provide birds with just the right nutrients for the season. Chock-full of sugars (carbohydrates), the berries ripen just when parent birds, busy with nestlings, need these kinds of nutrients. Soon after, the active fledglings, newly emerged from the nest, will also benefit from the berries.

As nestlings, young birds require the high protein content of insects and worms—the pursuit of which creates the high-carbohydrate needs of their parents. Fruits contain only 3 to 13% protein (dry weight), while insects may be up to 70% protein (dry weight). But once out of the nest and adult size, the young birds need more sugars and less protein, so fruits are the perfect answer to their needs at this time.

Basically, fruits provide three kinds of nutrient packages, each offering a well-balanced diet geared to the seasonal variations in the birds' activities. An avian dietician would be delighted! The summer fruits are usually high in sugar and low in fat. Fall ripening fruits, on the other hand, generally present two types of nutrient packages. Some fruits are high in fats and low in carbohydrates; others are low in both fats and carbohydrates.

The differences in these fall fruits can be significant. For example, the high-fat fruits of Spicebush have 47% fat; magnolias, 33–62% and Flowering Dogwood, 24%. The low-fat fruits, on the other hand, typically have less than 10% fat by weight. Hawthorns average about 6%, Choke Cherry has 5% and Cat Briar has 0–1%. All these nutrients, incidentally, are not used by the plants themselves and seem to have evolved solely to attract birds and other animals that help disperse their seeds.

Over 70% of the fruits of bird-distributed plants ripen in fall, perfectly timed for peak migration. Trees, shrubs and vines are laden with fruits ready to feed the masses of migrating birds, many returning from nesting sites in Canada and the northern states. Fruit-eating birds begin to move south in August, their numbers peaking in mid-September—which are precisely the months when the fruits ripen for them. "Clearly," says Kricher in *Eastern Forests*, "the plants have evolved the timing of fruit production to attain the maximum probability of being eaten by a bird."

Plants even accommodate the migrating schedules of birds, ripening first in the North, later in the South. For example, in New England, most tree and shrub fruits ripen in August and September, which coincides with the migration of thrushes and other birds. In the Carolinas, the fruits ripen a month later, providing these same migrants with a continuous food supply as they wing their way farther south. This timing is all the more remarkable considering plants in the South generally flower earlier in the spring, sometimes by as much as six weeks, and could reasonably be expected to produce ripe fruit a month earlier, rather than a month later.

THE MIDWEST'S MOST FRUGIVOROUS* BIRD

Cedar Waxwings love fruit and are one of the few temperate birds to specialize in fruit-eating. Fruit makes up about 70% of their diet, and nearly their entire diet from fall to early spring. From their bills to their behavior, waxwings show many adaptations and habits related to their specialty.

The bills of Cedar Waxwings are short, broad and slightly hooked—perfect for gripping and swallowing fruit.

Like many fruit-eating birds, Cedar Waxwings are almost always found in flocks. Because fruits are patchy in distribution, flocks of birds can more effectively search for patches of fruiting shrubs or trees than can an individual bird. This also explains why they are a nomadic, irruptive species—they show up where they find fruit.

Cedar Waxwings can survive on fruit alone for several months. They defecate the seeds in the fruits, unlike most birds, which regurgitate the seeds.

Cedar Waxwings sometimes succumb to alcohol intoxication and can even die by feeding on fermented fruit.

(continued)

Cedar Waxwings choose nesting sites near sources of fruit. Nestlings are fed insects at first; berries are added within a few days. The color of their tail tip is related to the fruit they eat. While normally yellow, the tip of the tail sometimes is orange, if waxwings have eaten berries of a nonnative honeysuckle. Ornithologists fear this could disrupt their social interactions.

Fruit is also important in waxwing courtship. The male hops toward the female with a berry in his beak. She may take the berry, hop away, then come back and pass the berry to him. This can be repeated up to fifteen minutes until one of them eats the berry. Mating often takes place after this courtship ritual. Watch for this behavior in late winter and early spring.

The "Cedar" in their name comes from their fondness for the berries of the Eastern Red Cedar (*Juniperus virginiana*), the most common juniper in the Midwest and eastern North America. "Waxwing" comes from the waxy red tips on their wings, which may play a part in mate selection.

Besides cedar berries, important fall and winter fruits for Cedar Waxwings include those of hawthorns, grapes, viburnums, mountain ash and crabs. Summer favorites include strawberry, serviceberry, mulberry, cherry, blueberry and blackberry.

*(Froo-jiv'-er-us) *adj.* feeding on fruit

To sustain them during the rigors of migration—literally to keep them airborne—birds need to build up large deposits of subcutaneous fats. High-fat fruits are ideal. Fats provide twice the amount of energy per unit dry weight as do carbohydrates and allow the birds to store more fuel for less weight than they could with the sugar-laden fruits of summer. Not surprisingly, the ravenous birds devour the high-fat fruits at each stop on their journey south. In a New Jersey study, the fruits of Spicebush which had ripened in the first two weeks of September were largely gone in less than two months. Birds dispersed 77% of the fruits by October 31 one year, 90% the next.

Other fall-ripening fruits are far less popular with migrating birds. Some, like sumac, are high in fat but have so little flesh that they don't offer much per beakful. These fruits, along with those that are low in both fat and carbohydrates, tend to hang on the plants well into winter and even into early spring. In a study in New Jersey, Maple-leaved Viburnum retained more than 70% of its fruit into January. Long-lasting fruits provide an important source of food for wintering birds and returning spring migrants.

Why aren't all fall-fruiting plants high in fats, since birds prefer them? The major problem for plants is that the fatty fruits, so popular with birds, are also popular with microbes and tend to rot more quickly. They must be eaten and dispersed quickly. To better balance supply and demand and ensure quick consumption, high-fat fruits tend not to ripen at the same time. In New Jersey, peak fruiting of high-fat Spicebush occurs before that of Flowering Dogwood, another high-fat species.

Low-fat species, on the other hand, use another tactic. Although their fruits are not eaten as readily by migrating birds, they don't rot as easily due to their low fat content. Their fruits persist until late fall and winter, and even into spring, when other fruits aren't available and the hungry birds readily eat them during these leaner seasons.

Perfect Pollinators

Besides the complex collaborations between birds and the fruits they eat, there is an equally intriguing coevolution between hummingbirds and the flowers they pollinate. Many of these flowers evolved to attract hummingbirds and many are brilliant red. How fortunate we are, for hummingbirds and many of the flowers on which they feed are unique to the Americas. No

Gray Dogwood berries

hummingbirds hover in the gardens of Europe and other parts of the world. I'll discuss more of the fascinating details about hummingbird/flower coevolution in chapter 8.

Insects, Plants & Birds

Another mutually beneficial interrelationship between birds and plants involves a third group of players: insects. Plants, as we know, are attacked by many insects and other invertebrates. The upside is that, by inadvertently harboring these insects, plants provide the insect food needed by birds, particularly during certain times in their life cycle. Birds, in turn, provide a critical service for plants by eating the insects that harm them. Thus, plants as insect hosts and birds as insect predators are intertwined in yet another complex collaboration advantageous to both.

Songbirds are particularly active as insect predators during nesting when young birds need copious servings of insect protein for their growth. Birds, in fact, seem to time their nesting to coincide with plentiful supplies of insects. As biologist Paul Ehrlich points out in *The Birder's Handbook,* "For most birds, the young hatch and grow when insects are abundant."

Parent birds favor the large, juicy, late-stage caterpillars for feeding their young and, in doing so, play a key role in controlling insect populations. One pair of Evening Grosbeaks can dispatch up to 50,000 caterpillars while raising a family. Studies

BIRD DIET STUDIES

Discovering what birds eat is not always an easy job. You may see a Downy Woodpecker catching insects as it forages on tree trunks—but which insects? Perhaps you spot an Eastern Phoebe darting out from its perch, time and time again, as it "fly-catches"—but is it catching true flies or some other flying insects? You might catch a Brown Thrasher pulling up a worm-like critter from the leaf litter in your yard—but is it a caterpillar, grub or earthworm?

Because of such difficulties, the early ornithologists in our country relied on careful examination of the content of birds' stomachs to get an accurate idea of their feeding habits. In 1885, the federal government officially began such research into food habits of wildlife. The data on stomach contents of various species of birds (as well as other animals) were recorded on examination cards, which eventually numbered over a quarter of a million. Since this kind of research involves the slaughter of many birds, stomach analysis is seldom used today.

Field observation of bird feeding habits supplemented stomach analysis studies even in the early days and is still an important method of study today. Another approach, the study of bird droppings, began to be used in the late 1930's and, like field observation, is harmless to birds.

Owls are among the easiest birds to study regarding their food preferences. They regurgitate the indigestible items in their meals, like bones and fur, in the form of a

(continued)

pellet. Examination of these pellets can identify the prey on which owls feed. (I discovered the bones of a vole in the pellet of a screech owl that roosted in a nest box in my yard.) Long-eared Owls may be the best studied of all. An estimated 30,000 prey items of this owl have been identified in pellets from North America, plus another 300,000 from Europe.

The results of 65 years of research, from 1885 to 1950, using these various methods, are interpreted and summarized in *American Wildlife and Plants: A Guide to Wildlife Food Habits,* by Alexander C. Martin, Herbert S. Zim and Arnold L. Nelson (Dover, 1951), a classic that is still widely used and referenced today.

In recent years, scientists have used a new technique to study the foods that nestlings eat. They gently place pipe cleaners around the throats of nestlings so that they can't swallow, but can still breathe. The food brought by the parent birds can then be taken for analysis. This difficult method must be carried out carefully so that the nestlings don't suffer injuries or malnutrition.

There is still much to learn about the foods birds eat, and field observation of the variations in avian diets continues to be important. All of us, as citizen-scientists, can aid in this research by recording and publishing our careful observations. (The journals of state ornithological societies often publish observations by local birders.) You may even make discoveries right in your own backyard!

have also shown that birds can eat 98% of spruce budworms, a pest of eastern forests that has periodic population explosions. During insect outbreaks, some bird species produce more offspring due to the abundant food supply.

Birds are also important predators of insects during their spring migration in the Midwest, researchers have found. On their journey north, many birds migrate in perfect timing with the emergence of caterpillars that devour the newly forming leaves on shrubs and trees. Later in the year, the leaves will develop tannins and tough cuticles to help protect them from the onslaught of insects. But meanwhile, the birds provide damage control while feasting at the avian sushi bars provided by oaks, hickories, willows and other plants.

This new research on migratory birds and insects has uncovered another important fact. Only native plants host abundant insects. Nonnative plants are significantly less popular with our native insects and could play a part in causing the declining populations of some insect-eating birds. More about this intriguing research in later chapters.

Evolutionary Lessons for Bird Lovers

This ancient collaboration, this long and complex co-evolution between plants and birds, embodies a lesson for all bird lovers. Simply put, *native plants are best for our native birds*. As Stephen Kress of the National Audubon Society has said, "Native plants, which have co-evolved with native wild birds, are more likely to provide a mix of foods—just the right size, and with just the right kind of nutrition—and just when the birds need them."

Not only are our native plants best for our native birds, they're best for the place we live and the easiest to grow because these plants evolved with the birds, climate, precipitation, soil, insects, other flora, fauna and physical characteristics of our area. When planted on sites similar to their natural habitats, natives will survive the gales and cold of our midwestern winters and the hot, desiccating days of summer without special care. They'll prosper in the soils to which they're accustomed—whether clay, sand, loam or muck. They'll survive the aphids, bugs and beetles with whom they've adapted through long centuries, or for some, over eons. Growing natives, in fact, is just what nature has done, without our help, since plants first graced our planet.

RESOURCES FOR READERS

Books

Kaufman, Kenn. 1996. *Lives of North American Birds*. Boston: Houghton Mifflin.

Kricher, John C., and Gordon Morrison. 1988. *A Field Guide to Eastern Forests: North America*. Boston: Houghton Mifflin.

Martin, Alexander C., Herbert S. Zim, and Arnold L. Nelson. 1951. *American Wildlife and Plants: A Guide to Wildlife Food Habits*. New York: Dover Publications.

Tallamy, Douglas W. 2007. *Bringing Nature Home*. Portland, OR: Timber Press.

Websites

Sterling, John. 2003. "How Birds Keep Our World Safe from Plagues of Insects." http://nationalzoo.si.edu/scbi/migratorybirds/fact_sheets/fxsht2.pdf

Downy Arrowwood berries

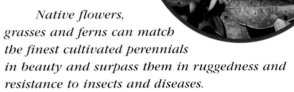

Native plants are those plants that existed in an area prior to European settlement. Since the time of settlement, however, plants have been introduced to the Midwest from other countries and from other regions of our own country. Once such exotic plants grow wild—on their own—they are said to be "naturalized."

Many of the plants growing along roadsides and in old fields, like Queen Anne's Lace, Ox-eye Daisy, Chicory and Smooth Brome Grass, are "naturalized" plants. Because they take over disturbed areas—areas where the native vegetation has been removed—they can become more abundant than native species. Some go on to become invasive in our natural areas. Naturalized plants are not native, nor should they be used in native habitat restorations.

There is also a great difference between natural landscaping with native plants and "naturalistic" landscaping. The latter is a trendy, popular style of gardening using great masses and sweeps of plants to imitate a wild natural look. But most of the plants used are non-native exotics, like ornamental grasses, daylilies and shrubs from abroad. These nonnative species don't offer any more value to wildlife in their new "naturalistic" arrangements than they did when

(continued)

photo: Field Sparrow

Native flowers, grasses and ferns can match the finest cultivated perennials in beauty and surpass them in ruggedness and resistance to insects and diseases.
— Jim Wilson, former co-host of PBS television's *The Victory Garden*

Now that you're ready to go native, you may be wondering—*just what is a native plant?*

Obviously, every plant is native to somewhere—to India or Africa, to Fiji or Hawaii, to California or Maine. Many of our houseplants are native to the tropics of South America or Africa. Our farm fields are filled with food crops from many parts of the world. While corn and squash are native to the Americas, rye and soybeans originated in Asia, oats in Western Europe and wheat is believed to have come from the Euphrates Valley in Iraq. Many garden plants, like lilacs and lilies-of-the-valley, were brought here by immigrants nostalgic for home.

Plants that are native to our own country are considered to be those that existed here prior to European settlement. Just a few hundred years ago, old growth forests, pristine wetlands and vast prairies swept across America from sea to sea, rich with such a variety and abundance of native plants that it astounded the early pioneers. Squirrels, it was said, could travel from the Atlantic to the Mississippi across the tops of the trees of our great eastern forests, without touching the ground. The beauty and breadth of our prairies, stretching from the eastern forests to the Rockies, amazed westbound travelers. Our wetlands and waterways were lush and beautiful with their own specialized flora, from great tamaracks and cypress trees to stunning orchids and huge beds of wild rice. And all these forests, wetlands and prairies offered habitat, shelter and food resources for our native birds and other wildlife.

Like all parts of our country, the Midwest has its own unique native flora, those plants that welcomed the first settlers from the East. We midwesterners are particularly lucky since we lie at the crossroads of the prairie/forest frontier. As a result, we enjoy a greater variety of native plant species, and their associated birds and wildlife, than many other parts of the country. We have the opportunity to reflect this bounty in our landscaping.

How Native Is Native?
The Question of Local Ecotype

In the Midwest, many species of plants are not native to the entire area. Some plants that are native to Wisconsin may not be native to Indiana. In fact, some species of plants may not be native to every part of your state. Plants grow in different geographic regions, sometimes called ecoregions, and these regions don't follow our artificially created state or county boundaries. In Wisconsin where I live there is a great difference between the species found in the northern half of Wisconsin—our North Woods—compared with those in the southern half of the state. Our North Woods vegetation is more like that of upper Michigan and northern Minnesota than that of Kenosha County in the southeastern corner of Wisconsin, where the vegetation is more akin to that of northern Illinois. There are other significant differences east to west.

The ecoregions within the United States have been delineated by the Environmental Protection Agency and by The Nature Conservancy, an organization dedicated to preserving the diversity of flora and fauna throughout the country, as well as worldwide. See the map on page 16 to determine your ecoregion.

Plants native to a particular locality or ecoregion are referred to as local ecotypes. (Sometimes, the term "local genotype" is used instead, with much the same meaning.) Plants or seeds derived from such local or regional sources and planted in similar environmental conditions will likely thrive.

A single plant species may have several ecotypes, each shaped by the local conditions in which it evolved. The Prairie Blazing Star in Minnesota is different from the same species in Indiana at the far eastern edge of its range. So what? In Minnesota, the Prairie Blazing Star has adapted to the special conditions in its native locale—the temperature extremes, the unique soil, the rainfall, the insects and humidity. If transplanted to Indiana, it may behave quite differently.

planted in the more regimented styles of the past.

Gardeners can achieve a more authentic natural look with native plants and get double the value for their efforts—a beautiful landscape, which also serves as natural habitat for birds, butterflies and small mammals.

American Cranberrybush Viburnum

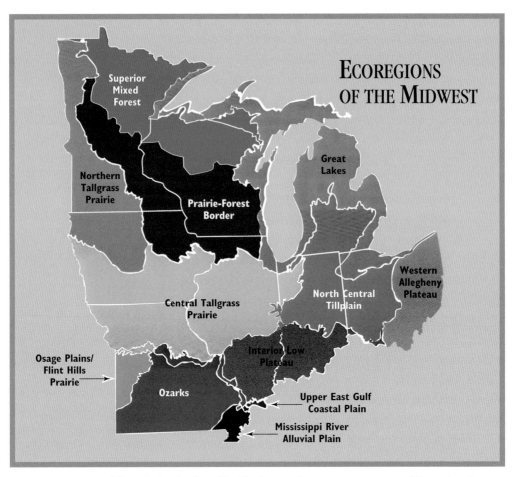

ECOREGIONS
OF THE MIDWEST

Superior
Mixed
Forest

Great
Lakes

Northern
Tallgrass
Prairie

Prairie-Forest
Border

Western
Allegheny
Plateau

North Central
Tillplain

Central Tallgrass
Prairie

Osage Plains/
Flint Hills
Prairie

Interior Low
Plateau

Ozarks

Upper East Gulf
Coastal Plain

Mississippi River
Alluvial Plain

Ecoregional boundaries developed by The Nature Conservancy as a part of Ecoregional Assessments in the continental United States, Alaska, Hawaii and Canada. Based on boundaries originally developed by Bailey (1995) and Environment Canada (Wilken, 1986). Data subject to continual revision and updates.

In a new location, a transplant from another ecoregion may not thrive at all or, in contrast, it may become aggressive, even invasive. The Red Maple is native throughout the eastern United States, but the Florida ecotype, transplanted to Minnesota, may well die during the tough northern winters.

On the other hand, Switchgrass grown from Nebraska seed is extremely aggressive in Wisconsin. Such seed was used in a prairie restoration at the Wehr Nature Center in Milwaukee County before local Switchgrass seed was available. Although prairie wildflower seeds had been included in the original seed mix, the Switchgrass was still dominant when I began to work there fifteen years later. For twenty years, it carpeted five acres and appeared to be a monoculture like a lawn or cornfield. Fortunately, the prairie forbs gradually gained a foothold, and today that restoration is a beautiful and varied quilt of prairie grasses and wildflowers.

Plants are also native to specific habitats within an ecoregion. Like cultivated perennials, some natives like it shady, some sunny, some dry, some moist, according to the habitats in which they are normally found. Some native species are found only in acidic bogs, others only in sunny prairies. Some thrive on dry cliffs, others on damp river banks.

True native plants not only are long-time residents of suitable habitats, but also retain their original genes. They have not been genetically engineered or hybridized. Corn, for example, has been cultivated and selectively improved for thousands of years. Recently, most of the corn grown in the U.S. has been genetically engineered to include Bt, which kills caterpillars that eat it. The original native corn is nearly nonexistent and has been found only in a few remote locations in Mexico.

Similarly, garden roses have long been selected and hybridized to enhance their beauty, blossom size or color. Unfortunately, most hybrid roses are difficult to grow and could not survive without the fertilizers, herbicides, water and winter protection that gardeners lavish on them. In the course of breeding, many cultivated plants have also lost much of their nectar and pollen so they provide little nourishment for hummingbirds, insects and other wildlife.

Cultivars of native plants are not usually local ecotypes. Cultivars are plants that are propagated asexually (generally by cuttings), instead of sexually by seed, and are actually clones of the original plant, with exactly the same genes. Usually the original plant was selected for showy blossoms, height, shape or some other desired characteristic. It is native only to its original location, not to other ecoregions. These cultivars would survive just fine in their original locales, but they are generally sold without any information about their local origins. As a result, they may require the same tender loving care as a tea rose in your yard. Or, like the transplanted Switchgrass, they could become quite aggressive in a new location.

Most important, by planting only the cultivars of a species, all having the same genes, we lose the genetic variation that gives that native species the flexibility to adapt to uncertain future occurrences, such as diseases, drought or global warming.

Most nursery stock, unfortunately, consists mainly of cultivars. Cultivars of the following species are widely sold but are unsuitable for a native habitat garden or restoration: asters, bergamot, goldenrods, sneezeweed, blazing stars, wild strawberries and Black-eyed Susan. A cultivar can usually be recognized by an added name, following its scientific name, that is capitalized, not italicized, and enclosed in single quotation marks. For example, the common Black-eyed Susan's scientific name is *Rudbeckia hirta*. A cultivar of this species is *Rudbeckia hirta* 'Indian Summer'.

HARDINESS ZONES, NATIVE RANGES AND ECOREGIONS

Can hardiness zones be used in selecting native plants? What about basing selections on native ranges or ecoregions? Is there a difference? These three approaches to selecting plants are described and contrasted below.

Hardiness Zones

Many gardening catalogs give information about hardiness zones for plants, based on the Plant Hardiness Zone Map published by the United States Department of Agriculture. This map divides most of North America into eleven climate zones, according to their average winter minimum temperatures. Subtropical Zone 11 has minimum temperatures above 40 degrees F., while Zone 1 has minimum temperatures of -50 degrees F. Because temperature is the single most important factor in determining whether a plant will survive, these zones help gardeners decide whether to select plants that are not native to their areas. Obviously, these hardiness zones are not useful for native plant gardeners who want to plant species native to their locale, where they are naturally hardy.

Native Ranges

Native ranges offer natural landscapers better criteria than hardiness zones for selecting plants. Most field guides and other books, including this one, give native ranges for plant species, listing the states in which the species are native. A plant, however, may not be native to all parts of a state.

(continued)

Prairie Blazing Star, like most plants, has different ecotypes in different parts of its range. Choose an ecotype of this species adapted to your area; it will thrive best in your garden.

Why Select Local Ecotypes

There are three important reasons for selecting local ecotype plants for your landscaping: to ensure your own success, to provide the best for birds and other wildlife and to ensure the genetic diversity of the plants themselves.

Successful landscaping. Any landscaping takes money and effort, so it makes sense to select native species that originate in your own ecoregion. Those plants are best adapted to your area and should thrive with minimal care, once established. Place the plants in sites that replicate the habitats in which the plants grow naturally. Take into consideration sun, shade, soil type, drainage, precipitation, slope and elevation. By doing so, you'll help ensure the success of your landscaping project.

Be sure to take advantage of seedlings of native species that serendipitously show up in your yard. Rick Darke, author of *The American Woodland Garden*, has discovered seedlings of American Beech, Pagoda Dogwood, Flowering Dogwood and Spicebush in his woodland garden. He uses them in his own landscaping and has given them as gifts to local gardeners.

Best for birds and other wildlife. The native plants of local origin are best for the birds native to your neighborhood. They also help the other local wildlife which, like the birds, co-evolved with these plants.

Local pollinators, insects, frogs, salamanders, squirrels and other animals—all depend on the native flora for food and shelter as do birds. Native plants may support 10 to 50 times as many species of native wildlife as nonnative plants, according to the National Wildlife Federation. You enrich the entire local ecosystem when you create native habitat for birds.

Genetic diversity. We need to preserve not only a diversity of species, but a diversity of genetic material within each species. Aldo Leopold wrote, "A species must be saved in many places if it is to be saved at all." Every local extinction brings a loss of genetic material for the species and threatens its survival. One ecotype might better compete with invasive species. Another might do better in our warming climate. Still another might be able to cope with a drought or flood. A diversity of genetic material offers many more options for a species, and it's more likely that some populations of the species will survive our present epoch of extinction. "To keep every cog and wheel," said Leopold, in *A Sand County Almanac*, "is the first precaution of intelligent tinkering."

Yellow Warblers nest in a Ninebark, a dense native shrub. Its spring flowers attract many insects for these insect-eating birds.

There is one exception to the rule of selecting plants of local ecotype. Very rare plants can become so inbred that their survival is jeopardized. In such cases, an infusion of new genes from plants from other ecoregions can sometimes help to save the species from extinction.

Sources of Native Plants of Local Ecotype

Nurseries. As native landscaping becomes more popular, many more sources of native plants become available. This is particularly true in the Midwest, which is in the forefront of the native landscaping movement. Even traditional garden centers and nurseries are beginning to offer native plants, albeit sometimes reluctantly, due to popular demand. You'll want to make sure you buy from reputable sources. See the source list in the appendix. Local nature centers, state natural resource agencies and local chapters of Wild Ones: Native Plants, Natural Landscapes can also help you locate nurseries.

Always ask about the origins of the plants. They should be nursery propagated from seeds or cuttings, not dug from the wild. Wild lilies, trilliums, ferns and orchids, especially lady-slipper orchids, are often collected from natural areas and then sold at high prices to unsuspecting customers.

In addition, plants should come from stock which originates in your ecoregion, ideally within a short distance of the site of planting. Avoid cultivars or other artificially selected varieties, in favor of genetically diverse plants.

Do not dig up plants in the wild. It is illegal without permission, unethical and mars the beauty of natural areas. The resulting bare soil is an invitation for invasive plants. Collecting from the wild also reduces the genetic variability and hardiness of the remaining plants and may even

Sumac berries are a useful late winter and early spring food for many birds.

cause local extinctions. The only exception is a plant rescue—with a landowner's permission—to save plants threatened by construction or other disturbances.

Seed collecting and propagating. Seed collecting is sometimes allowed, with special permission, in natural areas. If you are lucky to have such a source, be sure to collect only a small proportion of the available seed. This will help preserve the diversity and will leave seeds available for wildlife that depends on them. Also, try to collect from many plants of any one species. Don't take all your seed from the tallest or showiest. By collecting from many individuals, you will increase the genetic diversity in your restoration and be better assured of long-term success.

Seeds can be planted directly into the soil or propagated indoors in winter. Many good books are available to help you learn how to propagate the seeds, and it can be an enjoyable winter hobby.

Contract growing. Some nurseries will grow plants for you, from seed you either collect or purchase from them. This is a good way to get species that are not readily available as seedlings or if you need many plants.

Cuttings. Some wetland shrubs, such as willow and red-osier dogwood, are easily propagated from cuttings of young twigs. Stick the cuttings in moist soil and they will grow roots. See more information on this technique in chapter 7.

Reflections of place. By landscaping with natives of local origin, you will help preserve the "essence of place" being lauded today by an increasing number of landscape architects. In *Natural Landscapes*, John Brookes, one of most influential garden designers, writes: "Along with an increasing awareness of the importance of using regional plants, there is a desire to work in sympathy with the landscape."

Our midwestern landscapes should proclaim our heritage. They should radiate with the beauty of our savannas with their oaks and bluebirds, of our prairies with their purple coneflowers and meadowlarks and of our shrubberies with their dogwoods and catbirds. Rather than the monotony of yews, lawns and geraniums common to cities across the country, by landscaping with our native flora, we can ensure that our properties truly express our midwestern origins and preserve the diversity of unique flora and fauna.

Ladybird Johnson, former first lady and founder of the National Wildflower Research Center, praised and promoted this kind of locally flavored landscaping. In *Wildflowers across America*, she wrote, "Where I go in America, I like it when the land speaks its own language in its own regional accent."

RESOURCES FOR READERS

Books

Adelman, Charlotte, and Bernard L. Schwartz. 2011. *The Midwestern Native Garden: Native Alternatives to Nonnative Flowers and Plants; An Illustrated Guide*. Athens: Ohio University Press.

Bailey, Robert G. 1995. "Description of the Ecoregions of the United States." 2nd ed. Misc. Pub. No. 1391. Washington, DC: USDA Forest Service.

Leopold, Aldo. 2001. *A Sand County Almanac*. New York: Oxford University Press.

Marinelli, Janet, ed. 1994. *Going Native*. New York: Brooklyn Botanic Garden.

Stein, Sara. 1993. *Noah's Garden: Restoring the Ecology of Our Own Backyards*. Boston: Houghton Mifflin.

———. 1997. *Planting Noah's Garden: Further Adventures in Backyard Ecology*. Boston: Houghton Mifflin.

Wilken, E. 1986. "Terrestrial Ecozones of Canada." Ecological Land Classification 19. Canada Department of the Environment, Lands Directorate.

Websites

National Wildlife Federation. "Attracting Wildlife with Native Plants." http://www.nwf.org/Get-Outside/Outdoor-Activities/Garden-for-Wildlife/Gardening-Tips/Using-Native-Plants.aspx

Wild Ones: Native Plants, Natural Landscapes. "Landscaping with Native Plants." http://www.wildones.org/landscap.html

CHAPTER 3
The Case against Exotics

An equally important reason to use locally native plants is to lessen the possibility that exotic plants from our landscapes will run wild.

—National Wildlife Federation, *Native Plants and Your Habitat*

A growing body of research has begun to document the detrimental effects associated with exotic plants. Exotics include any plants that are not native to a particular area. All take up precious space that could be better used by their native counterparts which usually provide better shelter and nourishment for birds and other wildlife.

Some exotic plants become so invasive that they eventually outcompete and wipe out native species. These plants are increasing in alarming proportions throughout our country, including the Midwest. New research is beginning to reveal that some of these invasive plants have dire effects on our native birds.

Birds, Exotic Vegetation & Housing Density

Several studies have found fewer species and numbers of native birds in areas with exotics compared with areas with more native vegetation. In 1989, researchers G. Scott Mills, John Dunning Jr. and John M. Bates reported on a study of the effects of urbanization and its associated exotic vegetation in 34 neighborhoods in Tucson, Arizona. They discovered significantly more diversity and numbers of nesting native birds in areas with a greater amount of native vegetation. The native plants provided the birds with more of the resources—cover, nesting sites and food—than did the exotics. "Vegetation factors," the researchers found, "explained more of the variance in breeding bird densities than did measures of housing density." This suggests that "native bird populations may be better retained in areas of urban development by landscaping with native plants in such a way as to retain predevelopment distributions of vegetation volume."

While this research was done in the Southwest, it is likely the same results would be found in the Midwest. Additional studies have found reduced numbers of other wildlife, including birds, insects, reptiles and small mammals, in stands of exotic vegetation.

photo: Garlic Mustard

Exotics & Nesting

Research conducted in the heart of the Midwest, at the Morton Arboretum near Chicago, has uncovered disturbing news about the effects of exotic buckthorn and honeysuckle shrubs on bird populations. These shrubs were introduced as ornamentals from Eurasia and are now extremely invasive, dominating the understory of many midwestern woodlands. The study revealed that thrushes and robins nesting in these exotic shrubs lost many more eggs to predators than those nesting in comparable native shrubs, like hawthorns and viburnums.

Why? The researchers, who analyzed data collected from 585 nests during six years, from 1992 to 1997, found that the exotics don't offer the protection that native species do. Honeysuckles, for example, have heavier branches situated lower to the ground than many native shrubs. Unsuspecting birds may see these as perfect nesting sites, but the lower positioning of the branches allows easy access by predators, like raccoons, cats and opossums. In addition, the heavier limbs offer the marauders better support. Honeysuckle and buckthorn also lack the stout thorns of native hawthorns, which help deter the nest raiders.

Another factor is the early leaf flush of these exotic shrubs, which seems to attract birds looking for nest sites early in spring. "Here's an ecological trap if there ever was one," says Chris Whelan, a researcher and avian ecologist at the Illinois Natural History Survey. Whelan and his co-researcher, Kenneth Schmidt, a biologist at the University of Memphis, suggest restoring native, fruit-producing shrub species in order to restore plant diversity, increase songbird nesting success and provide the fruit resources birds need for migration.

Other invasive shrubs also can reduce nesting success. Marcus Schneck, a nature writer in Pennsylvania, observed a hedge of Japanese Barberry for 30 years. Northern Mockingbirds frequently nested in the shrubs, attracted by their dense branching and berries. Unfortunately, house cats easily climbed the low-growing shrubs and few nestlings survived.

Exotic grasses can also have adverse effects on birds. Experts at the Department of Natural Resources in Maryland report that, in many regions of the country, the use of native grasses in place of exotic grasses and legumes has resulted in extraordinary rebounds of some bird populations. When as little as 5% of typical hayfields of orchard grass and alfalfa—both exotics— were converted to native warm season grasses, the populations of game birds and songbirds increased as much as ten times. The warm season grasses, like Big Bluestem, Little Bluestem, Side-oats Grama, Indian Grass and Switchgrass, generally grow in clumps that provide corridors through which birds travel to forage for insects and avoid predators. In contrast, many exotics, including fescues, grow too densely for wildlife to move through them. Other factors are likely to be involved in the greater nesting success of birds in native vegetation.

Common Buckthorn, Rhamnus cathartica, *is one of the worst invasive shrubs in the Midwest. It lacks the stout thorns of native hawthorns which help deter bird nest predators.*

Explore Your Alter*Natives*

Many excellent locally native plants can be suitable replacements for exotic landscaping plants. These natives relieve the monotony those standard few exotics create and help to keep invasives from overwhelming our natural areas. Here are two exchanges to consider:

Serviceberry Instead of Ornamental Pears

Bradford Pear and the newer cultivar Autumn Blaze Pear offer showy masses of white blossoms in midspring and flashy red foliage in fall. But their blossoms are foul smelling and their greenish, brown-spotted fruits are eaten by few birds. Serviceberries (*Amelanchier* sp.), on the other hand, burst out with a profusion of white blossoms even earlier in spring. Later in spring and early summer, dozens of songbirds devour their fruit. Their fall foliage—blazing with reds, oranges and salmon—is just as outstanding as that of pears. Serviceberries of various species are native to the Midwest and include trees and shrubs, and offer gardeners a wide range of choices.

Native Roses Instead of Ornamental Roses

Most ornamental roses do best in cool, wet climes like that of England and consequently are some of the worst choices for garden plants in the Midwest. They require watering, winter protection, fertilization and pesticides to survive our hot dry summers and freezing winters. Our native roses have only a single set of petals but their profusion of blossoms can be very showy. Two good choices native to most of the Midwest are Pasture Rose, *Rosa carolina*, and Illinois Rose, *Rosa setigera*. These natives are hardier than the ornamentals, much less prone to disease, and tolerant of a wide range of soils and drainage conditions. Since they don't need to be covered in winter, their berries—"hips"—offer food for birds from late summer to late March.

Exotics & Cedar Waxwings

Other studies point to a second problem with honeysuckles—their effect on Cedar Waxwings. This common bird is a beauty, with silky-smooth gray plumage grading to a soft yellow blush on the belly, a "Lone Ranger" mask and red-tipped wing feathers. Normally, its tail is edged with a yellow band, a great aid to the quick identification of fly-by birds. But ornithologist Mark Witmer, as a graduate student at Cornell University, observed waxwings with orange rather than yellow bands and began to investigate.

At the Powdermill Nature Reserve in Pennsylvania, 30 years of banding provides the best historical record of the phenomenon. Since first observed in 1964, orange-tailed waxwings increased from fewer than 5% to 25% by 1985. Orange-tailed birds have now been documented throughout the Midwest and Northeast. In the late 1980s, biologists found that the color switch was linked to the berries of Morrow's Honeysuckle, a species imported from Japan and widely planted in the last 30 years.

Witmer conducted lab experiments that showed birds fed the honeysuckle's berries during molting grew orange tail feathers. Waxwings fed the berries during half of their molt developed bicolored tailbands. The honeysuckle's berries have a carotenoid with a red pigment which was incorporated into the tail feathers during molt, causing the color change.

OTHER SUBSTITUTIONS

Invasive Exotic	Possible Native Substitutes That Attract Birds
Common and Smooth Buckthorn, *Rhamnus cathartica* and *R. frangula*, and exotic Honeysuckle shrubs (*Lonicera* sp.)	Allegheny Serviceberry, *Amelanchier laevis* Alternate-leaved Dogwood, *Cornus alternifolia* Gray Dogwood, *Cornus racemosa* Silky Dogwood, *Cornus amomum* Red-osier Dogwood, *Cornus sericea (C. stolonifera)* American Cranberrybush *Viburnum, Viburnum opulus* var. *americanum (V. trilobum)* Nannyberry Viburnum, *Viburnum lentago* Red Cedar, *Juniperus virginiana*
Norway Maple, *Acer platanoides*	Red Maple, *Acer rubrum* Sugar Maple, *Acer saccharum* Northern Hackberry, *Celtis occidentalis* White Oak, *Quercus alba*
Russian Olive, *Eleagnus angustifolia*, and Autumn Olive, *E. umbellata*	Wild Plum, *Prunus americana* Pin Cherry, *Prunus pensylvanica* Choke Cherry, *Prunus virginiana* Nannyberry Viburnum, *Viburnum lentago*
Narrow-leaved Cattail, *Typha angustifolia*, and Hybrid Cattail, *T. x glauca*	Broad-leaved Cattail, *Typha latifolia*
Crown Vetch, *Coronilla varia* (frequently used to stabilize the soil)	Whorled Milkweed, *Asclepias verticillata* Canada Milk Vetch, *Astragalus canadensis* Pale-leaved Sunflower, *Helianthus strumosus* Common Mountain Mint, *Pycnanthemum virginianum*

Bird banders also discovered other bird species in which orange has replaced their original yellow color. Some Yellow-Breasted Chats had orange breasts. Kentucky Warblers were found with orange instead of yellow chins, throats, breasts and "spectacles." A few White throated Sparrows had orange instead of yellow feathers above their beaks. All three eat honeysuckle berries occasionally.

Thus, exotic honeysuckles are beginning to have a far-reaching impact on the coloration of some of our native bird species. And color is extremely important to birds. Audubon ornithologist Stephen Kress said, "Plumage colors are badges used for gender and species recognition, so the effect of food on birds' color could be very disruptive." Many birds also use color in territorial disputes, with the brighter bird generally getting the best sites. While the long-term effects of the honeysuckle-induced color changes are still unknown, caution suggests that we try to replace exotic honeysuckles with native shrubs that offer the birds their natural, long-evolved fare.

The Baltimore Oriole is a neotropical migrant that feeds primarily on insects in summer. The best way to provide it with insects is to landscape with native plants.

Exotics, Insects & Birds

Exotics are "junk food" for insects as well as birds. Ornithologist Vicki Piaskowski studies the needs of neotropical migrants in her position as the international coordinator for Birds Without Borders—Aves Sin Fronteras at the Zoological Society of Milwaukee. Many of these migrants are warblers, orioles and flycatchers that depend heavily on insects for nourishment, so any reduction in the availability of insects can endanger them.

At a migration stopover site in the town of Pewaukee in southern Wisconsin, Piaskowski and co-researcher Gene Albanese sampled populations of insects and other arthropods in both native and exotic vegetation. Flying insects and arthropods were collected on sticky (Tanglefoot-coated) boards, while nonflyers were collected by clipping branches randomly, sealing them in bags and later examining the insects present on them.

Both wetlands and woodlands were present on the site, which harbored some of the most invasive exotic plants in the Midwest—Tartarian Honeysuckle, Common Buckthorn, Smooth Buckthorn and Japanese Barberry. The native tree species on the site included Red Elm, Black Cherry, Yellow-bud Hickory, Ash species, Quaking Aspen, Red Oak, Pussy Willow and Box Elder, while the native shrubs included several species of viburnums and dogwoods, as well as Prickly Ash.

The researchers found that the native plants contained the highest numbers of insects and other arthropods, while the extremely invasive Common and Smooth Buckthorns had the lowest numbers. Tartarian Honeysuckle and Japanese Barberry showed more moderate levels of the critters. Among the native plants, Red Oak and Pussy Willow supported the most arthropods, the only two species with total numbers of over 300. (The next highest were in the hundreds.)

As a result of their studies, Piaskowski and Albanese stress the importance of conserving native plant species for the benefit of birds. Whenever possible, they write, recommendations should be made to landowners about the importance of planting native trees and shrubs and managing their land to preserve these plants.

A study in Pennsylvania in 2001 also found that insects prefer native plants. On an abandoned farm near Oxford, ecologist Doug Tallamy and undergraduate student Rebekah Baity from the University of Delaware investigated insect feeding on 12 exotic invasive species and 16 native species. They focused on the characteristic feeding scars made by "chewing" insects, and measured the amount of leaf area the insects consumed. ("Chewing" insects include true bugs, aphids, cicadas and leafhoppers.) Without exception, insects ate significantly more foliage from native plants than from exotics "regardless of plant morphology, habitat, or relatedness."

This is not surprising, given that at least 90% of all plant-eating insects are specialists that feed on only one or a few related plant species. These insect specialists have evolved, through long periods of time, to circumvent their host plant's defenses and to assimilate the plant's tissue efficiently. But they have not had time to deal with the evolutionarily novel exotics. Consequently most native insects, says Tallamy, "lack the enzymes needed to detoxify and digest non-native plants."

As in the Wisconsin study, oaks and willows were favorite native trees among insect gourmets, the particular species occurring on the Pennsylvania site being Black Oak and Black Willow. Black Walnut was another tree favorite, while arrowwoods were the insects' top choice among shrub species. These species, say the researchers, "were particularly valuable food sources for insects in our study and should be favored in native restoration projects that seek to bolster community richness."

Among related species, the native Red Maple was three times more popular with insects than the exotic Norway Maple. The Norway Maple was introduced to Philadelphia from Europe as a shade tree in 1756, 250 years ago, and is now a widespread invasive species throughout the eastern United States. Apparently, that is not long enough for the insects to adapt to it as a food source.

This Pennsylvania study quantified the differences in insect-feeding on native versus exotic plants, which, in turn, provided an estimate of the reduction in insect life that occurs when exotics invade natural areas. The insects ate 18 times more leaf area on native vine species than on exotic vine species. This

BRITISH INSECTS AVOID EXOTICS TOO

In Great Britain, insects avoid exotic plants, just as do insects in the United States, according to experts at the Natural History Museum in London. This is strikingly illustrated by examining native trees, such as oak or hawthorn, and aliens like horse chestnut and 'London' plane. Very few British insects and other invertebrates are found on the exotic species, whose leaves provide them with little nourishment. Plants native to Britain, on the other hand, host innumerable native invertebrates.

The horse chestnut and the London Plane tree (despite its name) were introduced into Great Britain from their original locations close to the Mediterranean. English oaks and hawthorns, incidentally, are different species from the oaks and hawthorns native to North America.

The museum encourages British gardeners to plant native plants which, they emphasize, are the backbone of local ecology, providing food and shelter for insects, birds and other animals.

means that when exotic vines replace native vines, 18 times less food energy is moving from plant to insect and, consequently, 18 times less insect biomass is produced.

Data for the study were gathered in June and early July, a time when nesting birds depend almost entirely on insects to feed their young. The reduction in insects on exotics could be contributing to the decline of many bird species. Although, to my knowledge, no other research in the U.S. has compared food resources for birds in native and exotic vegetation, studies of American redstarts overwintering in the tropics have shown that the birds in habitats with fewer insects lost weight, which they need for their migration north.

University of Delaware researchers point out that many well-meaning bird enthusiasts plant such invasive exotics as Multiflora Rose and Autumn Olive to provide birds with nesting sites and fall berries. "We do not deny," say the researchers, "that birds use such species in both ways, but benefits from well-protected nests and a copious supply of post-nesting berries are unlikely to counter the costs of a depauperate [impoverished] insect community if it reduces reproductive success." Basically, fewer native plants support fewer insects which, in turn, support fewer nesting birds.

It's also important for native plant gardeners to realize that, while our native insects favor native plants, they rarely do significant damage. Our native plants have adapted to keep insects from "over-eating," enabling most native plants to flourish despite hosting native insects. The new leaves of many trees, for example, are tender and juicy for emerging insects in spring—the same insects that feed migrating birds. But in a short time, the leaves develop tannins and other substances that make them less edible to insects for the rest of the season. Milkweeds, likewise, produce toxins to ward off insect attack. Monarch butterflies are one of the few insects that have developed adaptations to deal with these toxins, but the plant remains deadly to many others. This has enabled milkweed to thrive despite hosting the milkweed caterpillars.

The Bottom Line

Besides the effects documented in the above research, exotic plants degrade habitat for birds and wildlife in other ways. Exotics, especially invasive ones, can reduce the availability of

A native Yellow Swallowtail on a native Prairie Blazing Star

Purple Loosestrife (*Lythrum salicaria*)
Reed Grass (*Phragmites australis*)*
Reed Canary Grass (*Phalaris arundinacea*)*
Siberian Elm (*Ulmus pumila*)
Spotted Knapweed, Bachelor's Button (*Centaurea maculosa*)
Sweet Clover, White and Yellow (*Melilotus alba* and *M. officinalis*)
Teasel, Common and Cut-leaved (*Dipsacus sylvestris* and *D.laciniata*)
White Popular (*Populus alba*)
Wild Parsnip (*Pastinaca sativa*)

*These species or some of their ecotypes are native to some areas of the U.S., but can be very invasive:

Black Locust is native to the southeastern U.S. with outliers in southern Illinois, Indiana and Missouri. It can be invasive outside its native range.

Narrow-leaved Cattail is possibly an exotic from Europe. Both the Narrow-leaved Cattail and the Hybrid Cattail are invasive.

Reed Grass is native, but invasive in the Midwest.

Reed Canary Grass has both native and Eurasian ecotypes. Although the ecotypes cannot be distinguished, it is believed that most plants in the U.S. are the Eurasian ecotype and extremely aggressive.

water, decrease the diversity of soil organisms, deplete soil nutrients, cause soil erosion, compete with native vegetation—including endangered species—and affect the frequency of wildfires.

Monocultures of exotics also destroy the diversity of vegetation and structure in plant communities that many birds require. A Wood Thrush, for example, feeds by scratching in the leaf litter on the forest floor, nests in shrubs above and sings in spring from the treetops. In contrast to a multi-layered forest, a buckthorn woods forms a dense mass of shrubs of uniform height, shading out herbaceous species, other shrubs and even tree saplings.

You can help create better habitat for birds by removing exotics that exist on your property and replacing them with locally native species. Birds will spread the seeds of these natives, instead of the seeds of exotics, into the surrounding area, reversing the current pattern. (See chapter 7 for information on the best methods for eliminating exotics from your property.)

Suburban areas are fast becoming the dominant "ecosystems" in the country, points out Tallamy. If homeowners would use only plants that are native to their area, he says, "just imagine the future impact on wildlife populations and our natural heritage."

We must also change our laws to end exotic plant invasions. At the time of this writing, only Minnesota and Iowa have outlawed buckthorns. No states have prohibited the equally invasive exotic honeysuckles. These species and other invasives are still available for purchase at garden centers and nurseries. Clearly, we need to work to ban the sale of these invasives for the well-being of our native birds and other wildlife, and to save their natural habitats.

Resources for Readers

Books

Czarapata, Elizabeth J. 2005. *Invasive Plants of the Upper Midwest*. Madison: University of Wisconsin Press.

Websites

Plant Conservation Alliance's Alien Plant Working Group. "Weeds Gone Wild." http://www.nps.gov/plants/alien/

Federal and state noxious weed lists and an invasive plant list with links to more information: http://plants.usda.gov

Invasive Plants Association of Wisconsin. http://www.ipaw.org/

Michigan Invasive Plant Council. http://invasiveplantsmi.org/

Wild Ones: Native Plants, Natural Landscapes. "Invasive Plants." http://www.wildones.org/download/invasive.html

National Audubon Society. "Remove Exotic Plant Pests." http://athome.audubon.org/remove-exotic-plant-pests

Chicago Botanic Garden. "Invasive Plants." http://www.chicagobotanic.org/research/conservation/invasive/whatis

More websites on invasive plants and their control are given in chapter 7, which discusses how to remove invasives before planting a site.

Yellow and purple coneflowers brighten this yard.

2 Gallery of Bird Habitat Gardens

Swamp Milkweed

We wanted birds and diversity, beauty and interest.
—Nancy Small, Kalamazoo, Michigan

Agarden offering habitat for birds can be a small urban garden of a hundred square feet or a larger expanse within an entire subdivision or a rural property. It can feature woodland, prairie, savanna, shrubland, wetland, water habitats or a mix of habitat types.

More and more midwesterners are welcoming birds to their yards by creating bird habitat gardens rich in a diversity of native plants that offer shelter and nourishment. Here are a few representative gardens from throughout the Midwest. Each gardener has a story about the design and planting of his or her garden, and about the special birds and other wildlife it attracts and nurtures.

(previous page) The Damons of Saint Paul, Minnesota, have transformed their yard into a haven for birds and wildlife.

CHAPTER 4
The Gardens & Gardeners

ILLINOIS—Bird Garden in a City Subdivision

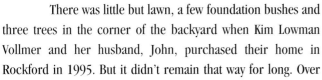

There was little but lawn, a few foundation bushes and three trees in the corner of the backyard when Kim Lowman Vollmer and her husband, John, purchased their home in Rockford in 1995. But it didn't remain that way for long. Over the first six years, they gradually introduced native plants and habitats to their property, an average-sized, 85-by-192-foot lot.

A beautiful prairie now graces over half of their front yard, and the round-ball Arbor Vitae foundation bushes have been replaced with Alternate-leaved Dogwood, American Hazelnut, Fragrant Sumac and Winterberry. Half the backyard has been landscaped for wildlife. Native shrubs and wildflowers line the boundary fence, and the back corner has become a mini-woodland. A large central area of their backyard is a play space for children.

With each expansion of their native plantings, the Vollmers eliminated the turf grass with several applications of the herbicide Roundup. In some areas, they spread newspaper topped with mulch to block the growth of weeds. Then they planted native species, using plants instead of seeds, because they wanted the yard "to look beautiful sooner and less weedy."

During the first few years, the Vollmers weeded and watered their new plantings carefully. They also developed a minor, and continuing, problem with Garlic Mustard. Usually, they simply pull out this invasive, but occasionally they've resorted to using Roundup. Today, they have very little maintenance—only minimal weeding and no watering. The Vollmers have also conducted a few controlled burns of their prairie in spring, after obtaining permits from city officials. (Such burns are highly recommended, where allowed by local code.)

The Vollmers were very careful in selecting the native plants for their yard. "We always consult books to make sure we are planting species indigenous to our exact area," says Kim, "what would have been growing on our lot 200 years ago." Today, their yard is sanctuary to 90 species of native plants. The many native wildflowers include both woodland and prairie species. An impressive variety of native shrubs encircle their backyard, including Ninebark, Witch Hazel, Winterberry, Red-berried Elderberry, Redbud, Buttonbush, plus several species of dogwoods, viburnums, serviceberries, sumacs and roses. In addition, they planted three low-growing prairie shrubs—New Jersey Tea, Leadplant and Indigo Bush. The Vollmer yard is 85% native, not counting the lawn.

This diversity of native plants provides birds with berries, nuts and seeds throughout the year. They attract American Goldfinches, Northern Cardinals, American Robins, House Finches, Mourning Doves, Downy Woodpeckers, Ruby-throated Hummingbirds, Black-capped Chickadees, Blue Jays,

Carly Vollmer is a budding scientist with an interest in butterflies she finds in her yard.

House Wrens, White-breasted Nuthatches, American Crows and Dark-eyed Juncos. Red-tailed Hawks and migrating Northern Goshawks come to hunt for prey.

Neighbors have enjoyed watching the birds as much as the Vollmers do, and a few have begun to plant some native species. The Vollmers have been careful to be "neighbor-friendly" in their natural landscaping. Signs state that they are members of the Wild Ones natural landscaping organization and that their yard is a wildlife sanctuary. A three-foot unobtrusive green wire fence keeps rabbits out their front-yard prairie garden. "It shows that we are keeping the garden contained and managed," says Kim. The Vollmers also maintain a lawn next to adjacent lawns to blend in with their neighbors' choice of landscaping.

The Vollmers love their naturally landscaped yard along with the birds, insects and other wildlife it attracts. Each member of the family has a favorite plant. John's favorite is the Pasque Flower because it's the first to blossom in spring. Kim's favorites are the Illinois Rose and the Common Milkweed because of their wonderful fragrance. Their daughter, Carly, is especially fond of all the milkweeds because she loves hunting for Monarch caterpillars.

The best reward of all for Kim and John is their great pleasure watching their daughter playing in the different natural areas—searching for caterpillars in the prairie or using her imagination in the little woodland to build forts from the dried plants. The family has raised and even overwintered many caterpillars. Carly has been an expert on their life cycle since she was four.

A Cooper's Hawk visits the front yard prairie of Kim and John Vollmer.

The diversity of prairie flowers in the Vollmers' front yard provides insects and nectar for birds in summer, and seeds in the fall and winter.

Button Bush blossoms provide nectar for hummingbirds and insects.

Winterberries are eaten by many birds, but are poisonous to humans.

Indiana

INDIANA—A Wildlife Habitat in a Community of Habitats

Elizabeth Mueller of Zionsville designed her first native habitat garden when she lived in a subdivision in town. She and her husband, Steve, kept a small lawn in front and landscaped the rest of their property with a wetland garden and native humming-bird/butterfly garden. Since then, Zionsville has become the first midwestern city to be certified as a wildlife habitat by the National Wildlife Federation, largely due to Elizabeth's inspirational leadership.

Now the Muellers live on a larger four-acre lot in a rural area of Zionsville, with woods, thickets, prairie, brush piles, a small pond, and a pasture of grasses, clover and wildflowers, which they mow as needed. They no longer maintain a lawn. Subdivisions are nearby, but immediately adjacent to their property are a ten-acre grassy quail habitat and a large wooded area.

When they purchased the property five years ago, the Muellers inherited the pasture, thickets and woods, plus plenty of invasive shrubs—Multiflora Roses, Russian Olives and honeysuckle. They are in the process of removing these invasives, one area at a time, cutting them down and treating the stumps with Roundup. Among the native shrubs, planted as replacements, are Ninebark, American Cranberrybush Viburnum, Gray Dogwood, Red-Osier Dogwood, Black Chokeberry and Downy Arrowhead Viburnum.

In the area disturbed by constructing their new home and septic field, the Muellers have planted gardens and installed a small pond. They've surrounded their home with perennials, shrubs and small trees, most of which are native. A prairie of native forbs and grasses grows on their septic field.

In some spots on the property where the clay soils stay wet, Elizabeth, the main gardener in the family, has planted wet-tolerant herbaceous plants like Great Blue Lobelia, Turtlehead, Joe Pye Weed, Queen of the Prairie, and Swamp Milkweed, along with Ninebark shrubs. Native Red Maple, River Birch, White Pine and Serviceberry have been introduced to supplement the ashes, cherries, oaks, maples and cedar that already grow there.

Elizabeth prefers using plants for her landscaping rather than seeds "because they grow better, require less maintenance, and support local wildlife." She uses some nonnatives for show.

The varied habitat on the Mueller property is a magnet for birds. So far, the couple has noted 53 species and each year brings more. They were particularly pleased that the addition of brush piles throughout the property attracted a lot of new birds—Gray Catbirds, Eastern Towhees and Fox Sparrows among them.

They've also noted more nesting birds every year and there are quite a few—Eastern Bluebirds, Black-capped Chickadees, Blue Jays, Northern Mockingbirds, Eastern Towhees, American Robins, Chipping Sparrows, Northern Cardinals, Gray Catbirds, Downy Woodpeckers, Carolina Wrens, House Wrens and American Crows. Elizabeth also thinks American Goldfinches and Ruby-throated Hummingbirds are nesting on their property. The Muellers have seen Barred Owls

The prairie garden in full blossom in the front yard of Elizabeth and Steve Mueller.

and have heard Great Horned Owls hooting. Green Herons, Great Blue Herons and Belted Kingfishers visit the pond looking for fish. Cedar Waxwings come for berries and Evening Grosbeaks for seeds.

"The best part of gardening for me," says Elizabeth, "is observing all of the wildlife in my garden." She enjoys monitoring Eastern Bluebird nest boxes, watching flocks of Cedar Waxwings drink and bathe in the shallows of the pond, seeing Blue Jays teach their young to eat from the feeders and catching sight of a Barred Owl in the evening.

The cottage garden bursts with sun-loving prairie plants.

The Muellers' pond, landscaped with an array of wetland plants, is regularly visited by Green Herons (below).

IOWA—Two Habitats

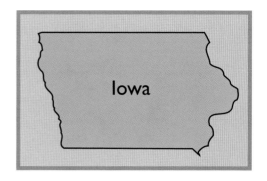

Iowa

An Urban Woodland

Kitty and Kevin Clasing's yard in Mason City features a woodland bird garden with a pond as its centerpiece. When they purchased the double-lot property, it had many mature trees, including hackberry, mountain ash, hawthorns, cedar, crabapple and pines. But most of the yard consisted of a large lawn bordered on one side with a lilac hedge. Over the years, they've replaced undesired species and enhanced the landscaping with native perennials, shrubs and smaller trees. Today, 60–70% of their plants are native. They also added three birdbaths with fountains or pumps circulating water, several "still" water birdbaths, a mister, dripper and bird feeders. They maintain a huge 20-foot brush pile for birds and wildlife, but it's hidden from the view of neighbors.

Once they started planting native species, Kitty says, the diversity of birds on their property nearly doubled, despite its location on a busy four-lane highway. Their bird count includes 52 species of birds, nine species of butterflies, five species of dragonflies, as well as frogs, toads and small mammals—chipmunks, squirrels, opossums and raccoons. Many birds, including cardinals, sparrows, catbirds, chickadees, wrens, jays, nuthatches, crows and woodpeckers, have found the yard an inviting place to nest. The rarest visitor was a White-winged Crossbill.

The Clasings' woodland garden is particularly lovely in spring when the trilliums, violets, Wild Ginger, Virginia Bluebells, Jack-in-the Pulpit, Wild Columbine, Marsh Marigold and other woodland flowers are at their peak. Butterfly/hummingbird gardens carry the color into summer and fall.

The viburnums, dogwoods, crabapple trees, mountain ash, hawthorns and hackberries provide a continuous abundance of fruits and berries for birds throughout the growing season. The recently added serviceberry tree has early-ripening berries, which will be among the first fruit for the birds next season. Virginia Creeper, which covers half their house and a fence, also provides berries favored by birds, especially Cedar Waxwings.

The pond is the focal point of the yard, making it a popular stop for local garden tours, as well as for birds. "Besides the robins and many other resident birds that use the pond," says Kitty, "we especially enjoy the birds that stop by on their spring and fall migrations." These include Cedar Waxwings, Yellow-rumped Warblers, Common Yellowthroats, Philadelphia Vireos, Eastern Towhees and American Redstarts. The Clasings put in a second pond so that each grandchild could add a fish and get up close to view them.

The Clasings are busiest maintaining their woodland garden in spring when they devote an average of four hours a week to it. The rest of the year, little work is necessary (outside of mowing the lawn).

While their beautiful yard brings many visitors, some of the Clasings' most memorable moments are those they share with their grandchildren, who enjoy the birds, wildlife and bugs. The Clasings' woodland garden is registered both as a National Wildlife Federation Habitat and a Windstar Institute Habitat.

The trickle of running water attracts birds to the Clasings' pond.

Prairie Hill Farm

Also in Iowa is a noteworthy certified habitat at the home of Mary and James Norton in New Hartford. In 1893, Mary Norton's great-grandparents homesteaded a corner of what is now their 200-acre Prairie Hill Farm. This cropland and pasture were once part of the vast prairie that covered three-fourths of Iowa.

When Mary and James returned to the farm in the 1970s, with their two children, the pastures were overgrazed and the invasive shrub Multiflora Rose (once a recommended plant) abounded. Ever since, Mary and James have been working to restore native prairie, woodlands and wetlands.

The Nortons used about half native species and half nonnative cultivars in the area around their house. On the rest of the property, they used only local ecotype seeds obtained within a 60-mile radius. Originally, they collected seeds from nearby natural area remnants, but now they harvest seeds from their property, which they use to expand their own plantings and share with nearby residents.

The Nortons delight in all the birds and wildlife. "We wake up each morning to a chorus of bird song and Wild Turkey chatter," says Mary, "and go to sleep each night listening to owls hoot and coo." They discovered the importance of native plants when they introduced a native reed to one pond. To their great pleasure, Green Herons immediately appeared.

In 2001, the National Wildlife Federation certified the Nortons' 45-acre restored tallgrass prairie as the nation's 30,000th Backyard Wildlife Habitat site. The Nortons share with the federation a deep concern about the loss of prairie wildlife and hope that their farm will help encourage others to restore habitat. Prairie birds, they note, are considered one of America's most rapidly and widely declining group of birds. They are pleased that meadowlarks, bobolinks, hawks, sparrows, finches and other prairie birds have found a home, once again, on their own farm. And the butterflies have been "phenomenal" since restoring the prairie, notes Mary.

Restored tallgrass prairie at Prairie Hill Farm.

The Nortons do not use chemicals to restore their land. They clean, clip and hoe several days each month. Occasionally they do major work, such as planting 8,000 small trees by hand in the wooded habitat along the stream. They also work one hour each early morning from May to October in the immediate, more formal yard around their house.

"We are in awe of what is happening on our island of restored native habitat," says Mary Norton. "None of this has ever seemed like work. It's just happened in a beautiful and natural way." James agrees, saying, "Much of our work is trial and error, but it's hard to make mistakes with prairie because it is so forgiving and strong."

Mary and James B. Norton's verdant yard invites woodland birds to visit.

MICHIGAN—An Urban Island of Diversity

One and a half miles from downtown Kalamazoo is a half-acre hotspot of diversity, the home of Tom and Nancy Small. The two former English professors have transformed their property from a landscape of invasive species interspersed with lawn to one lush with nearly 250 species of native plants.

I was amazed to find 50 species of native shrubs, two of which are rare (Species of Special Concern), and 15 species of native trees. Equally impressive are the 11 different kinds of sedges and 11 different ferns—a rare wealth of species for so small an area. Among the many wildflowers coloring their landscape are 13 Threatened, Special Concern or Extirpated Species (with Purple Coneflower in the last category, now reintroduced in Michigan).

The birds are as abundant as the plants. "People who visit our yard," write the Smalls, "marvel not so much at how unusual the wildlife is, but at how *prolific* it is. There's constant movement, birdsong, chattering of chipmunks and squirrels, cries and tapping of woodpeckers, always something to see and hear."

The habitat on their property is primarily woodland edge and oak savanna with a small prairie planting in their sunny front yard, a mini-wetland and a tiny pond. This is in keeping with the original vegetation of Kalamazoo, says Tom, which was "savanna and wetlands with patches of prairie." The Smalls are careful to use plants of local ecotype in their landscaping, many of which they grow from seed.

The couple began to restore their yard by tackling the invasive weeds. Woody plant culprits

Birdbath and feeders enhance the lush backyard of Tom and Nancy Small.

were barberry, honeysuckle, buckthorn and Multiflora Rose. All the flower beds were basically overgrown patches of periwinkle (ground myrtle) and pachysandra. Garlic Mustard added to the evil cauldron of invasives. Despite these challenges, they did not use herbicides; instead, they pulled, dug or smothered the invasives with leaves and brush, restoring one area at a time.

Downy Woodpecker, a frequent visitor to the shade garden at the Smalls' home.

The homes in their neighborhood surround a central woods, and the Smalls have extended the woodland into their backyard. Tom said, "We've learned to let fallen branches, twigs and leaves lie, and have noticed the fungi that now thrive in the yard."

"We also appreciate shrubs more—they are so useful to wildlife," added Nancy. "Spicebush, for example, feeds 48 different species of birds and animals." I was delighted to see this species, prized by migrant birds for its energy-rich berries. It's not native to Wisconsin where I live.

Their front yard prairie has dozens of wildflowers and native grasses, with signs identifying them, making it a popular spot with passers-by. The Smalls particularly prize the Silphiums. Cup Plant is Nancy's favorite, while Prairie Dock is Tom's favorite.

The diversity of habitat and plants in their yard has attracted 40 species of birds, including the Blue Jay, Yellow-bellied Sapsucker, Mallard, Tufted Titmouse and American Robin. The Cardinal Flower and other nectar-rich wildflowers bring Ruby-throated Hummingbirds.

The shade garden attracts woodland birds.

Goldfinches have nested in their Gray Dogwood and are particularly fond of the seeds of the native sunflowers. Downy, Hairy and Red-bellied Woodpeckers, Northern Cardinals, Black-capped Chickadees and Red-winged Blackbirds nest nearby and visit with their youngsters.

Migrants include the Indigo Bunting, Baltimore Oriole, Red-breasted Grosbeak, Scarlet Tanager, American Redstart, Blackburnian Warbler and a variety of sparrows. Winter brings Red-breasted Nuthatches and Carolina Wrens. Red-tailed Hawks make occasional appearances, and a Cooper's Hawk feasted on one of their Blue Jays.

Tom and Nancy love the vibrant, species-rich habitat they've created. "We wanted birds and diversity, beauty and interest," says Nancy. All their visitors—birds, wildlife, neighbors and guests—appreciate their success re-creating the landscape that once flourished in Kalamazoo.

This is a favorite place to relax and enjoy the tranquility and bird life in an urban yard.

MINNESOTA—Birdless Yard Transformed to Bird Haven

Minnesota

Susan and Paul Damon lived in their home in the city of Saint Paul for nine years before they saw the first American Goldfinch in their yard. It was the year they began to remove the invasive buckthorn shrubs that threatened to take over their yard.

In the disturbed soil around the buckthorn stumps, squirrels had planted a few annual sunflowers. Paul saw the first goldfinch while Susan was at work and was so surprised that he initially thought it was a canary. A male and female goldfinch returned many times to feed on the sunflowers during the late summer that year. In the following winter, a flock of goldfinches came to feed on the seeds of the Purple Coneflower that they had planted in their front yard.

Since then, they've expanded their native plantings and removed all their buckthorn. And the results have been more than they hoped. "We have been able to attract a number of native birds," says Susan, "which I find quite astounding for living in a large city."

The Damons started natural landscaping their 80-by-110-foot lot gradually, each year expanding to another area, and they suggest that others also start small. Their first native wild-flower garden was a 3-by-15-foot space on the south side of their house, planted in 1993, which they gradually expanded over the next five years. Then in 1999 and 2000, they removed the buckthorn in the midst of their backyard and planted the front garden as well, which includes primarily native plants, along with some nonnative cultivars. Their 2001 project was the challenging job of removing the huge buckthorn hedges border-ing two sides of their property. (Chapter 7 gives details of how they accomplished this Herculean task.)

The Damons planned and planted their gardens to ben-efit wildlife and the environment and, as Susan says, "because native plants are so incredibly beautiful!" The buckthorn hedges were transformed into havens for birds filled with grasses and shrubs that have begun to provide seeds, berries and nuts. Nectar-rich wildflowers were planted for hummingbirds and but-terflies. Other wildflowers were selected, not only for their beauty but for the seeds they offer to birds through fall and winter.

HUMMINGBIRD FAVORITES IN THE DAMON YARD
Cardinal Flower
Great Blue Lobelia
Royal Catchfly
Obedient Plant

GOLDFINCH FAVORITES IN THE DAMON YARD
Cup Plant
Yellow (Gray-headed) Coneflower
Wild Golden Glow (Green-headed Coneflower)
Giant Lavender (Fragrant) Hyssop
Western Sunflower
Woodland Sunflower

Great Blue Lobelia

Front of house with masses of Purple and Yellow Coneflowers.

Today, two-thirds of the Damons' property is native gardens, which they plan to increase to three-fourths. Their flourishing gardens now harbor five species of native grasses, sixty species of wildflowers, and a dozen species of native shrubs and trees. The bird habitats they've created range from a sunny prairie area to a shady woodland patch with an open savanna between the two.

As the native habitats on their property increase, birds come in ever greater numbers and variety. Chickadees nest in a box in their yard, and American Goldfinches flock in groups as large as 40. Baltimore Orioles drink from the Cup Plants. Common visitors include Dark-eyed Juncos, Downy and Hairy Woodpeckers, American Robins, Mourning Doves, Northern Cardinals, Red-winged Blackbirds and White-breasted Nuthatches. Occasional visitors include Ruby-throated Hummingbirds, Brown Creepers, Ruby-crowned Kinglets, Gray Catbirds, Brown Thrashers, House Wrens, House Finches, Ovenbirds and a variety of warblers, woodpeckers and native sparrows.

The birds aren't the only ones to appreciate their garden. "We love our garden, but so do people in the neighborhood," says Susan. "We have even gotten cards from people who tell us how much they like to walk by our house." Their beautifully landscaped yard is now a regular on tours of native gardens in the Saint Paul area.

Surprise Visitors to the Damon Yard

One of the Damons' biggest surprises was a Wild Turkey, which showed up one morning while Susan was drinking her morning coffee. Paul ran out and got a couple of photos before the bird walked down the driveway and out onto the sidewalk. Northern Goshawks and Cooper's Hawks are other rare visitors to their yard.

In 2003, warblers and kinglets showed up for the first time. Common Yellowthroats flitted through the Wild Golden Glow and Cup Plant searching for insects and the Damons spotted an Ovenbird and a Ruby-crowned Kinglet in other areas of their yard.

The latest additions to their yard bird list are a Fox Sparrow and Pileated Woodpecker. The Damons plan to add new shrubs to create more wildlife habitat, which is sure to bring more surprise visitors to their yard.

Goldfinches are attracted by the many seed-producing wildflowers in the Damons' front yard. Here, a male feeds his mate while she incubates the eggs.

The back and side yards are planted with hummingbird flowers and a wide variety of other native plants.

LANDSCAPE PLAN
DAMON YARD

20'

Landscape Plan: Paul Damon

NORTH

KEY TO DAMON LANDSCAPE PLAN

B   Boulevard Garden (Mainly Nonnatives)

D   Driveway Garden (Switchgrass & Big Bluestem Grass)

F   Front Garden (Prairie)

K   Kitchen Garden (Mix of Herbs & Wildflowers)

N   North Garden (Prairie)

SE Secret Garden (Violets & Raspberries)

SH Shade Garden (Woodland Wildflowers under a Basswood tree)

S   South Garden ("Goldfinch Garden" Prairie)

MISSOURI—A Floodplain Restoration

Missouri

Nathan Pate of Ellsville, a suburb of Saint Louis, began restoring natural habitat on his property, situated on the floodplain of a "wet weather" creek soon after buying it in 1994. At the time, the landscaping consisted of the "typical lawn with lots of 'professional' landscaping (i.e. exotics)."

Since then, he has created four ponds, a rain garden, a rock garden, a butterfly-hummingbird garden, and meadow/prairie areas on his one-and-one-half-acre property. The lawn has been completely eliminated and most of the exotics are gone. He has improved woodland and woodland edges along the creek as well. About 80% of his yard is native, with the aim of reaching 99%, with only a few tame exotics which his wife, Janet, insists on and which "have outstanding redeeming values."

The results are impressive. Scott Woodbury, horticultural supervisor of the Missouri Botanical Garden's Shaw Nature Reserve, calls Nathan "a local hero" whose beautiful and diverse natural landscaping serves to educate and inspire the many visitors who tour the Pate yard. Even passing motorists and visiting service people rave about the landscaping. Not surprisingly, some neighbors have followed suit and begun adding native plants themselves.

Like many others, Nathan has had to contend with a plethora of invasive plants. An invasive euonymous, *E. alatus*, is now banished to the far side of the creek, he reports, via "scads of manual pulling." Invasive honeysuckle shrubs have also been removed, but a neighbor still harbors many of them, so it's a continual battle to keep them out. Perhaps worst of all has been the Star of Bethlehem ("SOB"), which is resistant to Roundup, so it has meant a lot of digging up and the occasional use of a "meaner" herbicide.

Today, his property is largely free of invasives and flourishes with over 300 species of native plants. He's particularly fond of milkweeds and has ten different species, both common and rare. Other favorites are the hummingbird pleaser Fire Pink and other *Silene* species.

Nathan did all the landscaping work himself because, as he puts it, "I want intimate contact with dirt, plants and bugs." He delineated one area at a time and removed or killed the grass. Then he replanted with natives or constructed the ponds. The big pond in his yard was once a swimming pool. He sold all the material, but kept the hole, lined it and landscaped the edges. His smaller ponds were dug by hand and also lined. All the ponds are self-sustaining—no pumps, filters or chemical treatments. One of them is designed strictly for insects and frogs and has no fish.

The ponds have brought Mallards, Northern Shovelers, Wood Ducks, Great Blue Herons and Green Herons. Many songbirds have been attracted to nest in other habitat areas in his yard, including Northern Cardinals, Black-Capped Chickadees, American Robins and Mourning Doves. Carolina Wrens have nested in a plastic bag hanging in the garage.

One of the Pates' more memorable experiences has been watching House Wrens build a nest and raise young in a nest box with one clear plastic side hanging outside one of their windows. Nathan

also had the rare opportunity to watch a mink killing a rabbit and dragging it into the brushpile.

Experiences like those inspired Nathan to restore native habitat in his yard. "It has truth, beauty and a full complement of faunal activity—what more could a person want?"

A Rose-breasted Grosbeak is a special visitor to Nathan and Janet Pate's yard.

The rock garden provides visual interest and habitat for small creatures.

The pond is landscaped with a diversity of native plants.

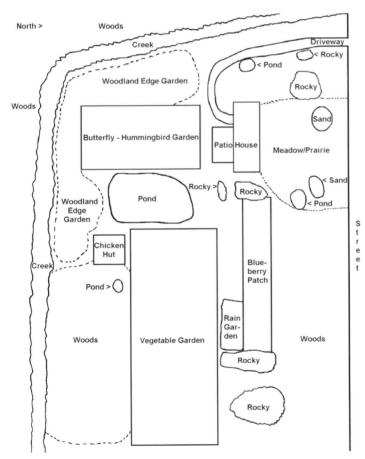

LANDSCAPE PLAN PATE YARD

With its great variety of habitats, the Pate yard in suburban Saint Louis attracts many birds, from hummingbirds and songbirds to herons and waterfowl.

Landscape Plan: Nathan Pate

Ohio

OHIO—Gardening on a Glacial Moraine

When Christine McCullough was a young girl, growing up in Ohio, she roamed what seemed to be limitless woods. "We said good-by to our parents in the morning," she says, "took our lunches and played all day in the woods, crawled on rock ledges, climbed trees, swung on grapevines, then came home for supper." She's worried that today's children (and their parents) don't know what a "real" woods looks like. To give them the opportunity to see an authentic-looking native woodland, Christine is restoring woodland habitat both on her own property and at a local school site.

Christine and her husband, Gordon, live on a half-acre lot in West Chester Township, about 20 miles from Cincinnati. The wooded property is situated on a terminal moraine left by glaciers that passed through Ohio 20,000 years ago. Among the many mature trees on their property are Shagbark Hickory, Slippery Elm, Northern Hackberry, Red Cedar, Redbud, Wild Black Cherry and Green Ash.

When the McCulloughs first purchased their home, however, a forest of invasive Amur and Japanese Honeysuckle grew beneath those trees. And unfortunately, shortly afterwards, the herbaceous invasive Garlic Mustard showed up. The only native wildflowers in the understory of the woods were Dwarf Larkspur and Spring Beauty, plus, "unbelievably," Chris says, "Adder's Tongue Fern."

Over several years, Christine worked on removing the invasive shrubs and Garlic Mustard. (See chapter 7 for details on how she accomplished this tremendous job.) Chris has even gone over

Hummingbird/butterfly garden at the home of Christine and Gordon McCullough.

BIRDSCAPING IN THE MIDWEST

Mourning doves nest in the McCulloughs' restored woodland.

her lot line to eradicate invasives on adjacent properties (with the permission of neighbors) to create a buffer for her woodland.

She has also eliminated aggressive grape vines which were harming the woodland canopy. (Although grapes are eaten by many birds, the vines can be extremely aggressive in some areas and may shade out valuable trees and shrubs. The best places for grape vines to grow are on snags, fences and arbors, where they will not be competing with live plants.)

In place of the invasive plants, Christine is filling her woods with the many native wildflowers and ferns that she saw as a child. She purchases her plants or swaps with friends. Jack-in-the-Pulpit, False Solomon's Seal, Wild Geranium, Wild Blue Phlox, Virginia Bluebells and four different species of violets are among the wildflowers flourishing in her woodland that are particularly valuable for birds, providing berries, nectar or seeds. But she has also many other woodland wildflowers, such as toothwort, twinleaf, hepatica, Spring Beauty, mayapple, ginger, two woodland anemones, four species of trillium and many others. These species, along with the woodland grasses and ferns that she's planted, provide a more complete complement of species native to Ohio woodlands and offer cover for ground-dwelling woodland birds.

While the woodland is completely native, other areas of the McCullough yard have a mix of natives and nonnatives (but no invasives). The front and side yards are landscaped traditionally, but Chris is proud to have none of the ubiquitous nonnative Taxus (yews). The small lawn, which she believes helps convince people that maintenance is taking place, is managed organically by a lawn care service.

Christine's pride and joy in the front are three Possum Haw, *Ilex decidua*, loaded with fruit for the birds. (The more common species in the Midwest is Winterberry or Michigan Holly, *Ilex verticillata*.) In both the front and back of the house, Chris has planted small hummingbird-butterfly

Dry wash of local river rock prevents erosion.

gardens. Among the native nectar-rich species in her yard are Beardtongue, Wild Bergamot, Prairie Blazing Star, Butterfly Milkweed, Cardinal Flower, Wild Columbine, Turk's Cap Lily, Oswego Tea (Bee Balm) and Great Blue Lobelia.

A great many birds, including a variety of songbirds, woodpeckers and hawks, enjoy the woodland and sunny gardens at the McCullough residence. Northern Cardinals, Mourning Doves, American Robins, wrens and sparrows nest on the property. The couple was able to confirm nesting Ruby-throated Hummingbirds when a baby hummer once found its way into their house.

Although it has taken a lot of work to get her yard free of invasives and restore the natural habitat, Christine has enjoyed many memorable moments in her yard, such as seeing an Indigo Bunting and Northern Cardinal in the same view, watching a Northern Mockingbird jealously guarding the Possum Haw berries, glimpsing a Ruby-throated Hummingbird taking a drink from a Cup Plant and then going on to nectar on the blossoms of native Trumpet Honeysuckle, and enjoying the sounds of woodpeckers, especially the Yellow-bellied Sapsucker, calling and hammering in the trees.

Restored woodland attracts many nesting species, including Mourning Doves.

WISCONSIN—An Oasis for Birds within the State's Largest Metropolitan Area

Pat and Carl Brust began with an oversize lawn and some trees on their one-acre property in Franklin, a suburb of Milwaukee. Today, they have a shrub border, a dense shrub bed as a backdrop to their bird feeders, a shade garden with woodland species, a large prairie planting, a woodland edge with shrubs and small trees, an open wooded area with little understory and a wet prairie area. And all this habitat was restored by a couple who weren't especially interested in gardening!

Instead, Pat and Carl were motivated primarily by their love for birds. They wanted to attract a diversity of birds by establishing a natural landscape of beauty and interest. The various habitat areas in their yard were created gradually, starting in the late 1980s, when they moved to their new home. As is often advised, they waited an entire year (which turned out to be the major drought year of 1988), to observe the landscaping they acquired.

Pat and Carl Brust's prairie is vibrant with wildflowers in midsummer.

Summer Tanager, a rare visitor, appeared in the Brusts' yard.

Pat, the main gardener in the family, studied their new property, noting the sunny and shady areas, the dry spots and wet ones, the spots with good rich soil and those near the streets with compacted soil. With that information, she drew up a rough plan for her planting projects. Later on, her plantings became more spontaneous. They were often done to address a problem, to create as much diversity as possible or to reduce mowing time for her husband. She also improvised to accommodate new plants she had acquired or admired in other yards and natural areas. As many native plant gardeners have discovered, Pat says, "Now, I realize that these plants will go where *they* want to go, not necessarily where I want to put them in."

The Brusts were fortunate that initially their property had no invasive plants. Over the years, however, several species appeared: buckthorn, honeysuckle, thistle, Garlic Mustard, Reed Canary Grass and others, testifying to the ever-increasing threat of invasives. "But since they were newly introduced to the plantings," says Pat, "I have been able to keep up with them by vigilance and hand weeding." Pat and her husband have used the herbicide Roundup only on a limited basis to treat stumps of invasive shrubs or to selectively treat clumps of Reed Canary Grass or thistles. They also used this chemical to prepare a seed bed for their prairie area.

The couple created their bird oasis on their own, only twice seeking professional advice. "For the most part," Pat says, "what they told me was not much more than what I had discovered on my own through reading and research, although they would have been quite helpful if I had not had the time or the inclination to do the research myself." Like most native plant gardeners, the major maintenance work is in spring and early summer, when it takes about 40 hours to prune shrubs, cut down and clean up the previous year's vegetation and rechip the wood paths and edges. For the rest of the season, several hours per week are spent monitoring and pulling weeds.

The rewards have been well worth the work. Their beautifully landscaped yard has attracted 96 species of birds to date, some of them Wisconsin records. The visit of an Orange-crowned Warbler, which spent several weeks in their yard, was the first time the warbler had been observed in Wisconsin in the winter. A Brambling, a European finch far from home, surprised them one year to become the second record in Wisconsin and brought 160 birders to their home, including this author, for a view. The Brusts were also delighted with the Summer Tanager, another rare bird for Wisconsin, that showed up for a brief visit.

Besides these "superstar" species, the Brusts enjoy the many, more common birds that visit their yard—from owls and woodpeckers to thrushes, sparrows, orioles, finches, a dozen species of warblers and many more. Pat, a careful observer of the plant preferences of the birds in her yard, has found that the berries of the Washington Hawthorn, Red-berried Elderberry and Alternate-leaved (or Pagoda) Dogwood are their favorites, with those of Nannyberry Viburnum and

The Brusts landscaped with prairie in the foreground and woodland near the house.

Serviceberry nearly as popular. Among the herbaceous plants, Pat discovered something I've never found in the literature: False Bugbane is a great plant for birds because of the insects it attracts. She's been delighted to see both Baltimore Orioles and Yellow Warblers feed on the insects nectaring on the blossoms crowding Bugbane's wandlike flower heads. (This woodland plant also brightens a summer shade garden, when little else is flowering.) I can testify that the hummingbirds love to nectar on the white blossoms of Foxglove Beardtongue in one of their prairie areas.

In her youth, Pat was depressed when she had to return home to Milwaukee after vacationing at a cottage in northern Wisconsin. Today, she cares for her elderly mother and is frequently house-bound as a result, but her beautiful garden has birds and wildflowers that both she and her mother can enjoy without a long drive to the country.

"It is difficult to step outside without being drawn into the observation of a flower or insect, bird song or berry, caterpillar or toad," she writes. "It can take a very long time to get from the house to the mailbox with all the distractions I find along the way and that is the real reward of this work—to have the opportunity to be in the middle of all this life and to be able to observe it close up."

A sign identifies this as "Conservation at Home."

A Buckeye rests on a prairie perch.

The weather vane makes a handy perch for a Baltimore Oriole at the Nortons' Prairie Hill Farm in Iowa.

3 NATIVE HABITATS FOR BIRDS: THE BASICS

If you don't have the habitat, you don't have the birds.
—Chandler S. Robbins, ornithologist and lead author
Birds of North America (Golden Field Guide)

Now that you've seen successful bird habitat gardens throughout the Midwest, it's time to discuss the basics of creating bird habitat in your own yard. In the first chapter in this section, you'll learn about the features every yard should have to attract birds. The following two chapters will provide planning and design tips, methods of site preparation and pointers on planting herbaceous species, shrubs and trees.

(previous page) This Northern Bobwhite looks out from low dense cover—its favorite habitat.
(top) Female Ruby-throated Hummingbirds raise their young with no help from the males.

CHAPTER 5
Getting Started

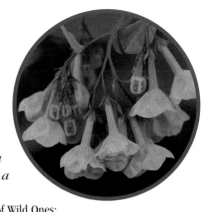

If nothing moves in your landscape but a lawnmower, it's time to think about designing a natural yard.

—Rochelle Whiteman of Wild Ones:
Native Plants, Natural Landscapes, Bayside, Wisconsin

Habitat is the single most important concept in the management of wildlife. Likewise, the creation of habitat is the most important means of providing for birds and other wildlife on your own property. Just as the realtor's phrase "location, location, location" applies to human real estate, the ecologist's emphasis on habitat reflects the importance of particular natural areas for birds and other wildlife.

Habitat, by definition, is the specific kind of natural community or environment where a plant or animal lives. A bird's natural habitat encompasses all the essentials of food, cover, nesting sites, space and water that it requires. Suitable habitat will vary with different species. A meadowlark prefers open grassland, a thrush needs a forest, while a duck requires a river, pond or lake. The habitat a bird needs might change with the seasons or the phases of its life cycle. A bird's nesting habitat, for example, may be different from its migratory stopover habitat, where it primarily needs food to fuel its migration. The Tennessee Warblers that feed high in my oaks in spring migration, nest on the ground in Canadian woodlands.

Tennessee Warblers use two different habitats: canopy trees in migration, and ground-level habitat for nesting.

The destruction and degradation of habitat, due to human population growth and consequent urban sprawl and development, are the major causes of the decline of birds and other wildlife. In an analysis of trends over 35 years (1966–2001), the U.S. Geological Survey reports that one in four bird species in the United States shows declines in populations.

Roads, buildings, airports and shopping centers are sprawling ever farther across the land. Home lawns alone now carpet over 40 million acres of land, according to the

photo: Virginia Bluebells

THE COST OF LAWNS

Lawns not only replace wildlife habitat, but are costly in time, resources and increased air pollution.

- Homeowners are using 50% more herbicides than they did 20 years ago, about 10 times more per acre than used on farms.

- Watering lawns amounts to as much as 2/3 of water use in some cities.

- The average homeowner spends the equivalent of a typical workweek (40 hours) simply mowing the lawn each year.

- $8.5 billion is spent annually on retail sales of residential lawn care products and equipment.

- Lawn mowing produces more than 5% of urban air pollution, according to the Environmental Protection Agency.

Sources:
http://athome.audubon.org
and *Windstar Wildlife Weekly*

U.S. News & World Report. Unfortunately, the typical home yard dominated by lawn offers little valuable habitat for wildlife and the native plants upon which they depend. As gardening guru Jim Wilson says in *Landscaping with Wildflowers: An Environmental Approach to Gardening,* "Mowed lawns, sheared shrubs, and neatly raked beds fail as wildlife magnets; most are inhospitable deserts to birds and butterflies."

Given the huge swath of inhospitable lawn engulfing our country, it is essential that we try to re-create some of the lost natural habitat in our yards. If even a fraction of lawn acreage could be landscaped for birds, we could help offset the devastating loss of habitat that has occurred as a result of development.

In his book, *Win-Win Ecology: How the Earth's Species Can Survive in the Midst of Human Enterprise,* ecologist Michael Rosenzweig shows that all the world's reserves, parks, refuges and natural areas are but a small fraction of the earth's surface. Even under the best projections, only 5% of the world's species will be secure. As the title suggests, natural habitat must also be provided in the midst of development, in home yards, as well as air force bases, golf courses and corporate headquarters. Renowned Stanford biologist Gretchen Daily agrees. In her review of the book, she says: "Save biodiversity in the hostile sea of development? You bet."

Habitat restoration for birds, wildlife and the plant species themselves needs to become the norm in every yard and in every community. While small-scale yard habitats won't eliminate the need to save the large blocks of habitat needed by some birds and larger animals, they will certainly welcome a great many species of birds, butterflies, frogs, small mammals and other wildlife. Ken Druse, internationally known author of *The Natural Habitat Garden,* said, "The simplest wildflower meadow is more complex, more botanically varied, than a grass lawn, offering a long season of pollens, nectars, and finally seeds, along with nesting sites and shelter for all those creatures that used to live somewhere before we arrived."

Now that you're eager to rip up some lawn and create outstanding bird habitat, here are some tips on how to begin.

Take an Inventory

Before you do anything, you need to know what you have, beyond lawn, in your yard. If you've just moved to a new home, it's good to simply sit back and observe for a whole growing season. Learn which of your plants are native, which are not, and which are invasive. Although most invasive species are exotics, a few native species also are invasive.

Most yards are likely to have some invasive exotic plants, which you must remove before planting your natives. But you might also discover some valuable native species, perhaps in a less developed corner of the yard. If you're lucky to have some natives, build your new bird habitat around these valuable plants.

A near fiasco taught me the importance of taking time and care landscaping in a new location. Young nonblossoming plants fooled me during the first spring. I nearly transplanted extremely invasive Spotted Knapweed from one spot in my new yard to another. I thought the plant was Prairie (Gray-headed) Coneflower, whose leaves, particularly the lower ones, are similar to that of knapweed. Both plants have leaves that are divided into narrow segments. Something didn't look quite right to me. The plant seemed a little lighter green and there was something about those leaves. I checked my field guides and discovered my error. At least a few of the lobes on the coneflower's leaves usually have teeth, while the knapweed's do not. Botanists would say that the knapweed's lobes are "entire." You don't know how glad I am that I didn't transplant it that day! After several seasons, we are still removing this amazingly prolific and devastating invader from the original site.

It would have been easier if I had waited until the knapweed was in flower, with its unmistakable pink and purple blossoms. It is best to identify plants when they are in bloom; botanists use floral characteristics as the basis for classifying plants.

A number of excellent field guides can help you in identifying your plants, both native and exotics, including the invasives (although they are not usually identified as invasive in field guides). There are also some excellent websites which have photographs and information on invasive plants. See books and websites listed in Resources for Readers at the end of this chapter.

University extension horticulturists or experts at your local nature center, museum or botanical garden may also be consulted. (You may be asked to clip a stem and send it in plastic to a staff botanist.) Local chapters of Wild Ones: Native Plants, Natural Landscapes or native plant societies may be able to assist in identification and some may even have experts among the membership who are willing to come to your yard. Some Wild Ones' chapters sponsor an annual "Help Me" day on which they visit the yards of members seeking assistance. Wild Ones has chapters in seven of the eight midwestern states covered by this book (none in Iowa). See the listing of chapters and locations in the appendix.

Native plant societies, under various names, are found in all eight states. Like Wild Ones, they promote the appreciation, preservation and sometimes cultivation of natives. But generally they are not as active in encouraging natural landscaping as is Wild Ones. For locations of native plant societies in your state, check the appendix.

As you check out the plants on your property, keep a record of the birds you see and note what seems to attract them to your yard. You may decide to enhance habitat for these birds as well as add missing habitat to attract new species native to your area. Later, you'll be able to compare the before-and-after bird life in your yard.

Habitat Features for Every Yard

The following is a list of the essential features to include in your landscape plans. They will be discussed in detail in the following pages. Check these basic habitat features against your inventory and make a list of what needs to be added.

Food
1. Plants that provide a variety of food throughout the seasons
2. Leaf litter
3. An area with gravel or sand
4. No herbicides, pesticides or rodenticides

Cover and Nesting Sites
1. Multiple layers of vegetation for a variety of habitat niches
2. At least one evergreen, or better, a clump of evergreens
3. Thorny shrubs
4. Dead branches and trees, standing or fallen
5. Dead and dying vegetation during winter
6. Log, brush and/or rock pile

Space

Water

White-throated Sparrows forage on the ground for insects, sometimes scratching in the leaf litter with both feet at once.

Food

1. Plants that provide a variety of food throughout the seasons

Species offering nuts, seeds, berries and nectar-rich flowers will provide food throughout the seasons. I'll provide much more information in later chapters on specific habitat gardens, but here's a brief overview.

Early Summer. The new young leaves of many species of trees and shrubs, as well as their flowers, are magnets for insects that will, in turn, attract migrating and insectivorous birds. Serviceberries and chokecherries are among our earliest fruiting species in the Midwest and attract many kinds of birds.

Summer. Cherries, mulberries, raspberries, blackberries, elderberries, currants, gooseberries, blueberries and more—berries galore will be available for birds if you plant some of these species in your yard. Blossoming wildflowers in your sunny areas will attract nectar-eating insects, essential food for the nestlings of most bird species. Hummingbirds also need nectar-rich flowers.

Late Summer/Fall. Dogwoods and viburnums are among the top fall-fruiting species which will fatten migrants for their long journeys. Seeds of native grasses and wildflowers feed finches and sparrows; nuts and acorns feed jays, woodpeckers, titmice and turkeys.

Winter. Fruits that remain attached long after ripening and remain available through the winter months include chokeberries, hawthorns, snowberries, native bittersweet and sumacs. Many seeds of native grasses and wildflowers also help to nourish your wintering birds.

2. Leaf litter

Leaf litter should be left in place wherever possible. Thrushes, towhees, thrashers and some sparrows are ground-feeders that forage in the fallen leaves to uncover insects. Leaf litter is also used for nest material.

3. An area with gravel or sand

Birds, having no teeth, ingest sand or gravel to aid them in grinding up food in their gizzards. Many birds also dust-bathe in sand or dust, which may help them remove parasites, oil and moisture and align the barbs on their feathers.

BIRD GARDENS A CENTURY AGO

Some of the country's first urban bird gardens were designed by Jens Jensen, a visionary landscape architect of the early 1900s. Two of his bird gardens in Chicago were featured in an article entitled "Bird Gardens in the City" in a 1914 issue of *Country Life in America*. The essentials of Jensen's bird gardens were "a food house, a bathing pool, and a belt of shrubs with edible berries." Obviously the gardens included the basics of food, water and cover, just as today. The "food house," what we now call a bird feeder, was invented by Baron von Berlepsch, an early pioneer in restoring Germany's birds. (Von Berlepsch also invented artificial nesting boxes for woodpeckers, based on his studies of actual tree hole nest sites.)

The shrubs Jensen chose for the bird gardens included a variety of dogwoods and viburnums—still stars of today's midwestern landscapes. The author praises them highly:

"Put your faith in Cornus [dogwood] and viburnum, the two genera in which America excels the whole world."

Jensen's bathing pool featured a number of shallow areas for birds to bathe in, and he designed it with an emphasis on the horizontal lines characteristic of prairie rivers.

The author sums up the value of the bird garden with these words: "It is very American and it harmonizes with the prairie."

4. No herbicides, pesticides or rodenticides

Probably the best single thing a gardener can do for wildlife is to minimize chemical use, say wildlife habitat experts at the U.S. Department of Agriculture's Natural Resources Conservation Service. Herbicides and pesticides will poison the natural foods you offer the birds, including berries and other plant foods, insects and even larger prey. In high concentrations, they kill the protein-rich insects so vital to birds. Rodenticides sicken, and sometimes kill, birds of prey when they feed on animals that have ingested the poisons. Dead birds tested for West Nile virus by the New York State Pathology Lab in 2000 revealed that over 48% died of chemical poisoning, not the virus.

A healthy birdscaped habitat will attract predator insects, like lacewings, praying mantises, and ladybugs, which reduce the need for toxics. Plant diseases are also less noticeable and widespread in a landscape with a diversity of species, since they will generally attack only one or a few species within a wide mix of plants, unlike the mass attacks which often occur in monocultures.

COVER AND NESTING SITES

Birds need cover to help them survive adverse weather conditions and to provide safe havens from predators like cats and dogs, fox or even larger birds like hawks. The importance of providing adequate cover, sometimes referred to as shelter, is often underestimated. If given a choice, wildlife will always choose shelter before food, according to the experts with the Wisconsin Department of Natural Resources.

The very best way to provide natural cover is to restore native plant communities. To maximize the value of the vegetation, choose native species that will provide food as well as cover. This is especially important for yards too small to accommodate a great variety of plants. Multipurpose plants will also give you "more birds for the buck"—very important for those on a limited budget.

1. Multiple layers of vegetation for a variety of habitat niches

Natural habitats typically have multiple layers of vegetation attractive to a wide variety of birds. Undisturbed natural woodlands have herbaceous plants as a groundcover, with shrubs, small trees and canopy trees in successive layers above. Tall grass prairies also show a layering in the various heights of grasses and wildflowers, ranging from ground-hugging rosettes to ten-foot tall grasses and sunflowers. Various species of birds prefer different layers of vegetation for cover, as well as for feeding, courting and nesting. Brown Thrashers, for example, sing in the treetops, nest on the ground or in shrubs and low trees and feed, as their name suggests, by thrashing aside dead leaves with their bills to find insects on the ground.

2. At least one evergreen, or better, a clump of evergreens

Evergreens have value as both cover and food for birds. Their thick needled branches offer cozy shelter for birds, which can be critical in harsh winter weather. Ideally, these evergreens should be placed on the northwest side of your property in the direction of our prevailing midwestern winds, which will help protect your yard birds, as well as your home, from the worst blasts of winter wind. Planted several trees deep, an evergreen windbreak can reduce wind impact on a house by as much as half and help reduce your winter heating bills. The perfect location for winter bird feeders is in the shelter of these evergreens. They'll also provide a beautiful green backdrop to enhance the view from your windows as you enjoy watching your winter birds. In addition, the nutritious oily seeds of pines are eaten by dozens of species of birds.

3. Thorny shrubs

Thorny shrubs offer great protection from predators, especially for nesting birds. Researchers in Illinois found that robins and thrushes were less apt to have their nests destroyed if they nested in shrubs with stout thorns, like our native hawthorns, instead of invasive shrubs like honeysuckle and buckthorn. Although other shrubs and trees in the Midwest have thorns, our native hawthorns are standouts, having both very stout thorns and berries perfectly sized for fruit-eating birds.

4. Dead branches and trees, standing or fallen

Dead branches and trees provide insect food, cavities and perching sites for birds. Nearly 50 species of midwestern birds are dependent on standing dead trees, often called snags. Hawks, owls, kingfishers and many other birds perch on them to scan for prey. On larger properties, Bald Eagles and Ospreys come to snags to survey their surroundings. In addition, Ospreys often build nests on snags near water.

Downy, Red-headed, Red-bellied and Pileated Woodpeckers and Flickers drill cavities in the trunks of dead trees for their nesting sites. Later, the old woodpecker holes, as well as natural cavities that form in snags, will be used by a host of other birds, including owls, nuthatches, wrens, bluebirds and wood ducks to name a few. Chickadees use these cavities, too, although they often drill their own dens in soft wood. They are the only midwestern species besides woodpeckers to do so.

Snags are also home to many beneficial native insects, which live in and under the bark and burrow into the wood. These insects and their larvae are prime, high-protein food for woodpeckers, nuthatches, creepers and other woodland birds.

Because most cavity-nesting birds feed on insects and play an important role in controlling insect pests, the U.S. Forest Service established a national snag policy in 1977 that requires all regions and forests to develop guidelines for snag management. The loss of snags has been shown to reduce the populations of some species of birds, including Red-headed Woodpeckers.

The most common yard birds attracted to snags and older trees with cavities include wrens, chickadees, nuthatches and woodpeckers. Experts recommend three to five snags per acre; at least one would be ideal for the average one-third acre lot.

Hardwood species such as oaks, maples, hickories, butternuts and beeches that grow to a large size and decay slowly have the best potential as snags. Willows, aspens and birch have shorter life spans and rot more quickly, making superior soft snags, also of great value to birds. They will produce cavities sooner than hardwoods and attract swarms of insects to their pulpy wood for insect-feeding birds.

You can create a snag by girdling an undesirable tree. Girdling involves removing a ring of bark around the circumference of a tree which will eventually kill it. (See chapter 7 for details on girdling.) You could choose an invasive tree or one that is already diseased, deformed or crowded by other trees.

If you don't have snags or trees with cavities, add nest boxes while you wait for natural ones

Great Crested Flycatcher

to occur. We did this on a small snag in the corner of our suburban yard. Within a short time, a screech-owl discovered and used it as a roost in winter, providing us great views from our windows.

For safety, decaying limbs can be removed when the snag is near a path or the boundary of a neighboring property. But the main trunk and major branches of a snag often have a long life span before there's any danger of their falling.

A snag that is in full view of neighbors may raise aesthetic concerns. Vines can help in such situations, adding blossoms and beauty through the growing season and a brushy tangle up the trunk in winter which can easily blend in with surrounding shrubs and trees. Virginia Creeper is an outstanding choice for a showy vine, providing dense greenery all summer and a scarlet blaze of color in fall, along with beautiful berries which are eaten by over 30 species of birds. Trumpet Creeper with its showy trumpet-shaped flowers, full of nectar for hummingbirds, is another possibility. Check the recommended vine species in chapter 17 to see which of these or other species will be best for your location and conditions.

Once fallen, a tree is equally valuable for enriching the bird life in your yard. Logs and stumps teem with ants, beetles, spiders, millipedes, worms and many more invertebrates, becoming virtual cafeterias for birds. Cavities in the decaying wood are home to many other critters, like salamanders, mice and snakes, which can nourish Cooper's Hawks, screech-owls and other birds of prey. In forests of the Upper Midwest, Ruffed Grouse use logs for courtship drumming, beating their wings rapidly to produce a muffled sound.

Decaying wood, stumps, snags and puddles here and there—all these are hotspots of life and diversity in native habitats. As Ken Druse points out, "The natural habitat gardener rejoices at such happenings and the creatures who come in to bathe, drink, feed or breed because of them. In the habitat garden, such 'imperfections' are reasons for celebration—not a bout of obsessive tidying up."

5. Dead and dying vegetation during winter

Don't tidy up your yard in fall by removing vegetation that has died back. Your spent wildflowers and grasses provide insulating ground cover and seeds and fruit for wintering sparrows and finches. The standing stems will look stunning after a winter storm when the seedheads are topped with powder puffs of snow and their dark stalks stand out on a winter-white canvas.

Old stalks and seed pods also harbor insects on which many birds feed. Wendy Walcott, land manager at the Schlitz Audubon Center in Milwaukee, found twenty-seven species of insects wintering on the stalks of Golden Glow, also called Green-headed Coneflower. The surviving insects on your plants will hatch in spring and attract hungry migrant birds to your yard.

6. Log, brush and/or rock piles

At least one such pile is a must for every yard. A brush pile is easy to build and a haven for many kinds of birds. Usually a great deal of material is readily available in a naturally land-scaped yard. For starters, you can pile up all the brush from the invasive shrubs you remove. We made a brush pile "fence" of the honeysuckle and buckthorn we removed from our woods. The brush pile has been popular ever since with sparrows, wrens and other birds. I was thrilled to spot a Winter Wren, rather rare for our area, moving mouse-like at the base of this brush pile in April.

Pruning can also produce suitable branches for your brush pile. While only limited pruning should be done in a natu-ral habitat, I recommend the selective pruning of shrubs to ensure continual and abundant fruiting. After the holidays your live Christmas tree can become a one-piece brush pile. And don't forget to use the evergreens from holiday wreaths.

Detailed descriptions for building brush piles follow, but I've found that birds aren't all that particular. So if you don't have time to fuss, don't worry. Just loosely throw together a pile of branches, stumps, logs and brush of any size. Place them hap-hazardly, so that there is space for shelter from storms and cover from predators. If available, a few evergreen branches on top will offer extra shelter.

If you have more time, experts recommend building a base, topped with brush. Bases are usually constructed of logs about four to six feet in length. Hardwood logs, like oak or cedar, rot slowly and are best for the base. Large size stones up to a foot in diameter also work. Metal or plastic pipes at the base will allow passages for mice, reptiles and amphibians that will feed hawks and owls. Once the base is in place, add brush on top, in crosswise layers, the bigger ones first, then smaller limbs last. Leave plenty of spaces in between for birds and other critters, by placing the branches at different angles and directions.

A pile six to eight feet high and wide is the perfect size,

Raptors
Turkey Vulture, Merlin, American Kestrel, Barn Owl, Eastern Screech-Owl, Barred Owl, Northern Saw-whet Owl, Bald Eagle, Osprey, Red-tailed Hawk

Woodland Birds
Carolina Wren, Winter Wren, Brown Creeper, Great Crested Flycatcher, Prothonotary Warbler, Red-breasted Nuthatch, White-breasted Nuthatch, Tufted Titmouse, Ruffed Grouse

Meadow or Savanna Birds
Bewick's Wren, Eastern Bluebird, Tree Swallow

Residential Birds
House Wren, Purple Martin

Snags benefit many creatures.

but may be too big for your lot. If so, make it smaller. My brush piles have never been carefully constructed; nonetheless, they have been immensely popular with wrens, sparrows, juncos, chickadees, towhees and other songbirds.

Log and rock piles may attract more rabbits and rodents than songbirds, but these critters will provide ready food for hawks and owls that may be attracted to your yard. If you have a fireplace, you probably already have a log pile on your property. Otherwise, just pile up some logs and you're set. Rocks and boulders can be used to construct simple rock piles or walls. Don't bother with mortar; wildlife will use the crevices for shelter.

As a final touch, plant a flowering or fruiting vine to sprawl over your pile. A large perching post (perhaps your snag) can also be added nearby as an invitation to birds of prey. Elizabeth Mueller of Indiana (see chapter 4, The Gardens & Gardeners), grew Virginia Creeper over her brush piles, to make them more attractive to neighbors (and birds).

A pile of brush, rocks or logs is an inexpensive way to create a natural food chain and attract a greater diversity of birds and other wildlife. Before you construct a brush pile, however, check local codes for any restrictions. I've never lived in a community that regulates brush piles, but I understand that some do.

Space

Birds need adequate space for all aspects of their life, including courtship, mating, nesting, roosting, feeding and drinking, so many birds establish and defend territories. Usually, these territories surround their nesting sites and cover an area large enough to raise a family. Other kinds of territories include feeding, roosting, winter and mating.

Some birds, like Purple Martins and Tree Swallows, defend only the area around their nest sites. Most need breeding territories of larger sizes. For example, the Ruby-throated Hummingbird needs 1/4 acre, the Common Loon, 60–200 acres, while the Great Horned Owl needs up to 2 square miles.

To maximize your yard's potential, encourage your neighbors to join you in habitat restoration. Together, you can enlarge the size of suitable habitat and attract a greater diversity of birds. Any habitat improvement will enhance the birdlife. Many birds may come to feed, bathe, roost or refuel during migration, even if your habitat is not large enough for their breeding requirements.

A small pond gives birds a place to drink and bathe.

Water

Birds need water for bathing and drinking and sometimes for feeding and breeding. If your property has any natural sources of water, you're fortunate. Even puddles, where water accumulates after rain or snowmelt, can attract flocks of birds.

Sadly, natural sources of water are disappearing at an alarming rate as we create drier sites for homes, businesses, roads and farm fields. Most of us will need to supply an artificial source of water (such as a birdbath or pond) for wildlife. If you have clay soil, you can simply dig shallow holes that will fill with rainwater. They drain slowly, but provide some water for drinking and bathing. Chapter 16 will provide more details on constructing ponds and other water features.

Survey the Physical Characteristics of Your Property

Examine the physical characteristics of your yard to determine which plant species will grow best on the site. The most important are the soil conditions and the amount of sun or shade. Other factors to consider are the topography of your property, whether it is flat, sloped or rolling, and its hydrology, particularly where water flows and accumulates after rains.

Soil

You should know three things about your soil: moisture, texture, and pH. There are likely to be differences in different parts, so check areas of your yard where you plan to restore habitat.

Moisture. The amount of moisture in your soil can be determined by simple observations. Is there seasonal flooding in any area? Are there patterns of flowage, such as gullies or streams? Do pools of water remain for several days after heavy rains? Or does the ground surface dry very quickly despite heavy rains?

Texture and pH. Soil texture can be determined simply by rubbing the moist soil between your fingers and checking for the following characteristics:

Sandy soil:	Very gritty	Not sticky	
Loams:	Slightly gritty	Slightly sticky	Smooth, flourlike feel when dry (due to silt, a soil particle size between sand and clay)
Clay soils:	Not gritty	More sticky	Some have flourlike feel when dry (due to silt)

The pH of the soil is a measure of its acidity or alkalinity. Test kits can be purchased from biological supply stores and are very easy to use. You simply mix soil with distilled water and a reagent tablet and match the resulting color of the solution to a color chart which indicates the corresponding pH. Soils east of the Mississippi that once supported prairies are generally neutral (midway between acid and alkaline). Those that were once forested are usually acidic, except where there are limestone outcrops.

Christine McCullough of Ohio (chapter 4) learned the importance of knowing soil pH when a landscaper decided to plant the acid-loving Bearberry in the alkaline clay soil on her property. "It was the first indicator that acid lovers do not survive here," Christine says. "As in traditional gardening, 'right plant, right place' applies to naturally landscaping your property."

If you're unsure about your soil texture and pH, the nearest university extension or soil testing service will do the tests. In addition to pH and textures, the tests can determine the amount of phosphorous, potassium and other minerals in soil. This is generally unnecessary in natural landscaping, since native plants of local origin grow well in their native soils.

Knowing the soil moisture, texture and pH will be invaluable in helping you select plants for your restoration.

Sun or Shade

Observe the amount of sunlight in various locations of your yard. Full sun means direct sunlight for at least six hours a day. Partial sun refers to three to six hours of sunlight, while shade means less than three hours. Often, the topography of your site will affect the amount of sun. A south-facing slope, for example, will get much more sun than a north-facing slope.

Most trees and shrubs do well in full sun, although some can tolerate shade. The amount of sunlight is even more critical to herbaceous plants—nonwoody flowers and grasses. An area with full sunlight is ideal for a prairie bird garden. Many plants for a bluebird savanna garden can tolerate a little shade provided by the occasional trees. Woodland understory plants, on the other hand, require shade cast by trees, shrubs or buildings.

Now you have accomplished the essential beginning steps for creating bird habitat. You've done a careful inventory of your yard and its characteristics. You know what you have in basic habitat features and what you want to add. Now it's time to get to the nitty-gritty of creating bird habitat in your yard.

RESOURCES FOR READERS

Books

Creating Habitats

Mizejewski, David. 2004. *National Wildlife Federation's Attracting Birds, Butterflies and Other Backyard Wildlife.* Upper Saddle River, NJ: Creative Homeowner.

Newman, D. S., R. E. Warner and P. C. Mankin. 2003. *Creating Habitats and Homes for Illinois Wildlife.* Springfield, IL: Illinois Department of Natural Resources and University of Illinois.

Identifying Herbaceous Plants

Brown, Lauren. 1979. *Grasses: An Identification Guide.* Boston: Houghton Mifflin.

Cobb, Boughton. 1963. *A Field Guide to the Ferns.* Boston: Houghton Mifflin.

Moyle, J. B., and Evelyn W. Moyle. 2001. *Northland Wildflowers: The Comprehensive Guide to the Minnesota Region.* Minneapolis: University of Minnesota Press.

Newcomb, Lawrence. 1977. *Newcomb's Wildflower Guide.* Boston: Little, Brown.

Peterson, Roger Tory, and Margaret McKenny. 1968. *A Field Guide to Wildflowers of Northeastern and North-Central North America.* Boston: Houghton Mifflin.

Identifying Woody Plants

Petrides, George A. 1958. *A Field Guide to Trees and Shrubs.* Boston: Houghton Mifflin.
Symonds, George W.D. 1958. *The Shrub Identification Book.* New York: William Morrow.
———. 1958. *The Tree Identification Book.* New York: William Morrow.

Websites

Creating Habitats

National Audubon Society. Audubon at Home. http://athome.audubon.org/

National Wildlife Federation. "Garden for Wildlife."
http://www.nwf.org/Get-Outside/Outdoor-Activities/Garden-for-Wildlife.aspx

Identifying Invasive Plants

This website has photos and information on many invasive species:
Plant Conservation Alliance. http://www.nps.gov/plants/alien/

CHAPTER 6
PLANNING & DESIGN

*Backyards are becoming repositories of
habitat and hope.*

—Janet Marinelli
The Naturally Elegant Home: Environmental Style

Before you plant your first serviceberry or cast the first wildflower seeds, you have a few more things to do. You'll need to map your yard, check local ordinances, consider neighbors and look into the plant community you want to restore for your bird habitat. There are also design elements to consider as you plan the locations of shrubs, trees and herbaceous plants that are the basic components of every natural landscape. This chapter will walk you through these important steps.

Map Your Yard

Using graph paper, you can make your map to scale. Indicate the location of the present vegetation, including areas of native vegetation that you plan to keep. Place the locations of your house, driveway, garage and septic field if you have one. Call your local "diggers' hot line" to flag power lines, buried cable and any other utilities. Take photos for future reference and indicate their location on your map. You may also want to locate slopes, drainage, depressions and other topography that will affect your landscaping. Map the shady and sunny areas, and areas of varying soil conditions. Now you have a snapshot of your present landscape.

With this in hand, it's time to consider the habitat possibilities for the "undeveloped" parts of your yard. Your plans should take into consideration people, as well as birds and other wildlife. Your family may need areas for play and entertaining, such as decks, patio and benches. Be sure to keep lawn to a minimum in accommodating these needs. Do you plan to have a vegetable garden? Where will paths be located? Consider views you may want to screen, as well as scenic views you wish to retain. Likewise, keep in mind the bird viewing possibilities from windows in your home. You'll want to keep the vegetation low in areas next to these windows. Add all these basic human habitat features to your map.

Check on Weed Laws and Permits

Early in your planning efforts, check with your local authorities about ordinances related

photo: Butterflyweed

to noxious weeds, brush piles and landscaping. Most state and local governments prohibit noxious weeds—usually plants that have been deemed invasive to cropland or that cause hay fever. Purple Loosestrife, *Lythrum virgatum*, and Canada Thistle, *Cirsium arvense*, for example, are designated as noxious weeds in all the midwestern states covered by this book. Multiflora Rose, *Rosa multiflora*, is so designated in Iowa, Illinois, Indiana, Missouri, Ohio and Wisconsin, and Field Bindweed, *Convolvulus arvensis,* in Iowa, Michigan, Minnesota, Missouri and Wisconsin.

Municipalities often have noxious weed lists specific to their locales. These lists are usually no problem for natural landscapers, who don't want these weedy species either. Just be careful to watch your yard for a possible invasion of these species to avoid future complaints.

Some communities require permits for natural landscaping and, occasionally, the approval of the majority of neighbors. White Bear Lake, Minnesota, once had a permit process, but now simply requires a setback from property lines. Similarly, Greendale, Wisconsin, where I formerly lived, required a 10-foot setback from the street. Other communities, like Boone County, Illinois, and Harvard, Illinois, have ordinances that expressly protect native landscapes. Still others, like Long Grove, Illinois, require developers to plant native vegetation in scenic easements between homes and streets. Prairie Crossing, north of Chicago, is an entire subdivision in which prairie, savannah and native wetlands have been established and maintained.

On the national level, natural landscaping received significant and far-reaching support when President Clinton, in 1994, directed federal facilities to use native plants in landscaping. It is encouraging to note the growing support at every level of government. Bret Rappaport, a lawyer and past president of Wild Ones: Native Plants, Natural Landscapes, has represented a number of natural landscapers charged with violating weed ordinances over the years. But today he fields far fewer complaints than in the late 1980s and early '90s. "The good news," he says, "is that committed pioneers and newer converts, willing to question the status quo and recognize the ecological and monetary consequences of landscape choices, are undermining the arbitrary legal and social barriers to gardening with Nature." Ideally, in the future, natural landscaping will be the norm, and instead, lawns will need permits.

Also check into ordinances on fencing and other physical features you may want to incorporate into your landscape plans. In Greendale, my husband and I had hoped to use a split rail fence as a border between our prairie and the lawn required for the setback. Fences in the front yard, however, were not permitted. (We knew of plenty in place on other properties, however, and gave a list to our local inspector. He wasn't too happy about this, saying that he would now need to require the homeowners to apply for variances.) Nonetheless, we chose not to push the issue and decided on a rock border instead. We were lucky to get permission to collect the rocks from a construction site only a few miles from our home and were very happy with the border we created for our front-yard prairie.

Be Neighborly

Let your neighbors know about your plans, particularly if you plan to naturally landscape your entire yard. Otherwise, they may think you've simply let your yard go "wild" and unattended. Tactfully explain what you plan to do and why, pointing out that they will enjoy more birds, less lawnmower noise, more greenery and beauty. A neighbor in Greendale said that our yard was like having a park next door.

Red-bellied Woodpecker

If neighbors remain unenthusiastic, plant a hedge to screen their view. Shrubs are often used as conventional borders; the only difference will be that yours will be completely native. But try to avoid a "fortress" look with shrubs circling your entire property.

Another approach is to border your landscape with a fence, stones, bricks or wood chips or to maintain an edging of lawn or other low groundcover as a sign that your property is being planned and managed. It can also make your landscaping more compatible with your neighbors. In Greendale, for example, my small front lawn, mandated by the setback requirement, blended in with the adjacent, albeit much more expansive, lawns of my neighbors.

You can also give your property a human touch by adding a winding path, a bench, a sundial, birdbath, garden gate or arbor. Pat and Carl Brust (chapter 4) have incorporated nearly all these features in their yard and have enjoyed many compliments from neighbors.

Signs can also do the trick. An example of the potent psychology of signs is told in the book *Redesigning the American Lawn,* by F. Herbert Bormann et al. The neighbors of a biologist in Athens, Georgia, complained to city authorities about his naturally landscaped acre-size yard. The officials' creative solution was a large sign declaring the yard a bird sanctuary. The complaints came to a halt!

Both Wild Ones and National Wildlife Federation offer yard signs that will inform your neighbors of your intention to live in harmony with nature and to create habitat for our sister species. Of course, you can always design your own sign, perhaps specifying the type of bird habitat you're creating, such as "Hummingbird Garden."

Above all, don't just let your yard go unattended. In addition to alienating neighbors, you may well be opening the door to a problem with invasive weeds, which can sneak in without your notice. Make your landscaping as beautiful and inviting as possible, especially areas in view of your neighbors. By doing so, you'll be an effective ambassador for natural landscaping.

Since natural landscaping is becoming more popular, you may be lucky enough to have neighbors who will support and perhaps even join in your efforts. Together you'll be able create larger bird habitat areas, more attractive to a greater variety of species. For some birds, just one yard is not enough. By linking your habitat with that of adjoining property owners, you'll be able to create greenways or environmental corridors, which can help ensure the free flow of seeds, birds and other animals throughout your neighborhood. Ideally, these corridors would provide connections to larger natural areas and preserves in your community and help reduce the harmful effects of habitat fragmentation.

One of the most exciting new projects related to this is the Community Wildlife Habitat certification program, begun only a few years ago by the National Wildlife Federation (NWF). This organization has long been involved in certifying individual backyard and school wildlife habitats, but now they have expanded to community-wide projects. Fifty-seven communities across the nation are now certified. The first was Zionsville, Indiana, with much of the credit due to Elizabeth Mueller (chapter 4). Zionsville, a small town of about 13,000 people, has certified nearly 150 individual habitats. Chesterfield, Missouri, has become the second midwestern community to achieve certification. Four of the communities—in Florida, California and Virginia—are entire counties. Many other communities are registered with NWF and are working toward full certification, including four in the Midwest. You can also certify your own backyard, as I have done. See further information on NWF habitat programs later in this chapter.

Choosing Plants and Plant Communities

Now that you have mapped your yard and checked with the laws and the neighbors, you are ready to begin considering the type of plant community that you'll feature in the bird habitat you'd like to create. In the Midwest, we are lucky to enjoy the most richly varied landscape in eastern North America, thanks to our location midway between the deciduous forests to the east and the grassland plains to the west. It gives a wide choice of plant communities for our habitat restorations, ranging from prairie to open woodland or savanna and forest.

Although I recommend making a master plan for your entire yard, it's best to start on a small scale when you begin to implement it. For example, you could begin your habitat restoration by expanding existing beds, gradually adding native wildflowers. Or you could remove grass from under trees, mulch and then add ferns or woodland-edge wildflowers.

Starting small will give you time to learn-by-doing and help you avoid mistakes that might affect your whole yard. If you've found many invasives during your inventory, it will be easier to begin work on a small area, thoroughly removing invasives and keeping them in check one patch at a time. Another big plus in starting small is that it will give your neighbors time to adjust to your yard's new look.

Let the Habitat Native to Your Area Be Your Guide

Study the nearby intact natural communities in your area—perhaps at a nature center or designated state or local natural area. Note the dominant plants, the companion plants, the layering of the vegetation. Try to find microclimates similar to those in your yard.

You may also be able to locate a map of the pre-settlement vegetation of your area by checking with your local university or state department of natural resources. These maps are based on the government land surveys in the mid-1800s. The surveyors made note of tree species along township lines and drew maps of each township showing prairies, swamplands, lakes, streams and other features. From these records, it has been possible to deduce a general picture of the vegetation at the time of survey.

Some of the bird habitat gardens described in part 4 may be representative of your particular area and could serve as the major focus of your restoration efforts. If wooded habitat is native to your area, for example, the woodland bird garden would obviously be most appropriate. If your area was originally prairie or oak savanna, the prairie or bluebird savanna gardens would be ideal. If

Robert Cashman of Munster, Indiana, has created woodland and savanna habitat on his property with nearly all native species.

you're lucky enough to have a wetland on your property, check out the wetland bird garden.

You can still feel free to add variety to your basic habitat choices. Natural prairies often have pockets of shrubs, and forests have openings and shrubby edges. Other bird gardens in part 4 represent various transitional areas like these and include the hummingbird garden, and the shrubland, migratory and winter bird gardens. A water garden welcomes birds in any type of habitat.

Regarding habitat choice, noted restorationists Stephen Packard and Laurel M. Ross, of the Illinois chapter of The Nature Conservancy, have this advice: When restoring a weedy quarter-acre on a home lot, it might be considered a matter of personal taste whether grassland or woodland is chosen as the goal. But even on small sites, choosing the most appropriate option can make a big difference in the amount of work necessary and in the quality of the result. In other words, don't fight your site. Plant in harmony with the particular parameters of your geographic location and the physical characteristics of your property. Try to complement the natural habitat near or adjacent to your yard.

Select Native Plants of Local Ecotype

Review chapter 2 on the value of natives and tips on selecting plants. Just as selecting appropriate habitat will help make your landscaping efforts easier and more successful, native plants of local ecotype will be hardier and easier to grow than plants less suitable to your site.

Choose As Many Species as Possible

A number of studies have shown that a more diverse plant community is more stable, more productive and less vulnerable to insect damage, invasion by weeds and environmental change (like global warming). In addition, it will offer more varied cover and food for birds. A diversity of plants also adds more seasonal interest and design potential.

No matter what habitat you want to expand or create, you can easily increase diversity. If your habitat is mostly woodland, add diversity by creating adjoining edge habitat of shrubbery and woodland edge herbaceous plants. If your habitat is primarily shrubs and lawn, you may want to add a few trees and replace some lawn with wildflowers and native grasses. As you create new habitat, try to get a diversity of species in your seed mixes or plant selections.

Designing Your Habitat

A few basic design principles can help you create a natural habitat that is as appealing to people as to birds. Here are a few tips to consider as you work on your new habitat plans.

Curving Lines

From the meanders of rivers to graceful undulating transitions between various communities of plants, nature is full of curving lines. Unless you plan to opt for a formal look to your landscaping, use flowing lines in the paths and habitat borders within your yard. Use irregular, curving shapes for your planting beds.

Layout

As in nature, keep your layout asymmetrical but balanced. Look at your garden from different viewpoints. Be sure to arrange the plants, spaces between plants, benches and birdbaths so they appear roughly equal.

Views & Focal Points

Retain beautiful views in your yard, such as the setting or rising sun, a picturesque tree or shrub, or attractive knoll or ridge, and of course, a pond, lake or stream if you're lucky enough to have that on or adjacent to your property. These views can be the focal points in your landscaping. Consider the views from windows, porches and outdoor benches. Keep backlighting and shadows in mind—they can greatly enhance views at different times of day.

Natural Forms

Let plants take their own natural forms. Topiary and sheared hedges are inappropriate for a natural habitat.

Connections

Make natural pathways between different areas of natural habitat. Not only will your landscaping look more natural, birds and other animals prefer gradual transitions. In particular, wildlife will avoid crossing large expanses of lawn.

Clumps & Drifts

For masses of color and texture, plant numbers of the same species in clumps or drifts, as is typically found in nature. Doing so also encourages cross-pollination of flowers.

Sense of Order

Use repeated patterns to create a sense of order—repeated colors, or repeated drifts of different species, with their varying textures, forms and heights.

Colors

Color can impart mood. When used together, colors opposite each other on the color wheel appear more vibrant and lively. Orange-and-blue or red-and-green are examples of opposite colors. Combinations of colors next to one another on the color wheel can appear more quiet and restful. Yellow, yellow-green, yellow-orange might be one such combination. Another would be blue-green and green. Loretta Hernday, who designed a beautiful prairie garden to grace the front of the Wehr Nature Center in Milwaukee County, carefully placed wildflowers with color combinations in mind.

Variety of Textures

Use different plant textures to add interest and depth to your landscape: plants of different sizes and shapes, plants with coarse and fine stems or branches, plants with patterned and smooth bark, plants with different-shaped leaves—lobed and unlobed, compound and simple.

Illusion

To make a small yard look bigger, plant small, fine-textured plants. Curving paths that lead the eye toward unseen areas beyond a bend also suggest spaciousness, as well as an element of mystery.

Use Wildflowers & Native Grasses Together

As a practical matter, wildflowers planted close together and with native grasses physically support one another. Doing so also enhances the look of your landscape.

Resist the Too-Tidy Look

Although we want to create well-designed beautiful natural habitats, we should not be too neat and tidy. Lorrie Otto, a founder of the natural landscaping movement, has warned about the "tyranny of the tidy yard." Brushy, even unkempt-looking areas can make great wildlife habitat. Your habitat can be both beautiful and wild.

Where to Get Help

Many resources are available to help you create natural habitat. Local nature centers, universities, university extension programs, native plant nurseries and native plant societies offer information specific to your area. In addition, there's an immense amount of information on the websites of environmental organizations and state departments of natural resources. Two of the most active nonprofit organizations promoting habitat enhancement are Wild Ones: Native Plants, Natural Landscapes and the National Wildlife Federation. Both encourage restoration or habitat creation in home yards, school grounds, business sites and community green areas.

Hanson and Ueberroth's front yard in Hales Corners, Wisconsin, is entirely landscaped with native plants. The porous driveway lets water seep into the ground rather than run off into the sewers, lessening the possibility of flooding and pollution in a nearby river.

Wild Ones: Native Plants, Natural Landscapes

Wild Ones: Native Plants, Natural Landscapes is a national, nonprofit organization whose mission is to promote environmentally sound landscaping practices to preserve biodiversity through the preservation, restoration and establishment of native plant communities. At the time of this writing, there are 43 chapters in the Midwest, in every state covered by this book except Iowa. See the list of chapters in Bird Gardener's Resources, pages 325–327. Wild Ones chapters offer workshops, lectures, help-me days, yard tours, seed collection and plant rescues. Some chapters have experienced mentors who work with new members, visiting their yards and helping with plant identification and selection. Wild Ones also publishes a bimonthly newsletter, the *Wild Ones Journal*, filled with timely and informative articles about every aspect of landscaping with native plants.

I have been actively involved with Wild Ones as a past national board member and vice president. The organization's forte, I believe, is its chapters, which provide support, camaraderie and hands-on expertise in habitat restoration at the local level.

National Wildlife Federation

The National Wildlife Federation actively promotes the creation of native habitats through its Wildlife Habitat Certification program. Started in 1973, the program has done an outstanding job in educating people on the value and basics of habitat creation and offers certification for yards with the requisite habitat features. Wild Birds Unlimited stores sell the NWF's Backyard Wildlife Habitat Starter Kit, which includes a planning guide, application, habitat tip sheets, a landscape stencil and graph paper, full color poster, kid's activities and more. It is also available directly through National Wildlife Federation.

Certification through National Wildlife Federation has proven to be immensely popular

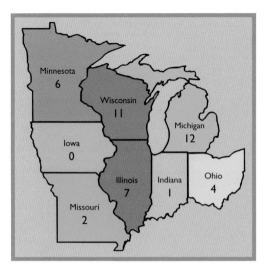

Wild Ones: Native Plants, Natural Landscapes. *Number of chapters in each of the midwestern states as of this writing. The chapters are listed in the Gardeners' Resources at the end of the book.*

and, as of this writing, 146,657 wildlife habitats, located mostly in the U.S. and Canada, are certified. Two of the midwestern states are in the top dozen: Ohio, with 6,449, ranks ninth, and Illinois, with 5,512, ranks twelfth. I encourage you to likewise certify the wildlife habitat you create in your yard, as I have done at my current and former homes.

NWF Wildlife Habitat certification signs have helped to educate the public on the value and beauty of natural landscaping. Certification may even increase your home's resale value. Ginny Widrick in northern Illinois attributes the quick sale of her family's home when they relocated to their certification with NWF. "We advertised our house as a certified wildlife habitat," she reports, "and had two offers in five hours! Both potential buyers wanted it because the landscaping was designed and already established for wildlife. We were thrilled that our birds would continue to be fed and cared for without us."

Summing It Up

In this chapter and the last, you've learned about habitat basics, what your yard has and what you want it to have. You've investigated plant community choices, as well as design features for creating a beautiful and diverse native habitat. You also know where to go for additional help as needed. Armed with all this knowledge, you're ready to bring out your yard map and complete plans for the creation of a beautiful and bird-filled natural habitat.

You can even go further than this, beyond simply providing general bird habitat, by designing habitats for a particular species of bird or groups of birds, as you'll see in part 4. By doing so, you can ensure that your yard

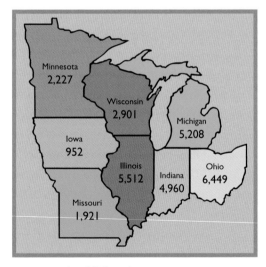

National Wildlife Federation. *Number of certified Wildlife Habitats in each of the midwestern states as of this writing.*

provides these particular birds with the essentials they'll need for their survival, generation after generation. If we can support robust, thriving populations of birds, they'll be better able to adapt and evolve to deal with new environmental challenges, like global warming and pollution. Ecologist

Spring Azure butterfly on Rattlesnake Master.

Michael Rosenzweig believes that by creating species-specific habitats for birds and other wildlife, we could "save the overwhelming majority of today's species." In this age of mass extinction, we need to try.

RESOURCES FOR READERS

Books

Bormann, H. F., D. Blamori and G. Geballe. 1993. *Redesigning the American Lawn.* New Haven, CT: Yale University Press.

Marinelli, Janet. 1992. *The Naturally Elegant Home, Environmental Style.* Boston: Little, Brown.

Organizations

National Wildlife Federation. 11100 Wildlife Center Drive, Reston, VA 20190-5362; phone: 1-800-822-9919; http://www.nwf.org/

Wild Ones: Native Plants, Natural Landscapes. PO Box 1274, Appleton, WI 54912-1274; phone: 920-730-3986 or toll-free 877-FYI-WILD (394-9453); www.wildones.org/

CHAPTER 7
Site Preparation & Planting

*In 30 years, the norm will be designing
and planting with this goal in mind of resource
conservation. You'll see less chemicals, more wildlife
enhancement, increased biodiversity. That will be what's
expected in yards, businesses, and roadsides. The water-consuming,
chemical-intensive landscapes will be rare. They'll be remnants,
almost like the native landscape is a remnant now.*

—Dr. David Northington, executive director of the National Wildflower Research Center

The information in this chapter on how to prepare your site, remove invasive species and plant native trees, shrubs and herbaceous species will be useful in creating either a general bird habitat garden or one of the specific bird gardens described in part 4.

Site Preparation

To establish your native plant bird garden, it is almost always essential to remove weeds, lawn grasses and other existing vegetation. This vegetation, especially nonnative weedy and invasive plants, will look unattractive, compete with your native plants and may be difficult to remove once your native plants are in place. An exception to this is when you are interplanting or interseeding in an area which already has mostly native vegetation.

Removing Invasive Plants

Review the list of the worst invasive plants in the Midwest in chapter 3, and look for these species in your inventory of plants on your property. Since they are so ubiquitous, you are likely to discover that you harbor a few of these troublesome plants. Some of the very worst are buckthorn, honeysuckle and Garlic Mustard.

Remove as many of the invasive plants as possible before doing any planting, since they will seriously compromise your landscaping efforts. This can be a difficult task, especially on larger properties with many invasives. In such cases, be sure to remove, at minimum, all the berry- and seed-producing invasives, since they will continue to revegetate your property with new recruits. Then, gradually attack the rest of your invasive plants, as time and energy permit. One approach is to work on only part of your yard, removing the invasives and creating native habitat there before

photo: Wild Petunias

proceeding to the other parts

Your goal is to control the invasives, since complete elimination can be difficult and may not be cost-effective. Some invasives may take several years of follow-up work to eradicate, due to seeds and roots remaining in the soil or to dispersal onto your property by wind or animals. Different invasive species require different removal techniques.

Herbaceous plants

Herbaceous species can often be removed by pulling or digging, especially in early spring or after rain when the soil is moist. Christine McCullough in Ohio (chapter 4) likes to use a circle-hoe (www.circlehoe.com) to control Garlic Mustard. As she explains: "While the rosettes were expanding, but before the flower stalk came up, I cut them with a circlehoe, just below the crown. I let the cut plant lay, and they simply shriveled up and disappeared. I went back a week or two later and cut the ones I missed. Hoeing the plants early works well since it cannot be done later, when the plants are blooming and have the ability to go to seed. The plants did not come back from the tap root."

Biennial weeds like sweet clover and some invasive thistles can be eliminated by mowing at the proper time to prevent seed production. You may choose to spray large areas of perennial invasives with a herbicide. It's best to do so when the surrounding native plants are dormant.

Woody plants

Small invasive shrubs and trees, especially shallow-rooted species like honeysuckle, can be pulled either by hand or with a Weed Wrench (www.weedwrench.com)—a tool with a big claw for grasping the shrub's stem or stems and a lever-like handle to yank it up.

When a shrub is too big for the Weed Wrench, its branches can be removed and its stump can be grubbed out with an ax. This avoids the use of herbicides, but because it exposes weed seeds in the soil and opens it up for weed invasion, the area should be seeded or planted as soon as possible.

Christine McCullough found it easier to use the root-cutting method on the shallow-rooted honeysuckle. Using a Japanese pruning saw, she cut two or three of the roots beneath the soil and then pushed over the shrub. She left the shrubs where they fell and they eventually disappeared.

Girdling. Girdling will kill some invasive trees and large shrubs with relatively few trunks. To girdle a tree or shrub, remove a three- to six-inch band of bark around the entire circumference of the trunk(s) just deep enough that the bark pops off easily when whacked or scraped. The idea is to cut through the phloem (inner bark) while leaving the xylem (sapwood) intact. There are tubes in the phloem through which food is sent down from the upper plant to the roots; in the xylem, the flow is reversed. The roots continue sending up nutrients, but receive nothing from the upper plant. Eventually the tree will die and become a snag.

Stump treatment. A common way of eradicating shrubs is to cut them down and treat their stumps immediately with a herbicide to prevent resprouting. A widely used method for honey-suckles and buckthorns is to paint or spray the stumps with a 20–25% solution of the chemical glyphosate after cutting.

Christine McCullough also had success using the drill method on honeysuckles. She drilled

Susan and Paul Damon took possession of a buckthorn-infested yard when they bought their home in the city of St. Paul in 1990. It had a row of buckthorn shrubs in the middle, a 100-foot hedge bordering the north side and a 25-foot hedge on the west side. The shrubs were 25 feet high and had probably been planted in 1924 when the house was built.

In 1999, they tackled the interior buckthorn first. They cut down smaller shrubs with loppers and handsaws. They used a chain saw for the biggest ones, whose trunks were up to 15 inches in diameter. After cutting the shrubs, they treated the stumps with Roundup. Although the couple rarely uses herbicides, they found it an effective way to deal with such a tough invasive. That summer, squirrels planted sunflower seeds in the disturbed soil, and when those sunflowers matured and formed seed, the Damons spotted American Goldfinches in their yard for the first time. A pair of goldfinches continued to visit, and that winter, a flock came to feed on the seeds of Purple Coneflower which the Damons had planted.

Encouraged by this success, the Damons decided to work on the rest of their buckthorn. It was a daunting task, but they managed to eliminate the huge hedges on the north and west borders. The following spring, the Damons planted native

(continued)

a 3/4-inch down-sloping hole into the base of the shrub and immediately filled it with the herbicide Finale. "It worked well," she reports, "and those plants never leafed out this spring."

Biological controls. For a few invasives, biological controls are becoming available. Biological controls are insects, other invertebrates, natural diseases or viruses that feed on or harm invasive plants and keep them from prospering and spreading. Beetles have been successfully used to wipe out Purple Loosestrife in some areas. Native weevils are helping control Eurasian Water Milfoil in many lakes. There have also been experimental releases of insects to control Leafy Spurge, Garlic Mustard and Spotted Knapweed. At the time of this writing, however, biological controls are rarely available for homeowners.

Resources. There are excellent sources of information on the preferred methods of controlling specific plants. *The Wisconsin Manual of Control Recommendations for Ecologically Invasive Plants* (available online) gives detailed coverage of over 25 invasive species in Wisconsin, as well other midwestern states.

The website of The Nature Conservancy (TNC) provides photographs and information on invasive weeds including their ecology and control. TNC also makes available online the *Weed Control Methods Handbook*, which reviews manual removal, fire, herbicide and other techniques.

See Resources for Readers at the end of this chapter for these websites and others, along with other useful sources of information.

Removing Lawn

Unless very sparse, lawn and other existing vegetation should be removed since they will compete with your newly planted native species, including trees and shrubs. Some grass species are allelopathic, that is, they produce chemicals that inhibit the growth of other nearby species. Where sparse (as in heavily shaded areas) grass and other vegetation are likely to gradually disappear as you incorporate native species.

Sod cutter or shovel. The most straightforward approach to eliminating your lawn is to remove the top three inches of grass sod, by hand or by renting a gas-powered sod cutter, and shake loose the soil into the cleared area. But as Pat and Carl Brust in Wisconsin (chapter 4) found, removing heavy rolls of sod with a sod cutter is a difficult, back-breaking job, and the site ends up several inches lower than adjacent areas. Bringing in topsoil to fill the area is not recommended, since it often contains weed seeds.

Typically, sod removal produces a nearly weed-free surface, but it may not eliminate perennial weeds that can cause problems. Susan and Paul Damon in Minnesota found that dandelions, with their deep roots, weren't removed with the sod and showed up later in their planting beds. The cut sod should be composted or used to patch bare areas of remaining lawn.

Smothering. Smothering involves placing material over a lawn after it has been mowed as short as possible. Spring is the ideal time to smother a lawn since weedy nonnative species like dandelions are at their peak growth and are best killed at this stage. Various materials can be used: black plastic, pieces of plywood, old carpeting, a thick layer of leaves (about 12 inches), or a thick layer of nonglossy newspapers (10–12 sheets) covered with leaves or grass clippings. Leave the material in place for a full season (5–6 months) until the underlying vegetation dies.

Smothering and planting can occur simultaneously. Cover unwanted vegetation with newspapers and 4 to 6 inches of quarried sand (which is weed-free, unlike beach sand) or sand and compost. Then immediately plant the area with seeds and/or small plugs placed directly into the sand or sand-compost. The roots of seedlings and plants grow right through the newspaper. Several school prairies in Wisconsin and Illinois have been established in this way, including one at Lincoln School, in Elmhurst, Illinois, under the direction of landscape designer Patricia Armstrong of Prairie Sun Consultants.

On a site for woodland habitat, smothering with a dozen layers of nonglossy newspaper, topped with three to four inches of wood chips, is an effective way of removing the grass and amending poor soil simultaneously. This mulch layer, along with the decaying sod, will help to build up the soil humus needed by woodland plants.

Tilling. A level site can also be prepared by rototilling the area two or three times about a week apart, until there is no regrowth. A full year of tilling may be needed if quack grass or Johnson grass is present. Both have rhizomes, lengthy horizontal stems beneath the surface of the ground with multiple roots. When broken up by cultivation, their stems break into many small pieces, each capable of producing a new plant, making these weeds extremely difficult to eradicate.

vegetation in their place. Along the driveway, on the west side of their yard, they decided to hide the buckthorn stumps with tall bushy prairie grasses. Plugs of Switchgrass were planted next to the drive, with Big Bluestem Grass behind it. By the end of the first summer, both grasses were four to five feet tall and hid the stumps. That winter and ever since, Dark-eyed Juncos have found it a favorite feeding spot and are particularly fond of the Switchgrass seed.

The Damons replaced the entire north border of their property with 30 native shrubs, including eight species, selected to provide birds with fruit and nuts: American Black Currant, Common Elderberry, American Hazelnut, American Cranberry-bush Viburnum, Black Raspberry, Gray Dogwood, Nannyberry Viburnum and Red-Osier Dogwood. Although the shrubs are still small, the Damons look forward to the day when they will feed and shelter the growing number of birds that now visit their yard.

Birds have not been the only ones to benefit from the buckthorn bust in the Damons' yard. Their neighbors were delighted that they no longer had to put up with the messy berries of these invasive shrubs.

You can smother nonnative vegetation by spreading shredded hardwood bark over newspapers. This method also helps improve the soil.

Using Herbicides

Many experts favor herbicide treatments in early fall or midspring when grass and other nonnative vegetation is growing actively. The Minnesota Department of Natural Resources recommends this method as the quickest and most cost-effective way of eradicating sod. Randy Powers of Prairie Future Seed in Wisconsin also prefers it. The Minnesota DNR recommends two organic herbicides, Scythe and Superfast Weed Killer; both contain naturally occurring fatty acids which kill sod by dehydrating the foliage and are accepted by most organic certification programs.

Roundup, a glyphosate-based chemical product, is one of the most commonly recommended herbicides for site preparation. Rodeo, a special formula of glyphosate, must be used in areas near water because it is nontoxic to fish. Although glyphosate-based herbicides are considered relatively safe to use, be sure to follow all the directions and precautions on the label.

All of these herbicides are nonselective and will kill any plant they contact, so take care when spraying. Most sod will die within two weeks after spraying and will look yellow. Spot-spray any remaining green areas.

After the sod is dead, the area can be planted. If using seedlings or transplants, you can plant them directly in the dead sod. But be sure to set their roots in the soil and not the dead lawn thatch. If you are planting seeds in spring, the dead sod must be tilled in or removed with a sod cutter before planting. In fall, however, the seeds can be planted directly onto the dead sod; they will work their way into the soil through the winter.

Preparing Slopes, Agricultural Fields & Old Fields

Slopes, while excellent sites for native plantings, must be prepared carefully to avoid erosion. Cultivation should be minimized. Herbicide application may be the best alternative. Replanting of the slope should be done immediately after the soil preparation. A cover crop (see below) is recommended. Better yet, stake a light erosion blanket containing straw or light excelsior over the planted area.

Use similar caution on easily eroded sites, such as areas with sandy soil or exposed ridge tops. In such cases, it is best to remove only vegetation around the new plants. The lack of moisture which results from the total removal of vegetation is worse than the competition from existing plants.

Agricultural fields that have been recently harvested are the easiest to prepare since the vegetation has already been removed and the surface is mostly weed-free. Carl Kurtz, an Iowa expert with over 25 years of experience, has excellent results with late fall seeding (from late October to November) in the stubble of a soybean field, without tillage. "Rain and snow will plant your seed," he explains.

Other experts advise shallow tilling of agricultural fields, no more than two inches deep, every three weeks in April, May and early June or for the full growing season, especially if there are rhizomatous weeds. It should be done whenever the weeds are over two inches high, to exhaust the weed seed bank and eliminate their competition with prairie seeds. Avoid deep tilling because it brings deep-lying weed seeds to the surface.

One caveat regarding agricultural fields: they cannot be planted if they have been treated with Atrazine or trifluralin chemicals (Treflan, Avadex) within the last two to four years, as these herbicides can inhibit the germination and growth of prairie plants.

Old fields, which are often full of aggressive weeds, are the most difficult to prepare for prairie planting. The field can be planted with crops such as corn or soybeans for one year to remove weeds prior to seeding with prairie plants. Some experts recommend a "spray, disk, spray" method in which a weedy acreage is sprayed with a herbicide, then shallowly disked and followed by another spraying as the next crop of weeds appears. Others recommend only herbicide applications every three to four weeks, until the weeds are under control. This work may have to be continued for one or two growing seasons.

Amending the Soil

Many native communities thrive in nutrient-poor soils

HERBICIDES: TO USE OR NOT TO USE?

Like most bird lovers, I am generally opposed to the use of herbicides or other chemicals, many of which, like DDT, have caused a great deal of harm to birds, other wildlife and humans.

Nonetheless, I have seen the advantage of using herbicides to control invasives and eradicate vegetation from a site to prepare it for planting with natives.

Invasive plants have burgeoned in recent years and their eradication can be a daunting task. In large areas with masses of invasives, the selective use of herbicides may be the only practical way to combat them. At the Wehr Nature Center, volunteers cut buckthorn and honeysuckle shrubs for several years, but were not allowed to apply an herbicide because they were not state-certified to do so (even though homeowners can use the same glyphosate-based herbicide). Nor was any certified staff person available to do this work. Consequently, the shrubs resprouted with great vigor—a dozen or more sprouts per cut stem. The volunteers were greatly discouraged and lost patience and interest in the work. Recently, certified staff has been available for this "stump treatment" and many more acres are being permanently cleared.

(continued)

Site preparation with herbicides has a number of advantages. This one-time application of a herbicide is usually the quickest and least expensive way to eradicate sod. Even more important are some of the environmental benefits.

A major advantage is that the soil structure remains intact and weed seeds in the soil are not brought to the surface to germinate. In addition, this method prevents soil erosion, retains organic matter, which enriches the soil, and saves the labor and the possible fuel costs of hauling the sod away.

Herbicide treatment also avoids the great environmental costs of intensive tilling, an alternate method of eradicating sod or old field vegetation. Tilling uses fuel and causes air pollution; heavy equipment compacts the soil. Herbicide treatment has none of these impacts.

Consider all the pros and cons of the various methods of site preparation. If herbicides seem like the best choice, then use them sparingly and selectively.

and soil amendments can damage them. Prairies, for example, are more readily established on soils of low fertility, since rich soils favor weeds over native prairie species during the early stages of a restoration. In addition, fertilizers can harm prairie plants.

Soil amendments, however, can be helpful under certain conditions, such as new home sites where the topsoil has been removed; shady wooded areas with poor soil; or sites with compacted soil, heavy clay soil or soil under excessively manicured lawns. Where topsoil has been removed, the best solution is to gradually add compost to improve the remaining soil. You can deal with compacted soil by tilling with compost, planting in raised beds and staying on paths as much as possible to avoid further compaction.

Under excessively manicured lawns, all the soil microorganisms needed for natural plant growth may have been killed off by overuse of pesticides and fertilizers. Sally Wasowski, in *Gardening with Prairie Plants*, says that if the soil has no earthworms or the lawn lacks that "fresh earth" smell shortly after a rain, you are likely to have dead soil. Wasowski recommends working several inches of compost into such sites. She's also had success with a commercial compost starter that has microorganisms to help with decomposition.

Heavy clay soils can also present problems. They compact easily if worked when wet, and they can get as hard as rock in the heat of summer, retarding root growth. Compost can help improve clay soils by creating a more porous structure, allowing air and water to move through the soil, which is critical to the health of the plant roots. Nonetheless, many native plants grow well in clay soils.

I don't recommend adding new topsoil. It often harbors the seeds of unwanted plants that can introduce an on-going problem with weeds.

For amending shady woodland soils, see chapter 11, The Woodland Bird Garden.

Planting

Planting

Herbaceous Species

Plants. Plants are more expensive than seeds but give quicker results. Many people opt to use them in their front yards where they want to have an attractive garden as soon as possible. Plants are also frequently used in clay soils, which tend to be either too wet (in spring) or too dry (in late summer) for good seed establishment. Plants work better, too, along shorelines and on slopes where seeds can easily be washed away by waves or rain. Woodland wildflowers are frequently installed as plants rather than seeds because many woodland species are very slow to grow and flower from seed.

The native plant nurseries can advise you on your purchases, but a few guidelines follow:

The best time to put in plants is when they are dormant or not in flower. Early spring or fall are generally good times for most species. Water potted plants thoroughly before planting, since dry root balls planted in the ground tend to repel water even if the ground is soaked after planting.

Potted plants generally come in small containers where their roots can become overgrown. Pull apart the roots before planting to encourage good plant growth. If the roots of small plants have formed tight interwoven masses, cut a slice off the bottom of the root ball and make a cut halfway up to the crown to stimulate growth. For larger plants (in four-inch or bigger pots) with extremely matted roots, cut the root ball two-thirds of the way up the plant in several places to encourage root growth.

Dig a hole the same depth as the soil surface of the potted plant. Firmly tamp down the soil around the plant and cover with a little garden soil or light mulch to prevent it from drying out. Then water thoroughly.

Continue to water thoroughly about once a week, through the first season, to encourage deep roots. More frequent shallow watering encourages shallow roots, which will not survive as well once watering stops.

Big-leaved Aster

Plants purchased as bare roots should never be allowed to dry out. Even a minute in sun or wind can damage or kill roots. When working on-site, cover them with damp burlap until they can be planted. Spread out the roots against the soil when planting to ensure good soil contact.

Label a few plants of each species, so that you can recognize them and avoid pulling them as you weed.

Seeds. Seeds take longer to produce results but are far less expensive and can provide a more diverse mix of species. Many native species are available only as seeds. For information on the propagation of particular plants see William Cullina's *Growing and Propagating Wildflowers*.

After seeding, mulch with a light application of weed-free straw, sawdust, cellulose fiber or compost, spreading it thin enough so that you can see the soil through the mulch. For prairie plantings, also seed a cover crop of quick-growing species so that the bare soil is covered quickly to prevent weeds from invading. Be sure to keep the soil moist for at least six weeks. Chapter 9, The Prairie Bird Garden, discusses seeding of prairies.

Letting Nature Do the Planting. If native plants are already growing adjacent to your newly chosen planting site, you can let nature do the planting and save yourself the effort and cost. They will expand into a new area if you eliminate competition from your lawn or other vegetation. By killing the sod or other vegetation, either by digging it up or using a herbicide (carefully, so it doesn't kill the nearby natives), you'll open up the area for colonization by the native plants.

This technique works best for strips five to ten feet in width adjacent to the native plants. Many native plants will spread by underground roots into the new area. Others may come in by seed. Gradually, over the years, you can continue this process until the entire site you want in natives is "planted." Be sure no invasive weeds are nearby, because they will quickly spread into your new area.

Woody Species

In the Midwest, the best time to plant trees and shrubs is during the early spring before growth begins, so they have an entire growing season to establish roots. The next best time is in fall after the leaves drop. The plants need time to develop good root systems before the extreme heat and drought of summer or the freezing temperatures of winter.

The spacing of woody plants is somewhat arbitrary, depending on the density you desire. You may want to feature those with particularly attractive forms, such as Alternate-leaved Dogwood or hawthorns, giving them sufficient space to display their beauty. Generally, smaller shrubs are spaced about two to three feet apart, large shrubs about four to six feet apart and trees about ten to thirteen feet apart.

Seeds. Planting acorns and the seeds of other woody species directly can be an effective method of planting shrublands and woodlands. There is evidence that this natural method can result in greater success than transplanting plants that germinated on other sites. See William Cullina's *Native Trees, Shrubs and Vines* for information on propagating woody plants from seed.

Bare root plants. Small bare root plants often are available in large quantities from state agencies and local nurseries. As with bare root herbaceous plants, it is essential to keep the roots moist until planted. For small plants, step on your spade, push the blade into the soil its full length, and force it forward to create an opening. Insert the plant's roots and press the soil back into place around them to ensure good contact with the soil and to eliminate any air pockets that could dry

Bright scarlet Cardinal Flowers attract hummingbirds and butterflies.

them out. For larger bare root plants, form a mound of soil in a hole and spread the roots out over the mound, cover with soil and tamp firmly around the plant.

Balled and burlapped and potted plants. Position the plant with its best side facing the direction you want. Then dig a hole a little more shallow than the root ball and two times as wide. A wide hole is recommended because the majority of roots are in the top foot of soil. Loosen up the sides and bottom of the hole so that the roots can penetrate the soil more easily.

With a potted plant, lay the plant on its side with the bottom of the pot near the hole and hit the pot until the root ball is loosened and the pot can be removed. With burlapped trees, remove the string or wire that ties the burlap around the root ball. The burlap itself need not be removed, but if the wrap is plastic, it must be removed since roots will not grow through plastic.

Examine the roots of the plant. If the roots encircle the root ball, slice through the ball on several sides. If the roots are much too long for the hole, extend them downward and outward. Work on the roots quickly to minimize their exposure to the sun and air.

When placing the plant in the hole, position it so that the top of the root ball or soil level in the container is about one inch above the soil. (This is in contrast to the rule for herbaceous species which are typically planted level with the soil in which they are grown.) Planting slightly above grade in this way ensures better drainage and oxygen for the roots of woody plants.

Fill the hole with soil gradually, settling with water as you go. Form a small mound of soil several inches high around the edge of the planting hole to retain water.

Cuttings from wetland trees and shrubs. Some wetland plants, like native willows and dogwoods, can be propagated from stem cuttings which are simply placed in moist soil, where they will take root on their own. The stems should be taken when the plants are dormant, in early spring, late fall or winter when the ground is not frozen. Stems should be about two to three feet long, with a diameter of about 1/2 to 1-1/2 inches. Cut the lower ends at an angle and the top ends flat so they can be pounded into the soil. After cutting, immediately place the stems in water and plant the same day or, at most, within a few days. Pound a rod into the soil first to make a hole for the cutting; then put a small block of wood over the flat end before pounding the cutting into the soil, so the stem does not split.

Native willows, including Pussy Willow, Black Willow and Peach-leaved Willow, will root easily from cuttings. Wet-loving dogwoods, such as Silky Dogwood and Red-Osier Dogwood, are also excellent choices. Other shrubs that root fairly well from cuttings include Prairie Willow, Common Elderberry, Meadowsweet, Downy Arrowwood Viburnum and Nannyberry Viburnum; Speckled Alder can be used, but doesn't root as well from cuttings.

Use this technique to create a shrubland bird garden in a wet to moist area. It is also an excellent way to provide erosion control along shorelines.

Mulching

Always mulch after installing plants. Mulch has many advantages. It suppresses weeds, helps keep the ground surface moist to prevent a hardpan from forming, prevents soil erosion and moderates soil temperatures.

Woody plants can receive up to three inches of mulch, while herbaceous plants should receive no more than one inch of mulch. The larger the mulched area around woody plants the better; a circle three feet in diameter around trees is common. Always keep the mulch away from direct contact with the stems of the plants to prevent stem rot.

One of the best mulches is shredded hardwood bark, which stays in place and does not blow or wash away in most situations. It can be used for herbaceous and woody plants. Other good mulches include weed-free straw, leaf mulch, compost and aged manure. These are not recommended for shorelines, however, since nutrients could be washed into the water. Wood chips tend to float and wash away in heavy rain. On steep slopes, keep mulch in place with an erosion-control net.

Watering

Your newly transplanted trees, shrubs and herbaceous species will need to be watered *deeply* immediately after planting, then every week for the first few weeks; thereafter, every other week for the first season until they become established. Most plants need about one inch of water per week. Sometimes woody species will also need watering through the second growing season.

Protecting from Herbivores

Herbivores, including mice, rabbits and deer, may damage new plantings. Fencing, sprays, tree shelters and wraps can deter them. See chapter 22 for details.

RESOURCES FOR READERS

Books/Brochure

Cullina, William. 2000. *The New England Wild Flower Society Guide to Growing and Propagating Wildflowers of the United States and Canada.* Boston: Houghton Mifflin.

——. 2002. *Native Trees, Shrubs and Vines: A Guide to Using, Growing, and Propagating North American Woody Plants.* Boston: Houghton Mifflin.

Henderson, Carrol L., Carolyn J. Dindorf and Fred J. Rozumalski. 1999. *Lakescaping for Wildlife and Water Quality.* St. Paul: Minnesota Department of Natural Resources.

"Tree Planting," a brochure available from the Natural Resources Conservation Service, USDA. For a copy, call 515-270-4864 or go to the website: http://www.nrcs.usda.gov/

Websites

Wisconsin Department of Natural Resources. "Wisconsin Manual of Control Recommendation for Ecologically Invasive Plants." http://dnr.wi.gov/invasives/publications/manual/manual_toc.htm

——. "Invasive Photo Gallery." http://dnr.wi.gov/topic/invasives/photos/

Plant Conservation Alliance. "Weeds Gone Wild" (Photographs and Fact Sheets). http://www.nps.gov/plants/

Missouri Botanical Garden. "Missouri Exotic Pest Plants." http://www.mobot.org/MOBOT/research/mepp/welcome.shtml

Minneapolis Park & Recreation Board. "Invasive Species." http://www.minneapolisparks.org/default.asp?PageID=879

Organizations

Invasive Plants Association of Wisconsin. PO Box 5274, Madison, WI 53705; http://ipaw.org/

Michigan Invasive Plant Council. PO Box 27036, Lansing, MI 48909-7036; http://invasiveplantsmi.org/

Midwest Invasive Plant Network. Contact: Kate Howe, Midwest Invasive Plant Coordinator, Purdue University, c/o The Nature Conservancy, 620 East Ohio Street, Indianapolis, IN 46202; http://mipn.org/

Wilson's Warblers feed in shrubs

A shrubland hedge offers shelter and food to migrating birds.

during their migration through the U.S.

4 Bird Habitat Gardens for Specific Birds

A Blue Jay puffs up to keep warm in the brisk October air.

Some habitats are of particular interest to backyard bird-watchers because small examples can be replicated in backyards, including freshwater marshes, ponds, brooks, wooded swamps, bogs, pine barrens, streamside forest, thickets, prairies, deserts, and alpine meadows.

—Donald S. Heintzelman
The Complete Backyard Birdwatcher's Home Companion

Different habitats will attract different species of birds. In the average yard, especially in an urban or suburban area, you may want to create several different small habitat areas for birds, as have many of the homeowners in the Gallery of Bird Habitat Gardens, part 2. A prairie patch in a sunny area, a small shrubland garden at the edge of your yard, and a little woodland in a shady back corner will attract a variety of bird species. The landscape design on the next page shows a representative yard with different habitat gardens.

(previous page) Prairie plants along a boundary fence attract birds and butterflies.

BIRDSCAPING IN THE MIDWEST

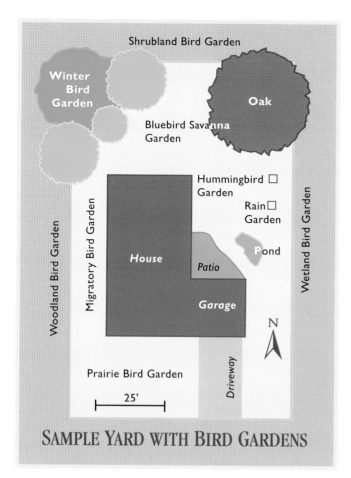

SAMPLE YARD WITH BIRD GARDENS

Labels in image: Shrubland Bird Garden, Winter Bird Garden, Oak, Bluebird Savanna Garden, Woodland Bird Garden, Migratory Bird Garden, Hummingbird Garden, Rain Garden, Wetland Bird Garden, Pond, House, Patio, Garage, N, Prairie Bird Garden, Driveway, 25'

A GARDEN SAMPLER

Here's a sample landscape design with several bird habitat gardens for an average-sized lot (80' x 130'). The six gardens within the lot are small, but together they offer a variety of bird habitats. Larger lots could include expanded gardens shown outside the lot lines.

If you live adjacent to a natural area, it would be best to create a similar habitat in your entire yard. It will enlarge that particular habitat in your community, increasing its value to birds and other wildlife. It has been well documented that our more rare birds require large habitats. Many prairie birds need large expanses of prairie to flourish. Similarly, some of our most threatened woodland birds require large tracts of forest for their survival.

Unfortunately, much of the natural habitat which still remains today is fragmented by subdivisions, roads, shopping centers, industrial parks, farms and other kinds of human development. Along with outright loss of habitat, fragmentation of habitat is a leading cause of the decline in bird diversity.

This section describes nine different kinds of bird habitat gardens you can create. Birds use the recommended plant species for food, cover, habitat, nesting sites or nesting material. There are many other plant species that provide food and habitat for insects and small animals that birds prey on, so don't hesitate to use the full array of native local flora for birdscaping. Also, because diversity is key to healthy habitats, try to include as many species as possible in your garden.

Descriptions of Bird Habitat Gardens

Hummingbird Garden

Target birds: Ruby-throated Hummingbird (only hummingbird species in most of Midwest)

Basic habitat: Woodland edge

Basic habitat components:

Primary: Nectar-rich wildflowers

Other: Trees and shrubs

Prairie Bird Garden

Target birds:

Small backyard sites: Many common species including finches, doves, sparrows and blackbirds

Large sites: Grassland specialists including Bobolinks and Meadowlarks

Basic habitat type: Prairie

Basic habitat components: Forbs (wildflowers), grasses, sedges

Bluebird Savanna Garden

Target birds: Eastern Bluebird and other savanna species such as Red-headed Woodpecker, Flicker and Loggerhead Shrike

Basic habitat type: Oak savanna

Basic habitat components: Forbs (wildflowers), grasses, scattered trees; also scattered shrubs and shrubby thickets

Woodland Bird Garden

Target birds: Owls, woodpeckers, tanagers, nuthatches, chickadees, wrens, many warblers and other woodland species

Basic habitat type: Woodland

Basic habitat components: Trees, shrubs, groundcover species

Wetland Bird Garden

Target birds:

Small rain gardens: Many common birds including finches, sparrows, black-birds, hummingbirds

Larger wetlands: Rails, herons, terns, waterfowl, sandpipers, plovers, sandhill cranes, blackbirds, swallows

Basic habitat type: Wetland

Basic habitat components: Wetland forbs, grasses, sedges, rushes, shrubs, trees

Migratory Bird Garden

Target birds: Neotropical migrants (birds wintering in tropics; nesting in Canada and U.S.), including warblers, thrushes, orioles and many others;

also, short-distance migrants

Basic habitat type: Woodland and woodland edge

Basic habitat components:

Primary: Trees and fruiting shrubs

Other: Wildflowers, grasses, sedges

Shrubland Bird Garden

Target birds: Shrubland specialists, including such species as Gray Catbird, Northern Cardinal, Song and Field Sparrows, Indigo Bunting and Eastern Towhee

Basic habitat type: Shrubland

Basic habitat components: Shrubs

Winter Bird Garden

Target birds: Resident nonmigratory birds and winter visitors, especially finches, siskins, juncos, chickadees, cardinals, woodpeckers and some sparrows

Basic habitat type: Coniferous and mixed woodland edge and prairie

Basic habitat components: Evergreen trees and shrubs; trees and shrubs with persistent seeds or berries; seed-producing wildflowers/grasses

Water Garden for Birds

Target birds:

Birdbaths and small ponds: All the common perching birds—robins, cardinals, grosbeaks, blue jays, warblers, hummingbirds, wrens and occasionally larger birds like herons Larger ponds: Herons, waterfowl, and many wetland species (see above) around edges

Basic habitat type: Pond/stream

Basic habitat components: Emergent plants, floating plants and submerged plants

Jack-in-the-Pulpit, a woodland species with bright red berries that sparrows and other songbirds eat.

CHAPTER 8
THE HUMMINGBIRD GARDEN

*Let a man plant a flower garden
almost anywhere from Canada to
Argentina and Chile, in the lowlands or
mountains, amid humid forest or in irrigated
deserts, and before long his bright blossoms will
be visited by a tiny flittering creature that hovers
before them with wings vibrated into twin halos while it sucks
their sweet nectar.*

—Alexander Skutch, *Life of the Hummingbird*

Hummingbirds, those winged jewels hovering about our flowers and feeders, are unique to the Americas. Nowhere else in the world do these beautiful birds bedazzle observers with their feats of flight and mind-boggling migrations. And nowhere else have wildflowers evolved shape and structure specially suited to hummingbirds. As with berries and birds, there has been a remarkable coevolution between wildflowers and hummingbirds, resulting in a mutually beneficial relationship between plant and pollinator.

Of the eight major species of hummingbirds in North America, only one, the Ruby-throated Hummingbird, is commonly found in the Midwest. The best way to attract this "glittering fragment of rainbow," as John J. Audubon described it, is to plant a rainbow of the hummingbird's favorite flowers.

A Coevolution of Bird and Bloom

The earliest hummingbirds, biologists believe, ate only insects that they snapped up as they probed among green leaves and especially among flowers abuzz with bees and other invertebrates. But over time, a reciprocal evolution between the flowers and hummingbirds began to emerge. The hummingbirds developed bill and tongue structures more suitable to feeding on nectar, the sweet secretion within flowers. Their tongues, for example, have grooves along the sides, through which nectar is drawn up by capillary action. Some hummingbirds also have fringes at the edges of their tongues, which may help them capture the minute insects in flowers—perhaps an adaptation retained from ancient times. Bills vary in length and curvature suited to the specific flowers, adaptations particularly pronounced in tropical hummingbirds. Today, hummingbirds feed primarily on flower nectar, although insects provide protein and constitute about 25% of their diet.

As the hummingbirds developed adaptations for nectar feeding, the plants evolved in ways more attractive to hummingbirds, producing flowers with copious amounts of nectar and "hummer

photo: Jewelweed

friendly" structure. What fueled this evolution? Why did the plants redesign their blossoms, when there already were insects around to pollinate them? Perhaps it was the prodigious appetites of hummingbirds, which devour half their weight in sugar each day and as much as eight times their weight in fluids. Such an appetite translates into a tremendous performance as a pollinator, since the hummers must feed so much and so often to prevent starvation.

Botanist Bastiaan Meeuse and Sean Morris, director of Oxford Scientific Films, in their book *The Sex Life of Flowers*, sum it up this way: Although few people who watch these jewel-like creatures flit from flower to flower in bright sunlight are aware of it, hummingbirds are constantly on the verge of death. This is what makes hummingbirds such magnificently efficient pollinators. They must visit, the authors say, hundreds, nay thousands, of nectar-rich flowers each day, simply to stay alive. As a way to conserve energy when their reserves are low, hummingbirds must also go into a state of torpor at night, during which their heartbeat slows and their breathing becomes irregular.

Hummingbirds pollinate flowers much as insects do. As they feast on nectar, they inadvertently get pollen, the male sex cells of the flower, on their heads, bills or breasts. When they feed on a second flower, some of this pollen sticks to the stigma, part of the female organ of that flower. Thus, cross-pollination occurs and the flower is fertilized. The pollen then grows a tube extending down to an egg in the ovary of the flower. A sperm from the pollen penetrates the egg and a seed begins to develop. The seed, formed from such cross-pollination, generally produces a more vigorous and healthier plant than one from a seed produced through self-pollination (pollen and egg from the same plant).

Hummingbird Flowers

Given the hummingbird's great appetite for nectar, some plants began to specialize in attracting hummingbirds in preference to other pollinators. Let's look at the unique features of "hummingbird" flowers in contrast to "insect" flowers. Typically, flowers are arranged in open inflorescences, about which hummingbirds can hover and feed without brushing their wings against leaves and twigs. Many hummingbird flowers are red, red and yellow, or have a red component such as orange-red, orange and pink. Red is a color that the birds see easily just as we do, but it does not attract bees, who see it only as black. Flowers pollinated by bees and other insects, in contrast, are more often blue or yellow.

While the flowers can vary considerably in shape, they generally have nectar at the base of a long tubular flower which is easy to reach with the long bill and tongue of hummingbirds, but difficult for bees and other insects. The flowers are thicker at the base of the floral tube, to prevent damage from the sharp beaks of the birds and to protect the blossoms from nectar thieves. Thievery occurs when a bee or a bird bypasses the standard entrance to the flower and instead cuts a hole at the base of the floral tube and robs the flower of nectar without pollinating it. Check your wildflowers for holes—I've found them on Virginia Bluebells and Jewelweed.

Hummingbird flowers also often have projecting stamens and pistils, making it more likely that hummingbirds will touch them while feeding, thus increasing the chances for pollination. Usually the flowers lack a scent, since hummingbirds have little or no sense of smell. Bees and butterflies, on the other hand, are often attracted to a flower's fragrance, while pollinating flies prefer a rotten odor. For the latter, try a quick whiff of the appropriately named Carrion Flower.

Many hummingbird flowers also point downward or to the side, rather than up, and they lack the horizontal, lip-like petals offering landing platforms that are found on many insect-pollinated plants. Hummingbirds can easily hover and turn their heads up or to the side to feed, while insects usually can't. The flowers also bloom during the day, unlike moth- and bat-attracting flowers that blossom at night. (For a list of wildflower species used by hummers, see pages 110–111.)

How to Create Your Hummingbird Garden

Regardless of the size of your yard, you have an excellent chance of attracting hummingbirds. The native habitat of hummers is woodland edge or openings within woodlands, a habitat that resembles many suburban and rural yards that typically have a mix of trees, shrubs and open areas with beds of wildflowers and lawn. Hummingbirds are less abundant in urban yards, but many city gardeners have been able to entice hummers with window boxes, patio planters or rooftop gardens brimming with nectar-filled blossoms, especially during migration. The following guidelines will help you plan the perfect hummingbird habitat for your yard, whether small or large.

Plant Natives

Besides the many reasons for planting natives mentioned earlier in this book, there's another persuasive reason to do so in hummingbird gardens. Wildflowers produce significantly more nectar than cultivated hybrids. Evidently, in developing these cultivars, the nectar has been reduced in the same way that the beautiful fragrance of roses has often been lost in hybrids.

Be sure not to plant nonnative honeysuckle shrubs. Although hummingbirds are attracted to honeysuckle flowers, these invasive shrubs crowd out our native, more beneficial shrubs and wildflowers. There are, however, several native honeysuckle vines whose flowers are equally attractive to birds and are not invasive.

Provide Both Sun and Shade

In order to create the best habitat for your hummingbirds, include areas of open sun, partial shade and dense shade. By doing so, you'll provide space for aerial displays, sites for perching, roosting and nesting, and sources of food and nesting material. A good mix is about half shade and half sun, which can include some lawn as well as flowerbeds.

Offer Varied and Continuous Bloom

Plant a variety of flowers that will bloom and offer nectar throughout the growing season. Be sure to include spring and fall blossoming species that will attract migrants. You will help hummingbirds withstand the stress of migration, and some of the spring migrants may choose to stay and nest in your yard.

The northward migration of hummingbirds, in fact, correlates with the flowering times of some of their favorite sources of nectar, especially Wild Columbine, which is common throughout the Midwest. Some other early-flowering hummingbird favorites include Beard Tongue, Paintbrush, Fire Pink and Virginia Bluebells.

For summer blooms, Wild Bergamot, Oswego Tea, Wood Lily and Turk's Cap Lily are good choices. On their fall migration, hummingbirds seem to follow closely the blossoming of Orange Jewelweed. Other early fall species include Cardinal Flower, Royal Catchfly and Great Blue Lobelia.

Hummingbirds have local preferences, so by planting a variety of species, you have a better chance of attracting hummers. A study of hummingbirds in New York found that they preferred to nest in areas where Oswego Tea was found. In North Dakota, they preferred areas with Jewelweed.

A final reason for variety is that nectar is not always available. It can be lost during adverse weather conditions—extreme heat, cold, wind or dryness—and to other pollinators and nectar thieves. Offering many flowers of numerous species helps minimize these problems.

Your flowers may also attract Baltimore Orioles. These radiant flame-colored birds have been known to sip nectar from the blossoms of at least two species of midwestern plants—Turk's Cap Lily and the vine Trumpet Creeper. Their cousins in the Midwest, the Orchard Orioles, occasionally eat tree blossoms.

Clumps, Curves and Other Considerations

Create large splashes of color by grouping each species of wildflower. Hummingbirds are best attracted by such vibrant visual displays. One year, migrating hummingbirds visited my feeder in early spring and then disappeared. But when the Oswego Tea blossomed in a beautiful, massed display, the hummingbirds returned and fed on the nectar of these flowers. If single blossoms had been scattered here and there, the hummingbirds may not have noticed.

As in any garden design, curved flowerbeds are more pleasing to the eye than beds with straight lines. Place taller species in back, shorter ones in front. By doing so, you'll be able to see the hummingbirds as they nectar, but more importantly, the birds will be able to hover, feed and fly with less restriction in the more open area.

Finally, plant your hummingbird flowers in different parts of your yard. Hummingbirds are territorial around their favorite nectaring sites and will be extremely aggressive towards any other hummers. By planting in different parts of the yard, you're likely to have more hummingbirds.

Plant a Rainbow of Colored Flowers

There is no doubt that red is the hummingbird's favorite color. A Ruby-throated Hummingbird once flew in to inspect my husband's red baseball cap as we were hiking in a park. Ruby-throats have also hovered over red hair ribbons and red ties. One even came in for a close look at someone's sunburned nose.

Scientists say that this preference for red is learned, not innate. Red flowers are often "hummer friendly" in shape and have nectar with the 20–25% sugar concentration hummingbirds prefer. By trial and error, the hummingbirds learn to associate red flowers with good food. The color red, moreover, is a complement to green and conspicuous against green vegetation. Red coloration, thus, serves as a convenient, easily recognized "flag" which helps the hummingbirds save energy in their search for sources of nectar. This flag can be particularly vital for tired, hungry migrants.

Some red flowers, like roses, lack the tubular shape and nectar of "hummingbird" flowers. While the red color may initially attract hummingbirds, they quickly realize the lack of food value for them and lose interest.

This hummingbird garden in Wisconsin has colorful flowers to attract ruby-throats.

Despite their preference for red, hummingbirds feed on the nectar of flowers of many other colors. The closely related color orange, for example, is showier than red in shaded settings and is found in many hummingbird-adapted flowers. Hummingbirds also feed on blue, purple and yellow flowers. In my yard, they prefer yellow Evening Primrose more than any other flower. I've also seen them feeding on the white flowers of Foxglove Beard Tongue and the greenish-white flowers of Solomon's Seal. Randy Powers of Prairie Future Seed Company in Wisconsin notes that hummingbirds tend to visit red and pink flowers during the day, but prefer white and blue flowers at dawn and dusk, when these colors are more conspicuous. In my yard, they've even come to flowers never mentioned in the books—yellow sunflowers and purple Hoary Vervain—whether for nectar or nearby insects, I'm not sure.

Offer Plants That Provide Nesting Materials

To encourage hummingbirds to nest, offer plants that will provide them with nesting material. Their walnut-sized nests are usually lined with soft fuzzy fibers to cushion their two tiny eggs, no bigger than beans. The outside of their nest is camouflaged with lichens attached by spider silk. For fibrous material, hummingbirds often search for Cinnamon Ferns, Thimbleweed, Pussy Willow or other shrub willows.

Hummers harvest the cinnamon-colored fuzz at the base of Cinnamon Fern leaves and the whitish down of Thimbleweed. The seeds of willow shrubs have cottony hairs that ripen in spring when hummingbirds are building their nests. Flowering willows also attract swarms of insects on which hummingbirds feed. In addition, several species of willow shrubs thrive in wet areas and are likely to offer the Ruby-throated Hummingbird one of its favorite nesting sites—a small, down-sloping branch near or over water.

You might also consider letting a few nonnative dandelions go to seed. Hummingbirds favor their fuzzy fibers for lining their nests.

Select Woody Plants with Hummingbirds in Mind

In addition to willow shrubs, a number of other woody plants, including trees, shrubs and vines, are particularly valuable.

Hummingbirds cover the outside of their nests with lichen from bark. Branches become perches and nesting sites. My candidate for the best "hummingbird tree" is the sugar maple. In spring, sapsuckers "tap" the sweet sap of this species by drilling rows of small holes through

Ever alert, a female hummer rests on a bare branch while she digests her food.

which the sap oozes. Hummingbirds sometimes follow sapsuckers around in the woods, dining on the sap after the woodpeckers leave. Insects, too, are attracted to the sap and offer an additional source of food.

Other species of trees, as well as shrubs and vines, have flowers that provide nectar and make excellent additions to your hummingbird garden. (See the list in this chapter.) Be sure to prune old wood from the shrubs and vines, to encourage production of more flowers, leaving a few dead branches for perches. Try to achieve a layered effect in your hummingbird habitat—a tall tree or trees, medium-high shrubs, with an understory of woodland wildflowers.

Finally, add an evergreen or two, to provide shelter for your hummingbirds, especially on chilly spring and frosty fall days. The Ruby-throated Hummingbird nests in both evergreens and deciduous trees.

The Importance of Perches
Hummingbirds are very territorial and love to perch up high to survey their domain. They also digest their food while perching. A full 80–85% of a hummingbird's day is spent perching. Typically, a hummingbird feeds on flowers for a few seconds, storing food in its crop (a food storage sac in its esophagus), and then perches for a while. It feeds again when its crop is half-empty.

Ruby-throats have perched on a clothesline in our yard as well as on power lines. A more natural perch is a dead branch of a tree or shrub, so be sure to leave a few dead branches on your woody plants. You'll not only accommodate the hummingbirds, but you'll see them more often. While bird watching in natural areas, I have discovered hummingbirds perching on tree branches just

The most important consideration in selecting a hummingbird feeder is ease of assembly and cleaning. The basin-style types are easier to clean than the inverted-bottle feeders. Two excellent brands are HummZinger and Hummerfest.

Most feeders have red parts to attract the hummers, so you don't need to tint the sugar water. Avoid any yellow trim, which attracts bees and wasps. Hummingbirds will tolerate a few of these insects, but will avoid feeders that have many. The best defense against bees and wasps is to select a feeder that has bee guards and will not drip sugar water, which will attract them. Another excellent method is to dab pure (not artificial) almond extract at each port to keep the insects away.

Ants can also be a problem. Buy a feeder with a built-in ant moat and keep it filled with water, to keep ants at bay. You can also suspend a plastic cup filled with water from your feeder's hanger. If the feeder is on a dowel, ants climb up and into the feeder. To prevent this, rub the dowel with vaseline, but don't put it on the feeder itself where the hummingbirds could get into it.

Perches on feeders aren't necessary, but are recommended. They eliminate the need for hummers to hover, saving them a great deal of energy.

as often as I find them feeding at flowers.

The bare branches you retain may also become nesting sites. Hummingbirds prefer to build their tiny nests on lichen-covered branches that match the lichen camouflage on their nests. If you don't have trees or shrubs in your yard, stick dead branches in the ground about 10 to 20 feet away from your hummingbird flowers. Make sure the branches have some small twigs around which hummingbirds can curl their tiny toes.

Avoid Pesticides

Avoid using pesticides in your garden and on your lawn. These chemicals can harm the very hummingbirds you're trying to attract, coating the flowers they feed on and contaminating or killing the insects they eat. Being so small in size, hummingbirds may be more susceptible to the harmful effects of pesticides than larger birds and animals.

Provide Water

Like most birds, hummingbirds love water and, in the wild, will often bathe in shallow puddles or flutter about in leaves laden with dew or raindrops. They'll also come to birdbaths in your yard if the water isn't too deep. Place flat rocks in the bath to accommodate the tiny hummers. They also love misters and have even been observed flying through the spray of a lawn sprinkler or a hand-held hose.

Add Feeders for Close-up Views

Nectar feeders can bring hummingbirds into close view so you can enjoy these tiny gems in grand detail. Feeders can also help keep the birds around when your flowers fail to bloom in sequence or their nectar has been diminished. But consider feeders only after you have provided all the natural amenities—flowers, shrubs, trees and perches in a nonpoisonous environment.

Feeders, however, can be more harmful than helpful unless they are carefully maintained. Liquid that sits too long and ferments can cause an enlarged liver in hummingbirds (just as excess alcohol does in humans), resulting in the death of the bird. A friend of mine conscientiously put fresh sugar water into her feeder every couple days, but forgot to clean the feeder, which became quite moldy. Other friends had a cottage that they visited only every few weeks, leaving a feeder up during the interim. Between visits, their feeder became black with mold and the syrup turned cloudy due to fermentation.

It is essential to clean the feeder each time you refill it and to do so often, at least once a week, says Stephen W. Kress, an ornithologist with the National Audubon Society. Others suggest doing so even more often—every two or three days when the temperature is above 80 degrees. It helps to hang the feeder in the shade; the sugar water is less likely to spoil. If you can't properly maintain a hummingbird feeder, it's best to rely on your hummingbird flowers to attract and feed the Ruby-throats.

Use a solution of one part sugar to four parts water, which mimics the typical sugar content of the nectar of hummingbird flowers. Don't use honey, which ferments more easily than sugar and supports the growth of a harmful fungus. Boil the sugar solution for a minute or two and cool before filling your feeder. Store the unused sugar water in the refrigerator.

Feeders can be safely hung within a foot or two of your windows but at least six feet high to keep the hummingbirds safe from cats. Since hummingbirds like to perch between meals, place your feeders near trees or shrubs if you have them. If not, tack up a dead branch with small twigs for perching near your feeders. To attract your first hummers, it is often helpful to place your feeder near your flowers and then gradually move it closer to your windows.

Put up your feeders in time for the arrival of Ruby-throats in spring. In the southern tier of Missouri, Illinois, Indiana and Ohio, the first birds usually return in early April. In the more northerly portions of the Midwest, they arrive in mid to late April.

The timing of fall migration is more diffuse, with some hummingbirds heading south as early as late July. Feeders don't usually cause the birds to delay their migration, so simply keep up your feeder until you have seen no hummingbirds for several weeks.

Hummingbirds have been known to come back year after year to their favorite nest and nectar sites. They are surprisingly long-lived for such tiny and seemingly fragile beings, frequently surviving nine or ten years, occasionally up to fourteen years. With luck, your hummingbird habitat garden could attract the same individuals and families of Ruby-throats to your yard for many springs to come.

ORIOLES AND OTHER VISITORS TO FEEDERS

Orioles frequently visit hummingbird feeders. Since orioles seem to favor orange over red, orange nectar feeders have been specially designed for them.

Orioles also come readily to orange halves on feeders or branches, particularly in early spring. After they eat the flesh of the oranges, you can fill the halves with grape jelly, another favorite food of orioles. Catbirds, cardinals and mockingbirds will also eat grape jelly.

Orioles eat grapes, watermelon and other fruit, as well as the fruits of many native plants. The major portion of the diet of orioles, however, is made up of insects, including many harmful pests, making them "naturals" as insect-control agents for your yard.

Besides orioles, nearly 60 other species of birds are occasionally seen at hummingbird feeders, including woodpeckers, jays, chickadees, titmice, nuthatches, wrens, mockingbirds, thrashers, robins, warblers, grackles, tanagers, cardinals, grosbeaks, buntings, finches and sparrows. Who will be on your yard list of nectar-feeders?

photo: Baltimore Oriole

Hummingbirds use all of the wildflowers listed below as a source of nectar, insects, water or nesting materials. The specific use is given except where unknown. Without binoculars, it can be difficult to determine whether a hummingbird is feeding on a flower's nectar, on the insects around the flowers or both.

Many of the less well-known hummingbird flowers on the list were provided by Randy Powers of Prairie Future Seed Company in Wisconsin (see Resources for Readers at the end of this chapter), based on his research over 30 years.

Most of these wildflowers will also attract butterflies, so even if hummingbirds are slow to show up or visit only during migration, your garden will be alive with winged beauty throughout the blossoming season. Finches and sparrows, among other birds, will visit many of these plants in late summer and fall to feast on their seeds. **Species in bold print are hummingbird favorites.** Consult the plant tables in part 5 for more information on the native range and cultural requirements of these species.

Prairie Alum Root, *Heuchera richardsonii*—a source of nectar

Foxglove Beard Tongue, *Penstemon digitalis*—a source of nectar

Large-flowered Beard Tongue, *Penstemon grandiflorus*—a source of nectar

Pale Beard Tongue, *Penstemon pallidus*—a source of nectar

Slender Beard Tongue, *Penstemon gracilis*—a source of nectar

Tall Bellflower, *Campanula americana*—a source of insects

Wild Bergamot, *Monarda fistulosa*—a source of nectar

Wood Betony or Lousewort, *Pedicularis canadensis*—a source of nectar

Cylindrical Blazing Star, *Liatris cylindracea*—a source of nectar

Marsh Blazing Star, *Liatris spicata*—a source of nectar

Meadow Blazing Star, *Liatris ligulistylis*—a source of nectar

Prairie Blazing Star, *Liatris pycnostachya*—a source of nectar

Rough Blazing Star, *Liatris aspera*—a source of nectar

Virginia Bluebells, *Mertensia virginica*—a source of nectar

Starry Campion, *Silene stellata*—a source of nectar

Cardinal Flower, *Lobelia cardinalis*—a source of nectar

Royal Catchfly, *Silene regia*—a source of nectar

Purple Prairie Clover, *Dalea purpurea* (*Petalostemum p.*)

Round-headed Bush Clover, *Lespedeza capitata*

White Prairie Clover, *Dalea candida* (*Petalostemum c.*)

Wild Columbine, *Aquilegia canadensis*—a source of nectar

Pale Purple Coneflower, *Echinacea pallida*—a source of insects & nectar

Purple Coneflower, *Echinacea purpurea*—a source of insects & nectar

Cup Plant, *Silphium perfoliatum*—a source of insects & water

Early Figwort, *Scrophularia lanceolata*—a source of insects

Late Figwort, *Scrophularia marilandica*—a source of insects

Fireweed, *Epilobium angustifolium*—a source of nectar

Fern-leaved False Foxglove, *Aureolaria pedicularia*

Yellow False Foxglove, *Aureolaria grandiflora*

Goats Rue, *Tephrosia virginiana*

Harebell, *Campanula rotundifolia*—a source of nectar

Hog Peanut, *Amphicarpaea bracteata*

Early Horse Gentian, *Triosteum aurantiacum*

Late Horse Gentian or Tinker's Weed, *Triosteum perfoliatum*

Lavender Giant Hyssop, *Agastache foeniculum*

Purple Giant Hyssop, *Agastache scrophulariifolia*—a source of insects

Yellow Giant Hyssop, *Agastache nepetoides*

Blue Wild Indigo, *Baptisia australis*—nectar

White Wild Indigo, *Baptisia alba (B. lactea; B. leucantha)*—a source of nectar

Northern Blue Flag Iris, *Iris versicolor*— a source of nectar

Southern Blue Flag Iris, *Iris virginica (I. shrevei)*—a source of nectar

Orange Jewelweed or **Spotted Touch-Me-Not**, *Impatiens capensis (I. biflora)*—a source of nectar

Yellow or Pale Touch-Me-Not Jewelweed, *Impatiens pallida*—a source of nectar

Prairie Larkspur, *Delphinium carolinianum (D. virescens)*—a source of nectar

Michigan Lily or **Turk's Cap Lily**, *Lilium michiganense (L. superbum)*—nectar

Prairie Lily, *Lilium philadelphicum*— a source of nectar

Great Blue Lobelia, *Lobelia siphilitica*— a source of nectar

Swamp Lousewort, *Pedicularis lanceolata*— a source of nectar

Wild Lupine, *Lupinus perennis*

Swamp Rose Mallow, *Hibiscus moscheutos (H. palustris)*—a source of nectar

Butterfly Milkweed, *Asclepias tuberosa*— a source of nectar

Common Milkweed, *Asclepias syriaca*— a source of nectar

Prairie Milkweed, *Asclepias sullivantii*— a source of nectar

Swamp or Marsh Milkweed, *Asclepias incarnata*—a source of nectar

Tall Green Milkweed, *Asclepias hirtella*— a source of nectar

Whorled Milkweed, *Asclepias verticillata*— a source of nectar

Horse Mint, *Monarda punctata*— a source of nectar

Monkey Flower, *Mimulus ringens*—nectar

Hedge Nettle, *Stachys palustris*

Obedient Plant or False Dragonhead, *Physostegia virginiana*—nectar

Oswego Tea or **Bee Balm**, *Monarda didyma*—nectar

Downy Paintbrush*, *Castilleja sessiliflora*— nectar

Indian Paintbrush*, *Castilleja coccinea*— nectar

Partridge Pea, *Chamaecrista fasciculata (Cassia f.)*

Wild Petunia or Hairy Ruellia, *Ruellia humilis*

Blue Phlox or **Woodland Phlox**, *Phlox divaricata*—nectar

Sand Prairie Phlox, *Phlox pilosa*—nectar

Smooth Phlox, *Phlox glaberrima*—nectar

Sweet William Phlox, *Phlox maculata*— nectar

Fire Pink, *Silene virginica*—nectar

Pale Indian Plantain, *Cacalia atriplicifolia*— a source of insects

Prairie Indian Plantain, *Cacalia plantiginea*— a source of insects

Common Evening Primrose, *Oenothera biennis*—a source of insects

Wild Senna, *Senna hebecarpa (Cassia h.)*

Smooth Solomon's Seal, *Polygonatum biflorum (P. caniculatum)*—nectar

False Sunflower or Oxeye, *Heliopsis helianthoides*

Thimbleweed, *Anemone virginiana*—downy seed head used for nesting material

Pasture Thistle, *Cirsium discolor*—a source of insects

Swamp Thistle, *Cirsium muticum*

Showy Tick Trefoil, *Desmodium canadense*

Turtlehead, *Chelone glabra*—nectar

Red Turtlehead, *Chelone obliqua*—nectar

Blue Vervain, *Verbena hastata*—insects

Hoary Vervain, *Verbena stricta*

American Vetch, *Vicia americana*

Canada Milk Vetch, *Astragalus canadensis*— nectar

Marsh Vetchling, *Lathyrus palustris*

*Difficult from seed (Cullina, *Growing and Propagating Wildflowers*)

Ferns

The Cinnamon Fern, *Osmunda cinnamomea*, is a beautiful addition to any garden. Hummers harvest its cinnamon-colored fuzz for nesting material. Adaptable and easy to grow, it does best in moist and shady to semishady locations. It is native to all midwestern states. For more information on this species, see the fern table in part 5.

Woody Plants

The flowers of Pussy Willow and other shrub willows attract swarms of insects. Hummingbirds eat the insects and use willow seed fuzz for nesting material. New Jersey Tea and Inland New Jersey Tea also attract tiny insects, perfect in size for hummingbirds. The sap of the Sugar Maple, oozing from holes drilled by sapsuckers, supplies early migrating hummingbirds with nutrients before many flowers bloom.

The other woody plants listed offer nectar-rich blossoms, which attract hummingbirds. Trumpet Creeper is said to have the richest hummingbird flowers in North America, with ten times more nectar than the average wildflower. Trumpet Honeysuckle is also a favorite of hummers.

For information on the native ranges and preferred growing conditions of these woody species, see the tables in part 5.

Vines

Red Honeysuckle, *Lonicera dioica*
Trumpet Honeysuckle, *Lonicera sempervirens*
Yellow Honeysuckle, *Lonicera prolifera*
Trumpet Creeper, *Campsis radicans*

Shrubs

Buttonbush, *Cephalanthus occidentalis*
Coralberry, *Symphoricarpos orbiculatus*
Currants and Gooseberries, *Ribes* species
American Fly Honeysuckle, *Lonicera canadensis*
New Jersey Tea, *Ceanothus americanus*
Inland New Jersey Tea, or Red Root, *Ceanothus herbaceus (C. ovatus)*
Willows, *Salix* species

Trees

Ohio Buckeye, *Aesculus glabra*
Crabtrees, *Malus* species
Hawthorns, *Crataegus* species
Sugar Maple, *Acer saccharum*
Tulip Tree, *Liriodendron tulipifera*

The bright red of Royal Catchfly attracts hummingbirds.

Hummingbird Garden

    This hummingbird garden is designed for the corner of a yard with moist soil. Its 28 species will provide color and bloom throughout the growing season. Each wildflower species has at least five square feet of space, so that it will provide a good show and draw for hummingbirds when it's in blossom. Those species requiring more shade are situated near the Pussy Willow in the corner.

    Most species are native to the entire Midwest. For those few that may not be represented in your local native flora, you'll find many excellent substitutions in the complete list of hummingbird plants on pages 110–112.

KEY TO PLANTS IN HUMMINGBIRD GARDEN

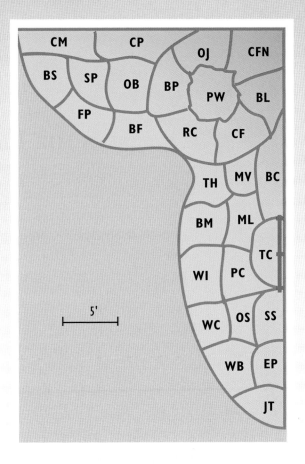

Wildflowers and Fern

BF	Beard Tongue Foxglove
BL	Great Blue Lobelia
BM	Butterfly Milkweed*
BP	Blue Phlox
BS	Prairie Blazing Star
CF	Cardinal Flower
CFN	Cinnamon Fern
CM	Common Milkweed
CP	Cup Plant
EP	Common Evening Primrose
FP	Fire Pink
ML	Michigan Lily
MV	Canada Milk Vetch
OB	Obedient Plant
OJ	Orange Jewelweed
OS	False Sunflower or Oxeye
PC	Purple Coneflower
RC	Royal Catchfly
SP	Sweet William Phlox
SS	Smooth Solomon's Seal
TH	Thimbleweed
WB	Wild Bergamot
WC	Wild Columbine
WI	White Wild Indigo

Woody Plants

PW	Pussy Willow
BC	Wild Black Currant
TC	Trumpet Creeper (on Trellis)
JT	New Jersey Tea

*Butterfly Milkweed for clay soils is available at some nurseries and can thrive in soils that are more moist. See the plant tables in part 5 for detailed information on the recommended species in this garden design.

A male Ruby-throated Hummingbird at a Red Honeysuckle.

RESOURCES FOR READERS

Books/Booklet

Kress, Stephen, ed. 2000. *Hummingbird Gardens.* Handbook #163. New York: Brooklyn Botanic Garden.

Powers, Randy R. "Wildflowers for Hummingbirds." Contact: Randy Powers, General Manager of Prairie Future Seed Co., PO Box 644, Menomonee Falls, WI 53052; phone: 262-820-0221; e-mail: pfsco@execpc.com. This booklet sums up the author's many years of observations of hummingbirds, with new insights into the effect of light on the hummingbird's color choices.

Skutch, Alexander F. 1973. *The Life of the Hummingbird.* New York: Crown Publishers. A detailed account of hummingbirds by a renowned ornithologist who spent most of his life in Costa Rica.

Website

http://www.hummingbirds.net
An excellent source of information on all aspects of hummingbirds. But stick to native plants and avoid the nonnatives suggested on the site.

CHAPTER 9
THE PRAIRIE BIRD GARDEN

*I was in the midst of a prairie! A world of
grass and flowers stretched around me, rising and
falling in gentle undulations....We passed whole
acres of blossoms all bearing one hue, as purple, perhaps, or masses of yellow or rose; and then again a carpet of every color intermixed, or narrow bands, as if a
rainbow had fallen upon the verdant slopes. When the sun flooded this
Mosaic Floor with light, and the summer breeze stirred among their
leaves the iridescent glow was beautiful and wondrous beyond anything I
had ever conceived.*

  —Eliza Steele, near Joliet, Illinois, in 1840, *Summer Journey in the West*

*The immense weed, grass, and fern grown marsh or low-land
prairie, which has been the breeding grounds for Henslow's sparrows and
short-billed marsh wrens since long, long before my time, is being slowly
reclaimed. The cornfields and pastures are eating into it on all sides, and
will, before many years, meet in its very center. What will become of ...
[these birds], as well as the hordes of bobolinks, the marsh hawks, the
prairie hens, and other characteristic nesting birds, when the last acre of
virgin sod is ploughed for corn?*

  —Ned Hollister, in 1919, *Some Changes in the Summer Bird Life of Delavan, Wisconsin*

When the pioneers wagoned westward, much of the Midwest was a magnificent tall-grass prairie. Thirty million acres of prairie graced the landscape of Iowa alone. The vast panorama and astounding diversity of the original tallgrass prairie will never again be seen. Only a mere one-tenth of 1% remains, most lost to the cow and plow, and now to development. Many of the birds have declined along with other prairie wildlife as a result of this loss of habitat. And many of the flowers are now rare where once a single species might have covered acres.

While we can never recreate the full complexity of the original tallgrass prairie, we can readily reconstruct a small representation of that prairie in our gardens and fields. "The prairie itself, though it once covered a vast area, is in many respects a small-featured, fine-textured community, so that it is possible to reproduce many—though certainly not all—of the attributes of a prairie in an area as small as an acre or even less," says William R. Jordan III, founder of the journal *Ecological Restoration*.

Even smaller, "postage stamp" prairies on as little as one-fourth acre have been shown to harbor an amazing diversity of insects, including rare species, according to the late Virginia Kline,

photo: Dickcissel

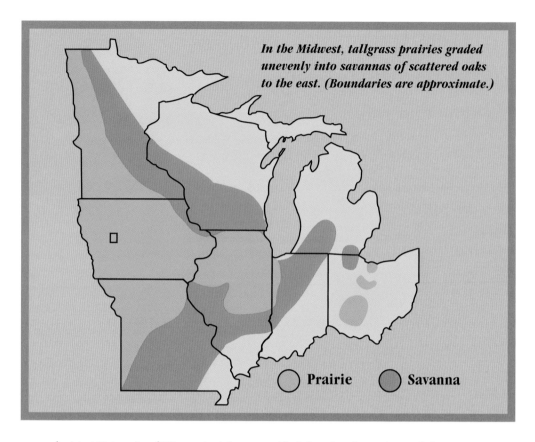

In the Midwest, tallgrass prairies graded unevenly into savannas of scattered oaks to the east. (Boundaries are approximate.)

⬤ Prairie   ⬤ Savanna

an ecologist at University of Wisconsin Arboretum. Their buzzing, humming and droning gave rise to the phrase "symphony grass."

Insects provide a major portion of the diet of many grassland birds. In addition, insects pollinate prairie plants which then produce seeds, the other major item on the menu of many prairie birds. Prairie habitats, whether small or large, in the backyard or the "back forty," provide insects, seeds, berries, rodents and cover for a variety of grassland birds.

Birds of the Prairies

Experts differ on which species they classify as prairie birds (or grassland birds, as they are often called). Wisconsin ecologists David W. Sample and Michael J. Mossman of the Wisconsin Department of Natural Resources broadly define grassland birds as species that use grasslands at any time during their life cycle—for courtship, nesting, foraging, rearing young, roosting or resting. Some of the birds they list as commonly using grasslands include such familiar backyard birds as Mourning Doves, Song Sparrows, Red-winged Blackbirds, Brown-headed Cowbirds and American Goldfinches. Many other common garden birds also occur in prairies, but less frequently. These are most apt to visit smaller prairie gardens, while larger expanses of prairies attract some of the less common grassland birds.

A stricter definition of grassland birds includes only grassland specialists—birds that require treeless prairie for most or all parts of their breeding cycle, including nesting and foraging. Many of these grassland specialists are relatively rare and show significant declines in the

Midwest, according to the Breeding Bird Survey, an annual bird-monitoring program. Unfortunately, they include some of our most colorful and beloved prairie birds, like Bobolinks and meadowlarks, as well as a variety of sparrows and other species.

The large tracts of prairie many grassland specialists require are beyond the scope of most individual property owners. Nonetheless, we should do all possible to support state and private groups active in preserving and restoring large grasslands for these birds. If your property is adjacent to a natural prairie, by all means maintain or reconstruct prairie on your own land to help create a larger site attractive to these increasingly rare species.

American Goldfinches are common in prairie gardens and stay all winter to feed on seeds of grasses and forbs.

How to Create Your Prairie

Prairie gardening has become so popular and well accepted that landscape designers have labeled it the "new American garden style." The style is quintessentially midwestern, since tallgrass prairie was the dominant natural community in presettlement times. Prairies consist primarily of grasses and wildflowers. (Prairie and savanna wildflowers are most often referred to as "forbs.") Only a few low shrubs are native to prairies.

Where to Plant

The prime requirement for a successful prairie habitat is a sunny open site. Most prairie plants need eight hours of sunlight to blossom and thrive, although some experts say six hours of full sun is sufficient. If no trees are nearby, a prairie planting will do well on the south, east and west sides of your home.

Here is a basic rule of thumb: the height to width ratio of the area should be no more than one to one. For example, if the narrowest part of the planting area is 15 feet wide, shade-producing elements (trees, buildings, fences) should be no more than 15 feet high to the immediate east, west or south. For sites that are not that sunny, consider establishing a savanna bird habitat garden, which features understory prairie plants more tolerant of a little shade (see chapter 10).

COMMON GARDEN BIRDS IN HOME PRAIRIES

Red-winged Blackbird
Indigo Bunting
Northern Cardinal
Gray Catbird
Black-capped Chickadee
Brown-headed Cowbird
American Crow
Mourning Dove
American Goldfinch
Ruby-throated Hummingbird
Blue Jay
Baltimore Oriole
American Robin
Chipping Sparrow
Song Sparrow
Tree Swallow
Eastern Towhee
Cedar Waxwing
Downy Woodpecker
House Wren

Although not considered prairie birds, the Dark-eyed Junco and American Tree Sparrow frequent prairie gardens in winter for seed and shelter.

Generally it's best to avoid the shadier north side of your house, which is better suited to a wooded habitat garden. But if the north side happens to be the best site you have for a prairie, don't despair. At our former home, we were able to create a successful prairie in our north-facing front yard, which happened to be the sunniest place on our property. The six-foot space immediately adjacent to the house was definitely too shady for prairie plants, and there we established a small herbaceous woodland wildflower garden. A narrow footpath separated this area from the prairie garden in the rest of the front yard. Away from the shade of the house, the prairie blossomed abundantly each summer.

Front lawns require the work of watering, fertilizing and mowing and are seldom used for playing or entertaining. What better place to plant a prairie, which would provide habitat for birds and butterflies and add so much beauty to our neighborhoods. We loved our front-yard prairie when we lived in a Milwaukee suburb and heard only compliments from neighbors and passers-by.

Hills also make excellent sites for prairies and can be more aesthetic than lawn since they offer superior views of the wildflower display. However, be sure to consider the direction the slope faces when selecting your plant species. South-facing slopes are hottest and driest. West-facing slopes are next in line, since they are exposed to desiccating westerly winds and the hot afternoon sun. East slopes are more cool and moist, since they receive less direct sunlight, while north slopes are shadiest. Plants for dry prairies are best suited for south- and west-facing slopes, while east-facing slopes favor more mesic prairie species, which require soils of medium moisture. If not too steep, the north side of a hill may support mesic prairie species, but steeper slopes are better suited to woodland wildflowers and ferns.

Septic fields and mounds are ideal locations for prairies. Studies have shown that the roots of herbaceous plants don't grow into the pipes or cause other problems with septic systems. (Avoid woody plants over septic sites. Their roots can grow into the system.) Herbaceous wildflowers and grasses actually enhance the operation of septic systems by using the wastewater and reducing the nutrients that enter the groundwater. The prairie at our pres-

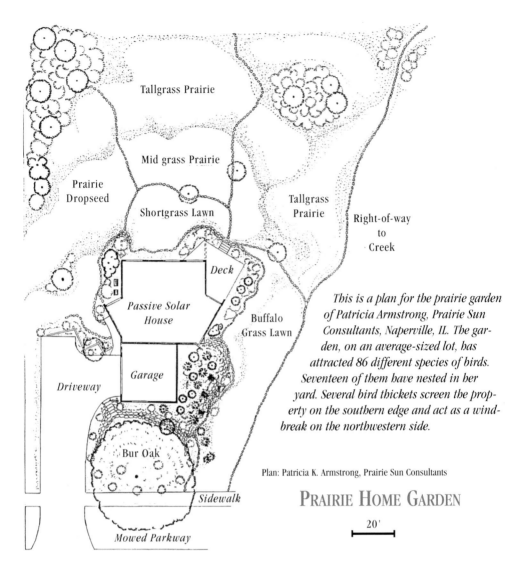

Tallgrass Prairie

Mid grass Prairie

Prairie
Dropseed

Shortgrass Lawn

Tallgrass
Prairie

Right-of-way
to
Creek

Deck

Passive Solar
House

Buffalo
Grass Lawn

Garage

Driveway

Bur Oak

*This is a plan for the prairie garden
of Patricia Armstrong, Prairie Sun
Consultants, Naperville, IL. The garden, on an average-sized lot, has
attracted 86 different species of birds.
Seventeen of them have nested in her
yard. Several bird thickets screen the property on the southern edge and act as a windbreak on the northwestern side.*

Plan: Patricia K. Armstrong, Prairie Sun Consultants

PRAIRIE HOME GARDEN

20'

Sidewalk

Mowed Parkway

ent home is located over our septic field. We enjoy a beautiful view with many birds and butterflies
and have never experienced any problems with the septic system.

Getting Started

There is no one way to create a prairie. Experts have their different methods; moreover,
different sites may demand different techniques. The most popular approach is to introduce seeds
and/or plants on a prepared site from which you have removed all vegetation. Interseeding is
another method in which you retain most or all of the original vegetation and enhance it with the
selective addition of new species. I'll provide basic information on the creation of both small yard-
size prairie habitats and field-size or larger prairie reconstructions using these various methods.

Establishing a Prairie after Removing Vegetation

Just as when you're seeding in a lawn or a farm field or transplanting perennial flowers
into a garden bed, the planting area for your prairie must be completely free of vegetation when

Prairie birds have adapted their life styles to their treeless habitat. Most nest near or on the ground. To foil the predation of their easily accessible nests, incubating adults are well camouflaged. If they lose their eggs, most prairie birds can renest in the same season.

Rough-legged Hawks (winter visitors to prairies) and American Kestrels hover above the prairie to scan for prey, while Northern Harriers and Short-eared Owls skim low over the vegetation and may momentarily hover before dropping on their prey. The Grassland Sparrow and Henslow's Sparrow weigh so little that they are able to perch and feed on the seeds of slender grass stalks without bending them to the ground.

Some species of prairie birds perform aerial courtship and territorial rituals, since they have no woody plants on which to perch as do birds in most other habitats. Bobolinks are well known for their bubbling "bobolink" song as they wing over the prairie in competition for space and mates. American Goldfinches have their own unique aerial display—an exuberant rollercoaster flight.

using this method. Any existing vegetation will compete with native seedlings and transplants for water, sun and nutrients. This competition can slow down or even prevent the establishment of your prairie plants. See chapter 7 for ways to eradicate a lawn or other vegetation.

Soil considerations. Prairie plants usually establish well on worn-out, nutrient-poor soils. As Loretta Hernday, a native-plant gardener in Wisconsin, puts it, prairie plants are the "original soil amenders. They have been making topsoil out of glacial clay," she explains, "ever since the Rocky Mountains pushed up into the clouds and stole the rain."

Rich soils, in fact, often encourage weeds over prairie plants. As a result, most restorationists do not recommend adding fertilizers or compost to improve soils. In time, prairies will improve the soil on their own through the decaying of dying roots and the return of the nutrients in the top vegetation through prairie fires or mulch-mowing. (For the few exceptions in which amending extremely poor soils is advised, see chapter 7.)

Prairies can be successfully established on many different types of soils and moisture conditions, from very dry sandy and gravelly sites, to mesic sites with loamy soils, to wetter sites with clay soils or high water tables. You may want to review the information in chapter 5 to determine your soil type. The important thing is to match the plants to the site.

Selecting species. The Midwest has three major types of prairies: dry, wet and mesic. They vary according to type of soil and related soil moisture, and each has its own unique suite of species.

Dry prairies are found on dry sandy or gravelly soils and the thin soils of steep slopes or ridges. The vegetation is generally rather short, no more than two to three feet in height. Dry prairie grasses in the Midwest include Little Bluestem and Side-oats Grama. Forbs include such dry-tolerant species as Rough Blazing Star, Bird's Foot Violet, Pasque Flower and Silky Aster.

Wet prairies are found in flood plains and other wet sites, on a variety of soil types. Typical plants include such wet-loving species as Prairie Cord Grass, New England Aster, Blue Flag Iris and Cup Plant.

Mesic prairies, as the name suggests, lie between wet and dry prairies in available soil moisture. They are found on flat to gently sloping sites with rich, moderately well-drained soils. Although mesic prairies were once widespread throughout much

The prairie grass is always greener over the septic system.

of the Midwest, almost all are now cultivated as farmland, with only a few small remnants in cemeteries, railroad rights-of-way and roadsides. Our tallest prairie grass, Big Bluestem, dominates the mesic prairies, along with Indian Grass. Characteristic forbs included Yellow Coneflower, Black-eyed Susan, Smooth Aster, Compass Plant, Flowering Spurge, White Wild Indigo and Rattlesnake Master.

Many plant species in each type of prairie provide seeds, nectar, cover and nesting materials for birds. See the tables of recommended bird-friendly species (many will also attract butterflies) on pages 130–138:

- *Bird-friendly Forbs (Wildflowers) for Prairies and Savannas*
- *Bird-friendly Grasses, Sedges and Rushes for Prairies and Savannas*
- *Bird-friendly Shrubs for Prairies*.

Often there is variation even within a small yard, so you may have the opportunity to use plants from several different prairie types. For example, you may have a gentle slope suited to dry or mesic prairie species on the top, grading to a wet area suited to wet prairie species at its base.

If conditions allow, the shorter dry prairie species are a good choice around homes and buildings. Taller mesic prairie species also create beautiful prairies in both front yards and backyards. Tallgrass prairie is native to most of southeastern Wisconsin where I live, and nearly all our home prairies feature its beautiful wildflowers and grasses.

Note that the plants in the tables are grouped into families. The prominent families in native prairies are grasses, composites (aster family), legumes (bean family) and milkweeds. Some other well-represented families are mints, lilies and roses. Evelyn Howell, a plant ecologist at the University of Wisconsin, suggests selecting at least one species from each of the major families, as well as some species from other families for a more varied, natural and successful prairie planting.

By planting a variety of species, you will have a year-round floral display. For the specific bloom times of the prairie forbs you've chosen, see the wildflower table in part 5, pages 267–275. Howell suggests selecting species for every season—about one-fourth for spring bloom; half for summer bloom and another one-fourth for fall bloom. By doing so, you'll be including both cool season (spring/fall) species and warm season (summer) plants.

Amounts. John A. Harrington, a landscape architect and restoration specialist at the University of Wisconsin, recommends planting "as many species as possible." The roots of different prairie plants are complementary and help form a sod, which will keep out weeds. Tap-rooted flowers grow better and produce more blossoms alongside clump-forming grasses.

Various species are interdependent in other ways. Most legumes are nitrogen-fixers, which means they are able to add nitrogen to the soil in excess of their own needs, making this invaluable soil nutrient available to other prairie plants.

Although much is still unknown about the relationships of prairie plants, studies have shown that a diversity of species can withstand environmental changes and pressures. Prairies with a greater number of species were best able to withstand the severe drought of 1988. Some of the many species in a diverse prairie succeed, whatever the circumstances. Some years more drought-tolerant plants in a mix of species do well, and other years plants able to tolerate mesic or wet conditions prevail. A variety of species will produce a more successful and long-lasting planting.

Virgin prairies can have from 40 to 400 species. A good mix for most prairie gardens, unless on very small urban sites, would include a minimum of 40 to 50 species. The majority should be forb species, as in native prairies. A mix of 50 species might have 45 forb species and 5 grass species.

Although grass species in native prairies are few, they represent up to 90% of the vegetative cover, with a great variety of forbs interspersed among them. To create a more natural prairie, Harrington and Howell advise maintaining at least 50% cover in grasses. Grasses help to unify a prairie restoration visually. They provide a beautiful backdrop to the forbs, as well as structural support for many of the taller ones.

Many prairie gardeners, however, prefer a greater proportion of the showy and colorful forbs. For such aesthetic pur-

A Red-spotted Purple basks on a Purple Coneflower.

poses, University of Wisconsin experts suggest planting a greater percentage of forbs in selected locations.

Neil Diboll, ecologist and president of Prairie Nursery in Wisconsin, has found that a mix of 50/50 or 60/40 forb to grass seed by weight provides a diverse prairie community with a good cover of both grasses and forbs. Since grass seed is heavier than forb seed, this proportion of forbs to grasses is quite a bit greater than it might seem. For example, a 50/50 mix of forb and grass seed by weight is equivalent to an 80/20 mix in terms of actual number of seeds.

Harrington recommends 6 pounds of seed per acre, a sharp contrast to the 20 pounds per acre recommended some years ago. Nowadays, seeding rates are usually given in number of seeds per area, not in weight. The nursery from which you purchase the seed should have a chart showing how many seeds of each species are needed to cover a given area. The number varies a great deal from species to species, depending on the size and viability of the seed.

You'll need a balance between too few seeds, which will

BUTTERFLY PLANTS

Many of the same prairie and savanna plants that attract birds also attract butterflies. In fact, prairie plants are essential elements of any native butterfly garden. Some serve as host plants for caterpillars, others as nectar sources for adult butterflies, and some do both. Among the plants recommended for prairie and savanna gardens, the following attract butterflies.

Caterpillar Plant Foods
Forbs & Grasses:
Showy Tick Trefoil, Wild Lupine, Wild Petunia, Canada Milk Vetch, Blue Vervain, Maryland Senna, Partridge Pea, Round-headed Bush Clover, milkweeds, prairie clovers, wild indigos, thistles, asters, violets, sedges, grasses.

Woody Plants:
Leadplant, New Jersey Tea, dogwoods, sumacs

Nectar Sources for Adult Butterflies
Forbs:
Canada Milk Vetch, Partridge Pea, Joe Pye Weed, Wild Bergamot, Black-eyed Susan, Cup Plant, Rosinweed, Prairie Dock, Compass Plant, sunflowers, vervains, asters, thistles, giant hyssops, milkweeds, blazing stars, coreopsis, phlox, goldenrods, purple coneflowers, bonesets

Woody Plants:
New Jersey Tea, Meadowsweet, hawthorns, sumacs

A MIX OF PLANTS AND SEEDS, FORBS AND GRASSES

Patricia K. Armstrong, of Prairie Sun Consultants has a favorite way of obtaining a good proportion of forbs and grasses in the prairie gardens she designs for small properties. She suggests planting plugs of forb species, then seeding prairie grasses around the plants. This gives the wildflowers a head start, increases their success, creates a better show in the early stages of a prairie garden and reduces the tendency for grasses to dominate in a prairie planting. I've seen several prairies where grasses over-whelmed the garden—to the dismay of the owners—so I highly recommend trying this method.

A Red Admiral butterfly nectars on Purple Coneflower.

allow room for weeds, and too many seeds, which will result in stunted plants. Harrington recommends a maximum of 50–60 seeds per square foot. To achieve a more diverse prairie, allowing time and space for the slower-growing, rarer, conservative prairie species to take hold, he suggests 10–25 seeds per square foot, though it may result in more weeds.

If you use container-grown transplants rather than seed, you can plant the grasses and forbs in the proportion you prefer.

Seeds or container-grown transplants? Cost and size of site determines whether to use seeds or transplants. For large sites, the cost of transplants is prohibitive and requires much more work than seeding. As a result, seed is used for most large-scale prairie reconstructions.

Live plants (rather than seeds) work well in small yards, in clay soils when seeds are slow to germinate and in front yards for an instant display to please the neighbors.

The density of planting container-grown transplants also affects cost. The most common recommendation is one plant per square foot. For a showy, colorful garden in prominent areas, plant two grasses for every eight forbs. To cut costs, the minimum planting density could be reduced to one plant for every 18 inches square. In contrast, UW restoration specialists have found that a dense planting of two plants per square foot, half forbs and half grasses, results in a more natural appearance. For prairie shrubs, one every 1,000 square feet is recommended.

A combination of seeding and transplants is another popular approach and has been used in many yards in Wisconsin and Illinois. It is less expensive and less labor intensive than using all transplants and gives some early color and interest for your prairie garden while waiting for the seeded species to develop and blossom. For guidelines on installing transplants, see chapter 7.

When to sow seeds. Seeding can be done in spring, fall or even late winter. Don't plant from mid July to mid October, since seedlings may not have sufficient time to become established before winter. Some experts recommend fall planting, as occurs in nature, especially for forbs, and in clay or sandy soils. Fall planting gives the seeds natural stratification (cold treatment) over the winter, which most native seeds require.

Frost seeding from late October to late March, although less common, also works well. Seed when there is no snow cover; the seeds work into the soil during later freeze and thaw cycles. Frost seeding is a good way to add new species to established plantings.

For spring planting of small areas that can be watered, stratify the seeds by mixing them with damp sand and placing them either outdoors or in a refrigerator for four to eight weeks prior to seeding to mimic natural winter conditions. Some experts no longer recommend stratification of seeds for use on large sites that can't be watered, since grasses and certain forbs that don't need irrigation will be favored.

Some seeds may require special processing, such as scarification or inoculation. For details on these matters, see *The Tallgrass Restoration Handbook*.

Seeding small sites. Small sites can be seeded by hand, broadcasting first in a north-south direction, then east-west, in order to distribute the seed evenly. You can add perlite or sawdust to the mix to help see where seed has been scattered. The seed should then be raked in or walked over a number of times to press it into the soil. Volunteers at the Wehr Nature Center in Milwaukee County successfully planted a small prairie of several acres as an Earth Day project by broadcasting the seed and then walking over the site several times.

Seeding large areas. For large sites, a drill for planting prairie seed is ideal because it places seed at the proper depth and distributes it evenly. Before seeding with a drill, you must pack the soil with a roller or cultipacker to remove air passages that can dry out seedlings.

Broadcasters, either hand or mechanical, are easier and cheaper to use but require more seed. When broadcasting, be sure to pack the soil after seeding. Double seeding in two directions is recommended, as with hand seeding. Rake or drag a chain over the ground to mix the seed and soil, then pack.

Cover crops. A cover crop of short-lived, quick-growing annuals or biennials will fill bare soil so there's no room for weeds to get started. A cover crop also lessens the chances for erosion on a sloping site and provides fuel for managed burns. Bob Ahrenhorster, owner of Prairie Seed Source in Wisconsin, suggests using native species such as Canada Wild Rye, Black-eyed Susans and Evening Primrose.

Enhancing a Site by Interseeding

Interseeding is used to restore remnants, oak savannas and old pastures where plowing would destroy the native species

PRAIRIE OR "MEADOW IN A CAN"?

Some commercial wildflower mixes have enticing names like Wedding Wildflowers, Sun Garden or Summer Magic. They come in a can or a bag and often tout Mother Nature, backyard biodiversity, native species and Earth Day.

But beware! Researchers from the University of Washington investigated 19 mixes from a variety of U.S. and Canadian sources and found each to contain invasive and/or noxious species. One-third of the packets had no content label and more than one-third had inaccurate labels. Only 5 of the 19 correctly identified their contents.

The researchers grew the wildflower mixes and identified the resulting plants. The best mix produced 106 plants total, of which 30 were invasive—a full 28%! The number of invasive species in various packets ranged from 3 to 13; in one packet, all the identified species were considered invasive in at least one part of the U.S.

At best, these mixes are inexpensive and provide short-lived results. They blossom well the first season or two, but most species soon disappear since they are not suited for local conditions. Far worse, other species may become invasive and require control measures.

Avoid even those packets that claim to have native species because while such species may be native to our country, they may not be native to your area. Instead, buy seed at a reliable native plant nursery. Well-planned seed mixes produce long-term results and plantings that improve with time.

Prairie birds are usually quick to discover new prairie plants. Susan Damon, whose garden is featured in chapter 4, gave a neighbor one of her Wild Golden Glow plants (Green-headed Coneflowers), and as soon as she planted it, goldfinches came to visit.

Both finches and sparrows will come to nibble at sunflowers and coneflowers, especially yellow ones. Later, the birds come to feast on the seeds.

Prairie birds also like to perch on the highest flower stalks. There in full view, they sing to attract mates and declare their territories. Some species scan for prey or predators from perches. A good way to attract grassland birds to your newly established prairie is to put up perches to supplement the plant stalks.

Lillian and Don Stokes, the well-known authors of many bird books and videos, attracted Bobolinks to their new property with a perch. First, they stopped mowing a large grassy field that had been regularly mowed. Then, they stuck a leafless, four-foot sapling in the ground as a perch. "No sooner had we turned our backs and walked away," they reported, "than a male Bobolink landed and began to sing."

Prairie Smoke is a handsome spring flower that adds color and dramatic seedheads to your prairie plantings.

already present, cause erosion or damage tree roots. An all-important first step is to remove highly aggressive species such as Reed Canary Grass, Purple Loosestrife, Teasel, Leafy Spurge and Garlic Mustard. Dense herbaceous vegetation should be burned or, if burning is not possible, mowed and then raked of thatch.

Seeds for interseeding are often collected from nearby prairie or savanna remnants and cleaned manually, resulting in rough-cleaned seed. Suggested seed quantities for interseeding are one cup of a mix of 50% rough-cleaned seed and 50% perlite for every 100 feet or one kitchen garbage bag per 18,000 square feet. Seeds can be hand-raked, disked, harrowed or drilled. If pure, clean seed from a local nursery is used, reduce the amount of seed by about a third.

How to Maintain Your Prairie

Weed control is important in prairies, as in all new native plant gardens. Water if possible, especially if you use transplants. After a few years, you should burn or mow to maintain your prairie. These management practices are covered in chapter 19.

Prairie Bird Garden

The garden on pages 128–129 is designed for a front yard with average soil of medium moisture in the central Midwest. The prairie is approximately 500 square feet which includes the larger prairie area directly in the front of the house and the prairie patch on the west side of the driveway. A split rail fence borders the garden in the front and on the sides, separating it from the lawn.

A lawn on the front and sides of the garden provides a more formal look and blends in with the lawns of adjacent neighbors. A narrow strip of lawn on each side of the driveway provides space to step out of cars without damaging wildflowers and to pile snow from the driveway in winter.

The planting layout along the borders has some symmetry and order to avoid a totally wild appearance in so visible a location. Place the rest of the recommended plants randomly in masses according to height. The intended overall effect of this garden layout is one of organized wildness. I suggest a total of 40 species, most of which are native to all midwestern states. Check local sources to insure that the species are native to your area.

You may want to install a good proportion of the species as live plants, rather than seed, in your front yard to create an attractive "instant" prairie garden to please neighbors. Plant one forb or grass plant per square foot. For a showy front yard, a good ratio is one grass clump for every four forbs. One prairie shrub (most of which are very small) or vine should be planted for every 1,000 square feet. In this plan, I've grouped two New Jersey Tea shrubs near the front door and an Illinois or Climbing Prairie Rose at two of the fence corners on the front lawn.

Prairie Dock is the native equivalent of Hollyhock for height and eye-catching blossoms, and I've placed it at the corner of the house. Blue Wild Indigo is directly in front of the house below the front windows. When mature, these showy plants are as big as small shrubs, about a yard wide, so three or four plants should easily fill the space. Indian Grass provides a backdrop to the prairie on both sides of the house.

I suggest shorter plants for the front of the garden adjacent to the split rail fence in a somewhat symmetrical pattern. Little Bluestem Grass is an attractive border plant. It makes a neat, orderly edge in any season and is especially lovely in autumn, when its leaves glow with copper colors and its fuzzy seedheads dance in the wind. Prairie Lily on the driveway side of the garden showcases its spectacular blossoms. If you use a lot of salt on your driveway, which can harm nearby plants, plant a hardier flower such as Purple Coneflower.

Reduce costs by using seed instead of live plants for the grasses. This also lessens the chance that the grasses will dominate in your prairie in its early stages. After you plant and mulch the forbs, you can sow the grass seed along with the cover crop species into the mulch.

Another way to reduce costs is to increase the spacing between plants. Some experts suggest the minimum number of plants would be one plant for every 18 inches square rather than one plant every square foot. To calculate the minimum number of plants using this spacing, divide the square footage of the site by 2.25. Thus, you would need 222 plants for this 500 square foot garden. If you planted only the forbs as live plants, you could subtract one-fifth of 222 (about 44) for the grasses which would be seeded in, leaving 178 forbs.

Another approach to reduce costs and labor is to plant only part of the garden one year, perhaps half, and do the rest the following year. Of course, if you have just built a new house and have bare ground, costs are often comparable or even less for planting a prairie than a lawn. It is definitely less expensive to plant a prairie in the long run, since fertilizers and watering are unnecessary.

The author's yard includes Prairie Blazing Star, Yellow Coneflower and Black-eyed Susan. Note the protective sleeve on the feeder post to discourage raiders.

KEY TO PLANTS IN PRAIRIE BIRD GARDEN

BG Little Bluestem Grass
BI   Blue Wild Indigo
DG Prairie Dropseed (Grass)
IG   Indian Grass
IR   Illinois or Climbing Prairie Rose
JT   New Jersey Tea
PC Purple Prairie Clover
PD Prairie Dock
PL   Prairie Lily
PV Prairie Violet
SG Showy Goldenrod
WP Wild Petunia
WS Wild Strawberry

Species to Be Planted Randomly in Center of Garden:

Forbs: Smooth and New England Asters, Rough Blazing Star, Purple Coneflower, Showy and Stiff Goldenrods, Rosin Weed, Prairie Indian Plantain, Thimbleweed, Foxglove Beard Tongue, Common Milkweed, Wild Bergamot, Sweet William Phlox, Starry Campion, Prairie Alum Root, Yellow Cone-flower, Prairie Coreopsis, Prairie Sunflower, Oxeye Sunflower, Obedient Plant, and Flowering Spurge

Grasses: Big Bluestem, Switchgrass

Cover Crop to Be Seeded In: Canada Wild Rye, Black-eyed Susan, Common Evening Primrose

See the plant tables at the end of this chapter and in part 5 for more information and the Latin names of the recommended species for this garden design.

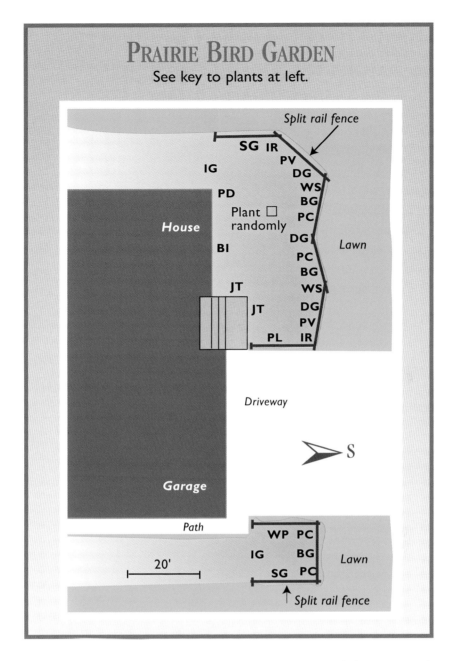

PRAIRIE BIRD GARDEN
See key to plants at left.

Split rail fence

SG IR

IG

PV

DG

WS

PD

BG

Plant ☐
randomly

PC

House

DG

BI

PC

Lawn

BG

JT

WS

JT

DG

PV

PL IR

Driveway

S

Garage

Path

WP PC

IG

BG

20'

Lawn

SG PC

Split rail fence

KEY TO TABLES FOR PRAIRIE AND SAVANNA PLANTS (pages 130–138)

To facilitate selection of either prairie or savanna plants, only two codes are given here for their light requirement:

S = Full Sun (for prairie plants)
P = Partial Sun (for savanna plants needing some shade)

Five categories for soil moisture are given to help you choose the very best plants for your site. Within each family and genus, the species are listed according to their soil moisture requirements from dry to wet.

Use this information to compile a list of potential species for your site. Once you have a list of potential species, you can then check for further information, including native range, color, and other characteristics in the appropriate tables in Part Five, which you can use to finalize your list.

Bird-Friendly Forbs (Wildflowers)
for Prairies and Savannas
Key to Tables on previous page.

Recommended plant species are grouped in families in the table below. Try to select species from every family when possible to provide a more natural and diverse mix of species for your prairie or savanna and to insure bloom throughout the season.

You may be surprised to find several species of thistles listed. While most of the thistles we usually see are invasive non-native species, there are a few beautiful native species that are not at all invasive and are wonderful for wildlife. Goldfinches seek out thistle down for nesting material and eat the thistle seeds. Goldfinch nestlings are fed primarily on seeds, including thistle seed. Thistles also provide nectar and food plants for butterflies. The two recommended thistle species are biennial, but they are likely to reseed themselves in your native habitat.

SPECIES		Dry	Medium Dry	Moist (Mesic)	Wet Mesic	Wet	Light Req.	
COMMON NAME	LATIN NAME	SOIL		MOIST	URE			VALUE FOR BIRDS
Acanthus Family								
Petunia, Wild or Hairy Ruellia	*Ruellia humilis*	x	x	x	–	–	S	Nectar for hummingbirds
Aster Family–Asters								
Aster, Silky	*Aster sericeus*	x	x	–	–	–	S,P	Seeds
Aster, Heath	*Aster ericoides*	x	x	x	–	–	S	Seeds
Aster, Sky Blue	*Aster oolentangiensis (A. azureus)*	x	x	x	–	–	S,P	Seeds
Aster, Side-flowering	*Aster lateriflorus*	–	x	x	x	–	P	Seeds
Aster, Smooth Blue	*Aster laevis*	–	x	x	x	–	S	Seeds
Aster, New England	*Aster novae-angliae*	–	–	x	x	x	S,P	Waterfowl cover; seeds
Aster, Panicled	*Aster lanceolatus (A. simplex)*	–	–	x	x	x	S	Waterfowl cover; seeds
Aster Family–Blazing Stars								
Blazing Star, Cylindrical	*Liatris cylindracea*	x	x	–	–	–	S	Seeds; nectar for hummingbirds
Blazing Star, Rough	*Liatris aspera*	x	x	x	–	–	S	Seeds; nectar for hummingbirds
Blazing Star, Prairie	*Liatris pycnostachya*	–	–	x	x	–	S	Seeds; nectar for hummingbirds & orioles
Blazing Star, Meadow	*Liatris ligulistylis*	–	–	x	x	–	S	Seeds; nectar for hummingbirds
Blazing Star, Marsh	*Liatris spicata*	–	–	x	x	x	S	Seeds; nectar for hummingbirds

Aster Family–Coneflowers

Coneflower, Pale Purple	*Echinacea pallida (E. angustifolia)*	x	x	x	–	–	S	Seeds; attracts insects for hummingbirds
Coneflower, Yellow or Grey-headed	*Ratibida pinnata*	–	x	x	–	–	S,P	Seeds
Coneflower, Purple	*Echinacea purpurea*	–	x	x	x	–	S,P	Seeds; attracts insects for hummingbirds

Aster Family–Goldenrods

Goldenrod, Old Field	*Solidago nemoralis*	x	x	–	–	–	S,P	All species provide seeds for goldfinches, juncos, & sparrows; their leaves are eaten by grouse
Goldenrod, Showy	*Solidago speciosa*	x	x	x	–	–	S,P	
Goldenrod, Stiff	*Solidago rigida*	x	x	x	x	–	S	
Goldenrod, Elm-leaved	*Solidago ulmifolia*	–	x	x	–	–	P	
Goldenrod, Broad-leaved or Zigzag	*Solidago flexicaulis*	–	–	x	–	–	P	

Aster Family–Silphiums

Rosin Weed	*Silphium integrifolium*	x	x	x	x	–	S	Seeds eaten by songbirds & grouse
Compass Plant	*Silphium laciniatum*	–	x	x	x	–	S	Seeds eaten by songbirds & grouse
Dock, Prairie	*Silphium terebinthinaceum*	–	x	x	x	–	S	Seeds eaten by goldfinches & grouse
Cup Plant	*Silphium perfoliatum*	–	–	x	x	–	S,P	Seeds eaten by goldfinches & grouse; nectar for hummingbirds; source of water (drinking & bathing); cover for songbirds

Aster Family–Sunflowers & Similar Species

Susan, Black-eyed	*Rudbeckia hirta*	x	x	x	x	–	S,P	Seeds & cover
Susan, Brown-eyed	*Rudbeckia triloba*	–	x	x	x	–	S,P	Seeds & cover
Golden Glow, Wild	*Rudbeckia laciniata*	–	–	x	x	–	S,P	Seeds & cover
Sunflower, Prairie	*Helianthus pauciflorus (H. rigidus; H. laetiflorus)*	x	x	–	–	–	S	Large nutritious seeds of outstanding value; eaten by gamebirds (doves, grouse, pheasants, bobwhites) & songbirds (blackbirds, crossbills, crows, finches & many sparrows)
Sunflower, Western	*Helianthus occidentalis*	x	x	x	–	–	S	
Sunflower, Pale-leaved or Woodland*	*Helianthus strumosis*	–	x	x	–	–	S,P	
Coreopsis, Sand	*Coreopsis lanceolata*	x	x	x	–	–	S	Both species provide seeds for birds
Coreopsis, Prairie	*Coreopsis palmata*	x	x	x	–	–	S	

| SPECIES | | | | | | | | VALUE FOR BIRDS |
COMMON NAME	LATIN NAME	Dry	Medium Dry	Moist (Mesic)	Wet Mesic	Wet	Light Req.	
		SOIL MOISTURE						
Sunflower, False or Oxeye*	*Heliopsis helian-thoides*	–	x	x	x	–	S,P	Seeds for birds
Sneezeweed	*Helenium autumnale*	–	–	x	x	x	S	Seeds for songbirds & game-birds

Aster Family–Thistles, Eupatoriums & Plantains

Thistle, Pasture	*Cirsium discolor*	–	x	x	–	–	S	Goldfinches use thistle down for nests and thistle seed for food; hummingbirds feed on insects attracted to thistles
Thistle, Swamp	*Cirsium muticum*	–	–	x	x	x	S	Same as above
Plaintain, Pale Indian*	*Cacalia atriplicifolia*	–	x	x	–	–	S,P	Source of insects for hummingbirds & other birds
Plaintain, Prairie Indian	*Cacalia plantiginea*	–	–	x	x	–	S	Same as above
Joe Pye Weed, Spotted	*Eupatorium maculatum*	–	–	–	x	–	S	Seeds eaten by Swamp Sparrows & Wild Turkeys
Boneset, Common	*Eupatorium perfoliatum*	–	–	–	x	x	S	Seeds eaten by Swamp Sparrows, Wild Turkeys, & some waterfowl; leaves eaten by Mallards & Ruffed Grouse

Bean Family

Goat's Rue*	*Tephrosia virginiana*	x	–	–	–	–	S,P	Attracts hummingbirds
Lupine, Wild*	*Lupinus perennis*	x	x	–	–	–	S,P	Nectar for hummingbirds
Clover, White Prairie	*Dalea candida (Petalostemum c.)*	x	x	x	–	–	S	Seeds eaten by songbirds
Clover, Purple Prairie	*Dalea purpurea (Petalostemum p.)*	x	x	x	–	–	S	Seeds eaten by songbirds
Clover, Round-headed Bush	*Lespedeza capitata*	x	x	x	–	–	S,P	Seeds eaten by gamebirds, especially bobwhites; used by hummingbirds
Pea, Partridge	*Chamaecrista fasci-culata (Cassia f.)*	x	x	x	–	–	S	Nectar for hummingbirds; seeds eaten by gamebirds, especially bobwhites
Indigo, White Wild	*Baptisia alba (B. lactea; B. leucantha)*	x	x	x	x	–	S,P	Nectar for hummingbirds
Senna, Maryland	*Senna marilandica (Cassia m.)*	–	x	x	x	–	S	Nectar for hummingbirds
Vetch, Canada Milk*	*Astragalus canadensis*	–	x	x	x	–	S	Nectar for hummingbirds

Tick Trefoil, Showy	*Desmodium canadense*	−	x	x	x	−	S	Seeds eaten by gamebirds, including turkeys & bobwhites; attracts hummingbirds
Indigo, Blue Wild	*Baptisia australis*	−	−	x	x	−	S,P	Nectar for hummingbirds

Bluebell Family

Harebell	*Campanula rotundifolia*	x	x	−	−	−	S,P	Nectar for hummingbirds

Buttercup Family

Pasque Flower	*Anemone patens* var. *multifida*	x	x	−	−	−	S	Used by hummingbirds
Thimbleweed*	*Anemone virginiana*	−	x	x	−	−	S,P	Downy seed head used by hummingbirds to make nests
Larkspur, Prairie	*Delphinium carolinianum* (*D. virescens*)	−	x	x	−	−	S,P	Nectar for hummingbirds
Anemone, Meadow or Canada	*Anemone canadensis*	−	−	x	x	x	S,P	Used by waterfowl

Evening Primrose Family

Primrose, Common Evening	*Oenothera biennis*	x	x	x	x	−	S,P	Nectar for hummingbirds; seeds eaten by goldfinches & other songbirds

Figwort Family

Foxglove, Fern-leaved False*	*Aureolaria pedicularia*	x	−	−	−	−	P	Source of insects for hummingbirds & other insect-eating birds
Foxglove, Yellow False*	*Aureolaria grandiflora*	x	−	−	−	−	P	Same as above
Beard Tongue, Pale	*Penstemon pallidus*	x	x	−	−	−	S,P	Nectar for hummingbirds
Beard Tongue, Large-Flowered	*Penstemon grandiflorus*	x	x	−	−	−	S	Nectar for hummingbirds
Beard Tongue, Slender	*Penstemon gracilis*	x	x	−	−	−	S,P	Nectar for hummingbirds
Beard Tongue, Foxglove	*Penstemon digitalis*	−	x	x	−	−	S,P	Nectar for hummingbirds
Paintbrush, Downy	*Castilleja sessiliflora*	x	x	−	−	−	S	Nectar for hummingbirds
Paintbrush, Indian	*Castilleja coccinea*	−	x	x	x	−	S	Nectar for hummingbirds
Figwort, Early	*Scrophularia lanceolata*	x	x	x	x	−	P	Source of insects for hummingbirds & other insect-eating birds
Figwort, Late	*Scrophularia marilandica*	−	x	x	−	−	P	Same as above

COMMON NAME	LATIN NAME	Dry	Medium Dry	Moist (Mesic)	Wet Mesic	Wet	Light Req.	VALUE FOR BIRDS
		SOIL		MOISTURE				
Betony, Wood or Lousewort*	*Pedicularis canadensis*	x	x	x	x	—	S,P	Nectar for hummingbirds
Lousewort, Swamp	*Pedicularis lanceolata*	—	—	—	x	x	S,P	Nectar for hummingbirds

Geranium Family

Geranium, Wild	*Geranium maculatum*	—	x	x	—	—	S,P	Seeds eaten by gamebirds & songbirds

Iris Family

Iris, Northern Blue Flag	*Iris versicolor*	—	—	x	x	x	S,P	Both species provide nectar for hummingbirds
Iris, Southern Blue Flag	*Iris virginica (I. shrevei)*	—	—	x	x	x	S,P	

Lily Family

Solomon's Seal, Starry False*	*Smilacina stellata*	x	x	x	x	—	S,P	Berries for birds
Solomon's Seal, Smooth	*Polygonatum biflorum (P. caniculatum)*	—	x	x	—	—	S,P	Provides nectar for hummingbirds; berries for birds
Lily, Prairie*	*Lilium philadelphicum*	—	x	x	x	—	S,P	Nectar for hummingbirds
Lily, Michigan or Turk's Cap Lily	*Lilium michiganse (L. superbum)*	—	—	x	x	x	S,P	Nectar for hummingbirds

Lobelia Family

Lobelia, Great Blue	*Lobelia siphilitica*	—	—	x	x	x	S,P	Nectar for hummingbirds
Cardinal Flower	*Lobelia cardinalis*	—	—	x	x	x	S,P	Nectar for hummingbirds

Milkweed Family

Milkweed, Tall Green	*Asclepias hirtella*	x	x	—	—	—	S	Nectar for hummingbirds
Milkweed, Butterfly	*Asclepias tuberosa*	x	x	x	—	—	S	Nectar for hummingbirds
Milkweed, Whorled	*Asclepias verticillata*	x	x	x	—	—	S	Nectar for hummingbirds
Milkweed, Common	*Asclepias syriaca*	x	x	x	x	—	S,P	Nectar for hummingbirds
Milkweed, Prairie	*Asclepias sullivantii*	—	—	x	x	—	S	Nectar for hummingbirds

Mint Family

Mint, Horse	*Monarda punctata*	x	x	—	—	—	S	Nectar for hummingbirds
Bergamot, Wild	*Monarda fistulosa*	x	x	x	x	—	S,P	Nectar for hummingbirds; early growth eaten by geese
Hyssop, Lavender Giant	*Agastache foeniculum*	—	x	x	x	—	S,P	Nectar for hummingbirds

Hyssop, Purple Giant	*Agastache scrophulariifolia*	–	x	x	x	–	S,P	Nectar for hummingbirds
Hyssop, Yellow Giant	*Agastache nepetoides*	–	x	x	x	–	S,P	Nectar for hummingbirds
Obedient Plant; False Dragonhead	*Physostegia virginiana*	–	–	x	x	x	S,P	Nectar for hummingbirds
Nettle, Hedge or Woundwort	*Stachys palustris*	–	–	x	x	x	S	Attracts hummingbirds

Phlox Family

Phlox, Sand Prairie*	*Phlox pilosa*	x	x	x	x	–	S,P	Nectar for hummingbirds
Phlox, Blue or Woodland	*Phlox divaricata*	–	x	x	x	–	P	Nectar for hummingbirds
Phlox, Sweet William	*Phlox maculata*	–	–	x	x	–	S,P	Nectar for hummingbirds
Phlox, Smooth	*Phlox glaberrima*	–	–	x	x	–	S	Nectar for hummingbirds

Pink Family

Catchfly, Royal	*Silene regia*	–	x	x	–	–	S	Nectar for hummingbirds
Campion, Starry*	*Silene stellata*	–	x	x	x	–	S,P	Nectar for hummingbirds

Rose Family

Prairie Smoke	*Geum triflorum*	x	x	–	–	–	S	Used by songbirds
Strawberry, Wild	*Fragaria virginiana*	x	x	x	x	–	S,P	Fruit eaten by songbirds & gamebirds

Saxifrage Family

Alum Root, Prairie*	*Heuchera richardsonii*	x	x	x	x	–	S,P	Provides habitat for birds; nectar for hummingbirds

Spurge Family

Spurge Flowering	*Euphorbia corollata*	x	x	x	–	–	S	Seeds eaten by gamebirds and songbirds

Vervain Family

Vervain, Hoary	*Verbena stricta*	x	x	–	–	–	S	Both species: seeds for sandpipers, buntings, cardinals, juncos & many sparrows; used by hummingbirds
Vervain, Blue	*Verbena hastata*	–	–	x	x	x	S	

Violet Family

Violet, Bird's Foot*	*Viola pedata*	x	x	–	–	–	S,P	Seeds of both species eaten by gamebirds
Violet, Prairie	*Viola palmata (V. pedatifida)*	–	x	x	–	–	S	

*These species grow well under the partial light below oaks in oak savannas and some are thought to be savanna specialists. Since so few undisturbed savanna remnants still exist, there is only limited knowledge of the original savanna vegetation. See chapter 10, The Bluebird Savanna Garden, for more information on savannas.

Bird-Friendly Grasses, Sedges & Rushes for Prairies and Savannas

Grasses, sedges and rushes provide nourishing seeds as well as wonderful habitat and cover for birds. For many species in the table below, specific information about bird use is known and described.

The table includes seventeen of the most common species in midwestern prairies and savannas. Select at least several species for your prairie or savanna garden. A natural-looking prairie garden will have at least 50% cover in grasses, but you may opt to have fewer grasses and more forbs in smaller gardens or in selected locations.

COMMON NAME	LATIN NAME	Dry	Medium Dry	Moist (Mesic)	Wet Mesic	Wet	Light Req.	VALUE FOR BIRDS
SPECIES		\multicolumn{5}{}{SOIL MOISTURE}					
Grass Family								
Grass, June	*Koeleria pyramidata (K. cristata; K. macrantha)*	X	X	–	–	–	S	
Grass, Porcupine	*Stipa spartea*	X	X	–	–	–	S,P	Important food for songbirds including buntings, sparrows & longspurs.
Grama, Side-oats	*Bouteloua curtipendula*	X	X	X	–	–	S	Seeds eaten by gamebirds & sparrows
Grass, Indian	*Sorghastrum nutans*	X	X	X	–	–	S,P	Good cover & seeds for songbirds
Grass, Little Bluestem	*Schizachyrium scoparium (Andropogon s.)*	X	X	X	–	–	S,P	Seeds are a principal food for songbirds, especially Field & Am. Tree Sparrows
Grass, Big Bluestem	*Andropogon gerardii*	X	X	X	X	–	S	Cover & seeds for gamebirds and songbirds (especially Field & Am. Tree Sparrows, finches, & juncos).
Dropseed, Prairie	*Sporobolus heterolepis*	X	X	X	X	–	S	Seeds important for ground-feeding birds including turkeys, buntings, juncos, larks, longspurs & sparrows
Rye, Canada Wild	*Elymus canadensis*	X	X	X	X	–	S,P	
Grass, Bottlebrush	*Elymus hystrix (Hystris patula)*	–	X	X	–	–	P	
Rye, Virginia Wild	*Elymus virginicus*	–	–	X	X	X	S,P	
Brome, Woodland	*Bromus pubescens (B. purgans)*	–	X	X	–	–	P	Large seeds eaten by gamebirds & songbirds

Common Name	Scientific Name						Code	Notes
Brome, Fringed	*Bromus ciliatus*	–	–	–	x	x	S,P	Large seeds eaten by game-birds & songbirds; geese consume young leaves & other plant parts
Switchgrass	*Panicum virgatum*	–	x	x	x	–	S,P	Important food for ground-feeding songbirds & game-birds: snipe, turkey, pheasant, blackbird, Bobolink, cardinal, cowbird, junco & sparrows. Teal, widgeon & Black Duck eat seeds & young leaves. Wonderful cover for birds.
Grass, Prairie Cord	*Spartina pectinata*	–	–	x	x	x	S	Seeds eaten by ducks (especially Am. Black Duck), Sora & Virginia Rails. Canada Geese eat early growth. Also provides habitat for Marsh Wrens.
Grass, Wood Reed	*Cinna arundinacea*	–	–	x	x	x	P	

Sedges & Rushes

Common Name	Scientific Name						Code	Notes
Sedge, Common Oak	*Carex pensylvanica*	x	x	x	–	–	S,P	Carex species provide seeds essential for many birds including sparrows, buntings, larks & grouse
Rush, Path	*Juncus tenuis*	x	x	x	x	–	S,P	Seeds of rushes are eaten by songbirds & gamebirds

It's important to plan your burns carefully and check with local authorities before setting off the blaze.

Bird-Friendly Shrubs for Prairies

(Shrubs for savannas are treated in the Bluebird Savanna Garden, pages 147–148.)

Prairies are open landscapes comprised primarily of forbs and grasses. The few shrubs that do occur are low-growing, with the exception of the Prairie Willow, and they look and act much like forbs in a prairie.

SPECIES		SOIL MOISTURE						
COMMON NAME	LATIN NAME	Dry	Medium Dry	Moist (Mesic)	Wet Mesic	Wet	Light Req.	VALUE FOR BIRDS
Tea, Inland New Jersey or	*Ceanothus herbaceus*	X	X	—	—	—	S,P	Flowers attract tiny insects, perfect size for humming-birds
Red Root Tea, New Jersey	*(C. ovatus) Ceanothus americanus*	X	X	X	—	—	S,P	Same as above.
Leadplant	*Amorpha canescens*	X	X	X	—	—	S	Called "Bird's Wood" by Lakota Indians because birds used it for perching in treeless prairies. Also provides cover.
Rose, Early Wild or Smooth	*Rose blanda*	X	X	X	—	—	S	Berry-like rosehips eaten by upland game birds in-cluding grouse, bobwhites, pheasants & some song birds. Excellent nesting habitat and cover.
Rose, Pasture	*Rosa carolina*	X	X	X	X	—	S	
Rose, Sunshine	*Rosa arkansana*	X	X	X	X	—	S	
Prairie, Willow	*Salix humilis*	X	X	X	X	—	S	Attracts swarms of insects for hummingbirds & other birds. Fuzz on seeds used by hummers in nests; buds & tender twigs eaten by grouse.
Meadowsweet	*Spirea alba*	—	—	—	X	X	S,P	Used for cover & nesting by many songbirds. Some gamebirds eat seeds, buds, or leaves.

Purple Prairie Clover

Shooting Star

Juncos are winter visitors that feed on prairie plant seeds.

Resources for Readers

Books and Booklets

Kurtz, Carl. 2001. *A Practical Guide to Prairie Reconstruction.* Iowa City: University of Iowa Press.

Madson, John. 1995. *Where the Sky Began: Land of the Tallgrass Prairie.* Ames: Iowa State University Press.

Packard, Stephen, and Cornelia F. Mutel, eds. 1997. *The Tallgrass Restoration Handbook for Prairies, Savannas, and Woodlands.* Washington, DC: Island Press.

Pauly, Wayne R. 1988. *How To Manage Small Prairie Fires.* Madison, WI: Dane County Park Environmental Council and Dane County Highway and Transportation Department.

Sample, Dave W., and Michael J. Mossman. 1997. *Managing Habitat for Grassland Birds: A Guide for Wisconsin.* PUBL-SS-925-97. Madison: Wisconsin Department of Natural Resources.

Shirley, Shirley. 1994. *Restoring the Tallgrass Prairie—An Illustrated Manual for Iowa and the Upper Midwest.* Iowa City: University of Iowa Press.

Smith, J. Robert, and Beatrice S. Smith. 1987. *The Prairie Garden.* Madison: University of Wisconsin Press.

Wasowski, Sally. 2002. *Gardening with Prairie Plants: How to Create Beautiful Native Landscapes.* Minneapolis: University of Minnesota Press.
An excellent book except for the maps, which are not accurate for Wisconsin and Michigan.

Organization

The Prairie Enthusiasts. This private nonprofit organization is committed to preserving and restoring prairies on both their own properties and other conservation lands. It has chapters in Illinois, Minnesota and Wisconsin. http://www.theprairieenthusiasts.org/

CHAPTER 10
THE BLUEBIRD SAVANNA GARDEN

*He carries on his back the blue of heaven
and the rich brown of the freshly turned earth on
his breast; but who has ever seen the bluest sky as
blue as the bluebird's back?*
—Arthur Cleveland Bent, *Life Histories of North American Birds*

*The Wisconsin oak openings were a summer paradise for
song birds, and a fine place to get acquainted with them; for the
trees stood wide apart, allowing one to see the happy home-seekers
as they arrived in the spring, their mating, nest-building, the
brooding and feeding of the young, and, after they were full-
fledged and strong, to see all the families of the neighborhood
gathering and getting ready to leave in the fall.*
—John Muir, *The Story of My Boyhood and Youth*

Oak savannas, or oak openings as they are often called, once covered approximately 30 million acres in the Midwest. The early settlers like Muir spoke not only of the diversity of birds in the oak openings, but also of their great beauty. Chauncy C. Olin's recollections in *The History of Waukesha County, Wisconsin*, published in 1880, were typical: "After crossing Poplar Creek, we came into the oak opening. I thought it the most lovely sight I had ever beheld. The country looked more like a modern park than anything else. How beautiful to look upon! How strange! We said in our enthusiasm, 'Who did this? by what race of people was it done, and where are they now?' for there were but very few people here."

Like prairies, oak savannas are fire-dependent communities, and when the pioneers suppressed fire, the savannas grew quickly into closed oak forests. John Muir described them in *The Story of My Boyhood and Youth*: "As soon as the oak openings in our neighborhood were settled, and the farmers had prevented running grass-fires, the grubs grew up into trees, and formed tall thickets so dense that it was difficult to walk through them and every trace of the sunny 'openings' vanished." As a result, midwestern oak savannas are one of the world's most threatened habitats.

Savanna habitat is basically scattered trees with a groundlayer of forbs (wildflowers) and grasses. It usually has only two layers of vegetation, in contrast to woodlands in the Midwest, which typically have three or four layers.

photo: Black-eyed Susans and Joe-Pye Weed

The "mini-savanna" at the author's former suburban home with Joe-Pye Weed and Black-eyed Susans.

Does this description of a savanna sound a little like the average yard? Most yards are savanna-like in structure—an expanse of lawn with a few trees and/or a few shrubs. If you substitute native species for the exotic lawn grasses and woody species, your yard can have approximately the same look as a traditional yard (although the "lawn" will be taller) but resemble more closely a native savanna.

We humans seem to have a penchant for savannas, which some anthropologists believe might stem from our origins in the African savannas. As it happens, the Eastern Bluebird also favors savannas and so does a cohort of other birds, as the young John Muir discovered during his early days in America.

This chapter tells you how to create habitats for bluebirds and other savanna birds.

The Eastern Bluebird

The Eastern Bluebird, one of three bluebird species in the U.S., benefited greatly during the early days of European settlement, when the eastern forests were decimated. The pastures, orchards and home sites of settlers created an abundance of savanna-like habitat ideal for bluebirds in the eastern states, which supplemented the original savanna habitat in the Midwest. By 1900, there were probably more bluebirds in North America than at any time before or since.

By the mid-twentieth century, both human-related and natural factors caused the population to plunge. The decline started with the introduction of two species of birds—House Sparrows in 1850 and starlings in 1890. These aggressive birds from Europe competed with bluebirds and other native birds for nesting cavities. Further declines were caused by the reduction of the open farmlands favored by bluebirds with increased urban development, the loss of snags with cavities, and the conversion of rotting fence posts with cavities to metal fences.

Ice storms also devastated the population. More than 50% of bluebirds in Illinois died during an ice storm in May 1940. Storms in the late 1970s caused similar losses throughout the eastern United States. Scientists think berries—bluebirds' major source of food in winter and early spring—became ice-covered and inaccessible.

By the late 1970s, the bluebird population had crashed, down an estimated 90% from their turn of the century numbers. But today, bluebird populations are rising, thanks to the many dedicated volunteers who put up bluebird nest boxes and monitor bluebird nest box trails.

Their work began as early as the 1920s, but really took off in 1964 on a national level with the formation of the National Association for the Protection and Propagation of the Purple Martin and Bluebirds of America. The group eventually disbanded and today the North American Bluebird Association, formed by bluebird expert Lawrence Zeleny in 1978, carries on the work of bluebird conservation. Thanks to these efforts, the Breeding Bird Survey, an annual survey taken throughout the U.S., shows that Eastern Bluebirds in the Midwest have steadily increased since the late 1970s.

How to Create Your Bluebird Habitat

Bluebirds have specific habitat needs in each season of the year. In summer, they require plenty of insects for food, perches from which to hunt insects, and natural nest cavities or boxes. In winter, most bluebirds migrate to escape the harsh weather in the northern Midwest, but some remain year-round in Missouri, Illinois, Indiana, Ohio and Wisconsin. At least some of the northern migrants pass over the resident bluebirds in the southern Midwest and winter farther south. Wherever they are, berries are the mainstay of their winter diet. You are likely to attract bluebirds to a large suburban or country yard if you provide for all of their habitat needs. Unfortunately, bluebirds rarely nest in cities, except in large parks or golf courses.

Vegetation

Bluebirds prefer a savanna-like habitat with scattered trees surrounded by relatively low or sparse herbaceous vegetation teeming with insects. Their favorite insect foods are ground insects, including grasshoppers, crickets, katydids and beetles. In an Illinois study, bluebirds were more likely to nest at the Morton Arboretum where the average height of the grass was 24 inches, than at Fermilab and McKee Marsh, where the grass height averaged 2 /-1/2 inches. Shorter grasses, apparently, make it easier for the bluebirds to forage for ground insects.

You can replicate these conditions on your property with a tree or two, surrounded by a prairie of short grasses and forbs (wildflowers). We have Little Bluestem and Side Oats Grama, both short prairie grasses about two feet high, plus dry-loving forbs in a prairie on our gravelly septic field, with a wooded area along the far edges of the field. To our delight, bluebirds nest in a box on the edge of this field, ignoring boxes in less open areas with taller plants.

A FEW FACTS ABOUT THE BLUEBIRD OF HAPPINESS

• Bluebirds are in the thrush family, as evidenced by the spotted breasts of their young; they are found only in America.

• The Eastern Bluebird's rich warbling song has been expressed as "Cheer, Cheerful Charmer."

• Eastern Bluebirds are feisty protectors of their nest sites. They fight, peck and chase competitors.

• A male Eastern Bluebird courts a female by performing a nest demonstration display, with nesting material in his beak, in front of a nesting cavity.

• The diet of Eastern Bluebirds consists of about 70% insects and other invertebrates, and about 30% fruit.

• Eastern Bluebirds usually have four to five young per brood and two broods per year in the Midwest.

• Female Eastern Bluebirds have a very distinctive tremble-thrusting behavior: they thrust their bills deep into the nesting material within their nesting cavity and shake with a trembling motion, apparently to shake out parasitic larvae.

(continued)

Skipper on Bergamot

Not everyone, however, has dry soils suitable for short-grass prairie species. You may have clay or moist loamy soil, common to many areas of the Midwest, which is more suited for tallgrass prairie species. If so, you can maintain a small area of shorter plants near the bluebirds' nest boxes by mowing several times a summer. Some people simply have old grassy fields with a few weeds and wildflowers that they mow occasionally to keep the area attractive to bluebirds. Even lawns, especially if they have some clover and other weeds to attract more insects, will work. If you maintain a lawn for children's play and entertaining, bluebirds may also use it.

It is essential to have a good variety of herbaceous plants, which will attract a diverse and plentiful supply of insects. Native plants will provide a greater variety of insects and are likely to be more beautiful. If you have a lawn, plant a nearby patch of wildflowers and native grasses to supply more insects. *Don't* spray pesticides on your lawn or other vegetation, which can contaminate the insects on which bluebirds feed. Instead, let the bluebirds serve as your natural pest control.

The same techniques used in planting a prairie can be used in planting the herbaceous species in a savanna. (See chapter 9 for details and tables on pages 130–137 and 147–148 for recommended species for savanna gardens.) Be sure to plant more shade-tolerant species beneath trees in your bluebird savanna garden by interseeding or careful transplanting, so you don't disturb the tree roots.

If you already have a few scattered native trees, you're in luck. Since trees take years to mature, you'll want to retain the ones you already have, no matter what the species. The exceptions are invasive species like Autumn Olive or Chinese Elm, which should be removed and replaced with native tree species.

On completely open sites, plant one or more trees or shrubs. Oaks of various species are the classic savanna trees and are ideal choices. Although not essential for bluebirds, oaks are important for attracting many of the other species of savanna birds, especially woodpeckers. Oaks also have good potential for forming cavities bluebirds and other cavity-nesters can use.

A few oaks have fairly shallow roots and are relatively easy to transplant, including Swamp White Oak, Red Oak and Pin Oak (not to be confused with Northern Pin Oak). Most other oaks have taproots which limit the size that can be successfully transplanted. The toughest and most adaptable oaks for yards are Bur

Oak, Swamp White Oak, Chinquapin Oak and Shingle Oak, according to Edith Makra of the Morton Arboretum in Illinois. Although most oaks grow slowly, give them serious consideration. It's been said that a society may be measured by its willingness to plant for the future.

Nancy Aten, a landscaper designer in Wisconsin, suggests planting a faster-growing species, like Black Cherry, in addition to oaks. It is a particularly good choice for bluebirds, since cherries are one of their preferred summer fruits. Another fast-growing tree choice with summer fruit is Red Mulberry.

The size of the trees is also a consideration, especially for small yards. Most oaks, as well as Black Cherry and Red Mulberry, can grow 50 feet high. Many smaller trees and shrubs can take the place of a large oak. The result will be a smaller scale, but similar, savanna-like setting.

Bluebirds need a plentiful supply of insects, especially when feeding their young.

For the best bluebird habitat, provide trees or shrubs that produce berries throughout the year. Savanna shrubs, although rarely

OAKS OF THE MIDWESTERN SAVANNAS

Oaks rank among the top wildlife plants in the country. Their acorns are the staff of life for many birds and other wildlife species. Acorns are eaten by at least 31 species of birds and are a choice food for the Blue Jay, Ruffed Grouse, Brown Thrasher, Common Grackle, Wild Turkey, Northern Bobwhite, and Eastern Towhee. The Red-headed Woodpecker and Red-bellied Woodpecker also eat many acorns, while most other woodpeckers will eat some. Wild Turkey, Ruffed Grouse, Northern Bobwhite and Rose-breasted Grosbeak eat oak flowers and buds.

Our deciduous midwestern oaks also provide valuable cover in the summer for birds and other wildlife. Oak twigs and leaves are favored nesting material. Oak trees also provide cavities for nesting birds.

For information on the native ranges and cultural requirements of oaks listed below, see part 5, pages 254–255.

Major Savanna Species
Black Oak, *Quercus velutina*
Bur Oak, *Quercus macrocarpa*
Northern Pin Oak, *Quercus ellipsoidalis*
Post Oak, *Quercus stellata*
White Oak, *Quercus alba*

Additional Species
Blackjack Oak, *Quercus marilandica*
Chinquapin Oak, *Quercus mulhenbergii*
Pin Oak, *Quercus palustris*
Red Oak, *Quercus rubra (Q. borealis)*
Shingle Oak. *Quercus imbricaria*
Swamp White Oak, *Quercus bicolor*

mentioned by pioneers, are thought to have been present but were stunted by frequent fires, and less noticeable in wet ravines and waterways protected from fire. If you plant a shrubby thicket at the border of your bluebird savanna garden with a variety of native berry-producing species, you'll provide fruit while still maintaining an open savanna-like area to supply insect prey.

Native berry-producing plants are especially important in the southern Midwest where bluebirds spend the winter surviving mainly on fruit. There's a good variety of shrub species listed on page 147. Plant those that are native to your area and suited to the conditions in your yard. Many are the same species suggested for the shrubland and winter habitat gardens, so you'll also attract the birds that frequent those habitats.

Perches

In summer, when bluebirds feed mainly on ground insects, they typically forage from perches. Sitting upright on open perches 18 inches to 50 feet high, bluebirds scan the ground and grasses for insects and then sally down to capture them. The easiest way to provide natural perches for bluebirds is to preserve snags (dead or dying standing trees) in your habitat area, as long as they are not dangerous. You can create a snag by girdling an undesirable tree (see chapter 7 for information on this technique). Dead branches on living trees are also readily used by bluebirds. If you have no natural perches, create some by clearing leaves from branches that offer good views of the ground.

Nest boxes help bluebirds where natural cavities are scarce.

Many people put up extra stakes in good feeding areas or stick small dead trees or large tree branches into the ground. Bluebirds perch on the tomato stakes and fence posts in our vegetable garden. They forage for insects in about a 20-foot radius around perches, so by providing more perches, you'll enable them to feed throughout your bluebird habitat garden. Hummingbirds, flycatchers, swallows and sparrows will also use them.

Cavities & Nest Boxes

In natural conditions, bluebirds nest in old woodpecker holes or in the cavities of dead and dying trees. John Muir wrote about the "knothole nests" of bluebirds that he discovered in his youth. This is a second good reason to keep your snags. You can encourage decay and cavity formation by drilling a small hole or two in your dead tree. That may also attract woodpeckers to excavate further.

If you don't have natural cavities or want to supplement the natural cavities you

TREES & SHRUBS FOR BLUEBIRDS
& OTHER SAVANNA BIRDS

BERRY-PRODUCING TREES AND SHRUBS

Bluebirds are known to eat the berries of species on this list. In many cases, there are several species within a genus that bluebirds eat. Other berry-eating savanna birds also feast on these fruits.

Among the listed species, those most commonly found in remnant oak savannas are Gray Dogwood, Smooth Sumac and the various wild roses. Cherries, hawthorns, serviceberries, crabapples, viburnums, snowberry, and other dogwoods and sumacs are all fairly common. Early records suggest that Red Cedar occurred in some savanna areas, although most restorationists today consider it a weed.

For information about specific species, their native ranges, and their habitat preferences, see the tree, shrub and vine tables, pages 252–263.

Winter Fruits

Coniferous Tree and Shrubs
Red Cedar, *Juniperus virginiana*
Juniper shrubs, *Juniperus* sp.
Deciduous Trees
Mountain Ash, *Sorbus* sp.
Crabapple, *Malus* sp.
Black Gum, *Nyssa sylvatica*
Hackberry, *Celtis* sp.
Hawthorn, *Crataegus* sp.
Deciduous Shrubs
Snowberry, *Symphoricarpos albus*
Sumac, *Rhus* sp.
Viburnum, *Viburnum* sp.
Winterberry, *Ilex verticillata*
Vines
Bittersweet, *Celastrus scandens*
Moonseed, *Menispermum canadense*
Poison Ivy, *Toxicodendron radicans*
   (*Rhus radicans*)
Virginia Creeper, *Parthenocissus*
   quinqulfolia

Summer and Autumn Fruits

Deciduous Trees
Cherry, *Prunus* sp.
Red Mulberry, *Morus rubra*
Serviceberry, *Amelanchier* sp.
Deciduous Shrubs
Blackberry, *Rubus* sp.
Blueberry, *Vaccinium* sp.
Cherries, *Prunus* sp.
Black Chokeberry, *Aronia melanocarpa*
Currant, *Ribes* sp.
Dogwood, *Cornus* sp.
Elderberry, *Sambucus* sp.
Raspberry, *Rubus* sp.
Serviceberry, *Amelanchier* sp.
Viburnum, *Viburnum* sp.
Vines
Grape, *Vitis* sp.
Bristly Cat Briar or Carrion Flower,
   Smilax sp.

have, add nest boxes. In suitable habitat, nest boxes sometimes attract bluebirds so quickly that the birds seem to "spontaneously generate" at the site of the boxes.

A basic nest box design for songbirds, along with specific dimensions for bluebirds, appears in chapter 20. There are, however, a great many designs for bluebird nest houses and experimentation is ongoing. A few details about the various designs follow.

Entry hole and dimensions. A horizontal oval entry hole no larger than 1-3/8 by 2-1/4 inches will exclude European Starlings and Brown-headed Cowbirds which occasionally parasitize nests.

Other Trees & Shrubs
for Savanna Birds

In addition to savanna oaks and the plants noted on the previous page, there are several other woody plants common to savannas that attract birds.

Trees

Shagbark Hickory, *Carya ovatus*: Eighteen bird species are known to eat hickory nuts. They are the preferred food of the Red-bellied Woodpecker, Carolina Chickadee, Tufted Titmouse, White-breasted Nuthatch, Yellow-rumped Warbler, Pine Warbler, Northern Cardinal, Eastern Towhee and Field Sparrow. Birds with tiny beaks must wait until the nuts split naturally or are opened by squirrels or other animals. Brown Creepers use crevices in the tree's shaggy bark as nesting sites. The tree also offers good cover for birds.

Shrubs

Hazelnuts, *Corylus* sp: Grouse and turkey eat the nuts, flowers and buds of hazelnuts. Red-bellied and Hairy Woodpeckers and Blue Jays eat the nuts. The shrubs' dense foliage provides excellent cover and nesting sites for birds.

New Jersey Tea, *Ceanothus* sp: The flowers on these shrubs attract insects for hummingbirds to eat.

The floor area should be about four to five inches square. The larger size may be better in winter when small groups of bluebirds roost together to keep warm. The circular floors for boxes made of PVC pipe should be approximately four inches in diameter.

Mounting and locating nest boxes. Mount the bluebird boxes with entry holes approximately five feet above ground on posts with predator guards to ward off raccoons, snakes and cats. Location is very important to discourage competition from nonnative House Sparrows and encourage peaceful coexistence among the native cavity nesters. Since House Sparrows prefer feedlots, barns and buildings, keep boxes a quarter mile or more away from them.

A number of native birds compete with bluebirds for nest sites, including Tufted Titmice, Tree Swallows, wrens and chickadees. By placing boxes in the habitat favored by each of these birds, you can provide for all of them and encourage a diversity of birds in your yard. Hang boxes for titmice in trees, and place small boxes for chickadees on posts under oak trees. Mount shallow wren boxes near porches, on low buildings or inside small barns and sheds.

Boxes for bluebirds should be in open areas, ideally facing at least one tree or shrub 25 to 100 feet away. The tree or shrub will provide perches for foraging adults and safe cover for fledglings when they first fly from the nesting box. This placement also reduces competition from Tree Swallows and House Wrens.

If you mount more than one bluebird box, place them at least 125 to 150 yards apart. Each nesting pair of bluebirds needs a territory about the size of a football field. Although pairing boxes for eastern Bluebirds and Tree Swallows has sometimes been recommended, recent studies by the Bluebird Restoration Association of Wisconsin show that the resulting competition from swallows

BIRDS OF THE SAVANNA

Birds that live in savanna habitats vary depending on the density and spacing of the trees, saplings, shrubs and herbaceous understory. Because of the transitional nature of savanna habitat, savanna birds also overlap those of prairies and woodlands. I found considerable variation among ornithologists in their designation of savanna birds. This list of birds typical to savanna habitats is based on a number of sources and personal experience. Birds that nest and breed primarily in shrubby habitats within savannas are discussed in the chapter on shrubland bird habitat.

Species	Midwestern Range
Eastern Bluebird	Throughout
Blue Jay	Throughout
Brown-headed Cowbird	Throughout
American Crow	Throughout
Mourning Dove	Throughout
Northern Flicker	Throughout
Great Crested Flycatcher	Throughout
Scissor-tailed Flycatcher	IA, MO
Common Grackle	Throughout
Sharp-tailed Grouse	IA, MN, WI
Red-tailed Hawk	Throughout
Swainson's Hawk	IA, MN, MO
American Kestrel	Throughout
Eastern Kingbird	Throughout
Western Kingbird	IA, MN
Black-billed Magpie	MN
Baltimore Oriole	Throughout
Orchard Oriole	Throughout
American Robin	Throughout
Loggerhead Shrike	Throughout
Chipping Sparrow	Throughout
Black Vulture	IL, IN, MO
Turkey Vulture	Throughout
Cedar Waxwing	Throughout
Red-headed Woodpecker	Throughout

Red-headed Woodpecker

reduces the chances for successful nesting by bluebirds.

Monitoring nest boxes. The North American Bluebird Society recommends monitoring bluebird boxes regularly, but not after the nestlings are about 12 days old, since you may frighten them into leaving the nest prematurely.

It is especially important to check the boxes weekly to remove House Sparrow nests and eggs. House Sparrows will attack and kill both adult and young bluebirds and destroy eggs. The nests of House Sparrows are messy and dome-shaped, often with bits of paper, plastic and other garbage; their eggs are whitish to greenish-white with gray, black or brown spots. (In contrast, bluebirds have rather deep nest cups built with fine grasses or pine needles; their eggs are usually powder blue, occasionally white.) Traps are available for catching House Sparrows, which are aliens and not protected by law, as are our native species.

The papery nests that wasps may build in spring on the lids of nest boxes should be removed. They can easily be crushed and scraped off when temperatures are 50 degrees F or lower, which is too cool for wasps to move actively.

Another insect pest in bluebird nests is the blowfly, whose larvae suck the blood of nestlings at night. Blowflies can weaken and sometimes kill the nestlings. A natural control of blowflies are parasitic wasps, also found in the nests, which feed on blowflies. Blowflies do not overwinter in the boxes, but wasps do. To ensure a good population of wasps for next year—and thus reduce blowfly infestations—leave old nesting materials in place until just before the new breeding season begins. A study in Michigan found significantly more blowfly problems when nests were removed before winter. In addition, bluebirds often roost in nest boxes in winter and the nesting material will add insulation.

Roosting Boxes

The usual winter roosting box is tall, with a hole at the bottom and perches near the top; heat rises and warms the birds. But this doesn't work for bluebirds, who prefer to huddle together at the bottom of the box where it is colder. In one study, bluebirds preferred natural cavities, but also used nest boxes for roosting. They never used roosting boxes.

Feeders

Bluebirds do not generally come to feeders, although feeders have been designed specifically for bluebirds. Bluebirds can be attracted with small bits of suet, berries, mealworms and raisins or currants softened in boiling water. You can buy mealworms at pet stores or order them online.

The most important time to feed bluebirds is when wild food is scarce, especially during ice storms and cold, rainy days early in the breeding season.

Water

Bluebirds can get enough water from the foods they eat. But like many songbirds, they are attracted to birdbaths. Place the birdbath in an open area, with a nearby perch.

Other Savanna Birds

John Muir described many of the savanna birds found on his farm in Wisconsin, often in relation to their oak-opening habitat. He spoke of the "plucky kingbird" whose "nest was usually built in a bur oak near a meadow where insects were abundant." He observed a "hawk in an oak tree" and a thrasher singing from the "top-most spray of an oak tree" and a male Red-winged Blackbird sitting on a nearby oak, while his "wife" was sitting on eggs in the swamp. He noted other savanna birds including Red-headed Woodpeckers, flickers, orioles and robins.

The savanna-like habitat you create for bluebirds may attract these and other savanna birds. We know much less about their specific habitat requirements than we do about bluebirds' needs. But in recent years, we've learned more about the habitats of two savanna species, Red-headed Woodpeckers and Loggerhead Shrikes.

Like Eastern Bluebirds, Red-headed Woodpeckers can be attracted to habitats that are structurally similar to oak savanna—scattered trees with a grassy park-like understory. This unexpected discovery occurred in a savanna restoration project at Necedah National Wildlife Refuge in Wisconsin.

Wildlife biologist Richard King restored five sites at the refuge to savanna habitat. All shrubs and trees were removed except the biggest oaks and pines—those with diameters (at chest height) of over 16 inches and 14 inches, respectively. Prescribed burns were also carried out. This thinning resulted in a "structural savanna"; no work was done to restore savanna understory vegetation.

Although the project was not undertaken specifically for the benefit of the Red-headed Woodpecker, a species of special concern in Wisconsin, the birds began to colonize the area immediately after the initial timber-thinning operations. Today, Red-headed Woodpeckers—more than 70 pairs—are the most common avian species in the restored savanna. Other birds attracted to the savanna habitat at Necedah include Field and Vesper Sparrows, Baltimore Orioles, Blue-Gray Gnatcatchers, Yellow-throated and Warbling Vireos, Eastern Kingbirds and Yellow-billed and Black-billed Cuckoos. King is also pleased that less common birds (for Wisconsin) showed up—the first singing male Northern Mockingbird and a migrant Olive-sided Flycatcher, as well as the first nesting of a Lark Sparrow.

The Loggerhead Shrike is listed as threatened or endangered in most midwestern states and in Canada and has been proposed for listing as a federally endangered species. In southern Florida, a simple habitat enhancement helped to more than double the population of Loggerhead Shrikes. The same technique might work here in the Midwest, too.

At the working ranch on the grounds of the MacArthur Agro-Ecology Research Center, a unit of Archbold Biological Station, Reuven Yosef, then a graduate student, made a thorough study of Loggerhead Shrikes. He observed that shrikes hunted only from perches, as bluebirds do. Because perches were relatively few and in great demand at the ranch, Yosef installed more—fence posts with barbed wire attached to give the birds some footing. These extra perches allowed the shrikes to utilize more of the available acreage for foraging and, in turn, resulted in an amazing 60% increase in the Loggerhead Shrike population.

For both the woodpecker and shrike, habitat improvements were key in increasing their numbers. Other savanna bird species are also likely to flourish when their habitat needs are met. Until we know more, our best recourse is to re-create, as much as possible, the original savanna that graced our midwestern plains.

How to Create a Savanna Bird Habitat on a Larger Site

The oaks of original midwestern savannas, especially bur oaks, had thick bark that could withstand the fires started by lightning or by Indians who hoped to create better hunting grounds. Beneath them was a variety of plants adapted to varying light conditions, some tolerant of the shade directly beneath the trees; others adapted to the partial shade at the periphery of the trees, while still others were sun-loving plants which thrived in the open areas between the far-flung trees.

This variety of light conditions, along with a wide range of soils, resulted in an astounding diversity of savanna species, far greater than that of the adjacent prairie and forest habitats. Mark Leach and Thomas Givnish, at the University of Wisconsin, found 507 species of plants in remnant oak savannas in the Midwest. This wealth of species can be used in creating your own mini-savanna. Some of those best known for attracting birds are among the recommended species in this book.

As in landscaping a small yard, you can create a large-scale savanna habitat by either enhancing the vegetation already present or planting from scratch.

If you have an oak woods that you believe was a remnant oak savanna, consider restoring it to its original condition by removing undesired trees and shrubs, including most of the midstory. (For bluebirds and other fruit-eating birds, however, you'll want to retain berry-producing shrubs, possibly on one edge of your savanna.) John Harrington of the University of Wisconsin suggests thinning the trees to create approximately 10–40% canopy cover to replicate the density in a native savanna. As always, remove invasive species. Wind damage to the remaining trees can sometimes be a problem, Harrington has found, resulting in the loss of large limbs, so he advises opening up a woodland gradually.

He also suggests burning the site regularly, protecting desirable trees less than one inch in diameter. If burning is not allowed where you live, mow instead. The understory can be interseeded with savanna grass and forb seed if needed, raking them into the soil, as described in chapter 9, The Prairie Bird Garden.

Often, a seedbank of native herbaceous savanna species remains in the soil below an overgrown woodland. When we removed the invasive honeysuckle and buckthorn shrubs from our small oak woodland, we were delighted to see Pennsylvania Sedge, Shooting Star and Violet Wood Sorrel show up on their own. All three have greatly increased over the last two years now that they get sufficient light. You may want to wait and see what comes up on its own before reseeding.

If you have an open site with little desirable vegetation, prepare and plant the site as described in chapter 7. Select tree species best suited for your area from the lists on pages 145, 147 and 148. Plant them randomly on your site, aiming for a canopy cover to be 10–40% in maturity (or with plans to harvest some trees as they mature to keep to this approximate percentage).

For the understory, select species of wildflowers, grasses and sedges from the tables on pages 130–137, keeping in mind the light conditions. As the canopy develops, you'll need to introduce more shade-tolerant savanna species beneath the trees.

To provide the best habitat for birds, add a shrubby edge with plenty of berry- and nut-producing species to feed the birds throughout the seasons. See pages 147–148 for recommendations.

Once your savanna is planted, be sure to follow the maintenance guidelines in chapter 19, especially for watering, weeding, burning and herbivore protection. Given time and patience, you should be able to recreate a "summer paradise for song birds" like the one John Muir enjoyed in his boyhood in Wisconsin. You may also want to get involved in establishing and monitoring a bluebird nest box trail, either on your own property, if you have an area large enough for five or more boxes, or on other private or public property with permission of the owners.

BLUEBIRD SAVANNA GARDEN

This bluebird savanna garden is based on my yard which has attracted nesting bluebirds for several years. The bluebird nest box faces the wooded edge, away from prevailing winds.

The woods are 50 to 60 feet away from the box—ideal for providing perches for foraging adults and for fledglings on their first flight. Several dead trees in the savanna area also offer perching sites.

The trees along the edge are Shagbark Hickories, Red Oaks and Black Cherry; there are also Choke Cherry shrubs. Both cherries provide fruit for the bluebirds in summer. The savanna area has a few native trees—a Bur Oak, a cottonwood, and a couple small Basswoods, plus scattered evergreens. All provide cover for birds.

The shortgrass prairie, located over the septic field, provides an excellent insect-hunting area. It is dominated by Side-oats Grama and Little Bluestem, both short prairie grasses. Prairie forbs include Pale Purple and Yellow Coneflowers, Prairie Coreopsis, Black-eyed Susan, Purple Prairie Clover, Whorled and Butterfly Milkweed, Horse Mint, Hoary Vervain, Stiff and Old Field Goldenrod, Hairy or Frost Aster, Prairie Smoke and Wild Bergamot.

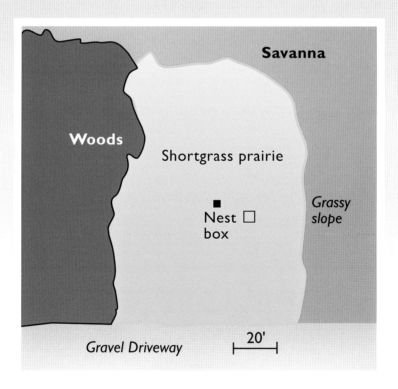

Resources for Readers

Books

Gowaty, P. A., and J. H. Plissner. 1998. *The Birds of North America: Eastern Bluebird*, No. 381. Washington, DC: American Ornithologists' Union.

Muir, John. 1913. *The Story of My Boyhood and Youth.* Boston: Houghton Mifflin.

Packard, Stephen, and Cornelia F. Mutel, editors. 1997. *The Tallgrass Restoration Handbook for Prairies, Savannas, and Woodlands.* Washington, DC: Island Press.

Stokes, Lillian, and Donald Stokes. 1991. *The Bluebird Book.* Boston: Little, Brown.

Organizations

North American Bluebird Society. 481 Athens Rd., Royston, GA 30662-5128; phone: 888-235-1331; www.nabluebirdsociety.org/

Bluebird Restoration Association of Wisconsin. 5221 Cheryl's Dr., Plover, WI 54467; phone: 715-341-5521; http://www.braw.org/

Compass plants in a savanna garden dwarf visitors.

CHAPTER 11
THE WOODLAND BIRD GARDEN

*Beneath our lawnmowers and asphalt is
an invisible forest that represents the richest and
most complex landscape type that can be attained,
given our climate.*

—Leslie J. Sauer, *The Once and Future Forest*

The forests of the Midwest are a magnet for a diversity of birds.* The North American Breeding Bird Survey lists over 70 species of birds nesting in midwestern woodlands, including warblers, woodpeckers, cuckoos, thrushes, flycatchers, nuthatches, jays, kinglets, vireos and many others. This birdlife reflects the diverse forests of the Midwest, ranging from deciduous forests dominated by sugar maple and mixed hardwoods or by oak-hickory; to coniferous forests dominated by spruce-fir or pine; mixed forests combining both deciduous and coniferous species; lowland forests with a mix of cottonwood, willow, silver maple and ash; and a southernmost fringe of oak, gum and cypress forest.

Among woodland breeding birds in the Midwest, 12 species declined significantly from 1966 to 2004, while another 9 show insignificant declines that may worsen in the future with continued fragmentation of habitat. This decline in birds is equally unfortunate for the trees and other woodland plants that depend on birds for insect control and seed dispersal. It behooves all of us whose lands were once wooded to re-create that lost woodland habitat on our properties, large or small, and do our part to stabilize or reverse these disheartening trends.

Restoring Existing Woodlands

Those fortunate to own existing woodlands can strive to restore them to their full potential as woodland bird habitat. A key strategy to maintaining a diversity of woodland birds is to maintain woodland plant diversity—a variety of trees, shrubs and herbaceous species. It is also important to manage woodlands by removing invasive species and, in the case of oak-hickory woodlands, by reintroducing fire.

In ongoing studies in Illinois at Swallow Cliff Woods and other sites in the Cook County

---

Although the words "forest" and "woodland" are often used interchangeably, generally "forest" refers to a large wooded area, "woodland" to a small wooded area.

photo: Canada Warbler

Forest Preserve District, restoration efforts are benefiting native woodland birds, including Red-headed Woodpeckers, Baltimore Orioles, Indigo Buntings and Summer Tanagers. Jeffrey Brawn, a scientist with the Illinois Natural History Survey, says, "The majority of bird species do better in the restored areas." The few that do not, require larger tracts of unfragmented forest. "Our results speak strongly in favor of woodland restoration as a way to conserve the diversity of our native bird populations," says Brawn.

Some of our most threatened woodland bird species require the larger forested areas that Brawn mentioned. To bene-fit these birds, try to team up with neighbors or nearby natural areas, to enlarge your woodland habitat and to make connecting corridors between segments of woodland. For advice on managing large tracts of forested land for birds, see the guides at the end of this chapter that are available from the Cornell Lab of Ornithology and the Minnesota Department of Natural Resources.

A Complexity of Needs and Preferences

Most bird species tend to prefer particular kinds of forests suited to their special needs. When R. R. Bond studied the southern upland forests of Wisconsin in 1955, he found that in Sugar Maple/mixed hardwood forests the characteristic birds were Cerulean Warblers, Red-eyed Vireos, Acadian Flycatchers, Hairy Woodpeckers, Ovenbirds, Red-bellied Woodpeckers, Pileated Woodpeckers and Cooper's Hawks. These species tended to be insectivores that foraged in foliage or on the ground and nested high in the canopy or in saplings.

The dry forests, dominated by White and Black Oaks, attracted a colorful array of birds that included Scarlet Tanagers, Black-capped Chickadees, Downy Woodpeckers, Rose-breasted Grosbeaks, Gray Catbirds, Northern Cardinals, Blue Jays, Indigo Buntings, Baltimore Orioles, Eastern Towhees, Red-tailed Hawks and Red-headed Woodpeckers. Bond noted that many of these birds preferred berries and nuts to insects, and commonly nested in shrubs.

Intermediate forests with White and Red Oaks as the dominant tree species had the greatest diversity of birds, mostly American Redstarts, Wood Thrushes, Least Flycatchers, Blue-gray Gnatcatchers, Yellow-throated Vireos, Ruby-throated Hummingbirds and Veeries. Many were sapling nesters.

Each woodland bird, Bond found, also has its own

particular niche in its favored forest type. The Cerulean Warbler, for example, likes to forage and nest high in the treetops, while the Ovenbird nests and feeds on the ground. Various cavity nesters showed well-defined "housing" preferences. Downy Woodpeckers excavate cavities in dead wood; Hairy Woodpeckers prefer to hollow out their nesting cavities in live wood at higher elevations than the Downy; Black-capped Chickadees, with their weaker beaks, require rotted wood to dig their cavities.

How to Create Your Woodland Bird Habitat

As these and other studies show, the kind of woodland habitat you establish will influence the kinds of birds you'll attract. Plan to re-create a woodland type that is native to your area and well suited to your site. Such a woodland habitat will be the easiest to plant and maintain, and it will also be the best habitat for the birds native to your neighborhood.

Look at nearby remnant woodlands to help you determine the woodland type native to your area. The northerly reaches of the Midwest support forests dominated by conifers or by a mix of conifers and hardwoods, while the southern forests are dominated by deciduous trees—the maple/hardwood mix on mesic (medium moisture) sites and oak/hickory forests on dry sites. Midwestern lowland forests have a mix of species tolerant of the high water tables that occur along rivers and other water bodies.

It can be somewhat difficult to replicate the relatively cool, moist and wind-protected interior typical of large wooded areas on a smaller site, such as a typical home yard. It's often easier to re-create the native woodland habitat found on drier sites in your region. For example, if both maple and oak woodlands grow in your area, an oak woodland may be a better choice than a maple woodland for your yard. Or simply choose the more dry-tolerant species native to your woodland type. The aim, of course, is to establish a community that will not need supplemental care and watering. Watering should only be needed to establish new plants and in extreme drought.

Make an assessment of your trees and large shrubs, since they require years of growth to mature and are difficult and expensive to bring in to a new landscape setting. Trees and/or large shrubs constitute the backbone of a woodland habitat and provide the shade required by other species. The

Wild Turkey
Veery
Vireos:
    Blue-headed, Red-eyed,
    Yellow-throated & Warbling
Warblers:
    Black-and-white,
    Blackburnian, Black-throated
    Blue, Black-throated Green,
    Canada, Cape May, Cerulean,
    Hooded, Kentucky, Magnolia,
    Pine, Prothonotary,
    Tennessee, Worm-eating,
    Yellow-rumped
    & Yellow-throated
Waterthrushes:
    Louisiana & Northern
Whip-poor-will
Woodpeckers:
    Downy, Hairy, Pileated
    & Red-bellied
Eastern Wood-Pewee
Winter Wren

Ranges vary; some breed only in northern tier of Midwest

DECLINING BREEDING BIRDS IN THE MIDWESTERN WOODLANDS

Chuck-will's-widow
Black-billed Cuckoo
Yellow-billed Cuckoo
Acadian Flycatcher
Least Flycatcher
Great Crested Flycatcher
Ruby-crowned Kinglet
Veery
Cerulean Warbler
Northern Waterthrush
Whip-poor-will
Eastern Wood-Pewee

—Results from the North American Breeding Bird Survey, 1966–2004

Eastern Screech Owl is a woodland breeding bird.

health of existing trees on your property and their very presence can give you clues about the conditions of your site, such as light, soil texture, moisture and drainage.

If you are lucky to have some large trees or shrubs growing well in your yard, build your woodland around them, adding other species to enhance the site. Most people will want to keep even the nonnative trees they have, given the time and expense of replacing them with natives. But it is essential to remove nonnative invasive trees like Norway Maple, Siberian Elm and White Poplar. The first two are prolific self-seeders that can create monocultures in which few other species can survive. The Norway Maple also produces heavy shade under which few things can grow. White Poplar spreads mainly by root suckers, which can quickly form dense colonies around a single tree.

Besides invasive trees, be sure to remove invasive shrubs and herbaceous plants. Some of the worst of these woodland invaders in the Midwest are the buckthorn and honeysuckle shrubs and the herbaceous species Garlic Mustard. For information on how to remove invasive plants, see chapter 7.

Be sure to retain any standing dead trees (snags) on your site which may provide existing or potential nesting sites for cavity-nesters, common to woodlands. Kitty Clasing of Mason City, Iowa, created snags by girdling (stripping a section of bark from the entire circumference of the tree) two large buckthorns, which interrupted the flow of water and nutrients through the plants. I've done the same thing with a large Siberian Elm. Now almost dead, it's a favorite perching spot for migrant warblers in spring and nesting bluebirds in summer. Girdling is an easy way to deal with invasive trees or tree-sized shrubs, and at the same time, use them to advantage. For more on girdling, see chapter 7.

Snags, as well as downed trees and branches, are also home to wood-feeding insects relished by woodpeckers and other insectivorous birds. In addition, dead wood and woody debris on the ground help build soil fungi essential for good tree growth.

Site and Soil Considerations

Unlike prairie plants, many woodland plants need soil rich in organic matter—partially or wholly decayed remains of plants and animals. Organic matter helps to retain water and nutrients and slowly releases those nutrients to plants. It helps to loosen and aerate clay soils, tightens up extremely sandy soils and prevents soil compaction. It also encourages the growth of beneficial soil microorganisms and helps to neutralize toxic substances. The best way to build up organic matter is to allow leaves, twigs, logs and other plant material to decompose naturally in your woodland and to add composted leaves and other material.

If the site for your woodland is now lawn, an examination of the lawn can often provide clues about the quality of your soil. If grass in a sunny area is thick and lush, you probably have adequate soil for woodland species; but if your grass is spotty and thin, your soil is likely to have insufficient organic matter. Heavy shade also weakens and thins grass. In that case, you'll have to test the soil to determine its quality.

You will need to eradicate the lawn or groundcover unless it is very sparse, using one of the methods described in chapter 7. If your soil is poor and compacted, the best method is smothering with newspapers and wood chips, which will help to enrich the soil.

The soil for your woodland garden can also be enriched by spreading the surface with three to six inches of compost and/or manure. This mix should not be tilled into the soil if trees already exist in the area, since this would disturb the tree and shrub roots. When planting, add a little of the mix into the hole of each plant. For degraded sites with poor soils, many experts, like Wisconsin landscape designer Don Vorpahl, recommend incorporating a small amount of "starter soil" from a mature woodland site similar to the one to be planted, as a source of native fungi and microorganisms.

Location and Layout

Generally, the shadier north side of your house is best for a woodland garden. The east side, which receives the less intense morning sunlight, is also a good location. Don't plant right next to the house under the overhang, where your plants will not receive the rainfall they need.

If you have a very small site, you can substitute the shade of your building for tree shade, suggests Jim Steffen, conservation ecologist at the Chicago Botanic Garden. He points out that many woodland wildflowers only require 15–20% full sun per day. Don't plant deciduous woodland plants known as spring ephemerals— such as Trout Lily, Dutchman's Breeches and Toothwort—which cannot tolerate shade. Named for their short-lived appearance each spring, ephemerals need the full sun of early spring woodlands to bloom, gather energy and set seed before they die back completely as the trees leaf out and shade them.

If you have space, plant the full spectrum of woodland flora. Multiple levels of vegetation are typical of wooded landscapes. Three to five levels of vegetation may be present: tall

EASY NO-FAIL HERBACEOUS PLANTS FOR WOODLAND BIRDS

Many of these plants are found in several types of woodlands (see the lists of recommended species for each woodland type.). All are hardy plants that thrive in a variety of conditions and will do well in the early stages of a woodland restoration. The Wild Columbine provides nectar for hummingbirds in spring. All the others have either seeds or fruits which attract birds. Violets not only have seeds enjoyed by gamebirds, but also have tuberous roots relished by turkeys.

Big-leaved Aster, *Aster macrophyllus*
Wild Columbine, *Aquilegia canadensis*
Wild Geranium, *Geranium maculatum*
Broad-leaved or Zigzag Goldenrod, *Solidago flexicaulis*
Elm-leaved Goldenrod, *Solidago ulmifolia*
Jack-in-the-Pulpit, *Arisaema triphyllum*
Downy Solomon's Seal, *Polygonatum pubescens*
Feathery False Solomon's Seal, *Smilacina racemosa*
Smooth Solomon's Seal, *Polygonatum biflorum* (*P. caniculatum*)
Starry False Solomon's Seal, *Smilacina stellata*

(continued)

Wild Strawberry, *Fragaria virginiana*

Pale-leaved or Woodland Sunflower, *Helianthus strumosus*

Common Blue Violet, *Viola sororia (V. papilionacea)*

Canada or White Tall Violet, *V. canadensis*

Yellow Violet, *Viola pubescens*

Ruby-throated Hummingbirds migrate north when Wild Columbine, one of their favorite sources of nectar, is in blossom.

canopy trees, understory trees, tall shrubs, short shrubs and groundcover vegetation of wildflowers, grasses, sedges, ferns and low-growing shrubs. You can mimic these multiple layers on a small scale with a single canopy tree, one or two understory trees or shrubs and various groundcover species.

Each woodland bird has its preference for a different level of vegetation. Turkeys forage on the woodland floor and roost high in the trees. Black-capped Chickadees and Ruby-throated Hummingbirds tend to nest in mid-canopy level. In larger forests, Scarlet Tanagers nest in the canopy, Wood Thrushes in the shrubs, while Ovenbirds are one of the few to nest on the forest floor. You'll attract the greatest diversity of birds by planting all the levels typical of your woodland type.

Some experts suggest planting a thick hedge of shrubs around the perimeter as a barrier to nest predators like raccoons and cats. Small woodlands offer much more access to such predators along edges and paths than the large expanses of forest in presettlement days. As a result, nest predation of woodland birds is high, causing precipitous declines in some species. A dense "wrap" of native shrubs is easily accessed by birds winging through the branches, but may hinder small mammals.

Providing Shade Trees

Your first goal is to provide sufficient shade for your woodland garden. If you have no trees, plant pioneering trees like aspen and birch, says Molly Murray, a landscape architect at the University of Wisconsin Arboretum. Black Cherry, Pin Cherry and Speckled Alder (a shrub) are also fast-growing woody plants. These species will act as a cover crop, producing early shade for your other plants.

Along with these species, you can plant the slow-growing, long-lived trees like Sugar Maple or oaks that will become the dominant trees in your landscape.

Be sure to include trees of different sizes to avoid a "plantation" look and insure the continuity of your woodland—as older trees die, the younger ones can replace them. Later you can thin some of your "cover crop," as the dominant trees develop their canopy.

When to Plant Shrubs

Restorationists disagree about when to plant. Many, like Steffen of the Chicago Botanic Garden, suggest planting the entire

The Tufted Titmouse nests in tree cavities or birdhouses.

community of plants at once to promote a healthy competition. Planting shrubs later can disturb tree roots and requires watering them longer as they compete with the trees for moisture.

Planting everything at one time, however, can cause problems. Evelyn Howell of the University of Wisconsin's Department of Landscape Architecture described a woodland construction project that failed because all species were planted simultaneously. The shrubs grew aggressively, she said, rivaling the trees in size, and "almost certainly interfering with their growth." The key seems to be to make sure that the shrubs do not outgrow and shade the developing trees. If you do decide to plant everything at the same time, make sure to plant small shrubs unlikely to outgrow the trees and prune them back if needed.

Groundlayer Plants

Once the trees and shrubs are in place, it's time to consider the groundlayer plants. If you have good soil, you can begin planting groundlayer species immediately. Otherwise, amend the soil as described above and wait a year or two before planting.

Select species according to the amount of shade available. If your woodland has little shade in the early stages, you will need to plant species that can tolerate sun, gradually replacing them with more shade-tolerant species as your woodland develops. Some excellent species for the early stages of woodland restoration include Virginia Creeper, a woody vine that often forms a groundcover, plus herbaceous species like Wild Strawberry, Broad-leaved or Zigzag Goldenrod, Big-leaved Aster, Wild Columbine and all of the Solomon's Seals.

Even at maturity, different types of woodlands create different light conditions for understory plants. Oaks, for example, allow much more light to reach the ground than do maples. As a result, oak woods have more understory species.

See the lists of bird-friendly trees, shrubs and herbaceous plants on pages 165–172.

The Woodland Bird Garden   161

FROM LAWN TO WOODLAND—3 PATHS

The Birds Were a Surprise

Donna VanBuecken, the executive director of Wild Ones: Native Plants, Natural Landscapes, wanted a place for woodland plants rescued from development sites.

Donna and her husband, John, had inherited a large lawn with scattered mature trees when they moved to Appleton, Wisconsin. Taking an inventory, Donna noted several trees relatively close together—three ash trees, a birch and a crabapple. They formed a roughly triangular area which became the target site for the woodland-to-be. Her husband mowed the lawn short in early summer, and then the couple spread six inches of wood chips over the entire area. In fall, they dumped chopped leaves on top of the wood chips. By the following spring, the heavy clay soil was showing improvement and the VanBueckens began transplanting rescued plants.

They rescued tree saplings like Ironwood and Sugar Maple as well as gooseberry, currant and other shrubs. They brought in a variety of woodland herbaceous species and planted them in the shade of the trees. Until the saplings are big enough to provide enough leaf litter for the herbaceous plants they've introduced, Donna and John continue to add chopped leaves from their other trees.

Their new woodland habitat had a surprise for them. Warblers and Cedar Waxwings find it a haven during migration. Red-headed and other woodpeckers are present year-round. Other visitors include goldfinches, robins, Red-tailed Hawks, Baltimore Orioles, Eastern Towhees, and the occasional American Kestrels and Cooper's Hawks.

•

Putting Words into Action

Marion and Larry Lopina started with only one tree—a crabapple in the backyard of their small suburban lot in Wauwatosa, a suburb of Milwaukee. Then they added a Bur Oak sapling, near the crabapple.

"I was teaching environmental education at the time and realized that our family should live up to the principles I was promoting at school," said Marion. So she and Larry decided to create a woodland. They purchased White Birches and a pine to add to their emerging woodland, and Marion planted herbaceous woodland species from plant rescues sponsored by Wild Ones. Luckily, their suburban home had been built on the site of a World War II victory garden, so the soil was excellent and they didn't need to amend it.

Like the VanBueckens, the Lopinas gradually expanded their woodland habitat.

Their "kitchen woodland" was started with five small White Birches and two White Oaks. But they didn't stop with the backyard. Pleased with the results, the Lopinas created a mini-woodland in front of their house around a large White Birch; they simply added a few shrubs, ferns and wildflowers.

Now the Lopinas' small yard has 125 trilliums, both Large-flowered and Red. Other spring woodland flowers include bloodroot, hepatica and goldenseal. Later

Large-flowered Trillium

in the season, Orange Jewelweed, Cardinal Flower and Tall Bellflower add color and provide nectar and insects for hummingbirds. A small backyard prairie includes sun-loving plants rich with nectar for hummingbirds and butterflies.

The Lopinas' habitat attracts a growing number of woodland birds. Baltimore Orioles, Ruby-throated Hummingbirds, Black-capped Chickadees, Northern Cardinals, Mourning Doves and several species of woodpeckers are regular visitors, while Rose-breasted Grosbeaks, Orchard Orioles and warblers visit during migration. Cardinals nest in their shrubs, while Tree Swallows and House Wrens nest in the birdhouses. The garden also appeals to fox, opossum, rabbits, chipmunks, squirrels and deer.

•

Starting from Scratch—Bare Lawn, No Trees

Pat and Carl Brust, whose yard is featured in chapter 4, have a corner lot in Franklin, a suburb of Milwaukee. The lawn was in poor shape at the corner near the street, the result of rocky fill dumped during road construction. They decided that a wooded triangle at the problem corner would be more attractive and decided to give it a try despite the soil.

Carl dug up a half-dozen saplings at a friend's rural property—four Quaking Aspen, a Sugar Maple and a Red Mulberry. After planting them, the Brusts put down a thick layer of cardboard and newspapers under the trees and covered it with wood chips. They didn't put in any herbaceous species because they had started a prairie restoration in another part of their yard and didn't have time to selectively weed another area. Carl simply whacked down all the weeds that came up through the woodchips. They also made sure they pruned carefully to insure good visibility at the corner for street traffic.

Over time, the birds and squirrels added additional species—a White Oak, a Bur Oak and a Choke Cherry. The Brusts bought other species at a Wild Ones plant sale—a White Pine for winter color (and bird cover), a Northern Hackberry for fall and winter fruit and an American Hazelnut for a supply of nuts until the oaks produced acorns.

After about 15 years, the fast-growing aspens are nearly 50 feet tall and the other trees are growing well. House Wrens and Black-capped Chickadees have raised families in nest boxes at the edge of their corner woodland. Pat was impressed by the chickadees, whose nest, she says, "was like a carefully-constructed layer cake with mosses at the bottom and layers of fine grasses and hairs above."

•

Woodland Phlox (purple) and Celadine Poppy (yellow) brighten a spring woodland garden.

A male American Redstart sings to declare his territory and attract a mate.

Design and Planting Considerations

Design your woodland habitat around existing trees if you have them; if not, decide on the location of your woodland garden. In either case, work out your basic design using the guidelines in chapter 6. Be sure to place trees and shrubs randomly for a natural look. Consider views from windows and patios.

Spacing of plants is another consideration. Traditionally, gardeners allow space for the mature size of plants, especially trees and shrubs. However, if you want to create a dense "wrap" of border shrubs, space them closer. Anyone walking in a naturally occurring woodland will see trees in closer proximity than recommended, and you can imitate this natural spacing in your yard. On the other hand, some species, like the Pagoda Dogwood, have particularly attractive forms when less confined. Give them sufficient space to display their full beauty.

Once your woodland is planted, be sure to follow the maintenance guidelines, especially regarding watering, weeding and protection from herbivores, as discussed in chapter 19. It will take time for a woodland restoration to fully develop. Prairie restorations take three to five years to resemble a natural prairie; but woodlands take considerably longer to develop the mature canopy and "look" of a native woodland. Nonetheless, your woodland—in all stages of growth—provides a healthier, more attractive habitat for birds than the thicket of invasive shrubs it very likely replaced.

BIRD-FRIENDLY PLANTS
FOR YOUR WOODLAND GARDEN

There are many types of forests in the Midwest and a vast variety of plants native to these forests. Here are five of the most common types, one of which is likely to be representative of the original forests in your locality. For each type of forest, I have listed plants which appeal to birds and could be included in a woodland garden.

Most woodland birds eat insects, especially leaf-chewing insects, in the summer, but in fall and winter they feed on berries and seeds. In oak woodlands where shrubs are abundant, some birds feed primarily on plant foods. The trees, shrubs and herbaceous species listed here provide berries, seeds, nuts or nesting sites for woodland birds. Many also attract insects, especially oaks and other trees when leafing out in spring. Shrubs often attract insects when they are in bloom in spring and early summer—the time birds most need insect protein for their young. Later in the season, these same plants produce fruits, nuts and seeds.

If you have a small yard, create a mini-woodland by selecting a shrub or smaller tree species from the lists below as your canopy tree. Plant appropriate herbaceous species in the shade beneath it. Alternate-leaved Dogwood or Round-leaved Dogwood are excellent choices for a small space.

The recommended trees and shrubs have rated good to very high for their value to birds. Most woodland herbaceous species have limited food value to birds, but provide essential cover and nesting sites on the woodland floor. All the herbaceous species listed offer berries, seeds or nectar used by some woodland birds.

Although these recommendations are limited to those plants known to be useful to birds, consider adding other species typical of the woodlands where you live. Trilliums, Wild Ginger and Wood Anemone have no recognized nutritional value for birds, but consider planting them for the beauty and diversity they offer. These plants also feed and shelter invertebrates and small mammals that provide sustenance for some woodland birds and are part of a complete woodland ecosystem. See the tables in part 5 for information on the native ranges and cultural requirements of the plants listed.

MAPLE FOREST

Maple forests, with Sugar Maple as the dominant tree, occur in all midwestern states.

Most of the species of trees in a maple forest are deciduous, but some evergreen conifers are found in northern maple forests. Soils in maple forests are generally moist and rich in humus.

The Sugar Maple, with its stunning fall colors and luxuriant foliage, is a magnificent tree to anchor this type of woodland garden. It is the the state tree of Wisconsin and birds like it as much as we do. In fact, maples are ranked in the top ten woody plants in the country for their value to wildlife. Grosbeaks, finches and other birds eat the seeds, buds and flowers of the Sugar Maple. Its leaves and seed stalks are used as nesting material. Its leafy branches provide cover and nesting sites. And its sweet sap, oozing from broken branches or sapsucker holes, nourishes both sapsuckers and early-migrating hummingbirds.

A frequent companion of the Sugar Maple in southern maple forests is the Tulip Tree, state tree of Indiana and the tallest hardwood tree in North America. Hummingbirds collect nectar from its showy tulip-shaped flowers. Sapsuckers tap its sap, and gamebirds and some songbirds eat its seeds. One of the smaller trees of the maple forest, the Flowering Dogwood, is the state tree of Missouri. It provides nutritious berries relished by nearly 40 species of birds. Among the birds of maple forests are the White-breasted Nuthatch, Red-eyed Vireo, Ovenbird, Cerulean Warbler, Acadian Flycatcher, and Hairy and Pileated Woodpeckers.

Trees for a Maple Woodland Garden

Trees Providing Fruit

Black Cherry, *Prunus serotina*; Choke Cherry, *Prunus virginiana*; Northern Hackberry, *Celtis occidentalis*; Alternate-leaved Dogwood, *Cornus alternifolia*; Flowering Dogwood, *Cornus florida*.

Trees Providing Seeds

Sugar Maple, *Acer saccharum*; Paper Birch, *Betula papyrifera*; Yellow Birch, *Betula alleghaniensis (B. lutea)*; Red Maple, *Acer rubrum;* Mountain Maple, *Acer spicatum*; White Pine, *Pinus strobus*.

Trees Providing Nuts

American Beech, *Fagus grandifolia*; Red Oak, *Quercus rubra (Q. borealis)*; White Oak, *Quercus alba*.

Trees Providing Cavities

White Oak, *Quercus alba*; Red Oak, *Quercus rubra*; Sugar Maple, *Acer saccharum*; Yellow Birch, *Betula alleghaniensis (B. lutea)*.

Trees Providing Shelter & Nest Sites

Sugar Maple, *Acer saccharum*; in north—Hemlock, *Tsuga canadensis* and White Cedar, *Thuja occidentalis*.

Trees Providing Sap or Nectar

Sugar Maple, *Acer saccharum*; Tulip Tree, *Liriodendron tulipifera*.

Shrubs for a Maple Woodland Garden

The dense shade of Sugar Maples limits the number of shrubs in maple-dominated forests. However, the following shrubs can thrive in gaps in maple forests, in areas where maples are less dominant, or at the edges of maple forests.

Shrubs and Vines Providing Fruit

American Bittersweet, *Celastrus scandens*; Virginia Creeper, *Parthenocissus quinquefolia*; Spicebush, *Lindera benzoin*; Maple-leaved Viburnum, *Viburnum aceri-*folium; Round-leaved Dogwood, *Cornus rugosa*; Red-berried Elderberry, *Sambucus racemosa (S. pubens)*; Prickly Wild Gooseberry, *Ribes cynosbati*.

Shrub Providing Nuts

Beaked Hazelnut, *Corylus cornuta* (mostly North).

Shrub Providing Nectar

American Fly Honeysuckle, *Lonicera canadensis*.

Herbaceous Plants for a Maple Woodland Garden

Like the shrubs, herbaceous plants are limited to sunnier areas of Sugar Maple woodlands (except for spring ephemerals, which are not known to attract birds).

Herbaceous Species Providing Fruit

White Baneberry, *Actaea alba*; Feathery False Solomon's Seal, *Smilacina racemosa*; Downy Solomon's Seal, *Polygonatum pubescens*; Jack-in-the-Pulpit, *Arisaema triphyllum*; Blue Cohosh, *Caulophyllum thalictroides*; Bluebead, *Clintonia borealis* (in North); Wild Sarsaparilla, *Aralia nudicaulis*; Spikenard, *Aralia racemosa*.

Yellow-bellied Sapsucker male

Herbaceous Groundcover Providing Fruit
Partridge Berry, *Mitchella repens*.

Herbaceous Species Attracting Insects
False Bugbane or Black Cohosh, *Cimicifuga racemosa*.

Herbaceous Species Providing Nectar
Blue Phlox, *Phlox divaricata*; Virginia Bluebells, *Mertensia virginica*.

Herbaceous Species Providing Seeds
Side-flowering Aster, *Aster lateriflorus*; Big-leaved Aster, *Aster macrophyllus*; Blue-stemmed Goldenrod, *Solidago caesia*; Broad-leaved or Zigzag Goldenrod, *Solidago flexicaulis*; Wild Geranium, *Geranium maculatum*; Purple Joe Pye Weed, *Eupatorium purpureum*; Bottlebrush Grass, *Elymus hystris (Hystris patula)*.

OAK FOREST

Oak forests, dominated by various species of oaks, are perhaps the most common forests in the Midwest; the three top species are the White Oak, Red Oak and Black Oak. The soil in an oak forest is generally drier, more acidic and lower in nutrients than in maple forests. An oak forest is also more open and less shady than a maple forest and consequently, has a more shrubs. Oak forests frequently grade into oak savanna on their drier side and maple forest on their more protected side.

The oak, tradition has it, is the king of trees and was chosen state tree of Iowa (no particular species selected). The White Oak is the state tree of Illinois. Called the "king of kings" by the late Chicago naturalist and writer Donald Culross Peattie, the White Oak is a mighty tree with great wide-spreading branches, a massive crown and colorful foliage—vivid red to pink in early spring, green in the summer and burgundy in fall. Wrote Peattie, "The fortunate possessor of an old White Oak owns a sort of second home, an outdoor mansion of shade and greenery and leafy music."

The fortunate possessors of oaks, whether White Oak or other species, will also enjoy an abundance of wildlife. Oaks are rated at the top of the list of wildlife foods for many birds and mammals. Birds feed on their buds, flowers and acorns, nest on their limbs and in their cavities, and use their twigs and leaves for nesting material.

Birds common to oak forests include the Scarlet Tanager, Black-capped Chickadee, Downy and Red-bellied Woodpeckers, Rose-breasted Grosbeak, Northern Cardinal, Blue Jay, Wild Turkey and Baltimore Oriole.

Trees for an Oak Woodland Garden

Trees Providing Fruit
Black Cherry, *Prunus serotina*; Red Mulberry, *Morus rubra*; Wild Plum, *Prunus americana*; Alternate-leaved Dogwood, *Cornus alternifolia*; Sassafras, *Sassafras albidum*; Alleghany or Smooth Serviceberry, *Amelanchier laevis*.

Trees Providing Seeds
Quaking Aspen, *Populus tremuloides*.

Trees Providing Nuts
Mainly White Oak, *Quercus alba*; Red Oak, *Q. rubra (Q. borealis)*; Bur Oak, *Q. macrocarpa*; Black Oak, *Q. velutina*. Also, Chinquapin Oak, *Q. muehlenbergii*; Northern Pin Oak, *Q. ellipsoidalis*; Shagbark Hickory, *Carya ovata*; Pignut Hickory, *Carya glabra*.

Trees Providing Shelter & Cavities
Oaks, *Quercus sp.*; Quaking Aspen, *Populus tremuloides*.

Tree Providing Sap
Sugar Maple, *Acer saccharum*.

Shrubs for an Oak Woodland Garden

Shrubs and Vines Providing Fruit
American Bittersweet, *Celastrus scandens*; Virginia Creeper, *Parthenocissus quinquefolia*; Downy Arrowwood

Viburnum, *Viburnum rafinesquianum*;
Nannyberry, *Viburnum lentago*; Choke
Cherry, *Prunus virginiana*; Gray
Dogwood, *Cornus racemosa*; Round-
leaved Dogwood, *Cornus rugosa*;
Common Elderberry, *Sambucus
canadensis*; Pasture Rose, *Rosa carolina*;
Common Blackberry, *Rubus alleghenien-
sis*; Red Raspberry, *Rubus idaeus var.
strigosus*; Blueberries, *Vaccinium* sp.; Box
Huckleberry, *Gaylussacia baccata*;
Summer Grape, *Vitis aestivalis*; Riverbank
Grape, *Vitis riparia*; Prickly Wild
Gooseberry, *Ribes cynosbati*.

Shrub Providing Nuts
American Hazelnut, *Corylus americana*.

Vines Providing Nectar
Yellow Honeysuckle, *Lonicera prolifera
(L. reticulata)*; Red Honeysuckle, *Lonicera
dioica*.

Herbaceous Plants for an Oak Woodland Garden

Herbaceous Species Providing Fruit
Red Baneberry, *Actaea rubra*; Wild
Sarsaparilla, *Aralia nudicaulis*; Spikenard,
Aralia racemosa; Feathery False
Solomon's Seal, *Smilacina racemosa*;
Starry False Solomon's Seal, *Smilacina
stellata*; Downy Solomon's Seal,
Polygonatum pubescens; Jack-in-the-
Pulpit, *Arisaema triphyllum*.

Herbaceous Groundcovers Providing Fruit
Wild Strawberry, *Fragaria virginiana*.

Herbaceous Species Providing Nectar
Late Horse Gentian or Tinker's Weed,
Triosteum perfoliatum; Early Horse
Gentian, *Triosteum aurantiacum*; Smooth
Solomon's Seal, *Polygonatum biflorum (P.
caniculatum)*; Fire Pink, *Silene virginica*;
Wild Bergamot, *Monarda fistulosa*.

Herbaceous Species Providing Seeds
Common Oak Sedge, *Carex*

pensylvanica; Elm-leaved Goldenrod,
Solidago ulmifolia; Short's Aster, *Aster
shortii*; Arrow-leaved Aster, *Aster sagittifolius*; Pale-leaved or Woodland
Sunflower, *Helianthus strumosus*;
Bottlebrush Grass, *Elymus hystris (Hystris
patula)*.

PINE FOREST
Pine forests, found primarily in the
three northern midwestern states of
Michigan, Minnesota and Wisconsin, are
dominated by various pine species. The
most representative pine of the north is
the majestic White Pine, the largest and
longest-lived species in the region and
state tree of Michigan. Unlike the glacially-
slow growth of the major trees in other
forests (Sugar Maple, White Oak and
Balsam Fir) White Pine grows relatively
quickly—up to two feet a year—which
makes the re-creation of pine woodland a
faster proposition for gardeners starting
with small trees.

The Red Pine, named for its reddish
bark, is a frequent companion of White
Pine and also grows fairly fast. Chosen as
the state tree of Minnesota, the Red Pine
is a handsome tree with a crown of foliage
topping a long, clean trunk.

Pines are one of the premier woodland
plants for wildlife, ranked second only to
oaks. Many birds eagerly consume their
nutritious, oily seeds; upland gamebirds
feed on their needles as well. Additionally,
several songbird species use the needles
for nesting material. The foliage of young
pines skirts the ground beneath them and
provides excellent cover for ground birds
and small mammals. Larger pines are
favorite roosting sites for robins during
migration and common nest sites for birds
small and large, from Mourning Doves to
Bald Eagles.

Some of the birds occurring in the pine
woodlands are the Hermit Thrush, Eastern
Bluebird, Ruffed Grouse, Bald Eagle and
Pine and Black-throated Green Warblers.
Of special note are the Red Crossbill, 50%
of whose diet consists of pine seeds, and
the Kirkland Warbler which nests only in

large stands of young Jack Pines, 8 to 20 years old, mainly in Michigan.

Trees for a Pine Woodland Garden

Trees Providing Fruit
Alternative-leaved Dogwood, *Cornus alternifolia*; Pin Cherry, *Prunus pensylvanica*.

Trees Providing Seeds
White Pine, *Pinus strobus*; Red Pine, *Pinus resinosa*; Jack Pine, *Pinus banksiana*; Quaking Aspen, *Populus tremuloides*; White Birch, *Betula papyrifera*.

Trees Providing Nuts
Northern Pin Oak, *Quercus ellipsoidalis*; Red Oak; *Quercus rubra (Q. borealis)*.

Tree Providing Shelter
Hemlock, *Tsuga canadensis*.

Trees Providing Cavities
White Pine, *Pinus strobus*; Northern Pin Oak, *Quercus ellipsoidalis*; Red Oak, *Quercus rubra (Q. borealis)*.

Shrubs for a Pine Woodland Garden

Shrubs and Vines Providing Fruit
Red Raspberry, *Rubus idaeus var. strigosus*; Common Blackberry, *Rubus alleghaeniensis*; Early Low Blueberry, *Vaccinium angustifolium*; Round-leaved Dogwood, *Cornus rugosa*; Rose, *Rosa* sp.; Maple-leaved Viburnum, *Viburnum acerifolium*; Sand Cherry, *Prunus pumila*; Prickly Gooseberry, *Ribes cynosbati*.

Groundcover Shrubs Providing Fruit
Bunchberry, *Cornus canadensis*; Wintergreen, *Gaultheria procumbens*.

Shrubs Providing Nuts
Beaked Hazelnut, *Corylus cornuta*; American Hazelnut, *Corylus americana*.

Shrub Providing Nectar:
American Fly Honeysuckle, *Lonicera canadensis*.

Ferns love a shady yard and provide groundcover for songbirds.

Herbaceous Plants for a Pine Woodland Garden

Herbaceous Species Providing Fruit
Red Baneberry, *Actaea rubra*; White Baneberry, *Actaea alba*; Bluebead, *Clintonia borealis*; Wild Sarsaparilla, *Aralia nudicaulis*; Downy Solomon's Seal, *Polygonatum pubescens*; Feathery False Solomon's Seal, *Smilacina racemosa*.

Herbaceous Groundcovers Providing Fruit
Partridge Berry, *Mitchella repens*; Wild Strawberry, *Fragaria virginiana*.

Herbaceous Species Providing Nectar
Wild Columbine, *Aquilegia canadensis*.

Herbaceous Species Providing Seeds
Big-leaved Aster, *Aster macrophyllus*; Common Oak Sedge, *Carex pensylvanica*.

In openings, prairie-associated species occur including these grasses: Big Bluestem Grass, *Andropogon gerardii*; Little Bluestem, *Schizachyrium scoparium*; June Grass, *Koeleria pyramidata (K. cristata; K. macrantha)* and Porcupine Grass, *Stipa spartea*.

LOWLAND FORESTS

Lowland forests occur along river valleys and lake plains throughout the Midwest. Unlike the other forest types, no tree species is dominant. Among the major trees, those most useful for birds are the Silver Maple, willows and ash.*

The Silver Maple is one of our fastest growing trees. It shoots up as much as three feet a year, making it ideal for gardeners wanting quick results. Moreover, it is a beautiful addition to any garden with graceful down-sweeping branches and red flush of flowers in early spring followed by winged seeds ready for migrating orioles, cardinals and robins. The Black Willow grows even faster—up to 6 feet a year—and with the Peach-leaved Willow, offers tender twigs and buds, and nest sites for returning birds. The Green Ash and Black Ash grow nearly as quickly as the Silver Maple but their seeds ripen later in summer and persist into winter. Thus, these five dominant trees of the lowland forests provision birds throughout the seasons.

Some birds common to lowland forests include the Baltimore Oriole, Northern Cardinal, Tufted Titmouse, Wood Duck, Wild Turkey, Warbling Vireo and Red-eyed Vireo. The declining Red-shouldered Hawk and still-widespread Barred Owl are raptors of the lowland forests. Three warblers of lowlands are the Prothonotary, Cerulean and Yellow-throated Warblers. Many woodpeckers, especially the Red-bellied, Red-headed and Pileated Woodpeckers, favor lowland forests, probably because of the many dead trees killed by flooding.

Trees for a Lowland Woods Garden

Trees Providing Fruit
Hackberry, *Celtis* sp.; Red Mulberry, *Morus rubra*; Black Gum, *Nyssa sylvatica*.

Ash (Fraxinus sp.) trees are no longer recommended for planting due to the Emerald Ash Borer, which has killed millions of ash trees in the Midwest.

Trees Providing Seeds
Silver maple, *Acer saccharinum*; Red Maple, *Acer rubrum*; Box Elder, *Acer negundo*; River Birch, *Betula nigra*.

Trees Providing Nuts
Swamp White Oak, *Quercus bicolor*; Bitternut Hickory, *Carya cordiformis*; Red Oak, *Quercus rubra (Q. borealis)*; Pin Oak, *Quercus palustris*.

Trees Providing Cavities
Black Willow, *Salix nigra*; Peach-leaved Willow, *Salix amygdaloides*; Sycamore, *Platanus occidentalis*.

Trees Providing Buds & Tender Twigs
Black Willow, *Salix nigra*; Peach-leaved Willow, *Salix amygdaloides*.

Tree Providing Nectar
Ohio Buckeye, *Aesculus glabra*.

Shrubs for a Lowland Woods Garden

Shrubs and Vines Providing Fruit
Virginia Creeper, *Parthenocissus quinquefolia*; Poison Ivy, *Toxicodendron radicans (Rhus radicans)*; Riverbank Grape, *Vitis riparia*; Moonseed, *Menispermum canadense*; Wild Black Currant, *Ribes americanum*; Common Elderberry, *Sambucus canadensis*; Spicebush, *Lindera benzoin*; Silky Dogwood, *Cornus amomum*.

Shrubs Providing Seeds
Buttonbush, *Cephalanthus occidentalis*; Ninebark, *Physocarpus opulifolius*.

Shrub Providing Nectar
Buttonbush, *Cephalanthus occidentalis*.

Herbaceous Plants for a Lowland Woods Garden

Herbaceous Species Providing Fruit
Jack-in-the-Pulpit, *Arisaema triphyllum*; Wild Sarsaparilla, *Aralia nudicaulis*; Downy Solomon's Seal, *Polygonatum pubescens*; Starry False Solomon's Seal,

A woodland typically has several layers of vegetation which provide a variety of habitat for wildlife.

Smilacina stellata; Carrion Flower, *Smilax herbacea*.

Herbaceous Species Providing Nectar

Cardinal Flower, *Lobelia cardinalis*; Orange Jewelweed, *Impatiens capensis*; Virginia Bluebells, *Mertensia virginica*; Monkey Flower, *Mimulus ringens*.

Herbaceous Species Providing Nesting Material

Cinnamon Fern, *Osmunda cinnamomea*.

Herbaceous Species Providing Seeds

Side-flowering or Calico Aster, *Aster lateriflorus*; Wild Golden Glow or Greenheaded Coneflower, *Rudbeckia laciniata*; Marsh Marigold, *Caltha palustris*; Virginia Wild Rye, *Elymus virginicus*; Fowl Manna Grass, *Glyceria striata*; Wood Reed Grass, *Cinna arundinacea*; Common Cattail Sedge, *Carex typhina*; Common Bur or Gray Sedge, *Carex grayi*.

SPRUCE-FIR FOREST

This woodland, dominated by Balsam Fir and White Spruce, occurs in northern Michigan, Minnesota and Wisconsin. The soils are generally more acidic than in other woodland types.

The Balsam Fir—a favorite Christmas tree with its lovely aroma and spire-like form—is one of the most popular trees of the North Woods. The White Spruce has uplifted branches that give it an airy, graceful appearance. Both are beautiful trees to use as the foundation for a reconstruction of a northern woodland and both provide food and shelter for northern birds. Their winged seeds are popular with many birds, plus a few birds feed on their needles. The dense evergreen foliage of both trees offer cover and nesting sites. Older trees may form cavities that birds use to nest and roost in.

Perhaps the most characteristic bird of the spruce-fir woodland is the Spruce Grouse. The Red-breasted Nuthatch, White-throated Sparrow, Gray Jay, Black-backed Woodpecker, Ruby- and Golden-crowned Kinglets, Red- and White-winged Crossbills and many species of warblers are also found there.

Trees for a Spruce-Fir Woodland Garden

Trees Providing Fruit

Mountain Ash, *Sorbus americana*; Pin Cherry, *Prunus pensylvanica*; Black Cherry, *Prunus serotina*.

False Dragonhead has bell-shaped flowers that provide nectar for hummingbirds.

Trees Providing Seeds
Sugar Maple, *Acer saccharum*; Mountain Maple, *Acer spicatum*; Red Maple, *Acer rubrum*; White Birch, *Betula papyrifera*; Yellow birch, *Betula alleghaniensis*; American Larch, *Larix laricina*; White Pine, *Pinus strobus*; Red Pine, *Pinus resinosa*; Quaking Aspen, *Populus tremuloides*; Balsam Poplar, *Populus balsamifera*.

Trees Providing Nuts
Red Oak, *Quercus rubra (Q. borealis)*; White Oak, *Quercus alba*.

Trees Providing Shelter and Nest Sites
White Spruce, *Picea glauca*; Balsam Fir, *Abies balsamea*; Hemlock, *Tsuga canadensis*; White Cedar, *Thuja occidentalis*.

Tree Providing Cavities
White Pine, *Pinus strobus*.

Shrubs for a Spruce-Fir Woodland Garden

Shrubs and Vines Providing Fruit
Rose, *Rosa* species; Red Raspberry, *Rubus idaeus var. strigosus*; Early Low Blueberry, *Vaccinium angustifolium*;

Round-leaved Dogwood, *Cornus rugosa*; Prickly gooseberry, *Ribes cynosbati*.

Groundcover Shrubs Providing Fruit
Bunchberry, *Cornus canadensis*; Wintergreen, *Gaultheria procumbens*.

Shrub Providing Seeds & Nest Sites
Speckled Alder, *Alnus rugosa (Alnus incana)*.

Shrub Providing Nuts
Beaked Hazelnut, *Corylus cornuta*.

Shrub Providing Nectar
American Fly Honeysuckle, *Lonicera canadensis*. Be sure not to plant the invasive non-native species of honeysuckles commonly sold.

Herbaceous Plants for a Spruce-Fir Woodland Garden

Herbaceous Species Providing Fruit
Red Baneberry, *Actaea rubra*; Downy Solomon's Seal, *Polygonatum pubescens*; Feathery False Solomon's Seal, *Smilacina racemosa*; Bluebead, *Clintonia borealis*; Wild Sarsaparilla, *Aralia nudicaulis*.

Herbaceous Groundcovers Providing Fruit
Partridge Berry, *Mitchella repens*; Wild Strawberry, *Fragaria virginiana*.

Herbaceous Species Providing Nectar
Orange Jewelweed, *Impatiens capensis*.

Herbaceous Species Providing Seeds
Big-leaved Aster, *Aster macrophyllus*; Sedges, *Carex* sp.

Virginia Bluebells provide a splash of blue in a woodland garden and nectar for hummingbirds.

A Great-crested Flycatcher's whiskers help him funnel flying insects into his beak.

White Baneberry berries are edible by wildlife, but they can sicken humans.

WOODLAND BIRD GARDEN

The following page features a maple woodland garden with species typical of maple forests in the southern Midwest. This 1/3 acre garden has been planned for a larger lot, with the house to the left and a neighbor's shrub border to the right. At the back of the lot (top) is a drainage way that is common property to the neighborhood and leads to a wooded parkway. Thus the woodland garden links to the neighbor's shrubbery and the drainageway, creating a larger area of continuous habitat so important to wildlife.

The soil on the lot is a loam of moderate quality and moisture. All the trees chosen are listed in *Bird-Friendly Plants for Your Woodland Garden* in this chapter under "Maple Forest." The three main trees in this design— the American Beech, Sugar Maple and Tulip Tree—are dominant in typical forests in Ohio and Indiana; the other tree species occur in much smaller numbers. The density of trees suggested here (70 trees for 1/3 acre) is similar to that found in some natural woodlands, although some experts suggest planting up to twice as many. Trees are spaced about 13 feet apart within the woods, with a 10-foot wide border around the periphery for shrubs.

The Eastern Wood-Peewee is a woodland summer resident more often heard than seen.

Few shrubs occur within maple forests, so the shrubs in this plan are mainly located along the borders where more light is available. The shrubs will provide food and shelter for birds more quickly than the slower-growing trees, and add beauty early in the restoration. Plant the large shrubs about 4–6 feet apart and the smaller shrubs about 2–3 feet apart.

Spicebush is very shade-tolerant and is one of the few that is common in maple woodlands. I've placed it both within the woodland garden and along its border. Spicebush produces high quality berries many species love, especially during migration.

You can often buy trees and shrubs in quantity as seedlings through states agencies at low prices. Some commercial nurseries offer clearance sales of their excess stock of small plants they are propagating, called "lining out stock." It is usually sold wholesale to other growers, but our Wild Ones chapter arranged to buy stock from a local nursery for members.

You may want to buy a few larger specimens for your woodland. A few large trees planted at the front (street-side) of the restoration area add more immediate visual interest, shade and structure to the garden.

Woodchips cover most of the garden. The chips enrich the soil and reduce competition for the newly planted trees. The border along the street side and to the left of the property is planted with groundcover species that do well in the early stages of woodland restoration. When the trees are more mature, many more woodland groundcover species should be planted. Good spacing for herbaceous plants is about one per square foot.

KEY TO PLANTS IN WOODLAND BIRD GARDEN

Trees

The numbers following the names are the suggested number of trees of each species in this design.

A   White Ash—3
B   American Beech—16
C   Black Cherry—3
D   Flowering Dogwood—3
H   Hackberry species—3
M   Sugar Maple—18
R   Red Oak—3
T   Tulip Tree—18
W   White Oak—3

Shrubs

The number of shrubs of each species in this design is optional. However, it is best to plant at least three of most shrub species for optimal cross-pollination and fruiting.

ah   American Hazelnut
av   American Cranberrybush Viburnum
bc   Black Chokeberry
bv   Blackhaw Viburnum
gd   Gray Dogwood
nv   Nannyberry Viburnum
nb   Ninebark
se   Serviceberry species
sp   Spicebush
wb   Winterberry or Common Blackberry

Groundcover Species

gc   Front along Street: Wild Strawberry, Wild Geranium, Wild Columbine, Elm-leaved Goldenrod and Starry False Solomon's Seal.

gc   On left, adjacent to home and patio: Virginia Creeper (as a groundcover not as vine), Pale-leaved or Woodland Sunflower, Broad-leaved Goldenrod, Jack-in-the-Pulpit, Feathery False Solomon's Seal, Big-leaved Aster and violets.

See the plant tables in part 5 for detailed information and the Latin names of the recommended species in this garden design.

Resources for Readers

Books

Art, Henry W. 1986. *A Garden of Wildflowers: 101 Native Species and How to Grow Them.* Pownal, VT: Storey Communications.

Cullina, William. 2002. *Native Trees, Shrubs, and Vines: A Guide to Using, Growing, and Propagating North American Woody Plants.* Boston: Houghton Mifflin.

Darke, Rick. 2002. *The American Woodland Garden.* Portland, OR: Timber Press.

Sperka, Marie. 1973. *Growing Wildflowers: A Gardener's Guide.* New York: Harper & Row.

Websites

Burns, Russell M., and Barbara H. Honkala. "Silvics of North America." http://na.fs.fed.us/spfo/pubs/silvics_manual/table_of_contents.htm. This two-volume handbook from the U.S. Forest Service gives detailed information on 200 tree species and varieties.

"How to Create a Woodland Garden." http://www.chicagobotanic.org/plantinfo/how-to/woodland_garden.php

Resources for Managing Large Tracts of Forested Land for Birds

Person, Carol W. 1998. *Planning for the Birds: Things to Consider When Managing Your Forest.* Minnesota Department of Natural Resources. 1-888-MINNDNR

Rosenberg, K. V., R. S. Hames, R. W. Rohrbaugh Jr., S. Barker Swarthout, J. D. Lowe and A. A. Dhondt. 2003. "A Land Manager's Guide to Improving Habitat for Forest Thrushes." http://www.birds.cornell.edu/conservation/thrush

Rosenberg, K. V., R. W. Rohrbaugh Jr., S. E. Barker, J. D. Lowe, R. S. Hames, and A. A. Dhondt. 1999. "A Land Manager's Guide to Improving Habitat for Scarlet Tanagers and Other Forest-interior Birds." http://www.birds.cornell.edu/conservation/tanager

Sauer, Leslie Jones. 1998. *The Once and Future Forest.* Washington, DC: Island Press.

Chapter 12
The Wetland Bird Garden

Wetland losses have been of staggering proportions in the Midwest.
—U.S. Department of Interior, Fish and Wildlife Service

Throughout the Midwest, families are discovering that mini-wetlands in the backyards, often in the form of rain gardens, can attract a diversity of birds and wildlife, and reduce water pollution. In Illinois, Mike Sands and his family are delighted with the hummingbirds that come to feast on the nectar of Cardinal Flowers in their rain garden. A neighbor who created a wetland swale was thrilled to spot the shy Virginia Rail feeding there.

In Wisconsin, Roger Bannerman, who heads the state's rain garden program, enjoys the finches and woodpeckers that feed among the wetland plants in his garden. Other common birds known to visit small rain gardens include blackbirds, cardinals, sparrows, catbirds and Common Yellowthroats. In my own little rain garden, I discovered one of my "best" yard birds early one spring—a woodcock probing the mud among the Marsh Marigolds. Many people are also amazed at the numbers of birds, butterflies, dragonflies and other beneficial insects that enliven their rain gardens.

A rain garden is basically a small-scale wetland, formed by making a depression where rainwater can soak into the soil. Rain gardens are designed to capture storm water runoff from rooftops, driveways and lawns. The plants in the garden filter and clean the water which then seeps slowly into the ground, as it would in a natural wetland. This helps to keep animal wastes, sediments and excess fertilizers, pesticides and herbicides from polluting our lakes and rivers. Just as important, rain gardens reduce flooding and replenish neighborhood groundwater with clean, filtered water.

photo: Red-winged Blackbird

**WETLAND LOSSES
IN THE MIDWEST
1780s to 1980s**

State	Acreage Lost
Illinois	**89%**
Indiana	**87%**
Iowa	**85%**
Michigan	**50%**
Minnesota	**42%**
Missouri	**87%**
Ohio	**90%**
Wisconsin	**46%**

(Source: Thomas E. Dahl. 1990. *Wetlands Losses in the United States, 1780's to 1980's.* U.S. Dept. of Interior, Fish & Wildlife Service.)

BIRDS OF RAIN GARDENS & LARGER WETLANDS

Rain Gardens

Since rain gardens are usually small and hold water only briefly after rains, they will attract primarily common yard birds including finches, sparrows, blackbirds, catbirds, cardinals, hummingbirds, yellowthroats and woodpeckers.

Larger wetlands

These larger-scale wetlands typically hold water longer, often permanently, and will attract a wide range of wetland birds including rails, herons, waterfowl, sandpipers, plovers, sandhill cranes, blackbirds and swallows.

A Common Yellowthroat is a welcome visitor to a rain garden.

Swamp Milkweed

Why can't our lawn grasses do the job as well as rain garden plants? Although lawn grasses are better than pavement and rooftops, they have very shallow roots and the soil on lawns is usually quite compacted, so rain does not soak in much and tends to run off quickly.

The cleaner surface waters produced by rain gardens and similar storm water management practices benefit us and the birds and wildlife that inhabit the wetlands along lakes and rivers. By establishing a rain garden, you can have a wide-reaching effect on birdlife. You'll be improving the diversity of birds in your own yard as well as in nearby wetlands.

You can grow a great variety of attractive wetland or wet prairie plants in these gardens, most of which provide birds with food, cover and nesting habitat. As the West Michigan Environmental Action Council points out, "Rain gardens are a beautiful solution to water pollution."

You'll also be glad to know that rain gardens don't breed mosquitoes, since the gardens are designed to hold water temporarily, just a few hours after most storms. Mosquitoes require a few days of standing water to lay and hatch their eggs.

Larger-scale retention ponds and rural wetlands, which are essentially large rain gardens, may have permanent or long-standing ponds. They will be discussed briefly at the end of this chapter.

How to Create Your Rain Garden

Choosing a Site

Wisconsin expert Roger Bannerman suggests placing your rain garden close to your house to catch roof runoff or farther out to catch both roof and lawn runoff. You can also divert water from your basement sump pump to your garden. Nathan Pate of suburban St. Louis goes a step further and channels water from both his basement sump pump and his clothes washer to his rain garden. Roof water can also be directed to rain barrels and the overflow sent to the garden. The barrel saves rainwater for a dry day.

Locate your rain garden at least 10 feet away and down slope from your house so that water does not seep into your foundation and basement. To select the site, observe your yard after a good rain to determine how water runs off your property. Put the garden where it will catch the natural flow of water, and any other water you may want to direct its way.

Naturally low spots might be good locations for rain gardens. If water pools in those areas, however, infiltration is probably slow and you may have to amend the soil to increase absorption. Soil is frequently compacted on building sites by heavy equipment. Often the soil is deliberately compacted in order to support foundations and prevent sinkholes. Rain gardens are even more vital when soil is compacted.

If you prefer not to amend the soil in a compacted area, find another, less compacted spot

Mandy Ploch's garden, which is 5 feet in diameter on a slight grade, catches rainwater from 40-foot-long gutters that run the length of her cabin roof. She built a small retaining wall of local stone on the low side of the garden, then took soil from the high side, mixed it with compost, and packed it on the low side against the stone wall, leaving a concave surface for the garden.

"The evening I finished, we had a good rain, and I watched as the water level rose to the top of the stones where it was held for about an hour, then seeped away. Ta da! Success, even without plants." The next day, Mandy added plants.

in your yard, perhaps near your front sidewalk or along the street. A rain garden near a hard surface can keep storm water from running down the street into the storm sewer. It can also be a beautiful addition to your front yard.

A Few Hints on Choosing a Site:

- Never place a rain garden over a septic field. The septic system doesn't need more water.
- Locate it in sun or partial sun for best success with your plants.
- Avoid trees. Digging around them can harm the roots. Not all trees tolerate wet soils and some can be weakened or killed by excess water. Trees are very good at absorbing rainwater and should be protected.
- Pay attention to views from the house, patio or deck. Bannerman suggests locating near a patio "where you can take advantage of the colors and fragrances for hours on end."
- Don't dismiss a site to which rainwater does not flow naturally. You can channel it underground via pipes or send it along attractive over-ground channels or swales, lined with stones or colorful wet-loving plants.
- A flat area is the easiest place to construct a rain garden. But if your land slopes, you can dig out a pocket. Another approach is to build a retaining wall and fill in behind it, as Mandy Ploch of Wild Ones: Native Plants, Natural Landscapes did at her vacation cottage in western Wisconsin. (See photo, p. 179.)

Evaluating Your Soil

Your soil type determines how quickly it will absorb rainwater. Sandy soils drain the fastest, silty soils drain a little more slowly, clay soils drain slowest and can become waterlogged. It's fairly easy to determine your soil type. If it's gritty, you probably have sandy soil. If it's smooth but not sticky, you most likely have silty soil. If it's smooth and sticky, you have clay soil.

You can test the drainage by digging a hole eight inches wide and deep where the rain garden will be. Fill it with water and watch how fast it drains away. If it takes more than an hour to go down an inch, you will need to improve the drainage at the site.

If slow drainage is due to clay soils, you will have to remove and replace the soil. Use a mix of 50–60% sand, 20–30% topsoil and 20–30% compost. (Don't add any clay.) The mix will improve drainage and help break down pollutants. Some people use this mix for their rain garden base regardless of their soil, to insure good drainage.

Slow drainage may also be due to compaction. Even sandy soils can drain slowly if they've been severely compacted. Compacted soil should be dug out and loosened to a depth of two feet. Doing so will create better drainage and better growing conditions for the plants. If you end up with extra soil, use it in another part of your yard.

In rare cases, soil is so sandy and porous that rain soaks in so quickly there is no runoff. Obviously, you would be wise to create a dry prairie habitat instead of a rain garden. Still, it's not impossible to grow wetland plants with bird appeal in porous soils. For example, many hummingbird plants, like Cardinal Flower and Jewelweed, need damp "feet." To create a wetland for these plants, dig a depression and spread a plastic liner over its surface to retain rainwater, as if constructing a pond. Poke a few pencil-sized holes through the lower half of the liner to allow slow drainage so the soil doesn't stay waterlogged for too long. Then fill the liner with a mix of soil and peat (which helps retain water), before planting wetland species. Tom and Nancy Small of Kalamazoo, Michigan (chapter 4), created their rain garden this way.

Garden Design

Determining size. Rain gardens in residential areas are typically about 100 to 400 square feet, but they can be any size (they can never be too large). Ideally, you size it to capture all the water that would otherwise run off your property. A garden can be up to 30% smaller than ideal and yet capture up to 90% of annual runoff, says Bannerman. Only the biggest storms will cause an overflow.

To determine the best size for your rain garden, first estimate the drainage area. Multiply the length times the width of your house to get the total roof area. Then check how much of your roof is drained by each downspout. Houses usually have four downspouts, each draining about 25% of the roof. If you plan to catch rain from one of those downspouts, the area of drainage will be one-fourth (25%) of your roof area. Similarly, estimate the square footage of other areas—lawn, sidewalk or driveway—and add them all together to get the total area of drainage.

Your soil type determines the size of the rain garden. If you have sandy soil, your garden should be 20–30% of the drain area. If you have clay soil, it will need to be about 60% of the drain area, since clay absorbs water poorly. If you have loosened compacted soil or replaced clay soil with the suggested mix, use the 20–30% size suggested for sandy soil.

Determining depth. The suggested depth of rain gardens is usually four to eight inches, although they can be as deep as one or two feet. Gentle drainage slopes need less depth than steeper slopes. Whatever the depth, it is important to keep the garden level. That may require adding soil on steep slopes. The bottom of the garden should be saucer-shaped, rather than bowl-shaped, so the water can spread out across the garden.

To avoid long-standing water that can breed mosquitoes, adjust the depth of the garden to the drainage capacity of the soil. If drainage is slow despite your preparations, make a shallower

EXAMPLE: ESTIMATING SIZE OF GARDEN

Dave's rain garden will receive rain water from one downspout which drains 25% of his roof equal to 800 square feet. He estimates that the area of lawn that will also drain into the garden is about 200 square feet. This makes a total drain area of 1,000 square feet. He has sandy soil, so the ideal size for his garden is 20–30% of 1,000 square feet. He decides on the mid-range 25%, so his rain garden will be 250 square feet (1,000 × .25).

Band-winged Meadowhawk dragonfly

garden so that there's less water to absorb. If drainage is fast, make a deeper garden with a larger capacity.

Building Your Rain Garden

Now that you know the dimensions, you're ready to get out the shovel and dig. Spring is the best time to build your rain garden. It's easier to dig the moist soil and the plants will have a long growing period ahead. Generally, it takes one person about half a day to dig a small rain garden. Or you might want to rent a backhoe to help with the job.

First, you'll need to define the borders of your garden. Be creative. I use a rope or a garden hose to work out the shape. Crescent or teardrop shapes are attractive possibilities. Bannerman recommends that the longer side of the garden face the upslope, perpendicular to the flowage area, so the garden will catch as much water as possible.

The next step is to remove existing lawn or vegetation. Kill the vegetation first by one of the methods described in chapter 7, or remove it as you dig the depression. Make sure to get out all the roots.

Use the soil from the high end of your garden to build up the edges of the low end. Make sure the garden is level from rim to rim. Pack the soil tightly on the low end and sides so the garden holds water long enough to percolate into the soil. Some experts, like Bannerman, suggest creating a berm—a low wall—of soil around all but the high end of the garden.

Once you've reached the desired depth, it's time to work the soil on the bottom. If you are not replacing the soil, loosen it and add compost. You'll probably have to remove some of the soil to accommodate the compost. If you are replacing clay or compacted soil, dig out 1 to 1-1/2 feet of soil and replace it with the compost. (See page 180.)

The final step is grading the base. It can be flat-bottomed with fairly steep sides or incline gradually toward the deeper midsection of the garden. If you decide on the latter, you will have several wetness zones to accommodate the preferences of different wetland plants.

Consider adding a stone border, rustic fencing or a bench to add to the garden's appeal.

Planting Your Rain Garden

Now comes the best part—choosing the plants. There are many native wetland plant species that are both beautiful and bird friendly. Daniel Shaw and Rusty Schmidt, in *Plants for Stormwater Design: Species Selection for the Upper Midwest,* name 131 species of wetland plants; all but 10 benefit birds by providing food, cover and/or nesting sites. Finches, sparrows, juncos, blackbirds, cardinals, woodpeckers, hummingbirds and grosbeaks are among the many birds that use wetland plants. Common birds known to nest in small rain gardens include cardinals, sparrows, catbirds and Common Yellowthroats.

In the wild, wetland plants grow in the floodplains along rivers. They are adapted to both flood and drought that typically occur through the seasons. And that makes them ideal for rain gardens, which will be flooded for short periods after rains, then very dry at other times.

If your rain garden has a gradually sloping basin, you can grow wetland plants that tolerate these extremes in the lower end and plants that like somewhat drier conditions in the higher end. Plant mesic (medium moisture) or dry-loving prairie plants on the outer edge or on the berm.

When selecting plant species, you can choose mainly wetland wildflowers for a colorful, traditional, "perennial garden" look, or you can mix in sedges and grasses with the wildflowers for a more natural habitat (I recommend the latter). Plant seedlings or full-grown plants in your rain garden rather than seeds, which can wash away in a storm. Some wetland shrubs can be propagated from cuttings, as described in chapter 7. (See page 93.)

You can also add wetland shrubs and trees to your rain garden. Shrubs are often planted at the center, surrounded by wildflowers, sedges and grasses.

Once your rain garden is planted, be sure to water and mulch as described in chapter 7. The best mulch for rain gardens is shredded hardwood, since it will not wash away in most circumstances. Don't let soil or debris run into your garden during rains; they can bury the plants and destroy your garden. A big boulder or dam of small stones can protect young plants from soil erosion if the water flow to your garden is particularly strong during thunderstorms. For guidelines on the maintenance of your garden, see chapter 19.

Now you're ready to sit back and watch the birds and blooms throughout the year. Each year brings its own surprises, and one spring you may even spot that rare woodcock or rail.

Retention Ponds and Rural Wetlands

Larger wetlands can be created around retention ponds common in many suburban areas. Rural areas also offer many opportunities to create large-scale wetlands. They will provide all the many benefits of small rain gardens but on a larger scale: purified rainwater as it filters into the soil, less flooding, less lake and river pollution, recharged groundwater and enhanced wildlife habitat.

Retention ponds, unfortunately, are often little more than sterile, lifeless bodies of water. But with the addition of wetland and aquatic vegetation, they could greatly benefit a variety of birds and other wildlife. Ideally, trees, shrubs, wildflowers and native grasses should be planted on at least half of the shoreline of retention ponds, and some aquatic plants should be introduced to the pond itself (see chapter 16 for suggestions).

Large-scale wetlands in rural areas can be established with methods similar to those used to create rain gardens, except that heavy machinery is generally needed for the basins and berms. Permits from local, state and/or federal authorities may be needed.

One of the best ways of creating wetlands in rural areas is to return marginally productive crop or pasture land in low areas to the fully functional wetlands they once were. Often it's accomplished by removing or blocking the tiles that drained the original marshes and swamps on those sites and reestablishing native wetland plants. Throughout the Midwest, many farmers are voluntarily doing this with the aid of the Wetlands Reserve Program, managed by the U.S. Department of Agriculture's Natural Resources Conservation Service. Currently, Iowa is one of the top states in terms of enrollment.

Larger wetlands can use not only the plants recommended for rain gardens but also a greater diversity of species, including plants that like having wet feet almost continuously. See the list in *Plants for Stormwater Design* (Resources for Readers, page 192).

BIRD-FRIENDLY HERBACEOUS PLANTS FOR RAIN GARDENS & WETLANDS

Most of these plants are available at nurseries. See the tables in part 5 for information on the cultural requirements and native ranges of these plants.

Forbs
Versatile Forbs for Both Side Slopes and Basins

Common Name	Latin Name	Value for Birds
Meadow Anemone	Anemone canadensis	Used by waterfowl
Hairy Aster	Aster pilosus	Waterfowl cover; seeds for songbirds & upland game birds
Panicled Aster	Aster lanceolatus (A. simplex)	Waterfowl cover; seeds for songbirds & upland game birds
Marsh Blazing Star	Liatris spicata	Seeds for birds; nectar for hummingbirds
Meadow Blazing Star	Liatris ligulistylis	Seeds for birds; nectar for hummingbirds
Prairie Blazing Star	Liatris pychnostachya	Seeds for birds; nectar for hummingbirds
Riddell's Goldenrod	Solidago riddellii	Seeds eaten by goldfinches, juncos, Swamp & Am. Tree sparrows; leaves eaten by grouse
White Wild Indigo	Baptisia alba	Attracts insects eaten by birds
Michigan or Turk's Cap Lily	Lilium michiganse (L. superbum)	Nectar for hummingbirds & orioles
Pale Spiked Lobelia	Lobelia spicata	Nectar for hummingbirds; seeds for songbirds
Common Mountain Mint	Pycnanthemum virginianum	Attracts insects eaten by birds
Nodding Wild Onion	Allium cernuum	Attracts insects eaten by birds
Sand Prairie Phlox	Phlox pilosa	Nectar for hummingbirds
Sweet Black-eyed Susan	Rudbeckia subtomentosa	Seeds and cover for birds

Additional Forbs for Side Slopes

Golden Alexander	Zizia aurea	Attracts insects eaten by birds
Prairie Alum Root	Heuchera richardsonii	Provides habitat for birds
Big-leaved Aster	Aster macrophyllus	Cover, nesting habitat & seeds for songbirds

Smooth Blue Aster	*Aster laevis*	Seeds for songbirds & upland game birds
Foxglove Beard Tongue	*Penstemon digitalis*	Nectar for hummingbirds
Tall Bellflower	*Campanula americana*	Attracts insects for birds
Wild Bergamot	*Monarda fistulosa*	Nectar for hummingbirds
Virginia Bluebells	*Mertensia virginica*	Nectar for hummingbirds
Butterfly Milkweed	*Asclepias tuberosa*	Nectar for hummingbirds
Pale Purple Coneflower	*Echinacea pallida*	Insects for hummingbirds
Purple Coneflower	*Echinacea purpurea*	Insects for hummingbirds
Yellow Coneflower	*Ratibida pinnata*	Seeds for goldfinch & other songbirds & gamebirds
Fireweed	*Epilobium angustifolium*	Nectar for hummingbirds
Broad-leaved or Zigzag Goldenrod	*Solidago flexicaulis*	Seeds for goldfinches, juncos, & Swamp & Am. Tree Sparrows; leaves eaten by grouse
Stiff Goldenrod	*Solidago rigida*	Same as above
Lavender Giant Hyssop	*Agastache foeniculum*	Attracts insects eaten by birds
Blue Wild Indigo	*Baptisia australis*	Attracts insects eaten by birds
Jack-in-the-Pulpit	*Arisaema triphyllum*	Fruit eaten by gamebirds (Ring-necked Pheasants & Wild Turkeys); Wood Thrushes & Wood Ducks
Prairie Onion	*Allium stellatum*	Attracts insects eaten by birds
White Sage	*Artemisia ludoviciana*	Habitat & cover for small birds
Feathery False Solomon's Seal	*Smilacina racemosa*	Fruit eaten by grouse & thrushes
Common Spiderwort	*Tradescantia ohiensis*	Attracts insects eaten by birds

Additional Forbs for Basins

Great Angelica	*Angelica atropurpurea*	Good habitat for gamebirds & songbirds
New England Aster	*Aster novae-angliae*	Cover & seeds for birds
Bristly or Red-Stemmed Aster	*Aster puniceus*	Cover & seeds for birds
Boltonia	*Boltonia asteroides*	Attracts insects eaten by birds
Boneset	*Eupatorium perfoliatum*	Seeds eaten by turkeys, waterfowl, Swamp Sparrows; leaves eaten by grouse and Mallards
Cardinal Flower	*Lobelia cardinalis*	Nectar for hummingbirds

(continued)

Wild Golden Glow or Green-headed Coneflower	*Rudbeckia laciniata*	Cover & seeds for birds
Culver's Root	*Veronicastrum virginicum*	Attracts insects eaten by birds
Cup Plant	*Silphium perfoliatum*	Seeds eaten by finches & grouse; nectar for hummingbirds; used for water (drinking & bathing)
Northern Blue Flag Iris	*Iris versicolor*	Nectar for hummingbirds; seeds for waterfowl & other birds; cover for marsh birds
Southern Blue Flag Iris	*Iris virginica*	Same as above
Common Ironweed	*Vernonia fasciculata*	Attracts insects eaten by birds
Orange Jewelweed	*Impatiens capensis*	Nectar for hummingbirds; seeds for gamebirds
Spotted Joe Pye Weed	*Eupatorium maculatum*	Seeds eaten by turkeys, waterfowl, Swamp Sparrows; leaves eaten by grouse and Mallards
Great Blue Lobelia	*Lobelia siphilitica*	Nectar for hummingbirds & orioles
Swamp Rose Mallow	*Hibiscus moscheutos (H. palustris)*	Nectar for hummingbirds
Marsh Marigold	*Caltha palustris*	Seeds eaten by upland game birds
Nodding Bur Marigold	*Bidens cernua*	Seeds eaten by waterfowl (esp. Wood Duck), shorebirds & songbirds
Purple or Tall Meadow Rue	*Thalictrum dasycarpum*	Attracts insects eaten by birds
Marsh Milkweed	*Asclepias incarnata*	Fibers from old stems for nests
Monkey Flower	*Mimulus ringens*	Nectar for hummingbirds
Obedient Plant or False Dragonhead	*Physostegia virginiana*	Nectar for hummingbirds
Sneezeweed	*Helenium autumnale*	Seeds for songbirds & gamebirds
False or Oxeye Sunflower	*Heliopsis helianthoides*	Attracts hummingbirds
Turtlehead	*Chelone glabra*	Nectar for hummingbirds
Blue Vervain	*Verbena hastata*	Seeds eaten by sandpipers, cardinals, juncos, Lark Buntings; and sparrows

Ferns for Side Slopes & Basins

Bracken Fern	*Pteridium aquilinum*	Leaves eaten by grouse; habitat cover for songbirds
Ostrich Fern	*Matteuccia struthiopteris*	Same as above
Royal Fern	*Osmunda regalis*	Same as above

For Basins

Marsh Fern	*Thelypteris palustris*	Same as Bracken Fern
Sensitive Fern	*Onoclea sensibilis*	Same as Bracken Fern

Grasses, Rushes & Sedges
For both Basins and Side Slopes

Fringed Brome	*Bromus ciliatus*	Good-size seeds eaten by many birds including grouse, sparrows & towhees; leaves eaten by geese
Switchgrass	*Panicum virgatum*	Seeds important for songbirds & gamebirds (snipe, turkey, pheasant, Mourning Dove), Redwing Blackbird, Bobolink, cardinal, cowbird, junco & sparrows; seeds & foliage eaten by ducks (teal, wigeon & black duck)

For Side Slopes

Common Bur Sedge or Gray's Sedge	*Carex grayi*	Seeds eaten by many birds including rails, grouse, marsh birds, shorebirds, songbirds (sparrows, buntings, cardinals, & redpolls) and most waterfowl; cover for ducks
Big Bluestem Grass	*Andropogon gerardii*	Cover and seeds for gamebirds & songbirds
Indian Grass	*Sorghastrum nutans*	Good winter cover & seeds for gamebirds and songbirds
Little Bluestem Grass	*Schizachyrium scoparium*	A principal food for songbirds, esp. Field & Am. Tree Sparrows
Switchgrass	*Panicum virgatum*	See uses for Switchgrass above

For Basins

Fowl Manna Grass	*Glyceria striata*	Good cover & food for waterfowl, especially Wood Ducks
Prairie Cord Grass	*Spartina pectinata*	Seeds for ducks (mainly black ducks) & rails; early growth eaten by Canada Geese; habitat for Marsh Wrens
Common or Soft Rush	*Juncus effusus*	Seeds eaten by waterfowl, gamebirds, marsh birds, & songbirds; nesting habitat for rails & ducks

(continued)

Bristly or Bottlebrush Sedge	*Carex comosa*	Seeds eaten by many birds including rails, grouse, marsh birds, shorebirds, songbirds (sparrows, buntings, cardinals, & redpolls) and most waterfowl; cover for ducks
Brown Fox Sedge	*Carex vulpinoidea*	Same as above
Fringed or Caterpillar Sedge	*Carex crinita*	Same as above
Porcupine Sedge	*Carex hystericina*	Same as above
Common Tussock Sedge	*Carex stricta*	Same as above
Woolgrass	*Scirpus cyperinus*	Habitat & nesting cover for waterfowl and marsh birds; seeds eaten by coots and many ducks (Am. Black, Canvasback, Mallard, N. Pintail, Redhead, Ring-necked, scaup, & teal); both seeds & rootstocks eaten by Sora & Virginia Rails; tender stems eaten by geese

Note: One native plant to avoid is the cattail, which can become (and is) invasive in

Leopard frogs are attracted to ponds, and in turn, attract bird predators like herons.

Bird-Friendly Shrubs for Rain Gardens & Wetlands

All these shrubs are very versatile and will grow in virtually any soil, except for Winterberry which prefers acidic soils. They all also grow well in sun or partial sun; Spicebush can grow in any light condition including shade. Some shrubs can be used both on the side slopes and in the basins of rain gardens. The shrubs are listed according to their value for birds. See the shrub table in part 5 for more information on these species.

Shrubs for Rain Garden Side Slopes
Shrubs for Berries
Black Chokeberry, *Aronia melanocarpa*

Gray Dogwood, *Cornus racemosa*

Red-Osier Dogwood, *Cornus sericea (C. stolonifera)*

Common Elderberry, *Sambucus canadensis*

Red-berried Elderberry, *Sambucus racemosa (S. pubens)*

Spicebush, *Lindera benzoin*

American Cranberrybush Viburnum, *Viburnum opulus var. americanum;*
    V. trilobum

Nannyberry Viburnum, *Viburnum lentago*

Winterberry, *Ilex verticillata*—Prefers acidic soils

Shrubs for Seeds, Buds or Catkins
Meadowsweet, *Spirea alba*

Ninebark, *Physocarpus opulifolius*

Shrubs for Insects
Pussy Willow, *Salix discolor*

Shrubs for Rain Garden Base
Shrubs for Berries
Black Chokeberry, *Aronia melanocarpa*

Red-Osier Dogwood, *Cornus sericea (C. stolonifera)*

Silky Dogwood, *Cornus amomum*

Common Elderberry, *Sambucus canadensis*

Winterberry, *Ilex verticillata*—Prefers acidic soils

Shrubs for Seeds, Buds or Catkins
Speckled Alder, *Alnus incana (A. rugosa)*

Buttonbush, *Cephalanthus occidentalis*

Hardhack or Steeplebush, *Spirea tomentosa*

Meadowsweet, *Spirea alba*

Ninebark, *Physocarpus opulifolius*

BIRD-FRIENDLY TREES FOR LARGER WETLANDS

All these trees are very versatile and will grow in virtually any soil. The trees are listed according to their value for birds. See the tree tables in part 5 for more information on these species.

Tree for Berries
Hackberry, *Celtis* sp.

Trees for Seeds
Quaking Aspen, *Populus tremuloides*
River Birch, *Betula nigra*
White Cedar, *Thuja occidentalis*
Red Maple, *Acer rubrum*
Silver Maple, *Acer saccharinum*
Tamarack, *Larix laricina*

Tree for Nuts
Swamp White Oak, *Quercus bicolor*

Tree for Buds, Tender Twigs
Black Willow, *Salix nigra*

Trees for Cavities
Swamp White Oak, *Quercus bicolor*
Black Willow, *Salix nigra*

Cardinal Flowers, Mountain Mints and Swamp-Rose Mallows brighten a rain garden.

RAIN GARDEN DESIGN

This rain garden is designed for a 300 square feet area located in full sun. All the species will do well in most soils and are native to most midwestern states. The sides of this rain garden slope gradually to a 6–8" basin. There is space in the middle for three Meadowsweet shrubs, valuable for songbirds and gamebirds. If you use larger shrub species, there will be less space available for the herbaceous species. The plants on the outer edge of the rain garden are those recommended for side slopes. The interior plants are those recommended for the basin of a rain garden. Plant one herbaceous species per square foot for good coverage.

KEY TO PLANTS IN RAIN GARDEN

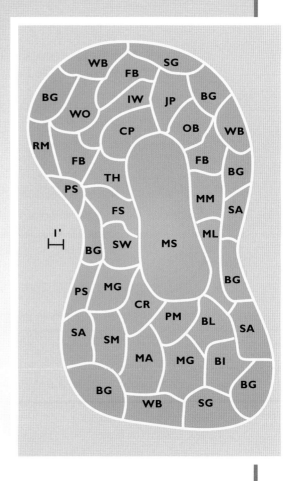

BG Little Bluestem Grass
BI   Southern Blue Flag Iris
BL   Great Blue Lobelia
CP Cup Plant
CR Culver's Root
FB   Fringed Brome
FS   Brown Fox Sedge
IW   Ironweed
JP Spotted Joe Pye Weed
MA   Meadow Anemone
MG   Fowl Manna Grass
ML   Michigan Lily
MM   Common Mountain Mint
MS   Meadowsweet
OB   Obedient Plant
PM   Purple Meadow Rue
PS Prairie Blazing Star
RM   Rattlesnake Master
SA Smooth Blue Aster
SG   Stiff Goldenrod
SM   Swamp or Marsh Milkweed
SW   Sneezeweed
TH   Turtlehead
WB   Wild Bergamot
WO White Wild Indigo

For detailed information on each species, see the plant tables in part 5.

RESOURCES FOR READERS

Books

Burrell, C. Colston. 1997. *The Natural Water Garden: Pools, Ponds, Bogs and Marshes for Backyards Everywhere.* Brooklyn Botanic Garden. Covers many aspects of water gardening, including ecology.

Eggers, Steve D., and Donald M. Reed. 1997. *Wetland Plants and Plant Communities of Minnesota and Wisconsin.* U.S. Army Corps of Engineers, St. Paul district. Color photos and descriptions of 144 plant species, along with information on wetland plant communities.

Galatowitsch, Susan M., and Arnold G. Vander Valk. 1994. *Restoring Prairie Wetlands: An Ecological Approach.* Ames: Iowa State University Press.

Henderson, Carrol L., Carolyn J. Dindorf and Fred J. Rozumalski. 1999. *Lakescaping for Wildlife and Water Quality.* St. Paul: Minnesota Department of Natural Resources. Discusses designing and planting wetlands along lakeshores.

Shaw, Daniel, and Rusty Schmidt. 2003. *Plants for Stormwater Design: Species Selection for the Upper Midwest.* St. Paul: Minnesota Pollution Control Agency. Out of print, but available through local interlibrary loan service.

Websites

Bannerman, Roger, and Ellen Considine. 2003. "Rain Gardens: A How-to Manual for Homeowners." University of Wisconsin–Extension. http://learningstore.uwex.edu/assets/pdfs/GWQ037.pdf

National Wildlife Federation. "How to Create a Mini-Wetland." http://www.nwf.org/News-and-Magazines/National-Wildlife/Gardening /Archives/1997/How-to-Create-a-Mini-Wetland.aspx

Rain Gardens of Western Michigan. http://www.raingardens.org/ An excellent source of detailed information about all aspects of rain gardens.

Wetlands Reserve Program. www.nrcs.usda.gov/programs/wrp/

CHAPTER 13
THE MIGRATORY BIRD GARDEN

In areas with high levels of disturbed or developed land, it helps to preserve or restore even the smallest fragment of natural habitat to provide helpful stopover sites for neotropical migrants.

—Ken Rosenberg, Cornell Lab of Ornithology

Small 'islands' of habitat can provide food resources to birds, particularly during migration.

—Victoria D. Piaskowski, international coordinator, Birds Without Borders, Zoological Society of Milwaukee

Avery high, thin "seet, seet, seet, seet" coming from the oaks caught my attention one spring. The trees were alive with Cape May Warblers. Soon I discovered Yellow-rumps, Palms, Black-and-Whites and many others. It turned out to be the best warbler wave I had ever witnessed, right in my own backyard—a total of 17 species visited that May 18th. Most stayed for only a day or two, resting and refueling before heading off to northern destinations, where they would spend the summer nesting and raising their young.

Ornithologist Paul Kerlinger, author of *How Birds Migrate*, has seen similar gatherings of warblers and other migrants in urban housing developments with large oaks and in Central Park in New York City. In Chicago, bird watchers have discovered a stand of shrubbery in a park on Lake Michigan's shores that is a similar magnet for migrants. Called the Magic Hedge by local birders, it's an important stopover for birds before they take their next long flight over Lake Michigan on their journey north each spring.

All such places offer valuable stopover habitat for Neotropical migrants, those birds that winter in the tropics of the Americas, then migrate north for the summer to escape the competition in the tropics for food and nest sites.

Declines in the numbers of Neotropical migratory bird species have been the concern of scientists for decades. At first, they focused on problems with the summer and winter habitats of migratory birds. Here in North America, for example, development has resulted in fragmentation and loss of habitat, while in South America, the destruction of the rain forests has played a major role.

Now scientists are also assessing the habitats that migratory birds need as they fly between their breeding and wintering grounds. The new field of study, called stopover ecology, is the subject of much ongoing research.

photo: Yellow-rumped Warbler

The Baltimore Oriole is one of the most beautiful of the tropical migrants. This female is searching for insects amid the blossoms of a crabapple tree.

Since birds can spend as much as half the year in migration, stopover habitat is critical to their survival. "Migration is a chain whose strength is that of its weakest link," says John Terborgh, author of *Where Have All the Birds Gone?*

Each spring and fall, millions of birds fly 600 miles nonstop across the Gulf of Mexico between the Yucatan Peninsula and the southern United States. Many of them pass through our midwestern states, to and from breeding sites as far north as the Canadian boreal forests and even the Arctic tundra.

The hazards birds face during these amazing journeys are growing greater every year. Predation and bad weather have always been challenges for these avian voyagers. Today, they also risk collisions with towers, buildings, windows, cars and hunters' bullets. But the greatest threat of all may be the loss and degradation of stopover habitat.

When you and I drive off on a vacation trip, we know we'll find plenty of gas stations, restaurants and motels along the way. Often migrating birds are not so lucky. Many of the woodlands, wetlands and prairies where they once rested and refueled have become parking lots, malls or housing developments. Although hungry and exhausted, just as we are after a long trip, they may need to travel on and on before finding suitable habitat in which to feed and rest for a day or two. And many birds don't make it. Researchers estimate that half of all birds migrating south in fall will not return to breed in the spring.

Migratory Oases in City and Country—
Discoveries in the Heart of the Midwest

Stopover ecologists are discovering that even small islands of habitat in urban and agricultural landscapes can help feed these famished migrants. Robb Diehl of the University of Illinois at Urbana-Champaign and Ron Larkin of the Illinois Natural History Survey's Center for Wildlife Ecology confirmed this by using the same radar that tracks storms and tornadoes to track migrating birds. Most songbirds take off for migration at nightfall; on radar, echoes suddenly erupt as millions of birds take off each evening for the next leg of their journey. Diehl and Larkin found that stronger echoes emanate from forest habitat in Illinois than from the sea of cornfields. The radar even identified the specific forest patches.

Another tool for tracking the migrants in Illinois is radio telemetry, a technique pioneered by scientists at the Illinois Natural History Survey. In one study, researchers attached tiny transmitters to the backs of two species of thrush, Veeries and Swainson's Thrushes, near Urbana. The continuous signals from the transmitters allowed researchers to follow the movements of the thrushes as they journeyed through the state. Their research has confirmed the importance of even the smallest pockets of habitat. One Swainson's Thrush, for example, was tracked to a tiny woods only 16 yards across, an avian oasis in the midst of miles of corn stubble.

A Swainson's Thrush stops in woods for shelter and food when migrating.

Illinois was dominated by tallgrass prairie before European colonization. Forests were never common. Diehl and Larkin report that today less than 5% of east-central Illinois is forested, down considerably from presettlement levels. Migrants use what remains, no matter the size.

Keeping up with the migrants in a radio tracking vehicle can be very challenging, say the two researchers, since the birds' paths are not limited by roads. Nonetheless, they followed a dozen migrating thrushes over 350 miles, tracking six of them until they landed. Three of six thrushes chose to stop within 55 yards of houses in urban and suburban areas, vividly illustrating the need for quality habitat in developed communities as well as in rural landscapes.

The telemetry tracking also enabled the researchers to determine the energy requirements of thrushes by taking blood samples from the birds before and after a seven-hour migratory night flight. Their conclusion: thrushes need the equivalent of more than a pound of insect larvae to fuel their 40-day migratory journey each spring. Obviously, a banquet of larvae must await these thrushes at every rest stop.

Like the Illinois studies, research around the country found that small pockets of quality stopover habitat in both city and country are vital to Neotropical migrants. This research also suggests what we can do to create such habitat.

How to Create Your Migratory Bird Garden
What Migrants Eat

Watch carefully, and you'll discover what spring migrants are eating. Perhaps you've seen some of the new leaves on your trees or shrubs peppered with many little holes. Most likely insect larvae, primarily caterpillars, chewed these holes. It is these caterpillars, usually about an inch long and light green, that many migrating birds feast on all their way north. With good binoculars, you can sometimes see green larvae in birds' bills.

Research in Illinois and elsewhere confirms that birds seem to time their spring migration to coincide with the emergence of these leaf-eating caterpillars. Most of the larvae feed on the tender new growth on trees, just as they begin to leaf out. Caterpillars emerge in waves from south to north each spring. Here in the Midwest, the month of May is peak for both migrating birds and the leaf-eating caterpillars on which they feed.

Researchers Jean and Richard Graber of the Illinois Natural History Survey's Center for Wildlife Ecology studied migrant warblers in the Shawnee National Forest in southern Illinois and in Allerton Park in east central Illinois. The warblers appeared to feed entirely on leaf-eating caterpillars—leaf rollers, loopers, fruit worms and others. That's not surprising since those insects constitute up to 98% of the invertebrates occurring at these sites. (Other groups of insects peak in late summer or fall.)

Shingle Oaks supplied most of the caterpillars for the warblers, the Grabers observed. Oaks in general supplied 60% of the food for warblers as a group and 90% for the Tennessee Warbler, the most numerous of the migrant warblers at those Illinois sites in May. Hickories, chiefly Pignut Hickory, were the second most important host of the caterpillars.

Volunteers in the Chicago Wilderness Region conducted a Migrant Bird Habitat Study under the auspices of the Urban Conservation Treaty for Migratory Birds partners during the springs of 2001–3. The tree species the spring migrating birds preferred included American Elm, Bur Oak and Hawthorn species. Sugar Maple was preferred at one site, but was underutilized at all other sites. Other trees used were Ohio Buckeye, crabapples, ashes, hickories, hackberry and honey locust. This and other Illinois studies highlight the importance of a diversity of tree species for migrating birds.

In Wisconsin, researchers Victoria Piaskowski, international coordinator of Birds Without Borders at Zoological Society of Milwaukee, and her associate Gene Albanese also found oak important, albeit a different species—Red Oak. This species of oak, along with Pussy Willow, hosted most of the insects in their study. As in the Illinois study, hickories ranked high, as the third top host for insects. But in Wisconsin, the species was Yellow-bud Hickory, not Pignut Hickory. An examination of fecal samples showed that, as in Illinois, leaf-eating caterpillars were the top food items for most warblers; flies also ranked high. Flies were the top choice for American Redstarts, warblers that feed like flycatchers, sallying out to catch insects in midair.

During fall migration, fruiting shrubs provide the best food sources for migrants. As noted in chapter 1, the majority of fruits ripen in fall in synchrony with bird migration. In the Midwest, this generally occurs from late August into September. Scientists are discovering that fruit eating in migrating landbirds is far more extensive than previously thought. In a study of 47 species of landbird migrants, ecologist Jeffrey D. Parrish of Brown University discovered that only the Winter Wren ate no fruit and fed strictly on insects. Even those species specially adapted for feeding on insects, like Brown Creepers

This Wisconsin garden features a variety of seed- and berry-producing groundcover plants below the tree in the foreground and fruit-bearing shrubs in the background.

and Black-and-White Warblers, ate some fruit during migration. The migrant that ate fruit almost exclusively (96% fruit by volume in fecal samples) was the Rose-breasted Grosbeak. Other species that eat a high percentage of fruit included flycatchers, thrushes, waxwings, vireos, warblers and sparrows.

Although migrating sparrows eat some fruits, they also thrive on the seeds of wildflowers and grasses, many of which also ripen in time for bird migration. Migrating Ruby-throated Hummingbirds require nectar-rich plants to fatten up for their 500-mile marathons across the Gulf of Mexico.

For the ideal migratory bird habitat, include plants in all of these categories, thus providing the multiple layers of plants usually found in the migrants' natural stopover sites. Plant tall canopy trees and/or hawthorns and Pussy Willows for spring insects, shrubs for abundant fall fruit and herbaceous plants for seed and nectar.

Woody Species for Spring and Fall Migrants

Trees. Oaks and hickories are the top choices for trees, since they are the best hosts for the caterpillars that feed spring migrants. Fortunately, a variety of oaks and hickories are now available at nurseries specializing in native plants.

Various species of oaks and hickories are native to every area of the Midwest and adapted to a variety of soil conditions. Three species of oak have very wide ranges covering nearly our whole area—White Oak, Bur Oak and Red Oak. Two of these, White and Bur, have deep taproots and must be transplanted when small. The same is true for most hickories. A few oaks, including Red, Swamp White and Pin Oak (not to be confused with Northern Pin Oak), have fairly shallow roots and are relatively easy to transplant.

Many species of oaks and hickories are slow growing. For quicker results, you may also want to plant other species attractive to migrant birds, such as most hawthorns, which can be readily planted as small trees. Or plant a fast-growing Pussy Willow.

This Chipping Sparrow has found a tasty insect among the leaves.

For a small urban yard, one specimen tree or even a large shrub can provide an attractive focus. For larger areas, use more trees to create a small grove or woodland.

Shrubs and vines. Shrubs bearing fruit are magnets for most migrating songbirds in fall, as birders have long known and research has now documented. In one study, two-thirds of all migrants were observed in shrubs and small understory trees. Because shrubs are also popular in home landscaping, "gardens can often provide good stopover habitat," says biologist Robert Askins, author of *Restoring North America's Birds*.

According to the University of Wisconsin Arboretum, many of the shrubs normally present in oak woods have berries, so they will be perfect under the oaks and hickories you plant for spring migrants. Those that provide fall fruit include several species of dogwoods and viburnums. (Other shrubs associated with oak woods, such as serviceberry, hazelnut, Choke Cherry, wild rose, elderberry and gooseberry, offer fruit or nuts for birds at other seasons. For fruit through the seasons for birds, you'll certainly want to include some of these in your landscaping.)

Vines that produce fall berries are also excellent choices for your migratory bird garden. Grapes are one of the best. More then 40 midwestern species of birds eat them. In my neighborhood, robins, waxwings and thrushes devour grapes each fall.

The fruits of some shrubs and vines are particularly high in the fats needed to fuel migrating birds. Although many species haven't been tested, the species known to have fruits high in fat include most dogwoods, Spicebush and Sassafras. Be sure to select some of these valuable plants for your migrant garden.

Herbaceous species

Grasses and wildflowers can provide seeds, fruit and nectar for migrants. Like many migrant songbirds, many sparrows eat fruits but also feed extensively on the seeds of herbaceous plants. Choose plants that flower in summer and produce seed or fruit by early fall. For hummingbirds, the best plants providing nectar for their migration are Wild Columbine in spring and Spotted Jewelweed in fall.

Ideas for Larger Rural Properties

On larger properties in rural areas, you can enhance fencerows or create shelterbelts as stopover habitat for migratory birds. If you're improving a fencerow, plant the larger trees in the middle and shrubs to the outside. For shelterbelts, especially where drifting winter snow is a problem, place the tall trees on the windward side and evergreens and shrubs on the leeward side. Five to eight "rows" about 10 to 15 feet apart are ideal, but strive for a natural arrangement. Stagger or

A migrating Hermit Thrush fattens up.

curve the rows and use plants of various sizes. Clumps or large blocks of shrubs and trees are better than rows because they provide less edge and more shelter.

Whether your garden is large or small, be sure to follow the guidelines for maintenance in chapter 19 in the first year or two, especially those for weeding, watering and protection from herbivores.

Avoid pesticides. Let the birds, as they fatten up for the breeding season, control the caterpillars in your yard. Later in the season, oaks and some other species develop tannins and chemicals in their leaves that make them less palatable to insects. Once established, your migratory bird habitat should need relatively little care, except for an occasional pruning of your shrubs to ensure abundant fruiting.

Migration Station

The importance of creating stopover habit for migratory birds cannot be overestimated. Donald S. Heintzelman, author of *The Complete Backyard Birdwatcher's Home Companion*, wrote, "Enhancing thousands of small yards with native vegetation, particularly species that produce fruits eaten by migratory songbirds, can help to compensate for the loss of larger habitats along North America's major coastal and inland songbird migration routes."

Your migratory bird habitat will offer a beautiful progression of flowers and fruits through the seasons. Best of all, you'll be doing your part to ensure that migratory flocks of birds—those "gatherings of angels," as scientists dubbed the puzzling radar echoes now understood to represent migrating birds—continue to wing their way across the continent each spring and fall.

Bird-Friendly Plants
for Your Migratory Bird Garden

WOODY PLANTS FOR SPRING MIGRANTS
Recommended Oaks Hosting Insects for Spring Migrants

Most widespread oaks in Midwest
Bur Oak, *Quercus macrocarpa*
Red Oak, *Quercus rubra (Q. borealis)*
White Oak, *Quercus alba*

Other excellent oaks
Chinquapin Oak, *Quercus muehlenbergi*
Northern Pin Oak, *Quercus ellipsoidalis*
Pin Oak, *Quercus palustris*
Shingle Oak, *Quercus imbricaria*
Swamp White Oak, *Quercus bicolor*

Other Recommended Tree Species Hosting Insects
Pignut Hickory, *Carya glabra*
Shagbark Hickory, *Carya ovata*
Pussy Willow, *Salix discolor*
Hawthorns, *Crataegus* sp.
Note: Other hickories and willows are also likely to host insects for migrants, but the species listed here are those known to attract migrants.

WOODY PLANTS FOR FALL MIGRANTS
Woody Plants Known to have High-Fat Berries
Gray Dogwood, *Cornus racemosa*
Flowering Dogwood, *Cornus florida*
Alternate-leaved or Pagoda Dogwood, *Cornus alternifolia*
Silky Dogwood, *Cornus amomum*
Sassafras, *Sassafras albidum*
Spicebush, *Lindera benzoin*

Other Woody Plants with Fall Berries
Note: Many of the species below retain their fruit into winter, providing winter fare for birds. See The Winter Bird Garden, chapter 15.

Dogwoods
(Both of the dogwoods below are likely to have high-fat berries.)
Roundleaf Dogwood, *Cornus rugosa*
Red-twigged Dogwood, *Cornus sericea (C. stolonifera)*

Other Shrub Species
Black Chokeberry, *Aronia melanocarpa*
Common Elder, *Sambucus canadensis*
Winterberry or Michigan Holly, *Ilex verticillata*
Common Juniper, *Juniperus communis*

Sumacs

Fragrant Sumac, *Rhus aromatica*

Smooth Sumac, *Rhus glabra*

Staghorn Sumac, *Rhus hirta (R. typhina)*

Shining or Winged Sumac, *Rhus copallina*

Roses

Illinois or Climbing Prairie Rose, *Rosa setigera*

Early Wild or Smooth Rose, *Rosa blanda*

Viburnums

American Cranberrybush Viburnum, *Viburnum opulus var. americanum (V. trilobum)*

Blackhaw Viburnum, *Viburnum prunifolium*

Downy Arrowwood Viburnum, *Viburnum rafinesquianum*

Maple-leaved Viburnum, *Viburnum acerifolium*

Nannyberry Viburnum, *Viburnum lentago*

Trees for Fall Berries

Red Cedar, *Juniperus virginia*

Black Cherry, *Prunus serotina*

Hackberry

Northern Hackberry, *Celtis occidentalis*

Southern Hackberry, *Celtis laevigata*

Hawthorns

Cockspur Hawthorn, *Crataegus crusgalli*

Dotted Hawthorn, *Crataegus punctata*

Downy Hawthorn, *Crataegus mollis*

Fleshy Hawthorn, *Crataegus succulent*

Washington Hawthorn, *Crataegus phaenopyrum*

Mountain Ash

American Mountain Ash, *Sorbus americana*

Showy Mountain Ash, *Sorbus decora*

Black or Sour Gum, *Nyssa sylvatica*

Vines for Fall Berries

American Bittersweet, *Celastrus scandens*

Moonseed, *Menispermum canadense*

Virginia Creeper, *Parthenocissus quinquefolia*

HERBACEOUS SPECIES FOR MIGRANTS

Nectar-Rich Flowers

Spring

Wild Columbine, *Aquilegia canadensis*

Fall

Orange Jewelweed, *Impatiens capensis (I. biflora)*

Cedar Waxwings as well as migratory birds relish the berries of this Silky Dogwood.

(continued)

Fall Berries

Feathery False Solomon's Seal, *Smilacina racemosa*
Smooth Solomon's Seal, *Polygonatum biflorum (P. caniculatum)*
Starry False Solomon's Seal, *Smilacina stellata*
White Baneberry, *Actaea alba*
Red Baneberry, *Actaea rubra*
Jack-in-the-Pulpit, *Arisaema triphyllum*

Seeds

Most prairie/savanna forbs and grasses provide seeds for seed-eating migrants. A few choice species are the Silphiums (Rosin Weed, Compass Plant, Prairie Dock, and Cup Plant), sunflowers and native grasses, especially Little and Big Bluestem Grasses, Switchgrass, Porcupine Grass and Prairie Dropseed.

MIGRATORY BIRD GARDEN

This garden is designed for an average-sized backyard about 75 feet wide with moist soil. The Pin Oak is a hotspot for both spring and fall migrants. In spring, the birds come to devour the leaf-eating caterpillars on its branches, while in fall the small acorns attract migrating Brown Thrashers, Common Grackles and Yellow-bellied Sapsuckers. In rural areas, resident gamebirds like Wild Turkeys, Ruffed Grouse and Northern Bobwhites, and a host of songbirds love the acorns, too.

Pin Oak does not have a taproot, so it is easy to transplant and is one of the faster growing oaks. We planted one and loved its beautiful symmetrical form and burgundy fall color. Its branches are low-swung, with an attractive, free-flowing look. There is little space below for shrubs, so I'd suggest only herbaceous species as a ground-cover below this particular oak. (Pin Oak is not recommended for highly alkaline soils. Bur Oak or Chinquapin Oak do better in such soils, but are difficult to transplant; move as balled and burlapped trees early in spring.)

All the other species of shrubs and trees in this design produce berries relished by many migrants. The Washington Hawthorn will become one of the most popular spots in your garden for fall migrants. In Pat and Carl Brust's yard, its berries attract robins, waxwings, cardinals and House Finches. Summer birds nest in the hawthorn, protected from predators by its hefty thorns.

The dogwoods in this garden have high-fat berries, which help migrants fatten up for their flight, while the viburnums retain their berries longer for late migrants. Red Cedars offer excellent cover as well as berries, and are a perfect backdrop to set off the Washington Hawthorn and red twigs of Red-Osier Dogwoods.

Plant a mix of woodland herbaceous species with cover, seeds, and berries below the trees and shrubs. Best choices for berries are: Jack-in-the-Pulpit, Blue Cohosh, Solomon's seals and baneberries. For hummingbirds, plant Wild Columbine, and if you have a damp spot (or you can dig a little depression), Orange Jewelweed. For seed-eaters, plant some shade-tolerant grasses like Wood Reed Grass, Virginia Wild Rye, and Woodland Brome and fall seed-producing wildflowers like Short's Aster, Side-flowering Aster, Big-leaved Aster, Broad-leaved Goldenrod and Blue-stemmed Goldenrod.

There's an island of savanna forbs and grasses in the middle of the lawn. These plants could also be placed as a border in front of the trees and shrubs so you have more lawn. If you don't want a lawn, you could replace it with native plants. That's what we did—we kept much of the yard as a play area until my sons outgrew it. Then we gradually installed native plants, keeping only lawn paths and borders. See the Prairie & Savanna Forbs and Grasses Tables on pages 130–135 for suggestions of species for this island of forbs and grasses.

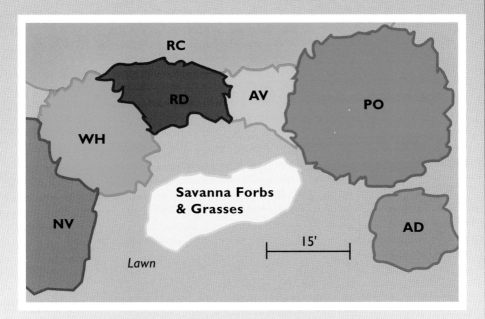

Key to Plants in Migratory Bird Garden

Following the names are the suggested number of each species to plant. Several individuals of shrub species will insure successful cross-pollination and fruiting. Red Cedars are dioecious, so five individuals will help increase the likelihood that at least one will be female and produce berries.

Trees
    AD   Alternate-leaved Dogwood—1
    PO   Pin Oak—1
    RC   Red Cedar—5
    WH   Washington Hawthorn—1

Shrubs
    AV   Downy Arrowhead Viburnum—5
    NV   Nannyberry Viburnum—5
    RD   Red-osier Dogwood—5

See the plant tables in part 5 for detailed information on the recommended species.

RESOURCES FOR READERS

Books

Able, Kenneth P., ed. 1999. *Gatherings of Angels: Migrating Birds and Their Ecology.* Ithaca, NY: Cornell University Press.

Kerlinger, Paul. 1995. *How Birds Migrate.* Mechanicsburg, PA: Stackpole Books.

Terborgh, John. 1989. *Where Have All the Birds Gone?* Princeton, NJ: Princeton University Press.

Websites

Smithsonian National Zoological Park. Migratory Bird Center. http://nationalzoo.si.edu/scbi/migratorybirds/

U.S. Fish and Wildlife Service. "Migratory Songbird Conservation." http://library.fws.gov/Bird_Publications/songbrd.html

Learn when your favorite birds will be returning to your region in spring at www.enature.com/birding/migration_home.asp

Migrating birds visit the Brusts' prairie grasses for nutritious prairie grass seeds.

CHAPTER 14
THE SHRUBLAND BIRD GARDEN

If you want to see birds, plant a thicket.
—Sally Wasowski, *Gardening with Prairie Plants*

A thicket is fast becoming a place you have to drive to see.
—Sara Stein, *Planting Noah's Garden*

Millions of spring migrants pass through the Midwest on their way to the spruce and fir forests of Canada or the Arctic tundra, but others make the Midwest their final destination. Among them are many shrub-loving species that thrive in the same thickets that furnish stopover habitat for long-distance migrants. The Gray Catbird mewing from the bushes, the House Wren scolding from your brush pile, the Indigo Bunting singing along shrubby roadsides—all are migrant birds that may be enticed to stay and nest in your neighborhood given sufficient habitat. So, too, will non-migratory shrubland birds, like Northern Cardinals and Song Sparrows, who remain through the winter in much of the Midwest.

Shrubland habitats and the birds associated with them are often overlooked in conservation efforts. As Robert Askins points out in his book *Restoring North America's Birds*, "This habitat is not usually the subject of Sierra Club calendar photos or poetry, but these birds, and a multitude of other species that depend on low shrubland and vine tangles, are an important part of biological diversity of North America."

Unfortunately, a number of shrubland species are declining along with their habitat. The North American Breeding Bird Survey, which has monitored bird populations since 1966, shows that the populations of nine midwestern species are declining. Many birders know only too well the declines in such species as the Prairie Warbler, Northern Bobwhite, Yellow-Breasted Chat and Golden-winged Warbler. In some areas of the Midwest they are rare enough to be considered "hotline" species—singled out for mention on hotlines and rare-bird alerts.

Several species still considered fairly common are also showing significant declines in the Midwest. These include the Field Sparrow, Brown Thrasher, Indigo Bunting, Eastern Towhee and Common Yellowthroat. The towhee, in fact, is losing ground not only in the Midwest but throughout most of its range in eastern North America (both U.S. and Canada). "Few people," says Askins, "are aware that the still-common Eastern Towhee may be declining more rapidly than any other bird species in eastern North America."

photo: Indigo Bunting

**BIRDS TO WATCH FOR
IN YOUR SHRUBLAND
GARDEN**

According to the North
American Breeding Bird
Survey, the following 31 species
of birds breed in shrubby habitats in the Midwest:

Northern Bobwhite

Indigo Bunting

Northern Cardinal

Gray Catbird

Flycatchers—
   Willow & Alder

American Goldfinch

Blue Grosbeak

Sparrows—Field, Lark, Clay-
   colored, White-throated,
   Song & Lincoln's

Eastern Towhee

Brown Thrasher

Vireos—Bell's and White-eyed

Warblers—Prairie Warbler,
   Yellow-breasted Chat,
   Golden-winged Warbler,
   Common Yellowthroat,
   Chestnut-sided Warbler,
   Yellow Warbler, Mourning,
   Nashville Warbler, Blue-
   winged Warbler &
   Connecticut Warbler

American Woodcock

Wrens—Bewick's, House
   & Carolina

(continued)

*Brown Thrasher, nesting here in dense shrubbery, is
one of the shrubland birds with a declining population.*

Shrublands of the Past

Historically, the most stable shrublands were found in wetlands along riverbanks and in bogs and beaver meadows. These areas provided dependable habitat for shrub-loving species.

Naturally occurring shrublands in drier locations were generally far more transitional in nature. They often sprang up randomly when a forest gap was created by windthrows, storms or dying canopy trees. Fires started by lightning or Indians to improve hunting also kept the forest in check and allowed shrublands to develop. But over time, without disturbances of this kind, shrublands reverted gradually back to woodland.

In presettlement days, these short-lived shrublands occurred throughout eastern North America. But the Midwest, located on the prairie-forest border, must have had an abundance of shrublands, suggests Askins. Here, tornadoes, fires and drought kept the advancing forest at bay, allowing shrubland and its associated birds to thrive.

Unfortunately, many of these shrublands have now been converted to farmland or overtaken by urban sprawl. Others have grown into forest. Today, few natural sites remain for colonization by shrubs. For this reason, and a lack of nearby seed sources, new shrublands have little chance to develop as in the past.

Consequently, many shrubland birds have become "fugitives without a destination," Askins notes. Shrubby thickets of all sizes are needed to help save these species.

How to Create Your Shrubland Garden

Most shrubs grow best in sunny locations and generally need plenty of light to flower and fruit. Their flowers will attract insects on which the birds can feed early in the season, and their fruits will nourish birds later in the season. Although trees can be included in your shrubland habitat, it is important to make sure they do not shade out the shrubs.

Shrubbery for Wet Areas

Shrubbery typical of natural wetlands is relatively easy to duplicate on a small scale in the typical yard. Often, the lot is graded to form a swale at one end of the property to keep water from draining toward the foundation of the house. This is usually the spot where homeowners want screening shrubs.

Shrubland hedges provide food, cover and nesting sites for birds.

Species more closely associated to other habitats will sometimes nest in shrubs and small trees in brushy areas. These include:

Eastern Bluebird

Chickadees—Black-capped & Carolina

Brown-headed Cowbird

Cuckoos—Black- & Yellow-billed

Mourning Dove

Northern Flicker

American Kestrel

Great Crested Flycatcher

Eastern Kingbird

Northern Mockingbird

Eastern Screech-Owl

Ring-necked Pheasant

Tree Swallow

Tufted Titmouse

Downy Woodpecker

Such a swale would be a perfect spot for native shrubs that do well in moist soil. Red-osier Dogwood, Pussy Willow, Ninebark and Common Elderberry are species of midwestern shrubs that thrive in such a situation. Many wetland shrubs can be propagated from cuttings. See chapter 7 for more details. Small shrub islands of this kind provide nesting sites for some of our favorite back-yard birds, like cardinals, wrens and Chipping Sparrows.

Many neighborhoods have potential for a much larger expanse of shrubland habitat. Often an entire block of homes shares a swale running along all lot lines. If the entire swale was planted with native shrubs, the expanded area could attract a far greater variety of shrub-loving birds. At the same time, a uniform stretch of shrubs will appeal to traditional gardeners who like an ordered look. Ideally, this lengthy thicket would connect to a natural area on one or both ends, creating an environmental corridor or passageway for birds and other wildlife.

Shrubbery for Drier Sites

Shrubbery in drier places on your property can replicate the historical shrublands formed in forest gaps or at the prairie-forest border. Any drier area would be suitable. Again, shrubbery along lot lines provides screening and also can serve as a backdrop for wildflowers and grasses. Gray Dogwood, Nannyberry Viburnum, Blackhaw Viburnum and Downy Arrowhead Viburnum are perfect for such sites.

Shrubbery for Large Sites

If you live in a rural area, consider improving existing fencerows to provide more habitat for shrubland birds. The Wisconsin Department of Natural Resources (WDNR) suggests increasing the width of a fencerow to 25–50 feet, planting on either side of the fence. Plant a row of large shrubs along the fence and a row of smaller shrubs alongside them. This will not only provide nest-ing sites for shrubland birds but will turn an open fencerow into a safe passageway for wildlife. The WDNR suggests spacing the shrubs about every 3 feet, with rows 6 to 16 feet apart.

Alternately, you may have existing islands of shrubbery that you could enlarge to provide more shrubland habitat. The larger the acreage, the more shrubland bird species you'll be able to attract.

However, if you expand the shrubbery into a large open grassland, you may actually be harming more birds (albeit different species) than helping. Grasslands and the grassland birds they support are very rare and need protection, just as shrubland species do. Prairie chickens need great stretches of prairie, with an unobscured view of the horizon. Even a few tall shrubs and trees are undesirable; they not only block the view but provide perching sites for predatory hawks.

General Guidelines for Shrubland Habitats of All Sizes

The size of the shrubby thickets you create will influence the kinds of birds you'll attract. Each shrubland bird has different requirements. Common backyard species, like the Northern Cardinal, Song Sparrow and Gray Catbird, can do well on relatively small yard-sized sites, while White-eyed Vireos and Brown Thrashers need areas of intermediate size. The Yellow-breasted Chat prefers to nest in dense thicket five acres or more in size. The Golden-winged Warbler and Prairie Warbler also require large sites.

Whatever size your site is, prepare the soil and plant large shrubs about 5 to 7 feet apart and small shrubs 2 to 3 feet apart. For best growth, avoid planting herbaceous species beneath the shrubs, at least for the first few years. A mulch of wood chips will conserve moisture, keep down weeds and harbor insects for ground-feeding birds like thrashers and sparrows.

Plant a variety of shrubs native to your area to provide flower and fruit throughout the season. For a feast of color and fragrance in spring, as well as plenty of insects for birds, plant such shrubs as elderberry or Spicebush. Midsummer, their fruits will feed the birds. For fall, viburnums and dogwoods offer vibrantly colored leaves and lush fruits. Even in the winter your shrubs can feed your backyard residents. The bright red plumes of sumac and ruby rosehips provide nourishment and beauty against a blanket of snow.

After planting your shrubland bird garden, be sure to follow the maintenance guidelines in chapter 19, especially for weeding, watering and protecting your shrubs from herbivores during the first year or two. Once established, your garden will need only periodic pruning. Overgrown shrubbery will not fruit well, since most flower and fruit production is on young branches. You may also have to eliminate the occasional tree sapling (which will eventually shade your shrubbery) or invasive shrub whose seeds may be brought in by the wind, birds or squirrels.

Conservation Note

Many of our rare shrubland birds need large blocks of habitat. Unfortunately, few expanses of such habitat are available today and most of us will not be able to reproduce them on our own properties. But two types of artificial habitat—forest clearcuts and powerline corridors—could be managed for shrubland specialists. Although considered unsightly and unnatural by many, they can provide critically needed habitat for shrubland species.

A clearcut involves cutting all the trees from a large area of forest. Robert Askins notes that the dense shrubby aftermath of a clearcut provides habitat for most of the declining shrubland birds of the East, including at least seven species of warblers. Not all forests are suitable for clear-cutting. Old growth forests, steep sloping forests or those having unique flora and fauna should not be harvested.

Powerline corridors can likewise be valuable. For access and safety reasons, power companies must keep the land beneath the lines clear of trees, typically by mowing and applying herbicides. But to reduce costs and objections to the health hazards of herbicides, some power companies are now trying to establish thick shrubbery that is resistant to invasion by trees. Studies of the resulting shrubland corridors have found that they support a variety of birds, including a number of warbler species, White-eyed Vireos and Field Sparrows.

Birders will want to support the creation of both of these artificial habitats where appropriate, so that a diversity of shrubland birds will always be with us.

Bird-Friendly Shrubs for Moist/Wet Sites

For more information on the shrubs below, see the shrub table in part 5. Some of these species tolerate a wide range of soil moisture and are also listed for dry sites.

All of these shrubs provide cover and nesting sites. Their other values for birds are described below. Try to select shrubs from every group.

Shrubs for Berries

Early Low Blueberry, *Vaccinium angustifolium**

Highbush Blueberry, *Vaccinium corymbosum**

Bunchberry, *Cornus canadensis**

Choke Cherry, *Prunus virginiana*

Sand Cherry, *Prunus pumila*

Black Chokeberry, *Aronia melanocarpa*

Coralberry, *Symphoricarpos orbiculatus*

Wild Black Currant, *Ribes americanum*

Common Dewberry, *Rubus flagellaris*

Gray Dogwood, *Cornus racemosa*

Red-Osier Dogwood, *Cornus sericea (C. stolonifera)*

Rough-Leaved Dogwood, *Cornus drummondii*

Round-leaved Dogwood, *Cornus rugosa*

Silky Dogwood, *Cornus amomum*

Elderberry, Common *(Sambucus canadensis)*

Red-berried Elderberry, *Sambucus racemosa (S. pubens)*

Prickly Wild Gooseberry, *Ribes cynosbati*

Missouri Gooseberry, *Ribes missouriense*

American Fly Honeysuckle, *Lonicera canadensis***

Black Raspberry or Blackcap, *Rubus occidentalis*

Red Raspberry, *Rubus idaeus var. strigosus*

Swamp Rose, *Rosa palustris*

Round-leaved Serviceberry, *Amelanchier sanguinea*

Snowberry, *Symphoricarpos albus*

Spicebush, *Lindera benzoin**

Sumacs, *Rhus* species

Viburnums, *Viburnum* species

Winterberry or Michigan Holly, *Ilex verticillata**

Shrubs for Seeds, Buds or Catkins

Alder, Speckled, *Alnus incana (A. rugosa)*

Dwarf Birch, *Betula pumila*

Buttonbush, *Cephalanthus occidentalis***

Hardhack or Steeplebush, *Spirea tomentosa**

Indigo Bush, *Amorpha fruticosa*

Shrubby St. John's Wort, *Hypericum prolificum*

Ninebark, *Physocarpus opulifolius*

Meadowsweet. *Spirea alba*

Shrubs for Nuts

American Hazelnut or American Filbert, *Corylus americana*

Beaked Hazelnut, *Corylus cornuta*

Shrub for Perching in Prairies

Leadplant, *Amorpha canescens*

Shrubs for Insects

Willow *Salix species*

*Require acidic conditions
**Flowers have nectar eaten by hummingbirds

For more information on the shrubs below, see the shrub tables in part 5. Some of these species tolerate a wide range of soil moisture levels and, as a result, are also listed for moist-wet sites. All of these shrubs offer cover and nesting sites for birds. Their other values for birds are described below. Try to select shrubs from every group.

Shrubs for Berries

Early Low Blueberry, *Vaccinium angustifolium**

Highbush Blueberry, *V. corymbosum**

Sand Cherry, *Prunus pumila*

Choke Cherry, *P. virginiana*

Black Chokeberry, *Aronia melanocarpa*

Coralberry, *Symphoricarpos orbiculatus*

Snowberry, *Symphoricarpos albus*

Common Dewberry, *Rubus flagellaris*

Prickly Wild Gooseberry, *Ribes cynosbati*

Box or Black Huckleberry, *Gaylussacia baccata**

Missouri Gooseberry, *Ribes missouriense*

Black Raspberry or Blackcap, *Rubus occidentalis*

Red Raspberry, *Rubus idaeus var. strigosus*

Early Wild or Smooth Rose, *Rosa blanda***

Pasture Rose, *Rosa carolina***

Sunshine Rose, *Rosa arkansana***

Dwarf Serviceberry, *Amelanchier spicata (A. stolonifera)*

Round-Leaved Serviceberry, *Amelanchier sanguinea*

Sumacs, *Rhus* species

Blackhaw Viburnum, *Viburnum prunifolium*

Downy Arrowhead Viburnum, *Viburnum rafinesquianum*

Maple-Leaved Viburnum, *Viburnum acerifolium*

Nannyberry Viburnum, *Viburnum lentago*

Wintergreen, *Gaultheria procumbens**

Wolfberry, *Symphoricarpos occidentalis*

Shrubs for Nuts

American Hazelnut or American Filbert, *Corylus americana*

Beaked Hazelnut, *Corylus cornuta*

Shrubs for Seeds

Indigo Bush, *Amorpha fruitcosa*

Shrubby St. John's Wort, *Hypericum prolificum*

Shrub for Perching Site

Leadplant, *Amorpha canescens*

Shrubs for Insects

New Jersey Tea, *Ceanothus americanus**

Inland New Jersey Tea, *Ceanothus herbaceous (C. ovatus)*.

Prairie Willow, *Salix humilis****

* Requires acidic conditions

** The fruit of a rose is a berry-like hip.

*** Hummingbirds use the fuzz on the seeds for nest material.

Nannyberry Viburnum

SHRUBLAND BIRD GARDEN

This garden is designed as a shrub island which could serve as an excellent backdrop for your pond or bird feeding station, as an island in the midst of your lawn, or even as a border along the edge of your property. Each species is native to all eight midwestern states and tolerates a wide range of soil moistures. There are twenty-three shrubs in this garden: three Ninebark shrubs and five each of the other species. Plant several individuals of each species to insure successful cross-pollination and fruiting.

The shrubs provide wonderful habitat for shrubland birds, along with a variety of seasonal foods. Their flowers blossom sequentially through spring and early summer, and will attract multitudes of insects for the birds to gorge on. Berries, nuts and seeds will follow the flowers, ripening successively to provide nourishment for birds from summer through winter.

Hazelnuts and currant berries ripen in summer, providing food for breeding birds. Ninebark pods, which contain three or four seeds each, also ripen in summer, but remain available for wintering birds. Gray Dogwood's high-fat berries ripen in late summer and fall in time for migrating birds. Rose hips ripen in fall and like Ninebark pods, stay on the shrub for months and feed birds through the winter. See part 5 for detailed information on the recommended species for this garden. Also, see the shrub border in the woodland bird garden design in chapter 11 for more ideas.

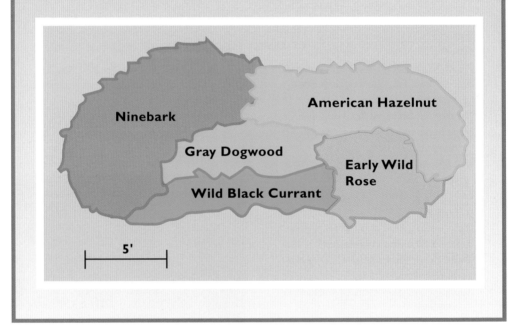

RESOURCE FOR READERS

Askins, Robert A. 2000. *Restoring North America's Birds.* New Haven, CT: Yale University Press. Excellent overview of the title subject, with one chapter on the restoration of shrubland birds.

CHAPTER 15
THE WINTER BIRD GARDEN

Feeding birds is certainly not as helpful as improving backyard habitat through landscaping, which provides food for a wider variety of birds, as well as shelter, nesting places, and perches.

—Stephen W. Kress, vice president of bird conservation,
National Audubon Society, *The Winter Banquet*

Winter is a favorite time for putting up bird feeders. Feeders bring birds close to our homes for easy and enjoyable bird watching. Winter is the ideal time to provide birds with extra nourishment since natural foods are scarce in the coldest season of the year.

But most bird species don't come to feeders. And the birds that do get a small fraction of their food from feeders—only 21% for Black-capped Chickadees, according to a Wisconsin study.

You can attract a greater variety of winter birds to your yard by providing habitat that offers their natural foods and adequate cover to shelter them from bitter cold and snowstorms. A source of water is also important, although wintering birds will eat snow when natural bodies of water are frozen. A heated birdbath is a magnet for winter birds, especially when little or no snow is available.

The ideal winter bird garden, then, provides habitat with cover, food plants and water as well as feeders.

How to Create Your Winter Bird Garden

Cover
Trees and shrubs. Cover is absolutely essential for wintering birds. In the coldest temperatures, birds conserve energy by hunkering down in a sheltered spot instead of hunting for food. Wildlife ecologist Margaret Clark Brittingham observed that "when the temperature dropped below minus 20 degrees F, we noticed that chickadees stopped searching for food. The birds simply slowed down, fluffed up and waited for warmer weather."

Evergreens provide ideal shelter for birds during frigid weather. They also make a beautiful backdrop to your feeding area. Place the evergreens so they block the prevailing winds, which generally blow from the west and north in the Midwest. Evergreens should comprise at least 10% of your total plantings, if possible.

photo: Pine Siskin

Red Cedar trees and juniper shrubs provide winter cover.

Fortunately, there are evergreens that do well in every part of the Midwest, and you can select those native to your area and suited to your soil and moisture conditions. Most evergreens do double duty since, in addition to providing dense cover, they offer food for birds through the winter months.

Dense shrubbery also provides shelter for wintering birds. Whenever possible, the shrub area should be a least six feet wide, so plant larger native shrubs. Many viburnums, for example, have a spread of six feet or more at maturity. A berm behind the shrubs, on the side of the prevailing winds, can create additional shelter in windy areas, but be careful not to create drainage problems or erosion.

For larger yards, a combination of conifers and deciduous trees, with shrubs to the forefront, makes an even more substantial barrier to winds, as well as an attractive border for your bird habitat.

Herbaceous plants. Sparrows, finches and doves are among the birds that seek cover in the dense dead stalks of grasses and wildflowers in winter. Wait until spring to burn or cut down herbaceous vegetation in your prairie patch, rain garden or native perennial bed.

Brush piles. Brush piles are especially valuable in

winter for additional shelter. Each autumn, as the vegetation dies back near our feeders and offers the birds less shelter, we construct a brush pile for the winter. It's truly amazing how much the birds love this feature. This year, chickadees were already exploring the base of the pile as my husband put on the final branches. In spring, we remove this brush to let the wildflowers blossom once again in that area.

You might want to do a bit of fall pruning on your shrubs for a supply of branches or use brush from the previous spring's pruning. Be sure to pile the brush loosely, leaving lots of nooks and crannies big enough for birds but too small for predators like cats, foxes or coyotes. After the holidays, your Christmas tree can make an attractive shelter next to your feeders. For details on how to build a brush pile, see chapter 5.

A place for roosting. In winter, birds roost in tree holes, as well as in dense vegetation and brush. In very cold weather, a dozen or more may crowd together in a single cavity to keep warm. The White-breasted Nuthatch, for example, usually sleeps alone in a tree cavity. But one winter evening, famed ornithologist Alexander Skutch saw 29 nuthatches arrive one by one and disappear into a crack in a dead pine.

If you don't have snags or old trees with cavities, birds may use your nest boxes. Although our yard has several tree cavities (perhaps used by other species), four Downy Woodpeckers peeked out from four different nest boxes in early morning last winter, as they woke from their night's slumber.

But nest boxes are not ideal for roosting birds. For one thing, they are usually too small for many birds to snuggle together in frigid weather. In addition, most birds perch or cling while roosting, and nest boxes lack perches.

Specially designed roosting boxes will keep birds warmer in winter. They are larger than most nest boxes and have perches inside. They lack ventilation holes, which helps keep the warm air inside, and have entrance holes near the bottom so rising warm air won't escape. Many small cavity-nesting birds, including nuthatches, titmice, chickadees, bluebirds and small woodpeckers, are likely to seek refuge in a roosting box. For more information on building a roosting box, see Resources for Readers at the end of this chapter.

Natural Foods

Insects and seeds, along with fruits, are the main natural foods of birds in winter. About half of our wintering birds feed

---

Owls: Most common are Eastern Screech-Owl and Great Horned Owl. Barred Owl is also fairly common. Snowy Owl, a northern owl, is seen some winters. Other owl species from Canada seen in northern tier.

Kingfisher: Belted Kingfisher, when open water is available.

Woodpeckers: Most common include Downy, Hairy, and Red-bellied Woodpeckers, and Northern Flicker.

Shrikes: Northern Shrike in the northern half of our area; the Loggerhead Shrike, more rarely, primarily in MO.

Jays, Crows & Ravens: Mainly Blue Jay and American Crow; Gray Jay and Raven in the far north.

Lark: Horned Lark

Chickadees & Titmice: Black-capped Chickadee to the north; Carolina Chickadee primarily in south; Boreal Chickadee at northern fringe. Tufted Titmouse throughout much of Midwest.

Nuthatches & Creeper: White-Breasted and Red-Breasted Nuthatches; Brown Creeper

Wrens: Carolina Wren and Winter Wren in southern half of the area.

Thrushes: Eastern Bluebird mainly south; American Robin, a few in most of the area.

Kinglets: Golden-Crowned Kinglet in most of area; Ruby-Crowned Kinglet to the south.

(continued)

---

primarily on insects, while fruits and seeds comprise the main menu for the rest.

Insects. The birds that eat mainly insects in winter include many of our familiar backyard birds—chickadees, creepers, kinglets, nuthatches, titmice and woodpeckers. These birds roam in mixed flocks through woodlands searching for hibernating insects in the bark of trees. Various insects spend the winter in different forms—as eggs, larvae, pupae or as dormant adults—and all provide excellent fare for wintering birds.

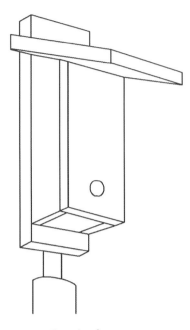

Roosting box

Woody plants furnish insect-laden tree trunks and branches for birds. Thus, the evergreens, deciduous trees and shrubs that you provide as a windbreaker can double as a food source in winter. Be sure to allow leaf litter to accumulate below your plants. It will insulate the ground and provide a warm blanket for the insects that ground-feeding birds prefer. Towhees and sparrows will scratch about in the leaves to uncover them.

The brush piles you provide for shelter will likewise create havens for beetles and spiders to entice wintering wrens. And don't forget the value of dead trees, called snags. They harbor an abundance of invertebrates—virtual avian sushi bars.

Some insects also spend the winter in the seedheads of wildflowers, like Black-eyed Susan and Evening Primrose. The dense heads of cattails are also warm winter hideaways for insects. A variety of herbaceous plants can add a source of insects for birds that prefer eating close to the ground.

Galls—growths on plants caused by insects that use them for shelter and food—are another source of insects for birds. Woodpeckers often dig into goldenrod galls, oak apples and other galls to snag the insects inside. (Ice fishermen sometimes use the larvae in goldenrod galls for bait.) Plant a variety of vegetation and you are more likely to attract these gall-forming insects.

Fruits. "Fruits are very important for overwintering birds," according to Christopher Whelan of the Illinois Natural

History Survey. Many birds that eat insects primarily in summer, including robins, mockingbirds, bluebirds and thrashers, turn to berries for a good part of their fall and winter diet, says Whelan. Even chickadees and titmice will eat some berries in winter.

Although most bird fruits ripen in late summer and fall, the fruits of some plants persist into winter and even spring, feeding both wintering birds and early spring migrants. One of the best evergreen trees for winter cover is Red Cedar, and it retains its fleshy pale blue berries as late as March. It is native to every state in the Midwest. Cedar Waxwings, as their name announces, devour the berries of the Red Cedar. Numerous other birds, including bluebirds, finches and grosbeaks, are also fond of its berries. Red Cedars are dioecious, that is, individual plants can be either male or female, so plant three or more cedars to increase the likelihood that some will be fruit-bearing females.

Among deciduous trees, Northern Hackberry—found throughout most of the Midwest—is an outstanding choice. Its purple-brown berries are often available until February and are eaten by nearly 50 species of birds. Cedar Waxwings will flock to the trees as long as the berries remain. Other wintering birds that feed on hackberries include bluebirds, cardinals, crows and titmice. The closely related Southern Hackberry, native to southern Missouri, Illinois and Indiana, is equally popular with birds.

Mountain ashes are beautiful trees with abundant fruit and are often recommended for winter birds, but their berries are frequently devoured well before winter arrives.

Hawthorns are smaller trees whose fruit persists into winter. A number of hawthorns do well in the Midwest, but the one that retains its berries the longest, into January, is the beautiful Cockspur Hawthorn. Its dense foliage and hooked thorns also provide safe nesting sites for summer birds. If you have small children who might run into the tree, a thornless variety is available.

A variety of shrubs have winter berries. The Common and Trailing Junipers are low-growing evergreen shrubs that offer food as well as cover for wintering birds. They retain their berries even longer than their tree-size cousin the Eastern Red Cedar, sometimes as late as April. Like Red Cedar, the shrub junipers are dioecious.

One of the loveliest of deciduous shrubs is Winterberry. It is very showy at Christmas, and its fruit lasts through late February. Winterberry shrubs are also dioecious.

Sumacs have attractive clusters of deep red berries. Four excellent midwestern species are Smooth Sumac, Staghorn Sumac,

BIRDS IN A FLOCK EAT DIFFERENT FARE

Birds often travel together in small flocks in winter. Although they feed together, the various species in these mixed flocks avoid competition by eating different insects, often based on the length and shape of their beaks. Even though several species of woodpeckers may "peck" on the same tree, for example, they harvest insects at different depths. The Downy Woodpecker feeds in shallow crevices with its short stubby bill, whereas the Hairy Woodpecker probes deeper with its longer, chisel-like bill.

Notice the different beaks of the other species in winter flocks. The Brown Creeper's curving sickle-like bill can probe in crevices which other species can't access. Kinglets sport short, tiny bills for the smallest of insects. Chickadees have small, stubby beaks, while those of titmice are a little longer. The Red-breasted Nuthatch has a shorter bill than its cousin, the White-breasted Nuthatch, which has a slim, up-turned bill. These variations allow each species to probe in different niches in tree bark.

White-breasted Nuthatch

Fragrant Sumac and Shining Sumac, all of which are dioecious. They provide nutritious winter fare for birds, although berries have little flesh. The sumacs also offer an added bonus for birds, since many insects use the berry clusters as a cover during the winter. As a result, birds often get both fat (berries) and protein (insects) in a single stop at one of these shrubs.

Native roses have bright red fruits called rose hips that last through late March. They are relished by bluebirds and mockingbirds, as well as upland game birds that visit yards in the more rural areas in the Midwest. These game birds include Ruffed Grouse, Ring-necked Pheasants and Bobwhites.

Snowberry and Coralberry have long-lasting berries that songbirds and game birds eat, but their fruit seems to be more popular with western birds than our midwestern species.

Chokeberry and some viburnums have berries that persist into the winter months. Black Chokeberry, native to wetlands, retains its berries through much of the winter; chickadees, waxwings and several other birds eat them. Berries of Maple-leaved Viburnum and Blackhaw Viburnum last into December. But the champions are Nannyberry Viburnum and American Cranberrybush Viburnum, whose fruits last into February. Avoid getting the nonnative, look-alike cousin to the latter, European Cranberrybush Viburnum.

Several native vines have attractive winter fruit for birds. Grape-like clusters of berries of Virginia Creeper often persist into February and are eaten by at least ten species of birds that winter in the Midwest. The beautiful orange and red fruit of American Bittersweet, which can last until Christmas, is decorative but somewhat less popular with birds. Be sure to avoid the invasive Asiatic Bittersweet.

Several vines in the genus *Smilax* are important sources of winter fruit for birds. Their dark blue clusters of berries can last into February in my area (southern Wisconsin). They are eaten extensively by cardinals, mockingbirds, catbirds and grouse. Carrion Flower, an herbaceous vine with smooth stems, and Bristly Cat Briar, a woody vine with spiny stems, are the two most common vines in this genus in the Midwest.

Poison ivy, although poisonous to us, is a premier wildlife plant, and ranks among the top ten species in our country. Its translucent white berries, which often persist into January, are eagerly sought by over 30 species of midwestern birds, as well as by many mammals, small and large. While I'm not suggesting that you deliberately plant poison ivy (it can cause severe skin rash and allergic reactions), consider leaving it if you happen to have it growing in an out-of-the-way corner of your yard. You'll be well rewarded with an avian hotspot that requires no work on your part.

Seeds. Seeds of trees, wildflowers and native grasses are the primary sources of food for many of our winter birds. Many of the same evergreens that you can plant for winter cover—pines, hemlocks and spruce—produce cones filled with nutritious seeds. These seeds are a favorite winter food of siskins, crossbills, chickadees and Pine Grosbeaks.

Pines are particularly valuable, ranked second only to oaks, as a source of food for wildlife. While oak acorns are primarily a fall food, pine seeds constitute a major winter food. Of all our winter birds, Red Crossbills are the top consumers of pine seeds which supply a full 50% of their diet.

Deciduous woody plants that provide seeds for winter birds in the Midwest include three species of birch, White Birch, Yellow Birch and Dwarf Birch, a shrub. All have seeds that often persist into winter and feed primarily redpolls during the season. Siskins, goldfinches, kinglets and chickadees also relish birch seeds. All three birch species are native to the Upper Midwest.

The Box Elder, often considered a weed tree, is nonetheless beloved by birds that flock to its seeds, which are often available until February. In southeastern Wisconsin, it is truly weedy, popping up all over. But I find it attractive and have kept several in my yard for diversity. It is found throughout most of the Midwest except in the northern tier.

A vine native to most of the Midwest that provides winter seed for birds is Moonseed. Songbirds and upland game birds devour its moon-shaped, blue-black seeds, which can persist into late December.

In addition to these woody plants, wildflowers and grasses are a major seed source for winter birds. Goldfinches and siskins will perch atop the stalks, acrobatically bending about to reach the seeds, while juncos eagerly harvest the fallen seeds. Other birds feeding on or near the ground include Mourning Doves and a variety of sparrows. Create a little (or large) prairie on your property and you'll provide a natural supply of these seeds. (See chapter 9, The Prairie Bird Garden.)

American Tree Sparrows are winter visitors that eat seeds of grasses and wildflowers.

Most important, don't deadhead or cut down your prairie plants in fall. Let them stand through the winter and you'll supply cover as well as seed for birds. The plants will also protect beneficial insects like butterflies that overwinter in, on or below such vegetation. Wait until spring, at the start of the new growth season, to mow (or burn) your herbaceous plants.

Water

Water is the third main feature to include, if possible, in your winter bird habitat. Birds really need it if neither open water nor snow is available. Southern Illinois photographer Susan Day had the pleasure of watching seven bluebirds using her birdbath daily during an icy winter. Other birds welcoming the water in her yard were titmice, Blue Jays, juncos, cardinals and mockingbirds.

The easiest way to provide water is to simply fill your bird bath regularly with warm water. I have friends who simply dump out the ice in their birdbath each morning and refill it with fresh water. But to keep the water from freezing, put a heater in your birdbath or use a birdbath with internal heating coils. Most models don't require much electricity and some are even solar heated.

Heated birdbaths can be placed on the ground or set atop pedestals. Some have clamps so you can attach them to porch or deck rails. We set our heated birdbath on a big tree stump. My husband hollowed out a depression on top of the stump just deep enough to hold the bath securely.

Heaters can also be used in ponds to keep the water open. In mild winter temperatures, you may be able to keep ice from forming with a recirculating pump or aerator.

We have a plastic birdbath with an internal heater that is very easy to clean—an important feature to look for in a birdbath. Birds often defecate in the water of a birdbath, contaminating it for other birds. To prevent disease from spreading, a birdbath should be scrubbed and rinsed at least every other day. In bitter weather, the faster you can clean the bath the better. I put on thick plastic gloves, toss out the dirty water, brush out the bath, rinse and refill with clean water—as quickly as I can in the cold. If you can't clean the birdbath frequently, it is best not to add it to your winter habitat.

Feeders

Bird feeders can supplement the foods produced by the native plants in your landscaping. See chapter 21 for details on setting up a feeding station in your yard.

Feeder food is particularly valuable in extremely cold weather, when snow covers the ground and in late winter when the supply of natural foods is diminishing. Research by wildlife ecologists Margaret Brittingham and Stanley Temple provide insights into the use of feeders by Black-capped Chickadees during different winter conditions. They kept track of 576 chickadees over three winters in Wisconsin, comparing those that lived near feeders and those that foraged entirely in the wild. The chickadees that visited feeders obtained only about 21% of their food from feeders, the rest in woods and fields. But these chickadees did not become dependent on the feeders. If people stopped feeding, the birds survived at the same rate as those that never visited the feeders.

However, it was a different story in severe weather. When temperatures plunged below 10 degrees F, chickadees that had access to feeders had double the survival rate of birds that foraged only in the wild.

Although we don't know a lot about the feeding habits of wintering birds, we do know that most wintering land birds congregate near feeders, and feeders in your habitat garden are likely to increase the survival of your visitors during the coldest weather.

The recent range expansion of several bird species, including the House Finch, Northern Cardinal, Tufted Titmouse, Red-bellied Woodpecker and Mourning Dove, is also thought to be related to supplemental feeding. Mourning Doves have even stopped migrating in a number of areas where bird feeders are plentiful in winter.

To help document trends like this, you can participate in Project FeederWatch, a winter-long survey of birds that visit feeders from November through early April. People throughout the country tally their feeder visitors to help scientists track the populations and movements of winter birds.

Another winter survey is the Great Backyard Bird Count, an annual four-day event that engages bird watchers of all levels in counting birds and recording their results to provide a mid-winter snapshot of the numbers and species of birds across the continent. The longest-running survey of wintering birds is the Christmas Bird Count, which began in 1900. This all-day count provides information on early-winter bird populations across America. For both counts, participants can simply watch their backyard feeders and submit the data, although other areas can also be surveyed. (See Resources for Readers at the end of this chapter for more information on these two counts, as well as Project FeederWatch.)

So sit back and keep a tally of your backyard birds, as you sip on a cup of shade-grown coffee.* By providing an inviting natural habitat, in addition to well-stocked feeders, you'll be able to attract the greatest possible variety of birds to your yard, adding to your pleasure all winter long.

Shade-grown coffee plantations support over 90% more species of birds than do the newer sun-grown coffee plantations. Shade-grown coffee is available through the internet and at specialty stores and many grocery stores.

NATURAL FOODS OF SOME NATIVE WINTERING LAND BIRDS

Northern Bobwhite	Seeds—95% of diet
Northern Cardinal	Seeds of trees & berries
Black-capped, Carolina & Boreal Chickadees	Insects eggs, pupae & larvae plus spiders in bark, seeds of conifers, also berries
Brown Creeper	Insect eggs and pupae under bark—nearly 100% of diet
Red & White-Winged Crossbills	Seeds of conifers primarily; also other seeds & insects
American Crow	Seeds of wildflowers & native grasses, berries, carrion
Mourning Dove	Seeds of wildflowers & native grasses, berries
House & Purple Finches	Seeds of wildflowers primarily; also tree buds & berries
American Goldfinch	Seeds of wildflowers & native grasses
Evening Grosbeak	Seeds of trees primarily; also some berries
Pine Grosbeak	Seeds of trees, esp. pines, & wildflowers; also berries
Ruffed Grouse	Tree buds, nuts, leaves
Spruce Grouse	Buds of spruces, pines, firs
Hawks	Voles—75–95% of diet; also mice, larger mammals & birds
Blue Jay	Acorns & other nuts, berries, insects
Gray Jay	Rodents, berries, insects
Dark-eyed Junco	Seeds on ground, primarily wildflower & grass seeds
Ruby-Crowned & Golden-Crowned Kinglets	Insect eggs & spiders
Horned Larks	Native grass & wildflower seeds
Northern Mockingbird	Berries
White-breasted Nuthatch	Nuts, acorns, insects
Red-breasted Nuthatch	Insects, seeds of conifers
Owls	Rodents, primarily. Larger owls will eat larger mammals (rabbits, skunks, squirrels), occasionally small birds
Common & Hoary Redpolls	Birch seeds primarily; also shrub, wildflower & grass seeds
Pine Siskins	Seeds of trees, esp. conifers, wildflowers and grass
Sparrows	Seeds of native grasses & wildflowers; some eat berries
Tufted Titmouse	Nuts, berries, wintering insects
Bohemian & Cedar Waxwings	Berries
Woodpeckers	Insects under tree bark primarily

The Winter Bird Garden

See the tables in part 5 for the native ranges and cultural requirements of the species listed below.

Conifers
Trees for Cover & Seeds
White Cedar, *Thuja occidentalis*
Balsam Fir, *Abies balsamea*
Hemlock, *Tsuga canadensis*
Jack Pine, *Pinus banksiana*
Red Pine, *Pinus resinosa*
White Pine, *Pinus strobus*
Tamarack or American Larch,
    Larix laricina
White Spruce, *Picea glauca*

Trees for Cover & Berries
Red Cedar, *Juniperus virginiana*

Shrubs for Cover & Berries
Common Juniper, *Juniperus communis*
Trailing Juniper, *Juniperus horizontalis*

Deciduous Trees
Trees For Berries
American Mountain Ash, *Sorbus americana*
Showy Mountain Ash, *Sorbus decora*
Northern Hackberry, *Celtis occidentalis*
Southern Hackberry, *Celtis laevigata*
Cockspur Hawthorn, *Crataegus crusgalli*
Washington Hawthorn, *Crataegus phaenopyrum*

Trees for Seeds
Box Elder, *Acer negundo*
Paper Birch, *Betula papyrifera*
Yellow Birch, *Betula alleghaniensis (B. lutea)*

Deciduous Shrubs
Shrubs for Berries
Black Chokeberry, *Aronia melanocarpa (A. prunifolia)*
Coralberry, *Symphoricarpos orbiculatus*
Early Wild or Smooth Rose, *Rosa blanda*
Sunshine Rose, *Rosa arkansana*
Swamp Rose, *Rosa palustris*
Pasture Rose, *Rosa carolina*
Snowberry, *Symphoricarpos albus*

Shining or Winged Sumac, *Rhus copallina*
Fragrant Sumac, *Rhus aromatica*
Smooth Sumac, *Rhus glabra*
Staghorn Sumac, *Rhus hirta (R. typhina)*
American Cranberrybush Viburnum
    Viburnum opulus var. *americanum*
    (Viburnum trilobum) (Avoid the nonnative species, European Cranberrybush Viburnum, *V. opulus* var. *opulus*. Birds are much less fond of the berries.)
Blackhaw Viburnum, *Viburnum prunifolium*
Maple-leaved Viburnum, *Viburnum acerifolium*
Nannyberry Viburnum, *Viburnum lentago*
Winterberry or Michigan Holly, *Ilex verticillata*

Shrub for Seeds
Dwarf Birch, *Betula pumila*

Vines for Berries
American Bittersweet, *Celastrus scandens* (Don't plant the related invasive species, Oriental Bittersweet, *Celastrus orbiculatus*.)
Bristly Cat Briar or Bristly Green Briar, *Smilax hispida (S. tamnoides)*
Carrion Flower, *Smilax herbacea*
Virginia Creeper, *Parthenocissus quinquefolia*
Poison Ivy, *Toxicodendron radicans (Rhus radicans)* (**CAUTION**: Poison ivy can cause severe skin rash and allergic reactions.)

Vine for Seeds
Moonseed, *Menispermum canadense*

Herbaceous Plants for Food & Cover
See the herbaceous plant list for the Prairie Bird Garden.

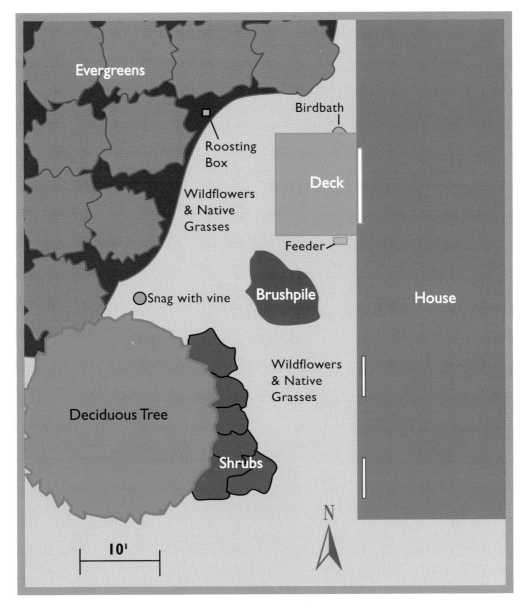

Winter Bird Garden

This garden provides all the essentials for wintering birds—cover, natural foods and water. Use the list of plants for your winter bird garden to choose species of evergreens, deciduous trees, vines, shrubs, wildflowers and grasses suited to the conditions in your yard. The evergreens will shelter the birds (and your home) from cold northwest winds. Plant them relatively close together (about 8–12 feet apart) to create a dense mass in their maturity. One of the smaller deciduous trees, such as a hawthorn or mountain ash, is appropriate for the space in this plan. Place woodchips under your trees and shrubs and allow leaf litter to accumulate. This natural mulch will speed the growth of your woody plants and create a haven for insects to nourish ground-feeding birds. The birdbath clamps to the rail of the deck, making it easy to maintain in winter. Place the bird feeder within a few feet of the house to lessen the chances of birds colliding with your windows.

Resources for Readers

Websites

BirdSource. www.birdsource.org/
Information on feeders, seed, identifying birds, Project FeederWatch, the Great
Backyard Bird Count and the Christmas Bird Count.

Cornell Lab of Ornithology. http://www.birds.cornell.edu/
Information on Project FeederWatch, the Great Backyard Bird Count and the
Christmas Count; on roosting boxes and landscaping for birds.

National Bird-Feeding Society. www.birdfeeding.org/
Information on all aspects of bird feeding.

Also see the resources on feeding at the end of chapter 21.

Frosted milkweed pods

CHAPTER 16
BIRDBATHS & WATER GARDENS

I woke the kids. I called my wife out of the shower. It was a Saturday morning and I discovered a Great Blue Heron by the pond in our yard!

—Mike Sands, Prairie Crossing, Grayslake, Illinois

Our little pond has changed our lives. It has added a living tapestry of motion, sound and color, an oasis of serenity and beauty to which we and the birds are attracted. More species of birds than we ever dreamed of have dropped by for a drink and a bath.

—Anne and Patrick Moretti, Dousman, Wisconsin

Whether it's a birdbath, pond, stream, waterfall, dripper or mister, the sight and sound of water is an irresistible magnet for birds. Since all birds require water for drinking and most need it for bathing, the variety of birds you can attract is limited mainly by the mix of species that live or travel in your neighborhood.

While water is a necessity for all, various species differ in the amount they need. Some, like raptors, get most of their liquids from the prey they eat. Likewise, many insect-eating birds get most of their water from juicy insect prey. Fruit-eating birds get some of their liquids from the berries they eat. Other birds get up to 80% of their fluids metabolically, through internal chemical processes, and need little additional water. Some seed-eating desert birds can go for months without drinking. But many other birds, especially those whose diet consists mainly of dry seeds, like finches and sparrows, need water.

Birds also vary in the way they drink. Most dip their beaks in the water and then lift their heads to the sky, letting the water flow down their throats. A few, like pigeons and doves, drink without lifting their heads by sucking up water through their beaks. Resourceful pelicans sometimes lift their huge beaks to catch rain, while many small species drink from dewdrops.

Birds bathe to clean their feathers, remove parasites and reduce itching. Most birds wade into shallow water, immerse their heads in water, then raise their heads and begin to splash in the water with their wings. At my home, the Tufted Titmouse simply dunks its head and breast, rather than indulging in a full bath. Some vireos and warblers prefer to bathe by skimming the water surface with their bellies several times in succession. Cedar Waxwings come in flocks to feed and bathe. Other species, like Northern Cardinal and Scarlet Tanager, prefer bathing alone. No matter what their style of bathing, birds usually alight on a nearby branch to preen their feathers afterward.

photo: Bathing Cardinal

Great Blue Heron, a handsome pond visitor.

Water features of any size in your yard can tempt birds to come to drink and bathe. Small yards can offer birdbaths and little pools. Larger yards in suburban and rural areas can accommodate ponds designed to be either permanent or ephemeral. This chapter will focus mainly on birdbaths and small ponds, although larger-scale ponds will be discussed briefly at the end of the chapter.

Birdbaths

Birdbaths, basically artificial puddles, are extremely appealing to birds and can fit into the tiniest yard or even on a porch or patio. They are far less expensive to maintain than bird feeders and will attract a wider variety of birds.

Styles

Birdbaths come in a great many styles—dish-shaped baths placed on the ground or deck, hanging baths, baths with suction cups that attach to windows and baths hollowed from rocks. The most popular style is a bath on a pedestal.

With a little creativity, you can easily make your own birdbath from saucers and dishes of any kind. Some people use a garbage can lid, burying the handle and rim so the top edge is flush with the soil. Others prefer to place the lid above ground on brick supports, so it's easier to clean. People also use rocks with natural depressions as birdbaths. I've placed the orange saucer from a large potted plant on an old stump next to bright orange Turk's Cap Lilies and ferns—a very harmonious effect.

The materials from which birdbaths are constructed are as varied as their styles. Those made of concrete withstand freezing better than those from terra cotta, ceramic or cement (unreinforced concrete). Wooden ones are attractive and popular with birds but difficult to clean. Even birdbaths of long-lasting woods like cedar and redwood deteriorate faster than those of other materials. Plastic and metal baths last indefinitely, but their smooth surfaces are slippery for birds. Metal baths of stainless steel or painted with rust-resistant paint could be used, but the paint will eventually chip and require repainting.

Whatever style birdbath you choose, here are a few additional points to keep in mind:

• A good width for a birdbath ranges from 12 to 36 inches. Narrower ones are generally too small for birds. Baths 12 to 18 inches wide are typically used by only one bird at a time. The wider ones can accommodate group bathing.

• Make sure the basin is not too deep. Many birds require very shallow water for bathing. Ideally, create several depths, 1/2 inch deep in some places to 2 inches deep in others, to accommodate birds of different sizes. Birdbaths that slope gradually to a deeper middle will naturally offer different depths. If not, an easy way to create different depths is to place a few flat rocks in the bath for the smaller species.

• The basin of the birdbath should have a rough texture so birds have secure footing. Algae-covered bottoms are too slippery for birds. If your basin lacks texture, you may be able to roughen the surface with coarse sandpaper or use a textured mat like those for bathtubs. Adding pebbles or rocks may also help.

• If you get the typical birdbath on a pedestal, make sure the basin is sturdy and can't be easily tipped by raccoons and other animals, or even worse, by children who could be seriously hurt if a heavy basin falls over on them. A one-piece birdbath could reduce the chances of its being tipped over. If you already have a two-piece birdbath, you could secure the basin to the pedestal with waterproof adhesive.

• Locate the birdbath near a shrub or small tree where the birds can perch before and after their baths to check for predators or fly to if danger arises. Birds with wet feathers can't fly well and are very vulnerable to lurking cats. A nearby perch also gives birds a chance to dry off and preen their feathers, typically done after bathing. Most birds prefer perches and dense cover about 15 feet away, but some forest birds, such as thrushes, like baths nestled close to dense vegetation. Baths in dense vegetation should be raised above ground to lessen the chances of cat attacks.

• Thoroughly scrub and refill your birdbath every few days, more often if it becomes visibly dirty. A stiff wire brush is a good tool. This will ensure fresh clean water for your birds and help prevent mosquito larvae from maturing, since the insects require only several days of standing water to mature.

• Movement of water also helps to keep mosquitoes from breeding. Drippers, misters and battery-operated water vibrators will keep the water moving in your birdbath or pond.

• If you have room for several baths and time to keep all of them clean, try to locate them at different heights: ground level, six inches above ground and the more typical two to three feet high. This gives more opportunities to birds, some of whom have distinct preferences for the height of baths and other habitat features. Place your birdbaths in different locations around your yard to benefit birds throughout your property.

• In winter, you may need to heat the water to keep it from freezing. Some people simply refill the birdbath with warm water on a daily basis in subzero temperatures. For more on winter birdbaths, see chapter 15, The Winter Bird Garden.

Drippers and Misters

By adding the sound of dripping water to your birdbath, you can greatly increase its attraction to birds. The attraction is so universal among birds that bird-banders often entice birds to their nets with dripping water.

Years ago we were amazed at the upsurge in visitors to our birdbath after we installed a dripper. It hooks onto the edge of the birdbath, and it came with thin tubing long enough to extend to our outdoor water spigot, plus a valve to control the rate of flow. The kit included a two-way adapter so we could easily use our regular hose without disconnecting the dripper. It uses about a gallon of water per hour. You can take advantage of the water that drips over the edge of the birdbath by planting moisture-loving plants at its base. Some birdbaths come with built-in drippers or fountains.

You can make a simple, low-cost dripper from a plastic gallon jug. Cut a very tiny hole in the bottom of the jug to drip water and a larger one at the top to vent air. Fill the jug with water and hang it above your birdbath from an overhanging branch or a shepherd's crook (like those used to hang plants or bird feeders). For an even simpler dripper, hang a hose from a branch above your birdbath and turn it on just enough so it drips slowly. The birds will appreciate these low tech drippers as much as any purchased one.

Drippers of any kind should be adjusted so that they create a gentle audible splash in the water, which is just what birds like. Great gushes and cascades of water will only scare off the very birds you want to attract.

Misters will also draw in birds and are often hung on a branch near or overhanging a birdbath or pond. A hose with a nozzle set on the mist spray can serve as a makeshift mister. Soaker hoses that spray mists of water can also be used. Hummingbirds and warblers are particularly attracted to mists and fly through them, preferring a shower to a bath. Songbirds like goldfinches, chickadees and nuthatches enjoy drinking droplets of water on the misted leaves.

A Ruby-crowned Kinglet enjoys a mister.

You can put your mister on a timer and set it to turn on when you are able to watch the action. Ann and Patrick Moretti of Wisconsin set theirs for lunch and dinner. Like other backyard bird-watchers with misters, they discovered that the birds learned to anticipate the treat.

Water Gardens

Water gardens used to be called simply ponds or pools. Whatever their name, birds love them and will show their appreciation by visiting more often and in greater numbers. As one Wisconsin pond owner says, "For birds, a pond is like a jacuzzi."

Water gardens can be as simple or complex as you like. A mini-water garden in a tub may be the ideal choice for a tiny yard, for a deck or for homes where young children may cause you to put your pond plans on hold. Small yards can also be enhanced by creating shallow, ground-level basins without extra "amenities"—basically artificial puddles. Larger yards can accommodate bigger ponds, which may include waterfalls, cascades or even associated streams and wetlands.

Tub Gardens

A half-barrel has been the traditional container for a tub garden, but similar-sized, less expensive plastic or terra cotta containers can be purchased at most garden centers. Tub kits are also available.

Barrels with drain holes and terra cotta containers must be made water-tight. The drain holes on barrels can be sealed with aquarium caulking. Premolded liners, readily available at water garden nurseries, could be used instead. Terra cotta containers will similarly require either a liner or a sealant, such as a concrete sealer or a urethane spray.

If the barrel has no drainage holes, you can use it directly with proper preparations. Garden consultant Judy Glattstein advises scrubbing the interior of the barrel thoroughly with a stiff brush and water, rinsing three or four times. Since water is heavy, place the barrel on a strong level spot before filling. The staves of the barrel will swell and become water-tight. Siphon the water out with a hose, fill once more and you're ready to plant.

To create varying depths on which to set your plants, you can use flat stones, sturdy plastic pails or plastic-coated shelf units found in office supply stores. Then arrange water lilies or emergent plants in your small tub garden. If the growth of algae becomes a problem, the addition of submerged plants should help.

Keep the water level close to the rim so birds can drink from the edge of the barrel, or provide a branch for them to perch on. To entice birds even more, consider adding a small spouting ornament, which will require a small submersible pump.

Ground-level Basins

Half-barrels can be set in the ground, but their staves will rot in just a few years. Easier and more long-lasting are shallow depressions dug in the soil and lined as you would a larger pond. The effect is a very natural-looking "mud puddle," just the kind to which birds typically flock to drink and bathe.

Bird photographer Gay Bumgarner made her miniature pool by digging a depression 3 inches deep and 24 inches in diameter and lining it with heavy black plastic. Suitable liners 3 to 6 mils thick are readily available at nursery or hardware stores. Several layers of black garbage bags would also work. Gay let the liner overlap the hole by at least 4 inches and cut off the excess. She placed natural, local rocks over the plastic overlap and inner edges of the pool to keep it in place. Then Gay added flat rocks, stones or gravel on the bottom to create depths of a fraction of an inch to one inch in order to accommodate the preferences of different species of birds. Her "puddle" has attracted a host of birds, including Baltimore Orioles and warblers like Yellow-breasted Chats and Common Yellowthroats, plus butterflies, dragonflies, frogs, toads, turtles, lizards, opossums and rabbits.

Ponds

Backyard ponds can be small or large, simple or elaborate. The most important feature needed to attract songbirds is a shallow area for them to drink and bathe. You can provide such an area at the edge of the pond or with a shallow basin below a waterfall or a fountain. Mallards and other waterfowl may be attracted initially by the water itself, but natural foods like plants and invertebrates in the water will keep them around. The Great Blue Heron discovered by Mike Sands, mentioned at the beginning of this chapter, was probably hunting for the tadpoles and frogs in his pond. In essence, your pond will be much more than a water-filled hole in the ground. It will be an artificially created ecosystem of plants, birds and other animals that mimics a natural pond.

Mallards take turns sitting in this little pond at the home of Nancy and Tom Small in Michigan.

A Mini-Wetland & Pond Combo in Kalamazoo

Tom and Nancy Small, whose landscaping is featured in chapter 4, created a mini-wetland bordered by a small pond in their yard. They used a similar approach in both constructions. The Smalls dug a hole to the desired depth and then used a liner in each of the depressions. For the wetland, the liner was punctured with some very small holes for slow drainage, but the pond liner was left intact.

The depth in the wetland ranges from a few inches at some of its margins to two feet, providing a variety of moisture conditions for the numerous sedges, rushes and wildflowers now thriving there. In the course of digging, Tom discovered that "the original topsoil was very thin, giving way to sandy glacial outwash." To improve this soil for the wetland plants, the couple mixed compost into the soil before adding it back into the lined depression.

There were no natural drainage patterns or depressions in the yard, so they chose the site for the wetland because it was one of the few sunny areas. The Smalls wanted to create a rain garden rather than a wetland, but constructing an artificial drainage way would have damaged tree roots and a sidewalk.

Many of the native plants in the mini-wetland were welcomed by their resident birds. Hummingbirds nectar at the Cardinal Flower, while finches, chickadees, wrens, blackbirds, titmice and others feed on the seeds of other forbs.

The little pond they constructed is not much more than a foot in diameter and its bottom is lined with stones among which wetland sedges are rooted. Blackbirds, robins and crows come to drink in this inviting little water garden and Mallards take turns sitting in the pond in spring.

Where to put your pond. Locate your pond so that you can see it from your deck, patio or windows. Blend it in with the other native habitats you've created. In my yard, a hummingbird garden surrounds the pond, both of which are in full view from my kitchen windows.

Most experts recommend placing a pool in a sunny area, since water plants, especially water lilies, flower best with six to eight hours of sun each day. Ponds under trees can be more difficult to construct. If you damage the tree roots, you may weaken or kill the trees. Such ponds also require more upkeep, since twigs and leaves are apt to fall in. Despite these drawbacks for the homeowner, many birds prefer the more intimate surroundings of a pond set within a woodland. The Morettis, quoted at the beginning of this chapter, built their pond in the midst of their wooded yard and have attracted 68 species of birds, including hummingbirds, woodpeckers, vireos, warblers, thrushes, finches and sparrows.

If you plan to use a pump for a waterfall, filter or fountain, be sure you have a safe source of electricity. Never use an extension cord. Have a qualified electrician put in a waterproof electrical outlet with a protective cover and ground-fault interrupter close to your pond. The outlet should be supplied by an underground conduit which is safely buried.

Ponds may also be regulated in your community. Check with your local officials; often ponds deeper than 18 to 24 inches require a fence. Such fencing can provide good perches for the birds that visit your pond. But don't despair, if you prefer not to fence in your pond. Helen Nash, who has written several books on water gardens, says it is possible to create a beautiful pond only 18 inches deep that can winter successfully in cold climates.

Although it may seem counter-intuitive, don't place your pond in a wet spot. Groundwater can push up a pond liner. To determine if this might be a problem, dig a hole at the pond site and watch through the spring, usually our wettest season. If water collects in the hole, you'll have to provide drainage away from the site.

Also, to avoid a flooded foundation or basement, make sure any drainage from the pond (such as during heavy rains) flows away from your house. It's also best to elevate the edges of the pond so that surface water doesn't flow into it (the opposite of a rain garden), bringing in dirt and debris.

Pond liners. Liners are rigid or flexible, and experts disagree about which is easier to use. Rigid liners are preformed pools. They can be rectangular, round, kidney shaped and a variety of other designs, some of which may have built-in shelves and waterfalls. Generally they are small, ranging from 11 to 17 inches deep, and hold from 65 to 550 gallons.

Flexible liners can be used for any size pond and allow you to design your pond any shape and size you want. My husband and I chose a flexible liner when we built our pond, and we think it's the easiest method for do-it-yourselfers like us. Flexible liners must be nontoxic and fish-grade. Be sure not to use swimming pool liners, which contain anti-algae chemicals harmful to plants and fish.

Liners of polyvinyl chloride (PVC) or laminated plastics are less expensive than synthetic rubber EPDM. EPDM, however, is longer-wearing, thicker and more resistant to UV degradation. If you want your pond to last for years, check the guarantees and go with the thickest and strongest liner you can find. Liners come in a variety of widths and lengths, but if your pond is large, you may have to piece together several sections, using special tape designed for the purpose.

To determine the size of the liner to buy, wait until you design and dig out your pond. Then measure its greatest depth, length and width. Add the maximum depth to both the length and

Leslie Cumming's pond in Wheaton, Illinois, is surrounded with prairie forbs and grasses.

width of your pond. Also, add an extra foot or two to the length and width, depending on how much overlap you want around the edge of your pond. This will give you the full length and width of liner you'll need.

Design and installation. If you go with a preformed pool liner, lay it on the ground and trace around it with a shovel. Dig a hole deep enough to allow about four inches of sand to be laid at the bottom to cushion the pond. Set the liner in the hole so it is at or slightly above grade. If it's too low, debris will wash in. Check to make sure the pond is level by using a carpenter's level supported on a board spanning the pond. Check the level both lengthwise and crosswise. Then begin to fill with water, and backfill with dirt around the sides so you get a snug fit. Iowa pond owner Kevin Clasing, whose landscaping is featured in chapter 4, found that sand packs in better than fill dirt. The liner edges can be concealed with rocks, logs or plants.

If you're using a flexible liner, start by laying out a hose or rope to create the shape and size pond you'd like. We chose to make a small pond about six feet by four feet. Once we were satisfied with the location and design, we called an electrician to put an outlet nearby, since we planned to get a pump for the waterfalls we wanted to create.

When that was completed, my husband began to dig the depression. Our pond is very shallow, averaging about one foot, with a deeper two-foot hole for the pump. But a slightly deeper pond averaging two to three feet is often recommended since it will allow a greater diversity of plants and fish. Don't forget to create an overflow depression to direct excess water away from your house. You can use the excavated soil to landscape around the pond, which can raise the level of the surrounding ground and result in less digging.

It's a good idea, especially in deeper ponds, to create shelves to hold your potted water plants. Many emergent plants, like arrowhead, iris and Sweet Flag, grow in 2 to 6 inches of water. Water lilies prefer slightly deeper water, with their crowns 6 to 12 inches below the surface.

Just as with preformed pools, it's important to level the top edge of the pond. Next, prepare the bottom surface by removing rocks and protruding roots. A one- or two-inch layer of sand, old carpeting or even a thick layer of newspaper on the bottom will prevent punctures in the liner. You may be able to skip this step, as we did, by making sure the surface is very smooth.

Now you're ready for the liner. If possible, lay it in a sunny spot for about 30 minutes to heat and soften it. Then spread the liner over the hole, centering it so there is enough overlap on all sides. Put a few rocks on the edges to hold it in place while you begin to fill the pond. When the pond is nearly full, remove the rocks and allow the liner to conform to the shape of the hole. An easy way to smooth out the wrinkles in the liner is to walk on it with bare feet. If you have chlorinated water, let your pond sit for several days so the chlorine dissipates, before putting in your plants and fish.

Complete your pond by covering the overlapping liner with flat-bottomed rocks. My husband has always disliked ponds where the edge of the liner is visible around the periphery and came up with his own method of minimizing this problem. He allowed for an extra amount of liner overlap, about 18 to 24 inches in all, and placed a layer of rocks over the liner all around the edge. He then wrapped the rest of the liner around and on top of these rocks, securing it with a second layer of rocks. Thus, the water can come up to the top edge of the bottom rocks, which helps to hide the liner without having a big and sometimes unsafe rock overhang. He concealed the fold of liner around the bottom rocks with another set of rocks. As a result, our pond is encircled by a double layer of rocks, with a single circle of rocks to the outside. The tiered effect looks quite natural and is also sturdy and safe for walking and kneeling when we're working with plants or cleaning the pond.

We also used rocks to build our waterfall. At a local quarry, we found a large limestone rock for the base of the waterfall and had it chiseled out to create a shallow basin. It serves the birds as a shallow "puddle" for bathing and drinking.

A small pump with a built-in filter, set in the deepest spot in our pond, circulates the water over the falls. A larger pond usually requires a separate pump and filter. Be sure to get a pump that is the proper size for the volume of water flow for your falls or fountain.

Unless you want to move water over falls or cascades, you can have a perfectly lovely pond without a pump. Mandy Ploch, a landscaper designer in Wisconsin, constructed two such ponds (8 by 10 feet and 12 by 16 feet) in her backyard. Both were dug to a depth of 1 foot. Then she installed a liner and returned six inches of soil over the liner. She needs no pump; the organisms in the soil keep the ponds clean. For mosquito control, she adds a few minnows from a bait shop each year. Goldfish can't be

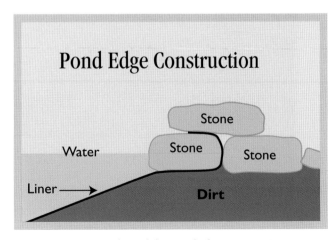

Dave Nowak used this pond edge construction method to hide the liner.

used in this kind of pond, since they'll root in the bottom and muddy the water. Mandy planted native aquatic plants in the muck. Her only maintenance involves raking off Hair Algae during warm spells and topping off the ponds with the hose during droughts.

Mandy and her husband have enjoyed the ponds immeasurably. "The best part," she says, "is watching the life in these small universes." Like Mike Sands's pond, her ponds attract Great Blue Herons occasionally as well as other birds, frogs, dragonflies and cherry-red mites. And she's found that her minnows are prolific.

Additional possibilities. Many other designs and elaborations can enhance your pond and increase its appeal to birds. The pond in Mike Sands's yard is adjacent to his rain garden, which consists of a small sedge meadow and swale. He estimates that the entire area for both pond and rain garden totals about 2,000 square feet. This arrangement mimics natural systems where ponds and lakes are bordered by wetlands and heightens the attraction of birds to his yard.

The Morettis purchased a three-tier cascade kit, which included a pump, a 5-by-6-foot liner, three preformed cascade sections, tubing, a waterfall rock and clear instructions. Using the kit, they constructed a natural-looking stream and small pond on the wooded slope at the back of their house within easy viewing. Water flows over the waterfall rock and cascades down the slope through three shallow pools, set one below the other, and then tumbles into a deeper pool that holds the pump and aquatic plants. "Since there is no nearby water source, the sound of running water acts as a magnet," say the Morettis. Among the many birds they've seen at Sylvan Cascades, as they call it, they particularly enjoyed the 23 species of warblers, including a rare Worm-eating Warbler, that have dropped in for a visit.

An old swimming pool was used as the basis for this lovely water garden at the home of Delene Hanson and Tom Ueberroth in Wisconsin.

Mosquito control. Just as with birdbaths, mosquito control is essential, particularly with the advent of West Nile disease, which has caused deaths of both birds and humans. In our pond, frogs came to the rescue. During the first few weeks after setting up our pond, we worried about the mosquito larvae we saw. Apparently our little waterfalls did not create enough water disturbance to keep them from breeding. Frogs, however, arrived within a week or two, and the mosquito larvae disappeared shortly. Fish, like Mandy's minnows, will also eat mosquito larvae and can be added to your pond, if frogs fail to show up. Other pond owners have used native fish, like bluegills and sunfish, which are particularly appropriate for native plant water gardens.

Although biscuit-like dunks containing Bt (Bacillus thuringiensis) will kill mosquito larvae in your pond, they will also kill the larvae of many beneficial insects. Leslie Jones Sauer, a landscape architect and adjunct professor at the University of Pennsylvania, warns that, although touted as safe and selective, Bt harms an entire order of insects, the Diptera. "In turn," she says, "it affects dragonflies and other predators and important pollinators such as craneflies, as well as many fish, bats, and insect-eating birds, including swallows, swifts, flycatchers, and hummingbirds."

Plants

Whether you have a tub garden or pond, aquatic plants are a beautiful addition to your water garden and offer food and habitat for birds. A healthy mix of plants is also important for maintaining a well-balanced ecosystem.

The three types. There are three groups of aquatic plants, each of which fulfills an important role in your water garden. For most people, water lilies are the quintessential water garden plants. They are more than just pretty blossoms, however. Like other floating plants, water lilies and their floating leaves shade the water, which discourages the growth of green algae. While water lilies and most other floating plants have roots, a few, like duckweed, are free floating.

Emergent or marginal plants are those whose roots are in the soil below water level, but their stems, leaves and flowers emerge (hence the name) above water. Plants like arrowhead, bulrush and iris are emergent plants. They also help shade the pond and sometimes take up nutrients in the water.

Most important of all are the submerged plants, which grow fully under water (although their flowers usually float to or on the surface). Although rooted in the soil from which they get some nourishment, most of their nutrients are absorbed directly from the water by their leaves. They also remove carbon dioxide, add oxygen and provide mats where fish can lay eggs and their young can hide. One of the best submerged plants for water gardens is the native Common Waterweed, which greens up early in the season in time to keep algae blooms from occurring. Experts suggest one bunch of submerged plants per square foot of water surface in your pond, particularly if you have fish.

It is generally recommended that plants should cover 50 to 70% of your pond surface to help maintain clean water. But this doesn't mean that the water needs to be crystal clear. As long as you can see your hand under five or six inches of water, you're doing fine. As pond expert Carol Franklin says, "Healthy water in a balanced-life pool is like good beer—clear, pale brown and well aged." She also advises adding a gallon of water from a natural pond to inoculate your water with bacteria, microscopic plants and insects, all of which will add biological complexity and help keep your water clean. Mulm, a dark organic layer, forms naturally on the bottom of ponds and is no problem as long as it's less than an inch or so thick.

BIRD-FRIENDLY PLANTS FOR YOUR POND

These plants are commonly available at nurseries. Check the tables on pages 240–242 for information on the cultural requirement and native ranges of these plants.

EMERGENT PLANTS

	Value for Birds
Common Arrowhead, *Sagittaria latifolia*	Wonderful waterfowl habitat & food (seeds & tubers)
Arrow Arum, *Peltandra virginica*	Berries relished by Wood Ducks & occasionally eaten by other birds
Wild Arum, *Calla palustris*	Berries
Common Bur Reed, *Sparganium eurycarpum*	Waterfowl & marsh birds eat the seeds in the bur-like seedheads; nesting cover for ducks & marsh birds
Soft Stem or Great Bulrush, *Scirpus validus*	Waterfowl habitat, nesting sites & food (seeds, stems, rootstocks)
Cardinal Flower, *Lobelia cardinalis*	Nectar for hummingbirds/orioles
Sweet Flag, *Acorus calamus*	Seeds, for waterfowl, esp. Wood Ducks; feeding cover & nesting sites for waterfowl, shorebirds
Fowl Manna Grass, *Glyceria striata*	Good food & cover for waterfowl, esp. Wood Ducks
Horsetail, *Equisetum fluviatile*	Food for geese, Ruffed Grouse, Trumpeter Swans
Northern Blue Flag Iris, *Iris versicolor*	Nectar for hummingbirds; seeds for waterfowl; cover for marsh birds
Southern Blue Flag Iris, *Iris virginica*	Same as above
Swamp Rose Mallow, *Hibiscus moscheutos* (*H. palustris*)	Nectar for hummingbirds
Marsh Marigold, *Caltha palustris*	Seeds for upland game birds
Pickerel Weed, *Pontederia cordata*	Seeds for waterfowl, esp. Wood & Am. Black Ducks
Common Water Plantain, *Alisma subcordatum, A. plantago-aquatica* var. *parviflorum*	Waterfowl eat tubers and nutlets; nutlets also eaten by pheasants; stalk is perch for song birds
Large-flowered Water Plantain *Alisma triviale; A. plantago-aquatica* var. *americanum*	Same as above
Needle Spike Rush, *Eleocharis ovata* (*E. obtusa*); *E. acicularis*	Waterfowl eat rhizomes & seeds; seeds also eaten by rails & shorebirds
Common or Soft Rush, *Juncus effusus*	Seeds for waterfowl, gamebirds, marsh birds, & songbirds; nesting habitat for rails, ducks
Bristly or Bottlebrush Sedge, *Carex comosa*	Cover for ducks; achenes eaten by wetland birds, waterfowl, cardinals & sparrows

FREE–FLOATING PLANTS

	Value for Birds
Small Duckweed, *Lemna minor*	Very nutritious—provides up to 90% of dietary needs of waterfowl; mats inhibit mosquito breeding.
Great Duckweed, *Spirodela polyrhiza*	Good food for waterfowl
Watermeal, *Wolffia* species	Good food for waterfowl, including scaup & Mallards

Floating-Leaf Plants

White Water Lily, *Nymphaea odorata*	Seeds eaten by waterfowl
Yellow Pond Lily or Spadderdock *Nuphar advena; N. variegata*	Seeds eaten by waterfowl
Lotus, *Nelumbo lutea*	Cover; acorn-like fruit eaten by variety of waterfowl
Water Smartweed, *Polygonum amphibium*	Seeds eaten by waterfowl; upland game birds

Submersed Plants

Wild Celery or Eel Grass *Vallisneria americana*	Premier food (foliage, rhizomes, tubers & fruit) for waterfowl, esp. Canvasbacks. Also, marsh birds and shore birds
Coontail, *Ceratophyllum demersum*	Foliage and fruit eaten by waterfowl
CommonWater Milfoil*, *Myriophyllum sibiricum*	Foliage and seeds eaten by waterfowl
Common Waterweed, *Elodea canadensis*	Waterfowl eat both the plant plus invertebrates that use it for habitat

*There are many other good native *Myriophyllum* species, but be sure not to use Eurasian Water Milfoil (*Myriophyllum spicatum*), an extremely invasive species.

Mallards are common visitors to backyard ponds in spring.

You'll also want to landscape around your pond, with sun-loving or shade-loving plants, depending on its location. These plants should be suited to the prairie, wetland or woodland habitats adjacent to the pond. For example, the pond in Kevin and Kitty Clasing's yard is in a woodland habitat; shade-tolerant ferns, sedges, Marsh Marigolds, Wild Columbine, Solomon's Seal and Turtlehead are among the plants that thrive along its borders.

Potting Aquatic Plants

Unless you have soil at the bottom of your pond, like Mandy's, you will need to pot most of your plants. Even in soil-lined ponds, plants may be potted to better contain them. Floating-leaf plants and emergent plants should be potted in light-weight shallow plastic pots or lined baskets. It is best to use heavy garden soil with some clay content. Typical potting soil is too light and will float away. After potting, cover the containers with a thin layer of gravel to help retain the soil. Emergent plants are best grown in two-gallon containers, but containers half this size are frequently used. Set the potted plants with their rims two to four inches below waterline. Water lilies do best in large five-gallon (or bigger) pots or baskets, but my local aquatic nursery suggests two-gallon, 12-inch-wide containers for general use, since the larger containers are heavy. Water lilies are set lower in the water than emergents, with their crowns between 6 and 18 inches below waterline. The Lotus will need an even bigger container, the recommended size being three feet wide by one foot deep.

Submerged plants are planted in various ways. Bunching plants, like Common Waterweed, can be tossed into the pond and allowed to sink. They will form roots on gravel or rocks at the bottom (when there is no soil). Their roots primarily anchor, rather than nourish the plants. If they fail to anchor and float to the surface, you can pot the plants in gravel. If left unanchored, they will turn mushy and die. Since they get most of their nutrients from water, they don't need soil. Wild Celery and Water Milfoil should be planted in a shallow pots or trays of soil covered with sand or gravel. Easiest of all is Coontail; it simply floats and never needs potting. In winter, it will sink to the bottom where it remains until spring.

Native plants usually don't need fertilization, which can cause unwanted algae blooms. Many experts, nonetheless, recommend fertilizing water lilies for good bloom. Native plants are hardy and able to survive the winter right in your pond. Since aquatic plants tend to grow fast, they may need to be thinned and repotted each year. See the tables in this chapter to make your selections. (Since most aquatic plants are unique to water gardens, the tables are given here, rather than in part 5.)

Rural and Ephemeral Ponds

Although large-scale ponds are beyond the scope of this chapter, they are often constructed in rural areas to great advantage. They can help check erosion and provide water and habitat for birds and other wildlife. Due to their size and location in a less developed landscape, rural ponds are likely to attract a great variety of birds.

Ephemeral ponds are a type of seasonal or temporary wetland that has become the focus of restoration efforts in recent years. They periodically dry up and do not contain fish. The wet-dry cycle prevents fish from becoming established, and thus these ponds provide critical breeding habitat for amphibians, crustaceans and dragonflies that fish would prey upon.

At the same time, ephemeral ponds provide important habitat for birds. Waterfowl, including Wood Ducks and Mallards, use these ponds during migration, feeding on insects, crustaceans and seeds to fuel their long journeys. Shorebirds, like Spotted Sandpipers and Lesser Yellowlegs, feed on the mudflats that are exposed as the ponds begin to dry.

Ephemeral ponds can be designed for almost any size site, says wildlife biologist Tom Biebighauser. His booklet (see Resources for Readers) describes techniques for constructing ponds of this type that have been successful in Ohio, Minnesota and Kentucky.

And the Birds Will Come

Although not as simple as filling a hole with water, water gardening is very rewarding and can attract a variety of birds. Some water gardens, like the Morettis', are visited primarily by songbirds, while larger ponds will attract waterfowl, herons, swallows and other open wetland birds. There is no one bird list to give you for water gardens. Different kinds and sizes of water gardens attract different sorts of birds; your neighborhood also affects the variety of birds that visit. The Morettis get many woodland birds in their wooded backyard but miss the bluebirds that visit my birdbath and the herons that fish occasionally in Mandy Ploch's and Mike Sands's ponds. Enjoy whatever birds arrive and you're certain to have some wonderful surprises.

Water lilies are the quintessential water garden plants.

Emergent Plants

Common Name	Lain Name	Plant Type	Bloom Dates	Color	Height	Light Requirement	Normal Water Level/soil Moisture	Native Range
Arrowhead, Common	*Sagittaria latifolia*	P	July–Sept	White	2'+	S, P	24" water	All 8 States
Arum, Arrow	*Peltandra virginica*	P	June–July	Greenish-white	3'	Sh	Shallow water	IA,IL,IN,MI, MO,OH
Arum, Wild	*Calla palustris*	P	June	White & gold	8–12"	S, P	Shallow water	IL,IN,MI, MN,OH,WI
Bur Reed, Common	*Sparganium eurycarpum*	P	June–Aug	White	To 4.5'	S, P	18" water or less to saturated soil	All 8 States
Bulrush, Soft Stem or Great	*Scirpus validus (S. tabernaemontani)*	P	June–Sept	Brown	3–9'	S, P	1–4' water; tolerates saturated soil	IA,IL,IN,MI, MN,OH,WI
Cardinal Flower	*Lobelia cardinalis*	P	July–Sept	Scarlet	2–5'	S, P	Moist to wet soil or pond water level below leaves	All 8 States
Flag, Sweet	*Acorus calamus (A. americanus)*	P	May–June	Greenish brown	2–6'	S, P	20" water or less to saturated soil	All 8 States
Grass, Fowl Manna	*Glyceria striata*	P	June–Aug	Purplish	1–4'	S, P	3–6" water	All 8 States
Horsetail	*Equisetum fluviatile*	P	June	Green	3'	S, P	3' water or less to saturated soil	IA,IL,IN,MI, MN,OH,WI
Iris, Northern Blue Flag	*Iris versicolor*	P	May–July	Blue-violet to Purple	2–4'	S, P	Shallow water to saturated soil	IL,OH,MI, MN,WI
Iris, Southern Blue Flag	*Iris virginica*	P	May–July	Light to dark to purple	2–3'	S, P	Shallow water to saturated soil	All 8 States
Mallow, Swamp Rose	*Hibiscus moscheutos (H.palustris)*	P	July–Sept	White to pink	5–7'	S	Shallow water to moist soil	IL,IN,MI, OH,WI
Marigold, Marsh	*Caltha palustris*	P	April–June	Yellow	1–2'	A	3' water or less to wet soil	All 8 States
Pickerel Weed	*Pontederia cordata*	P	June–Aug	Violet-blue	To 40"	S, P	12–18" water, but tolerates 3' water or saturated soil	All 8 States
Plantain, Common Water	*Alisma subcordatum (A. plantago-aquatica* var. *parviflorum)*	P	May–Sept	White or pinkish	3–4'	S, P	6" water or less to saturated soil	All 8 States

Common Name	Lain Name	Plant Type	Bloom Dates	Color	Height	Light Requirement	Normal Water Level/soil Moisture	Native Range
Plantain, Large-flowered Water	*Alisma triviale* (*A. plantago-aquatica* var. *americanum*)	P	May–Sept	White or pinkish	3–4'	S, P	Shallow water to saturated soil	All 8 States
Rush, Needle Spike	*Eleocharis ovata* or *E. acicularis* (*E. obtusa*)	A	June–Oct	Brown	12–20"	S	6" water to saturated soil	All 8 States
Rush, Common or Soft	*Juncus effusus*	P	July–Aug	Green, tawny or brown	2–4'	S, P	12" water or less to saturated conditions	All 8 States
Sedge, Bristly or Bottlebrush	*Carex comosa*	P	May–July	Green	1.5–4'	S, P	12" water or less to saturated conditions	All 8 States

KEY TO POND PLANTS

The plants on these tables are listed alphabetically according to their common name. The code letters used in the various categories are identified below.

Plant Type:
A = Annual
B = Biennial
P = Perennial

Light Requirement:
A = All (full sun, partial shade, shade)
P = Partial Shade
Sh = Full Shade
S = Full Sun

Latin names in parentheses are alternate names used by some botanists for the same plant.

Widow Skimmer Dragonfly

Floating & Submersed Plants

Common Name	Lain Name	Plant Type	Bloom Dates	Color	Light Requirement	Native Range
Free-Floating Plants						
Duckweed, Small	*Lemna minor*		Microscopic Flowers			All 8 states
Duckweed, Great	*Spirodela polyrhiza*					
Watermeal	*Wolffia* sp.					
Floating-Leaf Plants						
Lily, White Water	*Nymphaea odorata*	P	June–Sept	White	S, P	All 8 States
Lily, Yellow Pond; Spatterdock	*Nuphar* sp.	P	June–Sept	Yellow	A	All 8 States
Lotus	*Nelumbo lutea*	P	July–Aug	Yellow	S	All 8 States
Smartweed, Water	*Polygonum amphibium*	P	June–Sept	Pink	S, P	All 8 States
Submersed Plants[2]						
Celery, Wild[1] or Eel Grass	*Vallisneria americana*	P	July–Oct	White		All 8 States
Coontail[1]	*Ceratophyllum demersum*	P	July–Sept			All 8 States
Milfoil, Common Water	*Myriophyllum sibiricum*		July–Sept	Pinkish		All 8 States
Waterweed, Common[1]	*Elodea canadensis*	P	July–Sept	White		All 8 States

[1]*Dioecious: Some plants of this species bear male (staminate) flowers and others bear female (pistillate) flowers. Both sexes need to grow in relatively close proximity for fruit to form.*

[2]*Flowers: Although these are submersed plants, their flowers (or only the stamens of the male flowers in the case of Coontail) rise to or above the water surface.*

KEY TO POND PLANTS

The plants on these tables are listed alphabetically according to their common name. The code letters used in the various categories are identified below.

Plant Type:
A = Annual
B = Biennial
P = Perennial

Light Requirement:
A = All (full sun, partial shade, shade)
P = Partial Shade
Sh = Full Shade
S = Full Sun

Latin names in parentheses are alternate names used by some botanists for the same plant.

RESOURCES FOR READERS

Books and Booklets

Biebighauser, Thomas R. 2002. *A Guide to Creating Vernal Ponds.* Published by USDA Forest Service in cooperation with Ducks Unlimited, Inc., and the Izaak Walton League of America. Copies are available from the USDA Forest Service, 2375 KY Highway 801 South, Morehead, KY 40351. It is also available at http://herpcenter.ipfw.edu/outreach/VernalPonds/VernalPondGuide.pdf.

Borman, Susan, Robert Korth and Jo Temte. 1997. *Through the Looking Glass: A Field Guide to Aquatic Plants.* Madison: Wisconsin Department of Natural Resources. Publication #FH-207-97. Contact: Wisconsin Lakes Partnership, University of Wisconsin–Extension, University of Wisconsin–Stevens Point, College of Natural Resources, 1900 Franklin St., Stevens Point, WI 54481; phone: 715-346-2116. This guide focuses on Wisconsin plants that are widespread species found in waters across the U.S. and Canada.

Burrell, C. Colston, ed. 1997. *The Natural Water Garden.* Brooklyn Botanic Garden.

Nash, Helen, and Marilyn M. Cook. 1999. *Water Gardening Basics.* New York: Sterling Publishing. This book is packed with information for the beginning water gardener, but ignore the plant species recommendations. (Most are non-native and all the native species among them that are attractive to birds are on the plant lists in this chapter.)

Websites on Pond Construction

National Wildlife Federation. "Build a Backyard Pond." http://www.nwf.org /Get-Outside/Outdoor-Activities/Garden-for-Wildlife/Gardening-Tips/Build-a Backyard-Pond.aspx

Natural Resources Conservation Service. "Backyard Conservation—Backyard Ponds." http://www.nrcs.usda.gov/wps/portal/nrcs/detail/national /newsroom/features/?&cid=nrcs143_023601

A birdbath can be very simple.

5 MIDWESTERN PLANTS THAT ATTRACT BIRDS

One of the strongest reasons for using locally native plants is their inestimable value to myriad nonhuman organisms that have evolved with, and come to depend on, these plants for food and shelter.

—William Cullina,
Native Trees, Shrubs and Vines

Red-headed Woodpecker

This section consists primarily of tables that provide details on the characteristics, cultural requirements, native ranges and other pertinent information on midwestern native plants that attract birds. (Aquatic plants are treated separately in chapter 16, since they are unique to water gardens.) The plants are listed in each table in alphabetical order according to their common names. A "Latin Name to Common Name" list at the end of the chapter gives Latin names in alphabetical order followed by the common name(s) used in the tables.

(previous page) A Black-capped Chickadee gleans insects from the flowers of oaks.

Key to Tables in Chapters 17 & 18

The plants in these tables are listed alphabetically according to their common name.

Superscripts Following Common Names

D indicates plants are dioecious—that is, some plants of this species bear male (staminate) flowers and others bear female (pistillate) flowers. Plants of both sexes need to grow in relatively close proximity for fruit to form.

Numeric superscripts indicate that information is provided at the end of the table specific to those species.

Latin Names

Those in parentheses are alternate names used by some botanists.

Plant Type (Herbaceous Plants)

A = Annual: A plant that lives for only one season or year.

B = Biennial: A plant that lives for two years.

P = Perennial: A plant that lives three or more years.

Light Requirement

Based on the typical habitat of the species (i.e. woods–shade; prairie–sun, etc.) However, most need at least partial sun to bloom well.

A = All (full sun, partial shade,shade)

S = Full Sun

P = Partial Sun

Sh = Full Shade

Size

Height. The height range of a species is given; it will vary according to conditions. A height in parenthesis indicates a maximum height which is rarely attained.

Width. The average width range is also given for woody species. Vines vary greatly in height and width depending both on conditions and on the plant or structure on which they are growing.

Fruit/Seed Type (Woody Plants)

In botanical terms, a fruit is the structure which contains the seeds produced by a female plant and includes berries, nuts, samaras, etc. (A *Samara* is a dry seed with a membranous wing.) If the seeds of a plant are more notable than the fruits, such as hairy seeds dispersed by the wind, the seed description is given here in preference to that of the fruit.

Soil Requirements

Moisture. *Wet* soils are those with a high water table and are soggy much of the year. *Moist* soils rarely dry out completely. While the surface may be dry, the soil is damp within a few inches of the surface. Moist soils are ideal for most plants.

　　Dry soils are well-drained to excessively drained and are dry for a full foot below the surface for much of the year. Many native plants thrive in dry soils, which are commonly found through the Midwest.

Snowberry's flowers and fruit are an attractive addition to your garden.

Acidic or Alkaline

　　Most plants grow well in soil in the middle ranges of pH typical of many soils. In the table, only the exceptions, having specific preferences for acidic or alkaline soil, are mentioned. Acidic soils are those with a pH below 6.0 and alkaline are those with a pH above 7.

Parasitic Plants

　　A few plants are parasites, having roots which attach themselves to the roots of other plants to obtain water and possibly nutrients from the host plant. When known, the host plants are given.

Native Range

　　Lists those midwestern states in which the plant is native: IA (Iowa), IL (Illinois), IN (Indiana), MI (Michigan), MN (Minnesota), MO (Missouri), OH (Ohio) and WI (Wisconsin).

––

　　• The plant characteristics and cultural requirements of woody plants are based on my own experience, plus on those given in *Native Trees, Shrubs and Vines*, William Cullina. Those of herbaceous plants are based on my own experience, plus on those given in *Plants of the Chicago Region*, Swink and Wilhelm, and in the catalogs of Prairie Nursery (WI) and Prairie Moon Nursery (MN).

　　• The native ranges are based on the best available manuals and checklists of flora for each state.

　　• The value to birds for woody plants is based on information in *American Wildlife and Plants*, Martin, Zim and Nelson, 1951, and *Trees, Shrubs and Vines for Attracting Birds*, Richard M. DeGraaf, 2002 and *Native Trees, Shrubs and Vines in Urban and Rural America*, G. Hightshoe, 1988.

CHAPTER 17
TREES, SHRUBS & VINES

The tables in this chapter will help you choose the best species for your site. A few general tips, given below, are also important to keep in mind when selecting woody plants.

Male and Female Plants

Some species are dioecious—that is, some individual plants in the species bear only male (staminate) flowers and other plants of the same species bear only female (pistillate) flowers. At our first home, we unknowingly bought a male Green Ash that never produced seeds. Luckily, a wild female Green Ash later began growing on its own at the back of the lot and eventually produced seeds for cardinals, blackbirds and doves each fall and winter.

If you select a dioecious tree, shrub or vine, be sure that plants of both sexes will be in close proximity so that pollination will take place to produce fruit for birds.

Unfortunately, many nurseries sell only male trees, which do not produce seeds, and females can sometimes be hard to find. In addition, the sexes of some woody plants can't be determined until they are fairly large. In such cases, plant at least three individuals of the species for a 75% probability that at least one of each sex will be among them. Five plants are even better, giving a 94% probability.

Plant in Clumps

Unless your yard is small, always try to plant several individuals of any one species. Many species, even if they have both·male and female flowers on a single plant, are self-infertile. Consequently, they produce little or no fruit. (In botanical terms, the fruit is the ripened ovary and associated tissue and may be berries, nuts, seeds and seed pods.) Mike Yanny of Johnson's Nursery in Wisconsin has found that hazelnut and many viburnums, including Nannyberry Viburnum, Blackhaw Viburnum and American Cranberrybush Viburnum, are self-infertile.

Arboretums often plant only a single representative of each species, says Mike, many of which are similarly self-infertile. The unfortunate consequence is that the plant collections at many arboretums are, literally, fruitless. To address this problem at the University of Wisconsin–Madison, Ed Hasselkus of the Horticulture Department began planting three of each species at the university's arboretum and the plants are now valuable seed sources for Mike and other horticulturists.

photo: Bur Oak

Size Considerations

Despite the temptation to create an "instant" habitat, it is always best to purchase smaller-sized specimens, especially trees. As a general recommendation, a trunk diameter of two inches or less is best. Smaller trees always establish more quickly and successfully and often live longer than those transplanted at a larger size. Studies show that a 5-foot-tall tree will be as big or bigger than a 16-foot-tall tree after five years, if planted in similar conditions. The larger tree will try to rebuild its roots during that time, rather than put its energy into growing.

Also, consider the mature size of trees or shrubs. But remember, in natural settings like woodlands, they often grow fairly close to one another with overlapping branches, so feel free to imitate this more natural spacing. In some cases, however, trees or shrubs may have attractive forms best enjoyed in a more open setting. Hawthorns, Alternate-leaved or Pagoda Dogwood and Bur Oaks are my favorites in this category.

Field Grown vs. Container Grown

Woody plants that are field grown in local nurseries are generally more successful than plants that are container grown, says Rick Darke, a landscape designer and author of *The American Woodland Garden*. The soil in which plants are grown locally is more likely to resemble that in your own backyard, which can help the plants adapt more quickly to their new location.

Container-grown woody plants, on the other hand, are often grown in a light, porous medium to promote rapid drainage while at the nursery. Such plants can be extremely difficult to keep moist when transplanted, unless the soil medium is sufficiently loosened before planting.

Another serious problem with woody plants grown in containers is root girdling—roots that begin to grow in circles due to being constrained in the containers. This can eventually strangle the main stem, as the plants grow larger, killing the plant. Sometimes field-grown plants, which have been originally grown in containers, have this problem. Reject any plants that show signs of encircling roots just beneath the soil surface.

Information on how and when to plant trees and shrubs appears in chapter 7.

Midwestern Deciduous Trees for Attracting Birds

Deciduous trees (those that lose their leaves each year) constitute the major structural element of most midwestern bird gardens. Their fruits, whether berries, seeds, or nuts, are essential foods for many birds. Their leafy boughs offer cover and nesting sites. They serve as important hosts for insects, which are staples in the diet of many young birds and Neotropical migrants. And as they age, cavity nesters use them.

Oaks or maples are the classic, dominant species in most areas of the Midwest. Where I live, the Bur Oaks are awesome—huge and craggy with thick angled branching, particularly striking in winter. In some other areas, the White Oak is supreme. Mature open-grown White Oaks are picturesque hulks with massive, wide-spreading limbs. Ten other oak species native to the Midwest are listed in the table in this chapter, all having particular attributes and requirements that make them suitable to different areas and conditions.

Oaks are considered to be the top wildlife food plants in the Midwest and, indeed, throughout the country. Thirty-one species of midwestern birds are known to feed on the acorns, a preferred food of the Wild Turkey, Ruffed Grouse, Northern Bobwhite, Blue Jay, Brown Thrasher, Common Grackle and Eastern Towhee. Oaks have great potential for cavities for nesting birds. They also are the top hosts for the caterpillars that sustain so many of our migrating birds.

The Sugar Maple is the premier maple species, an outstanding tree with great horizontal limbs curving gracefully upward at their tips. It is valued for both its sweet sap in spring and its brilliant gold and scarlet colors in fall. Red Maple comes in a close second, sporting red color throughout the growing season—red flowers in spring, red samaras in early summer and brilliant crimson foliage in autumn. The Red Maple is also the widest

This House Wren hunts for a meal of small insects in the tree bark.

ranging and most adaptable of maples. Three other species of maple are listed in the table, providing a variety of choices for gardeners. Silver Maple, along with Red Maple, is typically found in river floodplains. Black and Mountain Maple, with Sugar Maple, are characteristic trees of rich deciduous woodlands. Box Elder is the major maple species native to prairie regions.

Maples as a group are rated among the top ten wildlife food plants in the country. Nineteen species of midwestern birds feed on the samaras, the winged seeds of maples, which ripen in different seasons depending on the species. These seeds are a preferred food of finches and grosbeaks. Many songbirds also eat maple buds and flowers. Upland game birds eat maple twigs and buds, in addition to the seeds. Yellow-bellied Sapsuckers are partial to the sweet sap of maples. In addition, the Sugar Maple is an excellent cavity-producing tree; Red Maple comes in second in this regard. Many nest-building birds also favor maple limbs for their nest sites.

Other trees with very high value for birds are serviceberries, cherries, dogwoods and hackberries. Their berries ripen in sequence to feed birds through the seasons. Serviceberries are the earliest and will attract droves of birds to your yard in spring. Cherries and dogwoods offer their berries in summer and early fall. Hackberries are available for birds from September through February, making them ideal selections for winter bird gardens. Trees in all four of these groups are also among our most beautiful native trees and will be treasured features in your bird garden.

In addition to the trees listed previously, the many other recommended species in the table similarly offer birds cover, nest sites, and nesting material, and their varied fruits have unique nutritional benefits for birds. Be sure to consider the full gamut of our diverse native tree flora when selecting specimens for your garden.

Trees, Shrubs & Vines

Midwestern Deciduous Trees
for Attracting Birds

See Key to Tables, pages 247–248, for abbreviations.

COMMON NAME	LATIN NAME	VALUE TO BIRDS	LIGHT REQ.	HEIGHT (FT.)	WIDTH (FT.)	BLOOM DATES	FRUIT/ SEED TYPE & DATE	SOIL REQ.	NATIVE RANGE
Ash, American Mountain	*Sorbus americana*	Good	S,P	15–35 (50)	8–20	May–June	Berry; Aug–Nov	Moist	IL,MI,MN, WI
Ash, Showy Mountain	*Sorbus decora*	Good	S,P	15–35 (50)	8–20	May–June	Berry; Aug–Nov	Moist	IL,IN,MI, MN,OH,WI
Ash, Wafer; Hop Tree	*Ptelea trifoliata*	Good	A	10–20 (25)		May–June	Samara; Aug–Nov	Moist to dry	IA,IL,IN,MI, MO,OH,WI
Aspen, Large-Toothed[D]	*Populus grandidentata*	Good	S,P	30–40 (80)		Mar–May	Cottony seeds; May–June	Moist to dry	All 8 States
Aspen, Quaking[D]	*Populus tremuloides*	Good	S,P	35–50	15–25	Mar–May	Cottony seeds; May	Moist to dry	All 8 States
Beech, American	*Fagus grandifolia*	High	A	50–70 (90)	25–50	Apr–May	Nut; Sept–Nov	Moist	IL,IN,MI, MO,OH,WI
Birch, Paper[2]	*Betula papyrifera*	High	S,P	50–75 (100)	20–30	Apr–May	Slender cluster; Aug–Oct	Moist; prefers acid	IA,IL,IN,MI, MN,WI
Birch, River[2]	*Betula nigra*	High	S,P	50–75	15–25	Apr–May	Cone-like fruit; June–Aug	Moist to medium dry; prefers acid	IA,IL,IN,MN MO,OH,WI
Birch, Yellow[2]	*Betula alleghaniensis (B. lutea)*	High	A	60–80 (100)	15–30	Apr–May	Cone-like fruit; June–Oct.	Moist; strongly acid to alkaline	IA,IL,IN,MI, MN,OH,WI
Box Elder[D,2]	*Acer negundo*	Very high	S,P	20–40 (60)	15–30	Mar–May	Samara; July–Feb	Moist to dry	All 8 States
Buckeye, Ohio	*Aesculus glabra*	High (Nectar)	S	30–40 (120)	20–35	Apr–May	Nut, poisonous; June–Sept	Moist; acid to alkaline	IA,IL,IN,MI, MO,OH
Cottonwood, Eastern[D]	*Populus deltoides*	Good	S,P	75–100	25–50	Apr–May	Cottony seeds	Moist	All 8 States
Cherry, Pin	*Prunus pensylvanica*	Very high	S,P	20–35	10–15	Apr–June	Berry; July–Sept	Moist to dry	IA,IL,IN,MI MN,OH,WI
Cherry, Wild Black	*Prunus serotina*	Very high	S,P	50–70 (90)	20–30	May–June	Berry; Aug–Sept	Moist to medium dry	All 8 States
Crabapple, Iowa[2]	*Malus ioensis (Pyrus i.)*	High	S,P	15–30 (35)	15–25	Apr–May	Apple-like berry; Sept–Oct	Moist to medium dry	IA,IL,IN, MN,MO,WI
Crabapple, Wild Sweet[2]	*Malus coronaria (Pyrus c.)*	High	S,P	10–25 (30)	8–20	Apr–May	Apple-like berry; Fall	Moist to medium dry	IL,IN,MI,MN MO,OH,WI

COMMON NAME	LATIN NAME	VALUE TO BIRDS	LIGHT REQ.	HEIGHT (FT.)	WIDTH (FT.)	BLOOM DATES	FRUIT/ SEED TYPE & DATE	SOIL REQ.	NATIVE RANGE
Dogwood, Alternate-leaved; Pagoda Dogwood	*Cornus alternifolia*	Very high	S,P	10–25	6–15	May–July	Berry; July–Aug	Moist to wet	All 8 States
Dogwood, Flowering[2]	*Cornus florida*	Very high	S,P	12–20 (35)	8–15	April–June	Berry; Sept–Nov	Moist; slightly acid	IL,IN,MI, MO,OH
Gum, Black; Sour Gum[D]	*Nyssa sylvatica*	Good	S,P	30–60 (80+)	20–35	May–July	Berry; Sept–Oct	Wet, tolerates some dryness	IL,IN,MI, MO,OH,WI
Hackberry, Northern	*Celtis occidentalis*	Very high	S,P	30–70 (100)	20–70	Apr–May	Berry; Sept–Feb	Wet to dry	All 8 States
Hackberry, Southern	*Celtis laevigata*	Very high	S,P	60–80 (100)	40–60		Berry	Moist to dry	IL,IN,MO
Hawthorn, Biltmore[2]	*Crataegus intricata*	High	S,P	10–25		May	Apple-like berry; Fall		IL,IN,MI, MO,OH,WI
Hawthorn, Cockspur[2]	*Crataegus crus-galli*	High	S	20–35	20–35	May–June	Apple-like berry; Aug–Jan	Moist to dry	IA,IL,IN,MI, MO,OH,WI
Hawthorn, Dotted[2]	*Crataegus punctata*	High	S	15–25	20–30	Apr–June	Apple-like berry; Aug–Oct	Moist to dry	IA,IL,IN,MI, MN,OH,WI
Hawthorn, Downy[2]	*Crataegus mollis*	High	S	20–40	20–35	Apr–June	Apple-like berry; Aug–Sept	Moist to dry	All 8 States
Hawthorn, Fireberry[2]	*Crataegus chrysocarpa*	High	S,P	To 25	To 25	May	Apple-like berry; Fall	Moist to dry	All 8 States
Hawthorn, Fleshy[2]	*Crataegus succulenta*	High	S,P	To 25	To 25	May	Apple-like berry; Fall	Moist to dry	All 8 States
Hawthorn, Frosted[2]	*Crataegus pruinosa*	High	S	20–35	10–20	May–June	Apple-like berry; Aug–Oct	Moist to dry	IA,IL,IN,MI, MO,OH,WI
Hawthorn, Large-seeded[2]	*Crataegus flabellata (C. macrosperma)*	High	S,P	To 25	To 25	Apr–May	Apple-like berry; Fall	Moist to dry	IL,IN,MI, MN,OH,WI
Hawthorn, Scarlet[2]	*Crataegus coccinea (C. pedicillata)*	High	S,P	To 30		May	Apple-like berry; Fall	Moist to dry	IA,IL,IN,MI, MN,OH,WI
Hawthorn, Washington[2]	*Crataegus phaenopyrum*	High	S	25–30	20–25	May–June	Apple-like berry; Sept–Mar	Moist to dry	IL,IN, MO,OH
Hickory, Bitternut	*Carya cordiformis*	Good	S,P	75–100 (160)	25–40	May–June	Nut; Aug–Oct	Moist to wet	All 8 States
Hickory, Mockernut	*Carya tomentosa (C. alba)*	Good	S,P	60–80 (100)	20–30	May	Nut; Sept–Oct	Moist to dry, well-drained	IA,IL,IN, MO,OH
Hickory, Pignut	*Carya glabra*	Good	S,P	60–80 (100)	25–35	May	Nut; Sept–Oct	Seasonally wet to dry	IL,IN,MI, MO,OH

COMMON NAME	LATIN NAME	VALUE TO BIRDS	LIGHT REQ.	HEIGHT (FT.)	WIDTH (FT.)	BLOOM DATES	FRUIT/ SEED TYPE & DATE	SOIL REQ.	NATIVE RANGE
Hickory, Shagbark	*Carya ovata*	Good	S,P	75–100	20–35	May	Nut; Sept–Oct	Wet to dry	All 8 States
Maple, Mountain	*Acer spicatum*	Very high	Sh	To 20	To 20	May– June	Samara; July–Sept	Moist to med; acidic	IA,MI,MN, OH,WI
Maple, Red[1]	*Acer rubrum*	Very high	S,P	40–75 (110)	20–50	Mar– May	Samara; Apr–June	Wet to moist	All 8 States
Maple, Silver[1]	*Acer saccharinum*	Very high	S,P	60–75 (100)	30–50	Mar– Apr	Samara; April/May	Moist to medium dry	All 8 States
Maple, Sugar[1]	*Acer saccharum*	Very high	A	60–80 (100)	25–50	Apr– May	Samara; Sept	Moist; pref- erably only slightly acid	All 8 States
Mulberry, Red[D]	*Morus rubra*	High	S,P	35–50 (80)	35–50	May– June	Berry; June–July	Prefers moist; tol- erates dry	All 8 States
Oak, Black[2]	*Quercus velutina*	Very high	S,P	70–80 (100)	50–60	Apr– June	Nut; Sept–Oct	Moist; tolerates dry	All 8 States
Oak, Blackjack[2]	*Quercus marilandica*	Very high	S	12–25 (40)	8–18	May– June	Nut; Sept–Oct	Dry	IA,IL,IN, MO,OH
Oak, Bur	*Quercus macrocarpa*	Very high	S,P	40–80 (120)	40–80	Apr– June	Nut; Sept–Oct	Wet to dry	All 8 States
Oak, Chinquapin	*Quercus muehlenbergii*	Very high	S,P	20–50 (160)	20–50	May	Nut; Sept–Oct	Dry	IA,IL,IN,MI, MO,OH,WI
Oak, Northern Pin[2]	*Quercus ellipsoidalis*	Very high	S	60–70	45–50	May	Nut; Sept–Oct	Moist to medium dry	All 8 States
Oak, Pin[2]	*Quercus palustris*	Very high	S,P	50–75	25–35	Apr– May	Nut; Sept–Oct	Moist to medium dry; intol- erant to high alkaline soils	IA,IL,IN,MI, MO,OH,WI
Oak, Post	*Quercus stellata*	Very high	S	25–50 (80)	20–30	May– June	Nut; Sept–Oct	Dry	IA,IL,IN, MO,OH
Oak, Red[2]	*Quercus rubra (Q. borealis)*	Very high	S,P	60–80 (100)	30–45	May	Nut; Sept–Oct	Moist	All 8 States
Oak, Scarlet[2]	*Quercus coccinea*	Very high	S,P	40–50 (80)	40–50	Apr– June	Nut; Sept–Oct	Medium to dry	IL,IN,MI, MO,OH,WI
Oak, Shingle	*Quercus imbricaria*	Very high	S,P	50–60	25–35	May	Nut; Sept–Oct	Moist to moderately dry	IA,IL,IN,MI, MO,OH
Oak, Swamp White	*Quercus bicolor*	Very high	S,P	60–80 (100)	15–40	May	Nut; Sept–Oct	Wet to moist	All 8 States
Oak, White	*Quercus alba*	Very high	S,P	60–80 (100)	30–40	Apr– June	Nut; Sept–Oct	Moist to dry	All 8 States
Poplar, Balsam	*Populus balsamerifa*	Fair	S,P	60–80	20–35	Apr– May	Seeds with silky hairs; May–July	Moist	IL,IN,MI, MN,WI

COMMON NAME	LATIN NAME	VALUE TO BIRDS	LIGHT REQ.	HEIGHT (FT.)	WIDTH (FT.)	BLOOM DATES	FRUIT/ SEED TYPE & DATE	SOIL REQ.	NATIVE RANGE
Persimmon, Common[D]	*Diospyros virginiana*	Good	S,P	30–50	15–25	June	Berry; Sept–Nov	Moist to dry	IA,IL,IN, MO,OH
Sassafras	*Sassafras albidum*	Good	S,P	30–60 (90)	12–25	Apr– May	Berry; Aug–Sept	Moist to dry	IA,IL,IN,MI, MO,OH,WI
Serviceberry, Alleghany or Smooth	*Amelanchier laevis*	Very high	S,P	25–40 (60)	8–18	Apr– June	Berry; June–July	Moist to dry	IA,IL,IN,MI, MN,OH,WI
Serviceberry; Juneberry; Shadbush	*Amelanchier arborea*	High	S,P	20–30 (50)	8–15	Apr	Berry	Moist, but well-drained to dry	All 8 States
Sycamore	*Platanus occidentalis*	Good	S,P	75–100 (l60)	40–60	May– June	Ball-shaped head of dry seeds; Aug–Dec	Moist	IA,IL,IN, MI,MO, OH,WI
Tulip Tree	*Liriodendron tulipifera*	Good (Nectar)	S,P	75–100 (175)	35–50	May– July	Samara; Aug–Nov	Moist	IL,IN,MI, MO,OH
Willow, Black[D]	*Salix nigra*	Good	S	35–50 (120)	20–35	Mar– Apr	Tufted seeds, Apr–May	Wet to moist	All 8 States
Willow, Peach-leaved[D]	*Salix amygdaloides*	Good	S	35–50	35–50	Mar– May	Apr– May	Wet to moist	All 8 States

[1]**Black, Red, Silver and Sugar Maples**: May be dioecious or monoecious (bearing both male and female flowers on same individual plant), so both sexes may need to grow in relatively close proximity for fruit to form.

[2]**Susceptibility:**

Birches: Borers commonly attack stressed trees, so be sure to avoid planting the wrong species for your site. With the exception of River Birch, birches do not do well on dry sites. Leaf minors can defoliate birches, but introduced predatory wasps are reducing this problem.

Box Elder: Female Box Elders have seeds attractive to birds, but also may harbor Box Elder Bugs in nuisance numbers. We had hundreds emerging in spring to sun on our siding last year and many got into the house. Avoid planting Box Elder close to the house to minimize this problem.

Crabapples are susceptible to Cedar Apple Rust. Don't plant in vicinity of cedars (*Juniper* species), the rust's alternate host. Some Iowa Crabs have limited resistance to this rust.

Flowering Dogwood is susceptible to anthracnose, most prevalent under cool, moist conditions. The disease is less likely to occur when the tree is grown in more open, sunny conditions.

Hawthorns are susceptible to Cedar Apple Rusts and should not be planted within 1/4 to l mile (depending on prevailing winds) from cedars (*Juniperus* sp.), the rust's alternate host. Cockspur Hawthorn and Washington Hawthorn are more resistant than other hawthorns. Due to the rusts and other diseases, most unimproved wild hawthorns are likely to lose their leaves early in the growing season, although their fruits, thorns and attractive forms will remain. As a result, this is one case where gardeners may want to select cultivars of the native hawthorns, whose fruits and cover will be equally attractive to birds. Also, there are thornless varieties available for locations where the thorns may be dangerous to people.

Oaks may be susceptible to oak wilt. The disease is more likely to occur in oaks in the Red Oak group (having pointed lobes). Those in the Red Oak group in the above table include Black, Blackjack, Northern Pin, Pin, Red and Scarlet Oaks. The other species listed are more resistant. Avoid pruning oaks during the growing season to reduce their chance of getting this disease.

[D]**Dioecious.** Some plants of this species bear male (staminate) flowers and others bear female (pistillate) flowers. Both sexes need to grow in relatively close proximity for fruit to form.

See Key to Tables, pages 247–248, for abbreviations.

A female Cardinal glows in the morning sun.

Midwestern Conifers for Attracting Birds

Most of our midwestern conifers, with the exception of tamarack, are evergreen and offer excellent protective cover for birds, a particularly valuable feature in winter when little other cover is available. All also provide nutritious berries or seeds for birds. Cedar berries (actually berry-like cones) and pine seeds are rated among the top ten wildlife foods in the country and are favorites of many birds, as well as many mammals.

Red Cedar is the most widespread conifer species in the Midwest and, indeed, in the entire eastern half of North America. Its berries are prized by at least 29 species of birds and are the preferred food of the Northern Mockingbird, Yellow-rumped Warbler, Evening Grosbeak, Purple Finch, Pine Grosbeak and, of course, the Cedar Waxwing, named for its fondness for cedar berries. Its dense branches are prime nesting sites and a large tree may have many nests in a single year. It offers cozy comfort for wintering birds as well. Since it can tolerate summer heat better than most evergreens, it is a good choice for southern areas of the Midwest except in prairies where it is considered a weed. The Common and Trailing Junipers are evergreen shrubs closely related to Red Cedar, with similar value for birds.

Pines have nutritious oily seeds tucked inside the scales of their cones. Pine seeds constitute a full 50% of the diet of the Red Crossbill, and they are the preferred food of 18 other species of midwestern birds, including many northern finches. Some birds even consume pine needles, including Mourning Doves, Northern Bobwhites and Wild Turkeys. The dense foliage of pines provides valuable cover for birds, and larger limbs are favorite nesting sites for Mourning Doves and favorite roosting places for American Robins during migration. Several species of birds use pine needles as nesting material.

Spruces provide excellent nesting, roosting and winter cover for birds, and their seeds are particularly important food for White-winged Crossbills. Hemlocks are favorite nesting sites for warblers, juncos and Veeries, and their seeds are a favorite food of Pine Siskins. Tamaracks provide nesting sites and seeds for Purple Finches and crossbills. Balsam firs offer nesting for many species and seeds for crossbills and finches. The dense foliage of White Cedars offers excellent cover and nesting sites, and their seeds are especially important food for Pine Siskins.

Midwestern Conifers for Attracting Birds

See Key to Tables, pages 247–248, for abbreviations.

COMMON NAME	LATIN NAME	VALUE TO BIRDS	LIGHT REQ.	HEIGHT (FT.)	WIDTH (FT.)	FRUIT/ SEED TYPE & DATE	SOIL REQ.	NATIVE RANGE
Cedar, Red[D,1]	*Juniperus virginiana*	Very high	S,P	15–35 (60)	3–12	Berry-like cone; July–March	Moist to dry	All 8 States
Cedar, White; Arborvitae	*Thuja occidentalis*	Good	S,P	20–40 (60)	5–20	Cone with seeds, Aug–Feb	Wet to dry; slightly acidic to alkaline	IL, IN, MI, MN, OH, WI
Fir, Balsam	*Abies balsamea*	High	All	60 (80)	12–18	Cone with seeds; July–Oct	Moist; acidic	IA, MI, MN, WI
Hemlock	*Tsuga candensis*	Good	All	60–80 (100)	25–40	Cone with seeds; Sept–Jan	Moist to medium dry acidic	IN, MI,MN OH,WI
Juniper, Common[D,1]	*Juniperus communis*	Very high	S,P	3–6	3–15	Berry-like cone; Aug–Apr	Moist to dry; well-drained; acidic to alkaline	IA, IL, IN, MI, MN, OH, WI
Juniper, Trailing[D,1]	*Juniperus horizontalis*	Very high	S	1/5–1	3–6	Berry-like cone; Aug–Apr	Moist to dry, well-drained; acidic to alkaline	IA, IL, MI, MN, WI
Jack Pine	*Pinus banksiana*	Very high	S	50–80 (85)	12–25 15–25	Cone with seeds; Persists for years	Moise to dry; acidic	IL, IN, MI MN, WI
Pine, Red	*Pinus resinosa*	Very high	S	50–80 (100)	12–25	Cone with seeds; Aug–Oct	Moist to dry, well-drained	IL, MI, MN, WI
Pine, White	*Pinus strobus*	Very high	S,P	60–90 (220)	25–40	Cone with seeds; Aug–Oct	Moist to dry acidic	IA, IL, IN, MI MN, OH, WI
Tamarack; American Larch	*Larix laricina*	Good	S	30–60	10–18	Cone with seeds; year-round	Wet to moist acidic	IL, IN, MI, MN, OH, WI
Spruce, White	*Picea glauca*	High	S,P	30–60 (90)	8–16	Cone with seeds; July–Jan	Moist; acidic	MI, MN, WI

[D]**Dioecious.** Some plants of this species bear male (staminate) flowers and others bear female (pistillate) flowers. Both sexes need to grow in relatively close proximity for fruit to form.

[1]**Susceptibility:** Junipers are susceptible to cedar-apple rust. Don't plant in vicinity of crabapples or hawthorns.

Midwestern Deciduous Shrubs for Attracting Birds

Midwestern shrubs offer a variety of nutritious berries, seeds and nuts for birds throughout the year, as well as good cover and nesting sites. Blackberries, cherries and dogwood berries are rated among the top ten wildlife food plants for many birds and other wildlife. Among shrubs in the northern reaches of the Midwest, blueberries also make the top ten.

As you'll note in the table, a number of other shrubs are highly valuable to birds. For the earliest fruit of the season, nothing can beat serviceberries, and birds will flock to your yard to devour them. If you're lucky, you'll be able to harvest a few of these delicious berries for yourself before they're eaten up. Elderberries and raspberries are top choices for summer fruit, while Spicebush provides its high-fat fruits a little later in summer and into fall, for migrating birds.

Although ranked less high than the shrubs mentioned above, roses and sumacs have fruits that are essential winter foods for birds and other wildlife.

Viburnums are also valuable for birds. Their fruits last into late fall and winter, providing berries for birds when other foods are no longer available. Many viburnums tolerate drier conditions than many dogwoods and as a result, might be better selections for some sites. Viburnums and dogwoods are two of the most showy and prolific of our native midwestern shrubs. All produce abundant fruit that will bring birds to your yard. Given the variety of species in each group, you're sure to find at least one that will thrive in your garden. Better yet—if you have room—choose several.

Midwestern Deciduous Shrubs for Attracting Birds

See Key to Tables, pages 247–248, for abbreviations.

COMMON NAME	LATIN NAME	VALUE TO BIRDS	LIGHT REQ.	HEIGHT (FT.)	WIDTH (FT.)	BLOOM DATES	FRUIT/ SEED TYPE & DATE	SOIL REQ.	NATIVE RANGE
Alder, Speckled	*Alnus incana* (*A. rugosa*)	High	S,P	8–15 (30)	6–20	Mar– Apr	Cone-like; Aug–Feb	Wet to moist	IA,IL,IN,MI, MN,OH,WI
Birch, Dwarf	*Betula pumila*	High	S	3–10	3–6	Apr– May	Cone-like, erect; Aug–Nov	Wet to moist	IA,IL,IN,MI, MN,OH,WI
Blackberry, Common	*Rubus allegheniensis*	Very high	S,P	3–6 (8)	4–8	May– July	Berry; July–Aug	Moist	All 8 States
Blueberry, Early Low	*Vaccinium angustifolium*	Very high	S,P	3/4–2	1–3	Apr– June	Berry; July–Sept	Moist to dry; acidic	IA,IL,IN,MI, MN,OH,WI
Blueberry, Highbush	*Vaccinium corymbosum*	Very high	S,P	6–12	6–12	Apr– June	Berry; June–Sept	Wet to dry; acidic	IL,IN,MI, OH,WI
Bunchberry	*Cornus canadensis*	Fair	P,Sh	1/4– 3/4	1/4	May– July	Berry; Aug– Oct	Moist; acidic	IA,IL,IN,MI MN,OH,WI
Buttonbush	*Cephalanthus occidentalis*	Good	S,P	3–8	3–6	June– Aug	Dry, ball- like pod Sept–Jan	Wet to moist	All 8 States

COMMON NAME	LATIN NAME	VALUE TO BIRDS	LIGHT REQ.	HEIGHT (FT.)	WIDTH (FT.)	BLOOM DATES	FRUIT/ SEED TYPE & DATE	SOIL REQ.	NATIVE RANGE
Cherry, Choke	*Prunus virginiana*	Very high	S,P	6–20 (30)	4–15	July– Aug	Berry; Aug–Sept	Moist to dry	All 8 States
Cherry, Sand	*Prunus pumila*	Very high	S	1–2 (3)	3–6	Apr– June	Berry; July–Sept	Moist to dry	IA,IL,IN,MI, MN,OH,WI
Chokeberry, Black	*Aronia melanocarpa (A. prunifolia)*	Good	S,P	3–8 (10)	3–6	Apr– June	Berry; Sept–Nov	Wet to dry	All 8 States
Coralberry	*Symphori- carpos orbiculatus*	Good	S,P	3–4	4–8	June– Aug	Berry; Oct–Jan	Moist to dry	IA,IL,IN, MO,OH
Currant, Wild Black[1]	*Ribes americanum*	High	S,P	3–5	3–4	Apr– June	Berry; July–Aug	Moist to medium- dry	All 8 States
Dewberry, Common	*Rubus flagellaris*	High	S	1–2		May– July	Berry; June–Aug	Moist to dry	All 8 States
Dogwood, Gray	*Cornus racemosa*	Very high	S,P	3–8	3–8	May– July	Berry; July–Oct	Moist to medium- dry	All 8 States
Dogwood, Red-osier	*Cornus sericea (C. stolonifera)*	Very high	S,P	3–10	4–8	June– Sept	Berry; Sept–Oct	Wet to medium- dry	IA,IL,IN,MI, MN,OH,WI
Dogwood, Rough-leaved	*Cornus drummondii*	Very high	S,P	4–15 (50)		May– June	Berry; Aug–Oct	Wet to dry	IA,IL,IN,MI, MO,OH,WI
Dogwood, Round-leaved	*Cornus rugosa*	Very high	P,Sh	6–10	4–7	May– July	Berry; Aug–Oct	Moist	IA,IL,IN,MI, MN,OH,WI
Dogwood, Silky	*Cornus amomum*	Very high	S,P	3–10	3–6	May– July	Berry; Aug–Oct	Wet to moist	All 8 States
Elderberry, Common	*Sambucus canadensis*	Very high	S,P	5–10	3–8	June– July	Berry; Aug–Oct	Moist to wet	All 8 States
Elderberry, Red-berried	*Sambucus racemosa (S. pubens)*	Very high	S,P	4–10	3–8	Apr– July	Berry; (poisonous) June–Sept	Moist	All 8 States
Gooseberry, Prickly Wild[1]	*Ribes cynosbati*	High	A	3–5	3–5	Apr– June	Berry; July–Sept	Moist to dry	All 8 States
Gooseberry, Missouri[1]	*Ribes missouriense*	High	A	3–6	3–6	Mar– May	Berry; June–Sept	Moist to dry	IA,IL,IN,MN MO,OH,WI
Hardhack; Steeplebush	*Spirea tomentosa*	Good	S,P	2–5	2–5	June– Sept	Dry capsule; Sept–Mar	Wet to medium- dry	IL,IN,MI, MN,MO, OH,WI
Hazelnut, Amer. or Amer. Filbert	*Corylus americana*	Good	S,P	5–12	4–8	Mar– May	Nut; July–Sept	Moist to dry	All 8 States
Hazelnut, Beaked	*Corylus cornuta*	Good	S,P	5–14	4–8	Mar– Apr	Nut; Aug–Sept	Moist to dry	IA,IL,MI, MN,OH,WI
Honeysuckle, Amer. Fly	*Lonicera canadensis*	Good (Nectar)	A	3–6	3–6	Apr– June	Berry; June–Aug	Moist	IL,IN,MI, MN,OH,WI
Huckleberry, Box or Black	*Gaylussacia baccata*	Good	S,P	1–2 (3)	2–4	Apr– June	Berry; July–Sept	Moist to dry; acidic	All 8 States
Indigo Bush	*Amorpha fruticosa*	Good	S	6	10	May– June	Pod (poisonous); Aug–Mar	Wet to dry	All 8 States

COMMON NAME	LATIN NAME	VALUE TO BIRDS	LIGHT REQ.	HEIGHT (FT.)	WIDTH (FT.)	BLOOM DATES	FRUIT/ SEED TYPE & DATE	SOIL REQ.	NATIVE RANGE
Leadplant	*Amorpha canescens*	Good	S	3	3	June–Aug	Pod; Aug–Feb	Moist to dry	IA,IL,IN,MI, MN,MO,WI
Meadowsweet	*Spiraea alba*	Good	S P	2–5	2–5	June–Sept	Dry capsule Sept–Mar	Wet to moist	All 8 States
Ninebark	*Physocarpus opulifolius*	Good	S,P	6–12	6–10	May–July	Dry capsule; July–Mar	Moist to dry	All 8 States
Plum, Wild	*Prunus americana*	Good	S,P	4–10 (18)	4–12	Apr–June	Large berry; Aug–Oct	Moist to medium-dry	All 8 States
Raspberry, Black; Black-cap	*Rubus occidentalis*	Very high	S,P	3–6	4–8	May–June	Berry; June–Aug	Moist to dry	All 8 States
Raspberry, Red	*Rubus idaeus var. strigosus*	Very high	S,P	2–6	3–5	May–July	Berry; July–Aug	Wet to dry	All 8 States
Rose, Early Wild or Smooth	*Rosa blanda*	Good	S,P	2–6	6–12	May–June	Berry (hip); Fall–winter	Moist to dry	All 8 States
Rose, Pasture	*Rosa carolina*	Good	S,P	2–3	3–4	June–July	Berry (hip); Aug–Mar	Moist to dry	IA,IL,IN,MI, MO,OH,WI
Rose, Sunshine	*Rosa arkans-ana*	Good	S	1–2	4–8	June–July	Berry (hip); Fall–winter	Moist to dry, well-drained	IA,IN,MI, MN,MO,OH WI
Rose, Swamp	*Rosa palustris*	Good	S	3–5	3–6	June–Aug	Berry (hip); Aug–winter	Moist to wet	IA,IL,IN,MI, MO,OH,WI
St. John's Wort, Shrubby or Kalm's	*Hypericum prolificum; H. kalmianum*	Good	S,P	3–6	3–6	June–Aug	Dry capsule; Oct–Apr	Moist to dry	IA,IL,IN,MI, MO,OH,WI
Serviceberry, Dwarf	*Amelanchier spicata (A. stolonifera)*	Very high	S	1–6	3–10	May–June	Berry; July–Aug	Dry	IA,MI,MN OH,WI
Serviceberry, Round-leaved	*Amelanchier sanguinea*	Very high	S,P	3–6	3–6	May–June	Berry; July–Aug	Moist to dry	IA,IL,IN, MI, MN, OH,WI
Spicebush[D]	*Lindera benzoin*	Very high	A	8–15	6–15	Mar–May	Berry; July–Sept	Wet to moist; strongly to slightly acidic	IL,IN,MI, MO,OH
Snowberry	*Symphori-carpos albus*	Good	S,P	2–3	3–4	May–July	Berry; Sept–Nov	Moist to dry	IA,IL,IN,MI, MN,OH,WI
Sumac, Fragrant[D]	*Rhus aromatica*	High	S,P	3–6	4–20	Apr–July	Berry; July–Mar	Moist to dry	IA,IL,IN,MI, MO,OH,WI
Sumac, Shining; Winged Sumac[D]	*Rhus copallina*	High	S,P	5–8 (15)	6–10	July–Aug	Berry; Aug–Mar	Moist to dry	IA,IL,IN,MI, MO,OH,WI
Sumac, Smooth[D]	*Rhus glabra*	High	S,P	8–16	10–12	June–July	Berry; Sept–Mar	Moist to dry	All 8 States
Sumac, Staghorn[D]	*Rhus hirta (R. typhina)*	High	S,P	8–18 (25)	8–20	June–July	Berry; Aug–Mar	Moist to dry	IA,IL,IN, MI,MN,OH WI

COMMON NAME	LATIN NAME	VALUE TO BIRDS	LIGHT REQ.	HEIGHT (FT.)	WIDTH (FT.)	BLOOM DATES	FRUIT/ SEED TYPE & DATE	SOIL REQ.	NATIVE RANGE
Tea, New Jersey	*Ceanothus americanus*	Good	S,P	2–3	2–3	June–Aug	Dry capsule; Sept–Nov	Well-drained, sandy or rocky; acidic	All 8 States
Tea, Inland New Jersey or Red Root	*Ceanothus herbaceus (C.ovatus)*	Good	S	2–3	2–3	June	Dry capsule	Well-drained, sandy or rocky	All 8 States
Viburnum, American Cranberrybush	*Viburnum opulus* var. *americanum (V. trilobum)*	High	S,P	5–15	4–10	May–July	Berry; Sept–Feb	Wet to moist	IA,IL,IN, MI,MN,OH, WI
Viburnum, Blackhaw	*Viburnum prunifolium*	High	S,P	8–15 (20)	6–15	Apr–June	Berry; Sept–Dec	Moist to dry	IA,IL,IN,MI, MO,OH,WI
Viburnum, Downy Arrowwood	*Viburnum rafinesqui-anum*	High	S,P	3–6	3–6	May–June	Berry; July–Nov	Moist to dry	All 8 States
Viburnum, Maple-Leaved	*Viburnum acerifolium*	High	S,P	3–6	3–6	May–July	Berry; Aug–Dec	Moist to dry	IL,IN,MI, OH,WI
Viburnum, Nannyberry	*Viburnum lentago*	High	S,P	8–15 (25)	6–12	Apr–June	Berry; Aug–Feb	Moist to dry	All 8 States
Willow, Beaked[D]	*Salix bebbiana*	Good	S	To 25	To 8	Apr–June	Tufted seeds; May–June	Wet to moist	IA,IL,IN,MI, MN,OH,WI
Willow, Prairie[D]	*Salix humilis*	Good	S	To 4	To 8	Mar–June	Cottony seeds; May–June	Wet to dry	All 8 States
Willow, Pussy[D]	*Salix discolor*	Good	S,P	6–15	4–8	Feb–May	Tufted seeds; Apr–May	Wet to moist	All 8 States
Willow, Shining[D]	*Salix lucida*	Good	S,P	6–20	4–8	Apr–June	Cottony seeds; June–July	Wet to moist	IA,IL,IN,MI, MN,OH,WI
Winterberry; Michigan Holly[D]	*Ilex verticillata*	High	S,P	6–10 (15)	6–10	June–July	Berries; Aug–Feb	Wet to moist; prefers acidic	All 8 States
Wintergreen	*Gaultheria procumbens*	Fair	P,Sh	To 1/2	1/4	May Sept	Dry Berries; July–April	Moist to dry; strongly to slightly acid	IL,IN,MI, MN,OH,WI
Wolfberry	*Symphori-carpos occidentalis*	Good	S,P	3–6	3–6	June–Aug	Berries; Sept–Dec	Moist to dry	IA,IL,IN, MN.MO,WI

[1]*Ribes* species are alternate hosts for White Pine blister rust. Don't plant with White Pine.

[D]**Dioecious.** Some plants of this species bear male (staminate) flowers and others bear female (pistillate) flowers. Both sexes need to grow in relatively close proximity for fruit to form.

See Key to Tables, pages 247–248, for abbreviations.

Midwestern Vines for Attracting Birds

Many of our native vines are outstanding "bird" plants. Most of those in the table produce berries for many species of birds. Flowers of the Trumpet Creeper have more nectar for hummingbirds than any other native flowers in North America.

The leafy tangles of vines make them ideal nesting sites for birds. Among our native species, grapevines are the top choice. Other native vines often used by birds for nest sites include Illinois Rose (Climbing Prairie Rose), Virginia Creeper, Trumpet Creeper and Poison Ivy.

Grapevines have an added use for birds. Its bark, in most species, peels easily into thin strips and catbirds, mockingbirds, thrashers, cardinals and finches use it as nesting material.

At least 33 species of birds devour Poison Ivy berries with impunity, and they are, in fact, a preferred food of the Wild Turkey, Northern Flicker, Red-bellied Woodpecker, Yellow-bellied Sapsucker, Hairy Woodpecker, Downy Woodpecker, Black-capped Chickadee, Carolina Chickadee, Northern Mockingbird, Gray Catbird, Hermit Thrush, Ruby-crowned Kinglet, Yellow-rumped Warbler and White-throated Sparrow. Many birds also nest within its leafy bowers. I don't advise you to plant it, since it's poisonous to about 70% of people, but I urge you to leave it in place if it happens to be growing in a corner of your lot, well away from contact with people. Not only is it invaluable to birds, it also is beautiful in fall with lovely translucent white berries set against orange to red leaves.

Both grapes and poison ivy berries are among the top ten foods for wildlife in the Midwest and across the country.

American Bittersweet vine

Midwestern Woody Vines
for Attracting Birds

See Key to Tables, pages 247–248, for abbreviations.

COMMON NAME	LATIN NAME	VALUE TO BIRDS	LIGHT REQ.	HEIGHT (FT.)	WIDTH (FT.)	BLOOM DATES	FRUIT/ SEED TYPE & DATE	SOIL REQ.	NATIVE RANGE
Bittersweet American[D]	*Celastrus scandens*	Fair	All	5–15	4–15	May–June	Berry; Sept–Dec	Dry to moist	All 8 States
Briar, Bristly Cat; Bristly Green Briar[D]	*Smilax hispida (S. tamnoides)*	Good	P, SH	High-climbing	Slender	May–June	Berry	Moist	All 8 States
Grape, Summer[D]	*Vitis aestivalis*	Very high	All	High-climbing		May–June	Berry	Moist to dry	All 8 States
Grape, Frost[D]	*Vitis vulpina*	Very high	All	High-climbing			Berry	Medium to	IA,IL,IN,MI, MO,OH,WI
Grape, Riverbank[D]	*Vitis riparia*	Very high	All	High-climbing		May–June	Berry; July–Aug	Dry to wet	All 8 States
Honeysuckle, Red	*Lonicera dioica*	High	S,P	3–9	3–4	May–June	Berry; July–Aug	Moist	All 8 States
Honeysuckle, Trumpet	*Lonicera sempervirens*	High	S,P	3–15	4–8	May–Fall	Berry; Aug–Sept	Moist	OH
Honeysuckle, Yellow	*Lonicera prolifera (L. reticulata*	High	Sh,P			May–July	Berry	Moist	IA,IL,IN MN,MO,OH, WI
Ivy, Poison[1]	*Toxicodendron radicans (Rhus radicans)*	High	All	to 35+		May–July	Berry; Sept–Jan	Wet to dry	All 8 States
Moonseed[1]	*Menispemum canadense*	High	Sh,P	3–12	6–12	June–July	Berry; Sept–Dec	Wet to dry	All 8 States
Raccoon-Grape; Heartleaf Ampelopsis[D]	*Ampelopsis cordata*	Good	S,P	To 35		June	Berry; Aug–Nov	Wet to medium	IA,IL,IN, MO,OH
Rose, Illinois; Climbing Prairie Rose	*Rosa setigera*	Good	S,P	4–8	5–10	June–July	Berry (hip); Sept–Mar	Moist	IA,IL,IN, MI,MO,OH
Thicket Creeper	*Parthenocissus vitacea*	High	S,P			June–Aug	Berry	Moist to dry	All 8 States
Trumpet Creeper	*Campsis quinquefolia*	High (nectar)	S,P	6–40	4–10	June–Sept	Dry capsules; Aug–Mar	Moist to dry	IL,IN, MO,OH
Virginia Creeper	*Parthenocissus quinquefolia*	High	All	4–40 (80)	3–15	June–Aug	Berry; Sept–Feb	Wet to dry	All 8 States

[1]**Poisonous**

  Poison Ivy—all parts including roots, poisonous to humans (but not birds). I don't recommend you plant it, but if you have a vine growing in an inconspicuous corner, you might consider leaving it for birds.

  Moonseed—fruit very poisonous to humans (but not birds).

[D]**Dioecious.** Some plants of this species bear male (staminate) flowers and others bear female (pistillate) flowers. Both sexes need to grow in relatively close proximity for fruit to form.

LATIN NAME TO COMMON NAME—
A CROSS-REFERENCE FOR WOODY PLANTS

Trees, Shrubs and Vines

This cross-reference gives the common names used in the tables and text of this book. The Latin names in parentheses are alternate names used by some botanists.

Abies balsamea—Balsam Fir
Acer negundo—Box Elder
Acer nigrum—Black Maple
Acer rubrum—Red Maple
Acer saccharinum—Silver Maple
Acer saccharum—Sugar Maple
Acer spicatum—Mountain Maple
Aesculus glabra—Ohio Buckeye
Alnus incana (A. rugosa)—Speckled Alder
Amelanchier arborea—Serviceberry; Juneberry; Shadbush
Amelanchier laevis –Alleghany Serviceberry; Smooth Serviceberry
Amelanchier sanguinea—Round-leaved Serviceberry
Amelanchier spicata (A. stolonifera)—Dwarf Serviceberry
Amorpha canescens—Leadplant
Amorpha fruticosa—Indigo Bush
Ampelopsis cordata—Raccoon-Grape; Heartleaf Ampelopsis
Aronia melanocarpa (A. prunifolia)—Black Chokeberry
Betula alleghaniensis (B. lutea)—Yellow Birch
Betula nigra—River Birch
Betula papyrifera—Paper Birch
Betula pumila—Dwarf Birch
Campsis radicans—Trumpet Creeper
Carya cordiformis—Bitternut Hickory
Carya glabra—Pignut Hickory
Carya ovata—Shagbark Hickory
Carya tomentosa (C. alba)—Mockernut Hickory
Ceanothus americanus—New Jersey Tea
Ceanothus herbaceus (C. ovatus)—Inland New Jersey Tea or Red Root
Celastrus scandens—American Bittersweet
Celtis laevigata—Southern Hackberry
Celtis occidentalis—Northern Hackberry
Cephalanthus occidentalis - Buttonbush
Cornus alternifolia—Alternate-leaved Dogwood; Pagoda Dogwood
Cornus amomum—Silky Dogwood
Cornus canadensis—Bunchberry
Cornus drummondii—Rough-leaved Dogwood

Cornus florida—Flowering Dogwood
Cornus racemosa—Gray Dogwood
Cornus rugosa—Round-leaved Dogwood
Cornus sericea (C. stolonifera)—Red-osier Dogwood
Corylus americana—American Hazelnut; American Filbert
Corylus cornuta—Beaked Hazelnut
Crataegus chrysocarpa—Fireberry Hawthorn
Crataegus coccinea (C. pedicillata)—Scarlet Hawthorn
Crataegus crus-galli—Cockspur Hawthorn
Crataegus flabellata (C. macrosperma)—Large-seeded Hawthorn
Crataegus intricata—Biltmore Hawthorn
Crataegus mollis—Downy Hawthorn
Crataegus phaenopyrum—Washington Hawthorn
Crataegus pruinosa—Frosted Hawthorn
Crataegus punctata—Dotted Hawthorn
Crataegus succulenta—Fleshy Hawthorn
Diospyros virginiana—Common Persimmon
Fagus grandifolia—American Beech
Gaultheria procumbens—Wintergreen
Gaylussacia baccata—Box Huckleberry; Black Huckleberry
Hypericum kalmianum—Kalm's St. John's Wort
Hypericum prolificum—Shrubby St. John's Wort
Ilex verticillata—Winterberry; Michigan Holly
Juniperus communis—Common Juniper
Juniperus horizontalis—Trailing Juniper
Juniperus virginiana—Red Cedar
Larix laricina—Tamarack; American Larch
Lindera benzoin—Spicebush
Liriodendron tulipifera—Tulip Tree
Lonicera canadensis—American Fly Honeysuckle
Lonicera dioica—Red Honeysuckle
Lonicera prolifera (L. reticulata)—Yellow Honeysuckle
Lonicera sempervirens—Trumpet Honeysuckle
Malus coronaria (Pyrus c.)—Wild Sweet Crabapple
Malus ioensis (Pyrus i.)—Iowa Crabapple
Menispermum canadense—Moonseed
Morus rubra—Red Mulberry
Nyssa sylvatica—Black Gum; Sour Gum
Parthenocissus quinquefolia—Virginia Creeper
Parthenocissus vitacea—Thicket Creeper
Physocarpus opulifolius—Ninebark
Picea glauca—White Spruce
Pinus banksiana—Jack Pine
Pinus resinosa—Red Pine
Pinus strobus—White Pine

Platanus occidentalis—Sycamore
Populus balsamifera—Balsam Poplar
Populus deltoides—Eastern Cottonwood
Populus grandidentata—Large-Toothed Aspen
Populus tremuloides—Quaking Aspen
Prunus americana—Wild Plum
Prunus pensylvanica—Pin Cherry
Prunus pumila—Sand Cherry
Prunus serotina—Wild Black Cherry
Prunus virginiana—Choke Cherry
Ptelea trifoliata—Wafer Ash; Hop Tree
Pyrus coronaria—See *Malus c.*
Pyrus ioensis—See *Malus i.*
Quercus alba—White Oak
Quercus bicolor—Swamp White Oak
Quercus coccinea—Scarlet Oak
Quercus ellipsoidalis—Northern Pin Oak
Quercus imbricaria—Shingle Oak
Quercus macrocarpa—Bur Oak
Quercus marilandica—Blackjack Oak
Quercus muehlenbergii—Chinquapin Oak
Quercus palustris—Pin Oak
Quercus rubra (Q. borealis)—Red Oak
Quercus stellata—Post Oak
Quercus velutina—Black Oak
Rhus aromatica—Fragrant Sumac
Rhus copallina—Shining Sumac; Winged Sumac
Rhus glabra—Smooth Sumac
Rhus hirta (R. typhina)—Staghorn Sumac
Rhus radicans—See *Toxicodendron r.*
Ribes americanum—Wild Black Currant
Ribes cynosbati—Prickly Wild Gooseberry
Ribes missouriense—Missouri Gooseberry
Rosa arkansana—Sunshine Rose
Rosa blanda—Early Wild Rose; Smooth Rose
Rosa carolina—Pasture Rose
Rosa palustris—Swamp Rose
Rosa setigera—Illinois Rose; Climbing Prairie Rose
Rubus allegheniensis—Common Blackberry
Rubus flagellaris—Common Dewberry
Rubus idaeus var. *strigosus*—Red Raspberry
Rubus occidentalis—Black Raspberry; Blackcap
Salix amygdaloides—Peach-leaved Willow
Salix bebbiana—Beaked Willow
Salix discolor—Pussy Willow
Salix humilis—Prairie Willow
Salix lucida—Shining Willow
Salix nigra—Black Willow
Sambucus canadensis—Common Elderberry
Sambucus racemosa (S. pubens)—Red-berried
    Elderberry
Sassafras albidum—Sassafras
Smilax hispida (S. tamnoides)—Bristly Cat Briar;

Virginia Creeper berries

    Bristly Green Briar
Sorbus americana—American Mountain Ash
Sorbus decora—Showy Mountain Ash
Spirea alba—Meadowsweet
Spirea tomentosa—Hardhack; Steeplebush
Symphoricarpos albus—Snowberry
Symphoricarpos occidentalis—Wolfberry
Symphoricarpos orbiculatus—Coralberry
Thuja occidentalis—White Cedar; Arborvitae
Toxicodendron radicans (Rhus r.)—Poison Ivy
Tsuga canadensis—Hemlock
Vaccinium angustifolium—Early Low Blueberry
Vaccinium corymbosum—Highbush Blueberry
Viburnum acerifolium—Maple-leaved Viburnum
Viburnum lentago—Nannyberry Viburnum
Viburnum opulus var. *americanum (V. trilobum)*—
    American Cranberrybush Viburnum
Viburnum prunifolium—Blackhaw Viburnum
Viburnum rafinesquianum—Downy Arrowwood
    Viburnum
Vitis aestivalis—Summer Grape
Vitis riparia—Riverbank Grape
Vitis vulpina—Frost Grape

Chapter 18
Wildflowers, Ferns, Grasses, Sedges & Rushes

The tables in this chapter will help you choose herbaceous species for your site. Herbaceous plants are nonwoody plants with stems that die at the end of the growing season. These tables, unlike those for woody plants, do not show the value of the plants for birds. That information appears in the chapters on the various bird gardens, where the specific benefits can be treated more thoroughly.

Generally speaking, the benefits to birds include primarily food, cover and nesting material. Many herbaceous plants, for example, are prairie and wetland species noteworthy for their seeds and cover. Many herbaceous plants also have nectar-rich flowers for hummingbirds. Some herbaceous species, mainly the woodland plants, produce berries, and others have flowers that attract insects on which birds like to feed. In addition, some herbaceous plants provide fibers or fluff that birds use to build nests.

As you'll note in these tables, the Midwest has a wealth of herbaceous species with known value to birds. In addition, many others indirectly benefit birds, plants whose leaves or fruits are eaten by insects or small mammals on which birds, in turn, may feed. Trilliums, for instance, have seeds with appendages eaten by ants, a favorite food of flickers. Don't hesitate to consider the whole gamut of midwestern species for your garden. Every species of our native flora is likely to have value, although sometimes unknown, for birds and other wildlife.

Chapter 7 tells how and when to plant herbaceous plants.

Wildflowers

All the recommended wildflowers in the table have documented value for birds.

Perhaps one of the most amazing is the Cup Plant, a one-stop avian supermarket that provides birds with three of their basic needs at once. Its nutritious seeds attract great flocks of finches in fall. The opposite leaves form a cup, as its name suggests, which collects and holds water after a rainfall. Hummingbirds, orioles and other birds are commonly seen taking a drink from the Cup Plant on hot, dry days. Cup Plants are also big and bushy, offering valuable cover for birds in their leafy hideaways.

The other recommended wildflowers also have their unique attractions for birds. All will add beauty and interest to your landscaping. By using the full palette of their colors and textures, you are likely to host the greatest potential variety of avian visitors in your garden.

photo: Cup Plant

Midwestern Wildflowers
for Attracting Birds

See Key to Tables, pages 247–248, for abbreviations.

COMMON NAME	LATIN NAME	PLANT TYPE	BLOOM DATES	COLOR	HEIGHT	LIGHT REQ.	SOIL REQ.	NATIVE RANGE IN MIDWEST
Alexanders, Golden	*Zizia aurea*	P	Apr–June	Yellow	1–3'	S, P to wet	Moist	All 8 States
Alum Root, Prairie	*Heuchera richardsonii*	P	May–July	Greenish-white	2–3'	S, P	Moist to dry	All 8 States
Anemone, Meadow or Canada	*Anemone canadensis*	P	May–June	White	1–2'	S, P	Moist to wet	All 8 States
Angelica, Great	*Angelica atropurpurea*	P	May–June	White	To 7'	S, P	Moist to wet; prefers alkaline	IA,IL,IN,MI, MN,OH,WI
Aster, Arrow-leaved	*Aster sagittifolius*	P	Aug–Oct	Light blue	2–4'	A	Moist to medium dry	All 8 States
Aster, Big-leaved	*Aster macrophyllus*	P	Aug–Oct	Light lilac	1'	P, Sh	Moist to dry	All 8 States
Aster, Bristly or Red-Stemmed	*Aster puniceus*	P	Aug–Oct	Light blue	1–6'	S	Wet	All 8 States
Aster, Hairy or Frost	*Aster pilosus*	P	Aug–Sept	White	2–4'	S	Dry	All 8 States
Aster, Heath	*Aster ericoides*	P	Aug–Oct	White	1–3'	S, P	Moist to dry	All 8 States
Aster, New England	*Aster novae-angliae*	P	Aug–Oct	Pink or purple	2–5'	S, P	Moist to wet	All 8 States
Aster, Panicled	*Aster lanceolatus (A. simplex)*	P	Aug–Oct	White	2–4'	S	Moist to wet	All 8 States
Aster, Short's	*Aster shortii*	P	Aug–Oct	Blue	1–4'	P, Sh	Moist to dry	IA,IL,IN,MI MN,OH,WI
Aster, Side-Flowering or Calico	*Aster lateriflorus*	P	Aug–Oct	White	1–3'	P, Sh	Medium-dry to moist	All 8 States
Aster, Silky	*Aster sericeus*	P	Sept–Oct	Purple	1–2'	S, P	Medium-dry to dry	IA,IL,IN,MI, MN,MO,WI
Aster, Sky Blue	*Aster oolentangiensis (A. azureus)*	P	Aug–Oct	Blue	1–4'	S, P	Moist to dry	All 8 States
Aster, Smooth Blue	*Aster laevis*	P	Aug–Oct	Blue	2–4'	S	Medium-dry to moist	All 8 States
Baneberry, Red	*Actaea rubra*	P	Apr–June	White	1–3'	P, Sh	Moist	IA,IL,IN,MI, MN,OH,WI
Baneberry, White	*Actaea alba (A. pachypoda)*	P	May–June	White	1–3'	P, Sh	Moist	All 8 States

COMMON NAME	LATIN NAME	PLANT TYPE	BLOOM DATES	COLOR	HEIGHT	LIGHT REQ.	SOIL REQ.	NATIVE RANGE IN MIDWEST
Beard Tongue, Foxglove	*Penstemon digitalis*	P	June–July	White	2–5'	S, P	Moist to medium-dry	IA,IL,IN,MI, MO,OH
Beard Tongue, Large-Flowered	*Penstemon grandiflorus*	B, P	May–June	Pale purple	2–3.5'	S	Dry to medium-dry; sandy	IA,IL,MN, MO,WI
Beard Tongue, Pale	*Penstemon pallidus*	P	May–July	Cream	1–3'	S, P	Dry to medium-dry; sandy	All 8 States
Beard Tongue, Slender	*Penstemon gracilis*	P	May–July	Lavender	8–24"	S, P	Dry to medium-dry	IA,IL,MI, MN,WI
Bedstraw, Northern	*Galium boreale*	P	June–July	White	20–30"	S	Moist to wet	All 8 States
Bellflower, Tall	*Campanula americana*	A, B	July–Oct	Blue	2–6'	P, Sh	Moist	All 8 States
Bergamot, Wild	*Monarda fistulosa*	P	July–Sept	Lavender	2–4'	S, P	Moist to dry	All 8 States
Berry, Partridge	*Mitchella repens*	P	June–July	White	1–2"	P, Sh	Moist to dry	All 8 States
Betony, Wood; Lousewort	*Pedicularis canadensis*	P	Apr–May	Yellow	4–12"	S, P	Moist to dry; parasitic on grass	All 8 States
Blazing Star, Cylindrical	*Liatris cylindracea*	P	July–Oct	Pink-purple	8–24"	S	Medium-dry to dry	All 8 States
Blazing Star, Marsh	*Liatris spicata*	P	July–Sept	Pink-purple	3–6'	S	Moist to wet	IL,IN,MI, MO,OH,WI
Blazing Star, Meadow	*Liatris ligulistylis*	P	Aug–Sept	Pink-purple	3–5'	S	Moist	IA,MN,WI
Blazing Star, Prairie	*Liatris pycno-stachya*	P	July–Sept	Pink-purple	2–4'	S	Moist	IA,IL,IN,MN, MO,OH,WI
Blazing Star, Rough	*Liatris aspera*	P	July–Oct	Pink-purple	2–3'	S	Moist to dry	All 8 States
Bluebead	*Clintonia borealis*	P	May–June	Yellow	8–12"	Sh	Moist; acid	IL,IN,MI, MN, OH,WI
Bluebells, Virginia	*Mertensia virginica*	P	Apr–May	Blue	1–2'	P, Sh	Moist	All 8 States
Boltonia	*Boltonia asteroides*	P	Aug–Oct	White	3–5'	S, P	Wet to dry	All 8 States
Boneset	*Eupatorium perfoliatum*	P	July–Sept	White	2–4'	S	Moist to wet	All 8 States
Bugbane, False; Black Cohosh	*Cimicifuga racemosa*	P	June–Aug	White	3–5'	P, Sh	Moist	IA,IL,IN,MI, MO,OH
Campion, Starry	*Silene stellata*	P	June–Oct	White	1–2'	S, P	Moist to medium-dry	All 8 States
Cardinal Flower	*Lobelia cardinalis*	P	July–Sept	Scarlet	2–5'	S, P	Moist to wet	All 8 States

COMMON NAME	LATIN NAME	PLANT TYPE	BLOOM DATES	COLOR	HEIGHT	LIGHT REQ.	SOIL REQ.	NATIVE RANGE IN MIDWEST
Carrion Flower[D]	*Smilax herbecea*	P	Apr–June	Greenish-yellow	Vine–8'	P	Moist	All 8 States
Catchfly, Royal	*Silene regia*	P	July–Aug	Crimson	2–4'	S	Moist to medium-dry	IL,IN,OH, MO
Clover, Purple Prairie	*Dalea purpurea (Petalostemum p.)*	P	July–Sept	Purple	1–3'	S	Moist to dry	All 8 states
Clover, Round-headed Bush	*Lespedeza capitata*	P	Aug–Sept	Creamy-white	2–4'	S, P	Moist to dry	All 8 States
Clover, White Prairie	*Dalea candida (Petalostemum c.)*	P	June–Sept	White	1–3'	S	Moist to dry	IA,IL,IN,MN, MO,OH,WI
Cohosh, Blue	*Caulophyllum thalictroides*	P	Apr–May	Yellow-green	1–3'	Sh	Moist	All 8 States
Columbine, Wild	*Aquilegia canadensis*	P	Apr–June	Red & yellow	1–3'	S, P	Dry to moist	All 8 States
Compass Plant	*Silphium laciniatum*	P	June–Sept	Yellow	3–10'	S	Moist to medium-dry	All 8 States
Coneflower, Pale Purple	*Echinacea pallida (E. angustifolia)*	P	June–July	Pale Purple	2–4'	S	Dry to moist	IA,IL,IN,MI, MN,MO,WI
Coneflower, Purple	*Echinacea purpurea*	P	July–Sept	Reddish purple	3–4'	P, S	Moist	IA,IL,IN,MI, MO,OH
Coneflower, Yellow or Grey-headed	*Ratibida pinnata*	P	July–Sept	Yellow	2–4'	S, P	Moist to medium-dry	All 8 States
Coreopsis, Prairie	*Coreopsis palmata*	P	June–Aug	Yellow	18–30"	S	Moist to dry	IA,IL,IN,MI, MN,MO,WI
Coreopsis, Sand	*Coreopsis lanceolata*	P	May–Aug	Yellow	2–3'	S	Moist to dry	IL,IN,MI, MO,OH,WI
Culver's Root	*Veronicastrum virginicum*	P	July–Aug	White	3–6'	S, P	Moist	All 8 States
Cup Plant	*Silphium perfoliatum*	P	July–Sept	Yellow	3–8'	S, P	Moist	All 8 States
Dock, Prairie	*Silphium terebinthinaceum*	P	July–Sept	Yellow	2–10'	S	Moist to medium dry	IA,IL,IN,MI, MO,OII,WI
Figwort, Early	*Scrophularia lanceolata*	P	May–July	Reddish brown	4–7'	P, Sh	Moist to dry	All 8 States
Figwort, Late	*Scrophularia marilandica*	P	June–Oct	Reddish brown	4–7'	P	Moist to medium-dry	All 8 States
Fireweed	*Epilobium angustifolium*	P	June–Aug	Pink	2–4'	S, P	Moist	IA,IL,IN,MI, MN,OH,WI
Foxglove, Fern-leaved False	*Aureolaria pedicularia*	A	July–Sept	Yellow	1–3'	P	Dry; sand, under oaks	All 8 States
Foxglove, Yellow False	*Aureolaria grandiflora*	P	Aug–Oct	Yellow	3–4'	P	Dry; parasitic on White Oak	IA,IL,IN, MN,MO,WI

COMMON NAME	LATIN NAME	PLANT TYPE	BLOOM DATES	COLOR	HEIGHT	LIGHT REQ.	SOIL REQ.	NATIVE RANGE IN MIDWEST
Gentian, Early Horse	*Triosteum aurantiacum*	P	Apr–July	Purplish red	To 4'	P	Medium to dry	All 8 States
Gentian, Late Horse; Tinker's Weed	*Triosteum perfoliatum*	P	May–July	Purplish to greenish-yellow	To 4'	P	Dry	All 8 States
Geranium, Wild	*Geranium maculatum*	P	Apr–June	Pink	1–2'	A	Moist to medium-dry	All 8 States
Goat's Rue	*Tephrosia virginiana*	P	June–July	Cream & mauve	8–20"	S, P	Dry; acidic, sand	All 8 States
Golden Glow, Wild; Green-headed Coneflower	*Rudbeckia laciniata*	P	July–Oct	Yellow	3–6'	S, P	Moist	All 8 States
Goldenrod, Blue-Stemmed	*Solidago caesia*	P	Aug–Sept	Yellow	2–4'	P, Sh	Dry to moist	IL,IN,MI, MO,OH,WI
Goldenrod, Broad-leaved or Zigzag	*Solidago flexicaulis*	P	Aug–Oct	Yellow	1–3'	P, Sh	Moist	All 8 States
Goldenrod, Elm-leaved	*Solidago ulmifolia*	P	July–Oct	Yellow	2–4'	P	Moist to medium-dry	All 8 States
Goldenrod, Old-field	*Solidago nemoralis*	P	Aug–Oct	Yellow	1–3'	S, P	Dry	All 8 States
Goldenrod, Riddell's	*Solidago riddellii*	P	Sept–Oct	Yellow	2–3'	S	Moist to wet	All 8 States
Goldenrod, Showy	*Solidago speciosa*	P	Aug–Oct	Yellow	2–5'	S, P	Moist to dry	All 8 States
Goldenrod, Stiff	*Solidago rigida*	P	Aug–Oct	Golden yellow	2–5'	S	Moist to dry	All 8 states
Harebell	*Campanula rotundifolia*	P	June–Sept	Blue	6–14"	S, P	Dry to medium-dry	All 8 States
Hog Peanut	*Amphicarpaea bracteata*	A	July–Sept	Purplish to whitish	Vine	P, Sh	Moist to dry	All 8 States
Hyssop, Lavender Giant	*Agastache foeniculum*	P	June–Sept	Blue-violet	3'	S, P	Moist to medium-dry	IA,IL,MN, WI
Hyssop, Purple Giant	*Agastache scrophulariifolia*	P	July–Oct	Purple	4–7'	S,P	Moist to medium-dry	All 8 States
Hyssop, Yellow Giant	*Agastache nepetoides*	P	July–Oct	Yellow	4–7'	S, P	Moist to medium-dry	All 8 States
Indigo, Blue Wild	*Baptisia australis*	P	May–July	Violet-blue	2–4'	S, P	Moist	IA,IL,IN, MO,OH
Indigo, White Wild	*Baptisia alba (B. lactea; B. leucantha)*	P	June–July	White	3–4'	S, P	Moist to dry	All 8 States

COMMON NAME	LATIN NAME	PLANT TYPE	BLOOM DATES	COLOR	HEIGHT	LIGHT REQ.	SOIL REQ.	NATIVE RANGE IN MIDWEST
Iris; Northern Blue Flag	*Iris versicolor*	P	May–July	Blue-violet to purple	2–4'	S, P	Moist to wet	IA,IL,OH,MI, MN,WI
Iris, Southern Blue Flag	*Iris virginica (I. shrevei)*	P	May–July	Light to dark purple	2–3'	S, P	Moist to wet	All 8 States
Ironweed	*Vernonia fasciculata*	P	July–Sept	Deep-purple	3–6'	S	Moist to wet	IA,IL,IN,MN, MO,OH,WI
Jack-in-the-Pulpit	*Arisaema triphyllum*	P	Apr–July	Green & brown or mahogany	1–2'	Sh	Moist; rich	All 8 States
Jewelweed, Orange; Spotted Touch-Me-Not	*Impatiens capensis (I. biflora)*	A	June–Sept	Orange-yellow	2–5'	A	Moist to wet	All 8 States
Jewelweed, Yellow; Pale Touch-Me-Not	*Impatiens pallida*	A	June–Oct	Yellow	3–5'	A	Moist to wet	All 8 States
Joe Pye Weed, Purple or Sweet	*Eupatorium purpureum*	P	July–Sept	Pink	3–8'	A	Moist	All 8 States
Joe Pye Weed, Spotted	*Eupatorium maculatum*	P	July–Aug	Rose to pink	4–6'	S	Moist to wet	All 8 States
Larkspur, Prairie	*Delphinium carolinianum (D. virescens)*	P	May–June	Blue	2–4'	S, P	Moist to medium-dry	IA,IL,MN MO,WI
Lily, Michigan; Turk's Cap Lily	*Lilium michiganense (L. superbum)*	P	June–Aug	Orange	3–7'	S, P	Moist to wet	All 8 States
Lily, Prairie	*Lilium philadelphicum*	P	June–July	Red-orange	1–3'	S, P	Moist to medium-dry	All 8 States
Lobelia, Great Blue	*Lobelia siphilitica*	P	July–Oct	Blue	1–4'	S, P	Moist to wet	All 8 States
Lobelia, Pale Spiked	*Lobelia spicata*	P	May–Aug	Lavender	8–40"	S	Moist	All 8 States
Loosestrife, Tufted	*Lysimachia thyrsiflora*	P	May–June	Yellow	1–2'	S, P	Wet	All 8 States
Lousewort, Swamp	*Pedicularis lanceolata*	P	Aug–Sept	Yellow	1–3'	S, P	Wet; parasitic on grass	All 8 States
Lupine, Wild	*Lupinus perennis*	P	May–July	Blue to violet	1–2'	S, P	Dry to medium-dry; sand	IA,IL,IN,MI, MN,OH,WI
Mallow, Swamp Rose	*Hibiscus moscheutos (H. palustris)*	P	July–Sept	White to pink	5–7'	S	Moist to wet	IL,IN,MI, OH,WI
Marigold, Marsh	*Caltha palustris*	P	Apr–June	Yellow	1–2'	A	Moist to wet	All 8 States
Marigold, Nodding Bur	*Bidens cernua*	A	June–Sept	Yellow	1–3'	S	Wet	All 8 States
Meadow Rue, Purple or Tall	*Thalictrum dasycarpum*	P	June–July	Cream	3–7'	S	Moist	All 8 States

COMMON NAME	LATIN NAME	PLANT TYPE	BLOOM DATES	COLOR	HEIGHT	LIGHT REQ.	SOIL REQ.	NATIVE RANGE IN MIDWEST
Milkweed, Butterfly	*Asclepias tuberosa*	P	June–Aug	Orange	2'	S	Moist to dry	All 8 States
Milkweed, Common	*Asclepias syriaca*	P	June–Aug	Purple	3–4'	S, P	Moist to dry	All 8 States
Milkweed, Prairie	*Asclepias sullivantii*	P	June–Aug	Pink	2–3'	S	Moist	All 8 States
Milkweed, Swamp or Marsh	*Asclepias incarnata*	P	June–Aug	Pink, rose-purple	2–5'	S, P	Moist to wet	All 8 States
Milkweed, Tall Green	*Asclepias hirtella*	P	June–Aug	Greenish-white	2–3'	S	Dry to medium-dry	All 8 States
Milkweed, Whorled	*Asclepias verticillata*	P	July–Sept	White	1–2'	S	Moist to dry	All 8 States
Mint, Horse	*Monarda punctata*	B	July–Sept	Lavender	6–30"	S	Dry to medium-dry; sand	All 8 States
Mint, Common Mountain	*Pycnanthemum virginianum*	P	June–Sept	White	20–36"	S, P	Moist to wet	All 8 States
Monkey Flower	*Mimulus ringens*	P	June–Sept	Light violet	1–3'	S	Moist to wet	All 8 States
Nettle, Hedge; Woundwort	*Stachys palustris*	P	June–Sept	Magenta	2–3'	S	Moist to wet	All 8 States
Obedient Plant; False Dragon-head	*Physostegia virginiana*	P	Aug–Sept	Pale purple or rose	2–5'	S, P	Moist to wet	All 8 States
Onion, Nodding Wild	*Alliium cernuum*	P	July–Aug	Lavender	1–2'	S	Moist to medium-dry	All 8 States
Onion, Prairie	*Allium stellatum*	P	July–Aug	Lavender	1–2'	S	Moist to dry	IA,IL,MI,MN, MO,OH,WI
Oswego Tea; Bee Balm	*Monarda didyma*	P	July–Sept	Scarlet	2–4'	P, Sh	Moist	MI, OH
Paintbrush, Downy	*Castilleja sessiliflora*	P	May–June	Cream	6–24"	S	Dry to medium-dry; parasitic	IA,IL,MN, MO,WI
Paintbrush, Indian	*Castilleja coccinea*	A, B	Apr–Sept	Scarlet with yellow	1–2'	S	Moist to medium-dry; parasitic	All 8 States
Pasque Flower	*Anemone patens* var. *multifida*	P	April–May	Lavender	6"	S	Dry to medium-dry	IA,IL,MN, WI
Pea, Partridge	*Chamaecrista fasciculata (Cassia fasciculata)*	A	July–Sept	Yellow	6–36"	S	Dry to moist; sand	All 8 States
Petunia, Wild; Hairy Ruellia	*Ruellia humilis*	P	June–Aug	Violet	6–24"	S	Dry to moist	All 8 States

COMMON NAME	LATIN NAME	PLANT TYPE	BLOOM DATES	COLOR	HEIGHT	LIGHT REQ.	SOIL REQ.	NATIVE RANGE IN MIDWEST
Phlox, Blue; Woodland Phlox	*Phlox divaricata*	P	Apr–June	Blue	6–24"	Sh, P	Moist to medium-dry	All 8 States
Phlox, Sand Prairie	*Phlox pilosa*	P	Apr–July	Pink	1–2'	S, P	Moist to dry	All 8 States
Phlox, Smooth	*Phlox glaberrima*	P	June–Sept	Pink	20–30"	S	Moist	IL,IN,MO,OH,WI
Phlox, Sweet William	*Phlox maculata*	P	June–Aug	Pink	1–3'	S, P	Moist	IA,IL,IN,MI,MN,MO,OH
Pink, Fire	*Silene virginica*	P	May–July	Crimson	6–14"	P, Sh	Moist	IL,IN,MI,MO, OH,WI
Plantain, Pale Indian	*Cacalia atriplicifolia*	P	July–Sept	White	3–7'	S, P	Moist to medium-dry	All 8 States
Plantain, Prairie Indian	*Cacalia plantiginea*	P	June–July	White	3–5'	S	Moist	All 8 States
Prairie Smoke	*Geum triflorum*	P	April–June	Pink	6–13"	S	Dry	IA IL,MI,MN,OH, WI
Primrose, Common Evening	*Oenothera biennis*	B	June–Sept	Yellow	2–6'	S, P	Moist to dry	All 8 States
Rattlesnake Master	*Eryngium yuccifolium*	P	June–Sept	White	2–5'	S	Moist	All 8 States
Rosin Weed	*Silphium integrifolium*	P	July–Sept	Yellow	2–6'	S	Moist to dry	IA,IL,IN,MI,MO,OH,WI
Sage, White	*Artemisia ludoviciana*	P	July–Sept	Greenish-white	2–4'	S	Moist to dry	IA,MI,MN,MO,WI
Sarsaparilla, Wild	*Aralia nudicaulis*	P	May–June	Greenish-white	6–12"	P, Sh	Moist to dry	All 8 States
Senna, Maryland	*Senna marilandica (Cassia marilandica)*	P	July–Aug	Yellow	2–4'	S	Moist	IA,IL,IN,MO,OH,WI
Senna, Wild	*Senna hebecarpa (Cassia hebecarpa)*	P	July–Aug	Yellow	3–7'	S	Moist to medium-dry	IL,IN,MI,OH,WI
Sneezeweed	*Helenium autumnale*	P	Aug–Oct	Yellow	2–5'	S	Moist to wet	All 8 States
Solomon's Seal, Downy	*Polygonatum pubescens*	P	May–July	White with green edge	1–2'	Sh	Moist	IA,IL,IN,MI,MN,OH,WI
Solomon's Seal, Feathery False	*Smilacina racemosa*	P	Apr–June	White	1–3'	P, Sh	Moist to dry	All 8 States
Solomon's Seal, Smooth	*Polygonatum biflorum (P. caniculatum)*	P	May–June	White with green edge	1–4'	A	Moist to medium-dry	All 8 States
Solomon's Seal, Starry False	*Smilacina stellata*	P	Apr–June	White	1–3'	A	Moist to dry	All 8 States
Spiderwort, Common	*Tradescantia ohiensis*	P	May–July	Blue	2–4'	S, P	Dry to moist	All 8 States

Wildflowers

273

COMMON NAME	LATIN NAME	PLANT TYPE	BLOOM DATES	COLOR	HEIGHT	LIGHT REQ.	SOIL REQ.	NATIVE RANGE IN MIDWEST
Spikenard	*Aralia racemosa*	P	July	Greenish-white	3–6'	P, Sh	Moist	All 8 States
Spurge, Flowering	*Euphorbia corollata*	P	June–Aug	White	2–4'	S	Moist to dry	All 8 States
Strawberry, Wild	*Fragaria virginiana*	P	Apr–June	White	4–6"	A	Moist to dry	All 8 States
Sunflower, False or Oxeye	*Heliopsis helianthoides*	P	June–Sept	Yellow	2–5'	S, P	Moist to medium-dry	All 8 States
Sunflower, Pale-leaved or Woodland	*Helianthus strumosus*	P	July–Sept	Yellow	3–6'	S, P	Moist to medium-dry	All 8 States
Sunflower, Prairie	*Helianthus pauciflorus (H. rigidus; H. laetiflorus)*	P	July–Sept	Yellow	2–6'	S	Dry to medium-dry	All 8 States
Sunflower, Western	*Helianthus occidentalis*	P	July–Sept	Yellow	2–3'	S	Moist to dry	All 8 States
Susan, Black-eyed	*Rudbeckia hirta*	B	June–Oct	Yellow	1–3'	S, P	Moist to dry	All 8 States
Susan, Brown-eyed	*Rudbeckia triloba*	B	Aug–Oct	Yellow	2–5'	S, P	Moist	All 8 States
Susan, Sweet Black-eyed	*Rudbeckia subtomentosa*	P	Aug–Oct	Yellow	3–5'	S, P	Moist	IA,IL,IN,MI, MN,MO,WI
Thimbleweed	*Anemone virginiana*	P	June–Aug	White	12–30"	A	Moist to medium-dry	All 8 States
Thistle, Pasture	*Cirsium discolor*	B	July–Oct	Purple	3–7'	S	Moist to medium-dry	All 8 States
Thistle, Swamp	*Cirsium muticum*	B	July–Sept	Rose-purple	3–9'	S	Moist to wet	All 8 States
Tick Trefoil, Showy	*Desmodium canadense*	P	June–Aug	Purple or pink	2–5'	S	Moist to medium-dry	All 8 States
Turtlehead	*Chelone glabra*	P	July–Sept	White	3–4'	S, P	Moist to wet	All 8 States
Turtlehead, Red	*Chelone obliqua*	P	Aug–Oct	Rose-pink	1–3'	S, P	Moist to wet	IA IL,IN,MI, MN,MO
Vervain, Blue	*Verbena hastata*	P	July–Sept	Purple	2–6'	S	Moist to wet	All 8 States
Vervain, Hoary	*Verbena stricta*	P	June–Sept	Purple	2–3'	S	Dry to medium-dry	All 8 States
Vetch, American	*Vicia americana*	P	May–July	Blue-purple	Vine to 3'	S, P	Moist	All 8 States
Vetch, Canada Milk	*Astragalus canadensis*	P	June–Aug	Cream	1–4'	S	Moist to medium-dry	All 8 States

COMMON NAME	LATIN NAME	PLANT TYPE	BLOOM DATES	COLOR	HEIGHT	LIGHT REQ.	SOIL REQ.	NATIVE RANGE IN MIDWEST
Vetchling, Marsh	*Lathyrus palustris*	P	June–Sept	Red-purple	Vine	S	Moist	All 8 States
Violet, Canada or Tall White	*Viola canadensis*	P	Apr–July	White	8–16"	P, Sh	Moist	IA,IL,IN,MI, MN,OH,WI
Violet, Bird's Foot	*Viola pedata*	P	Apr–June	Violet	3–6"	S, P	Dry to medium-dry, sand	All 8 States
Violet, Prairie	*Viola palmata (V. pedatifida)*	P	Apr–June	Violet	6–12"	S	Moist to medium-dry	All 8 States
Violet, Yellow	*Viola pubescens*	P	Apr–July	Yellow	8–16"	P, Sh	Moist	All 8 States
Violet, Common Blue	*Viola sororia (V. papilionacea)*	P	Apr–July	Violet	4–12"	A	Moist	All 8 States

Ferns

Ferns provide good cover for songbirds and are graceful complements to your wildflowers. The Cinnamon Fern has an added appeal to hummingbirds: it has cinnamon-colored fuzz that hummers use for nesting materials.

Ferns for Attracting Birds

COMMON NAME	LATIN NAME	LIGHT REQ.	HEIGHT (FT.)	SOIL REQ.	NATIVE RANGE
Bracken Fern	*Pteridium aquilinum*	S, P	1–5 or 6	Moist to dry	All 8 States
Cinnamon Fern	*Osmunda cinnamomea*	Sh, P	3	Moist	All 8 States
Marsh Fern	*Thelypteris palustris*	S	2	Wet to moist	All 8 States
Ostrich Fern	*Matteuccia struthiopteris*	P, Sh	to 6	Moist to wet	All 8 States
Royal Fern	*Osmunda regalis*	A (prefers P)	3+	Wet, acidic	All 8 States
Sensitive Fern	*Onoclea sensibilis*	P, Sh	1–2	Moist to Wet	All 8 States

Latin Name to Common Name—
A Cross-Reference for Ferns & Wildflowers

This cross-reference gives the common names used in the tables and text of this book. The Latin names in parentheses are alternate names used by some botanists.

Actea alba—White Baneberry

Actaea rubra—Red Baneberry

Agastache foeniculum—Lavender Giant Hyssop

Agastache nepetoides—Yellow Giant Hyssop

Agastache scrophulariifolia—Purple Giant Hyssop

Allium cernuum—Nodding Wild Onion

Allium stellatum—Prairie Onion

Amphicarpaea bracteata—Hog Peanut

Anemone canadensis—Meadow Anemone; Canada Anemone

Anemone patens var. *multifida*—Pasque Flower

Anemone virginiana—Thimbleweed

Angelica atropurpurea—Great Angelica

Aquilegia canadensis—Wild Columbine

Aralia nudicaulis—Wild Sarsaparilla

Aralia racemosa—Spikenard

Arisaema triphyllum—Jack-in-the-Pulpit

Artemisia ludoviciana—White Sage

Asclepias hirtella—Tall Green Milkweed

Asclepias incarnata—Swamp Milkweed; Marsh Milkweed

Asclepias sullivantii—Prairie Milkweed

Asclepias syriaca—Common Milkweed

Asclepias tuberosa—Butterfly Milkweed

Asclepias verticillata—Whorled Milkweed

Aster ericoides—Heath Aster

Aster laevis—Smooth Blue Aster

Aster lanceolatus (A. simplex)—Panicled Aster

Aster lateriflorus—Side-flowering Aster; Calico Aster

Aster macrophyllus—Big-leaved Aster

Aster novae-angliae—New England Aster

Aster oolentangiensis (A. azureus)—Sky Blue Aster

Aster pilosus—Hairy Aster; Frost Aster

Aster puniceus—Bristly Aster; Red-stemmed Aster

Aster sagittifolius—Arrow-leaved Aster

Aster sericeus—Silky Aster

Aster shortii—Short's Aster

Astragalus canadensis—Canada Milk Vetch

Aureolaria grandiflora—Yellow False Foxglove

Aureolaria pedicularia—Fern-leaved False Foxglove

Baptisia alba (B. lactea; B. leucantha)—White Wild Indigo

Baptisia australis—Blue Wild Indigo

Bidens cernua—Nodding Bur Marigold

Boltonia asteroides—Boltonia

Cacalia atriplicifolia—Pale Indian Plantain

Cacalia plantiginea—Prairie Indian Plantain

Caltha palustris—Marsh Marigold

Campanula americana—Tall Bellflower

Campanula rotundifolia—Harebell

Cassia fasciculata—See *Chamaecrista f.*

Cassia hebecarpa—See *Senna h.*

Cassia marilandica—See *Senna m.*

Castilleja coccinea—Indian Paintbrush

Castilleja sessiliflora—Downy Paintbrush

Caulophyllum thalictroides—Blue Cohosh

Chamaecrista fasciculata (Cassia f.)—Partridge Pea

Chelone glabra—Turtlehead

Chelone obliqua—Red Turtlehead

Cimicifuga racemosa—False Bugbane; Black Cohosh

Cirsium discolor—Pasture Thistle

Cirsium muticum—Swamp Thistle

Clintonia borealis—Bluebead

Coreopsis lanceolata—Sand Coreopsis

Coreopsis palmata—Prairie Coreopsis

Dalea candida (Petalostemum c.)—White Prairie Clover

Dalea purpurea (Petalostemum p.)—Purple Prairie Clover

Delphinium carolinianum (D. virescens)—Prairie Larkspur

Desmodium canadense—Showy Tick Trefoil

Echinacea pallida (E. angustifolia)—Pale Purple Coneflower

Echinacea purpurea—Purple coneflower

Epilobium angustifolium—Fireweed

Eryngium yuccifolium—Rattlesnake Master

Eupatorium maculatum—Spotted Joe Pye Weed

Eupatorium perfoliatum—Boneset

Eupatorium purpureum—Purple or Sweet Joe Pye Weed

Euphorbia corollata—Flowering Spurge

Fragaria virginiana—Wild Strawberry

Galium boreale—Northern Bedstraw

Geranium maculatum—Wild Geranium

Geum triflorum—Prairie Smoke

Helenium autumnale—Sneezeweed

Helianthus pauciflorus (H. rigidus; H. laetiflorus)—Prairie Sunflower

Helianthus occidentalis—Western Sunflower

Helianthus strumosus—Pale-leaved Sunflower; Woodland Sunflower

Heliopsis helianthoides— False Sunflower; Oxeye

Heuchera richardsonii—Prairie Alum Root

Hibiscus moscheutos (H. palustris)—Swamp Rose Mallow

Impatiens capensis (I. biflora)—Orange Jewelweed; Spotted Touch-Me-Not

Impatiens pallida—Yellow Jewelweed; Pale Touch-Me-Not

Iris versicolor—Northern Blue Flag Iris

Iris virginica (I. shrevei)—Southern Blue Flag Iris

Lathyrus palustris—Marsh Vetchling

Lespedeza capitata—Round-headed Bush Clover

Liatris aspera—Rough Blazing Star

Liatris cylindracea—Cylindrical Blazing Star

Liatris ligulistylis—Meadow Blazing Star

Liatris pycnostachya—Prairie Blazing Star

Liatris spicata—Marsh Blazing Star

Lilium michiganense (L. superbum)—Michigan Lily; Turk's Cap Lily

Lilium philadelphicum—Prairie Lily

Lobelia cardinalis—Cardinal Flower

Lobelia siphilitica—Great Blue Lobelia

Lobelia spicata—Pale Spiked Lobelia

Lupinus perennis—Wild Lupine

Lysimachia thyrsiflora—Tufted Loosestrife

Matteuccia struthiopteris—Ostrich Fern

Mertensia virginica—Virginia Bluebells

Mimulus ringens—Monkey Flower

Mitchella repens—Partridge Berry

Monarda didyma—Oswego Tea; Bee Balm

Monarda fistulosa—Wild Bergamot

Monarda punctata—Horse Mint

Oenothera biennis—Common Evening Primrose

Onoclea sensibilis—Sensitive Fern

Osmunda cinnamomea—Cinnamon Fern

Osmunda regalis—Royal Fern

Pedicularis canadensis—Wood Betony; Lousewort

Pedicularis lanceolata—Swamp Lousewort

Penstemon digitalis—Foxglove Beard Tongue

Penstemon gracilis—Slender Beard Tongue

Penstemon grandiflorus—Large-flowered Beard Tongue

Penstemon pallidus—Pale Beard Tongue

Petalostemum candida—See *Dalea c.*

Petalostemum purpurea—See *Dalea p.*

Phlox divaricata—Blue Phlox; Woodland Phlox

Phlox glaberrima—Smooth Phlox

Phlox maculata—Sweet William Phlox

Phlox pilosa—Sand Prairie Phlox

Physostegia virginiana—Obedient Plant; False Dragonhead

Polygonatum biflorum (P. canaliculatum)—Smooth Solomon's Seal

Polygonatum pubescens—Downy Solomon's Seal

Pteridium aquilinum—Bracken Fern

Pycnanthemum virginianum—Common Mountain Mint

Ratibida pinnata—Yellow Coneflower; Grey-headed Coneflower

Rudbeckia hirta—Black-eyed Susan

Rudbeckia laciniata—Wild Golden Glow; Green-headed Coneflower

Rudbeckia subtomentosa—Sweet Black-eyed Susan

Rudbeckia triloba—Brown-eyed Susan

Ruellia humilis—Wild Petunia; Hairy Ruellia

Scrophularia lanceolata—Early Figwort

Scrophularia marilandica—Late Figwort

Senna hebecarpa (Cassia h.)—Wild Senna

Senna marilandica (Cassia m.)—Maryland Senna

Silene regia—Royal Catchfly

Silene stellata—Starry Campion

Silene virginica—Fire Pink

Silphium integrifolium—Rosin Weed

Silphium laciniatum—Compass Plant

Silphium perfoliatum—Cup Plant

Silphium terebinthinaceum—Prairie Dock

Smilacina racemosa—Feathery False Solomon's Seal

Smilacina stellata—Starry False Solomon's Seal

Smilax herbacea—Carrion Flower

Solidago caesia—Blue-stemmed Goldenrod

Solidago flexicaulis—Broad-leaved Goldenrod; Zigzag Goldenrod

Solidago nemoralis—Old-field Goldenrod

Solidago riddellii—Riddell's Goldenrod

Solidago rigida—Stiff Goldenrod

Solidago speciosa—Showy Goldenrod

Solidago ulmifolia—Elm-leaved Goldenrod

Stachys palustris—Hedge Nettle; Woundwort

Tephrosia virginiana—Goat's Rue

Thalictrum dasycarpum—Purple Meadow Rue; Tall Meadow Rue

Thelypteris palustris—Marsh Fern

Tradescantia ohiensis—Common Spiderwort

Triosteum aurantiacum—Early Horse Gentian

Triosteum perfoliatum—Late Horse Gentian or Tinker's Weed

Verbena hastata—Blue Vervain

Verbena stricta—Hoary Vervain

Vernonia fasciculata—Ironweed

Veronicastrum virginicum—Culver's Root

Vicia americana—American Vetch

Viola canadensis—Canada or Tall White Violet

Viola palmata (V. pedatifida)—Prairie Violet

Viola papilionacea—See *V. sororia*

Viola pedata—Bird's Foot Violet

Viola pubescens—Yellow Violet

Viola sororia (V. papilionacea)—Common Blue Violet

Zizia aurea—Golden Alexanders

Grasses

The seeds of grasses are eaten by many species of birds. In addition, grasses offer invaluable cover, especially for grassland nesting birds.

Grasses for Attracting Birds

See Key to Tables, pages 247–248, for abbreviations.

COMMON NAME	LATIN NAME	FALL COLOR	TIME OF COLOR	HEIGHT	LIGHT REQ	SOIL REQ	NATIVE RANGE
Brome, Fringed	*Bromus ciliatus*			2–4'	A	Moist to to wet; tolerates drought	IA,IL,IN,MI, MN,OH,WI
Brome, Woodland	*Bromus pubescens (B. purgans)*			2–5'	P, SH	Moist to medium dry	All 8 States
Dropseed, Prairie	*Sporobolus heterolepus*	Gold	Aug–Sept	2–4'	S, P	Moist to dry	All 8 States
Grama, Side-oats	*Bouteloua curtipendula*	Straw	Aug–Sept	2–3'	S, P	Medium to dry	All 8 States
Grass, Big Bluestem	*Andropogon gerardii*	Bronze/red	Aug–Oct	3–8'	S, P	Dry to moist	All 8 States
Grass, Bottlebrush	*Elymus hystrix (Hystrix patula)*	Straw	June–Aug	2–5'	P, SH	Dry to moist	All 8 States
Grass, Fowl Manna	*Glyceria striata*	Straw	Jul–Aug	1–4'	S, P	Moist to wet	All 8 States
Grass, Indian	*Sorghastrum nutans*	Gold	Aug–Sept	4–7'	S, P	Dry to moist	All 8 States
Grass, June	*Koeleria pyramidata (K. cristata; K. macrantha*	Gold	May–June	2–3'	S	Dry; sand	All 8 States
Grass, Little Bluestem	*Schizachyrium scoparium (Andropogon s.)*	Copper	Aug–Oct	2–3'	S, P	Dry to moist	All 8 States
Grass, Porcupine	*Stipa spartea*			3–4'	S, P	Dry	All 8 States
Grass, Prairie Cord	*Spartina pectinata*	Gold	Aug–Sept	5–7'	S, P	Moist to dry	All 8 States
Grass, Wood Reed	*Cinna arundinacea*			3–4'	P, SH	Moist	All 8 States
Rye, Canada Rye	*Elymus canadense*	Straw	Jul–Aug	4–5'	S	Dry to moist	All 8 States
Rye, Virginia Wild	*Elymus virginicus*	Straw	Jul–Aug	4–5'	A	Moist	All 8 States
Switchgrass	*Panicum virgatum*	Gold	Aug–Sep	3–6'	S, P	Moist	All 8 States

Rushes and Sedges

Rushes and sedges provide food, cover and nesting habitat. Their seeds are relished by many birds, including rails, waterfowl, grouse, marsh birds, shorebirds, sparrows (Swamp, American Tree, Song), Snow Buntings, cardinals and redpolls. Waterfowl and rails eat the rootstocks and stems of some species.

Rushes & Sedges for Attracting Birds

See Key to Tables, pages 247–248, for abbreviations.

COMMON NAME	LATIN NAME	HEIGHT	LIGHT REQ	SOIL REQ	NATIVE RANGE
Rush, Common or Soft	*Juncus effusus*	2–4'	S, P	Moist to wet	All 8 States
Rush, Path	*Juncus tenuis*	2–14"	S, P	Moist to dry	All 8 States
Sedge, Bristly or Bottlebrush	*Carex comosa*	1.5–4'	S, P	Moist to wet	All 8 States
Sedge, Brown Fox	*Carex vulpinoidea*	To 3'	S, P	Wet	All 8 States
Sedge, Commor Bur or Gray's	*Carex grayi*	1–3'	SH	Moist	All 8 States
Sedge, Common Cattail	*Carex typhina*	1–2'	S, P	Wet to moist	All 8 States
Sedge, Common Oak; Pennsylvania Sedge	*Carex pensylvanica*	6–12"	A	Moist to dry	All 8 States
Sedge, Common Tussock	*Carex stricta*	To 30"	S, P	Wet	All 8 States
Sedge, Fringed or Caterpillar	*Carex crinita*	2–5'	S, P	Wet to moist	All 8 States
Sedge, Porcupine	*Carex hystericina*	2–3.5'	S, P	Wet to moist	All 8 States
Woolgrass	*Scirpus cyperinus*	3–4'	S, P	Wet	All 8 States

Indigo Bunting

A Song Sparrow perches on Big Bluestem Grass.

LATIN NAME TO COMMON NAME—
A CROSS-REFERENCE FOR GRASSES, RUSHES & SEDGES

This cross-reference gives the common names used in the text and tables of this book. The Latin names in parentheses are alternate names used by some botanists.

Andropogon gerardii—Big Bluestem Grass
Andropogon scoparium—See *Schizachyrium s.*
Bouteloua curtipendula—Side-oats Grama
Bromus ciliatus—Fringed Brome
Bromus pubescens (B. purgans)—Woodland Brome
Carex comosa—Bristly Sedge; Bottlebrush Sedge
Carex crinita—Fringed Sedge; Caterpillar Sedge
Carex grayi—Common Bur Sedge; Gray's Sedge
Carex hystericina—Porcupine Sedge
Carex pensylvanica—Common Oak Sedge;
    Pennsylvania Sedge
Carex stricta—Common Tussock Sedge
Carex typhina—Common Cattail Sedge
Carex vulpinoidea—Brown Fox Sedge
Cinna arundinacea—Wood Reed Grass
Elymus canadense—Canada Wild Rye

Elymus hystrix (Hystrix patula)—Bottlebrush Grass
Elymus virginicus—Virginia Wild Rye
Glyceria striata—Fowl Manna Grass
Hystrix patula—See *Elymus hystrix*
Juncus effusus—Common Rush; Soft Rush
Juncus tenuis—Path Rush
Koeleria pyramidata (K. cristata; K. macrantha)—
    June Grass
Panicum virgatum—Switchgrass
Schizachyrium scoparium (Andropogon s.)—
    Little Bluestem Grass
Scirpus cyperinus—Woolgrass
Sorghastrum nutans—Indian Grass
Spartina pectinata—Prairie Cord Grass
Sporobolus heterolepis—Prairie Dropseed
Stipa spartea—Porcupine Grass

6 Maintaining & Enhancing Your Bird Habitat Garden

This drake Wood Duck is at home in the trees.

A life without birds is like meat without seasoning.
—Henry David Thoreau

This section provides tips on how to maintain your bird habitat garden and how to enhance it with bird houses and bird feeders. It also addresses some of the problems that may arise, such as damage to plants by deer and other herbivores, cat predation, window collisions, woodpecker drilling on houses, bird diseases and deaths, orphaned and injured birds and feeder pests.

(previous page) A sunny front yard filled with prairie flowers welcomes visitors—both human and wildlife.

BIRDSCAPING IN THE MIDWEST

CHAPTER 19
GARDEN HABITAT MAINTENANCE

As we transformed the land, it transformed us; this is how a sense of place is nurtured. My father once wrote that restoration can be a ritual of self-renewal, and so it was. This place taught me how to look, how to live, and at last to sing its poetry.

—Nina Leopold Bradley, *A Sense of Place*

A native plant garden involves effort initially, but once established it is easier and less expensive to maintain than a traditional garden. There is no need for watering, herbicides, insecticides, fertilizers or weekly mowing.

Nonetheless, some maintenance is needed as a result of human-induced changes to the environment. In long-gone pristine times, natural areas needed no care. But now, exotic weeds from around the world invade natural areas everywhere, their seeds brought in by wind or on feet and in animal droppings. As a result, even after removing all existing invasive plants on your property, you will need to continually monitor your garden and remove new invaders. Weeding will be your main job in managing the bird habitat garden.

Prairie and savanna gardens need occasional controlled burns or mowing. Judicious pruning of your woody plants can help increase the production of berries and seeds for birds. Creating openings that simulate the activity of animals will allow self-seeding species to find suitable sites to germinate and grow.

A seasonal maintenance checklist at the end of the chapter sums up the suggested maintenance work and can serve as a handy reference for you.

Watering

In the first two or three weeks after planting, it's a good idea to water your seeds or plants twice a week. For the rest of the first growing season, once a week is usually sufficient. Most plants require an inch of water a week, and anytime it rains less than that amount, you'll need to make up the difference. The best way to water trees and shrubs is to give them a slow soaking once a week. Always water cautiously on slopes to avoid erosion.

In the second year, water plants only during droughts. If you continue to water plants unnecessarily, you will favor those that require extra water. The plants that can adapt to the rainfall on your site will rot from the excess water, or get crowded out by the water-tolerant plants.

photo: Black-billed Cuckoo

This gardener is adding transplants to her yard.

Your garden should not need watering after the first two years. If you've planted the right species for the conditions, they should be able to tolerate any droughts that occur. The plants may go dormant, but they are unlikely to die. Nonetheless, in severe droughts, you may need to water your garden, especially a front yard garden, to appease the neighbors.

Weeding

Fighting weeds is particularly important during the first few years, while your garden is getting established. Doing so will pay big dividends later. Weeds are always easier to deal with when they are small. But you don't have to waste your time removing weeds that are not invasive—they are usually annuals that will die out as your native plants grow and mature.

The trick is being able to identify weeds when they are small. Try to get help from your local Wild Ones chapter, native plant society or nature center. I know of no books that identify weed seedlings, but several books have pictures of prairie seedlings (see Resources for Readers at the end of this chapter). Another technique to use if you're seeding a new site cleared of vegetation is to plant a few seeds of each species in a pot, so you can distinguish the "invited" seedlings from unwelcome ones. In established areas, however, I wouldn't advise pulling out unknowns. Wonderful native asters and sunflowers have seeded on their own in my yard.

In the first year, scout for weeds every two weeks and pull or dig any you find. To remove deep-rooted species or large ones you've overlooked in the past, you may want to use a herbicide. (See chapter 7 for details on using herbicides to eliminate invasive plants.)

If you find numerous weeds in a new prairie planting, mow to about six inches with a weed whip or flail mower. Prairie plants never get above six inches in the first year, since they are busy growing roots to sustain them during dry times. If the mower does not chop the cuttings into small pieces, you may have to mow more frequently so cuttings don't smother the native seedlings.

Do a spring cleanup of weeds in the second year. Mow the vegetation in new prairies to the ground to encourage ungerminated seeds to sprout. Then, in all gardens, scout for weeds every three weeks. After the first two years, a spring weeding followed by a once-a-month check for weeds should be sufficient.

Burning or Mowing
Prescribed Burns

Prescribed burns are the ideal way to maintain prairie and savanna. Likewise, rain and wetland gardens benefit from burns since, in most cases, they are essentially wet prairies. Many woodlands, especially oak-hickory communities, also benefit from fire. Before European settlement, fires were started by lightning, or by Indians to attract animals that graze on the tender new growth after a fire.

Don't burn new plantings for two or three years. By then they should be fairly well established and there should be enough dead plant material to carry a fire. Fire has many benefits for prairies and savannas. It burns off the accumulated plant litter and exposes the darkened soil to the warming rays of the sun. This extends the growing season for most prairie species and slows the growth of nonnative European grasses, like Kentucky Bluegrass, Quack Grass and Brome Grass, whose roots stop growing in warm soil. Fire also slows the invasion of shrubs and trees. It stimulates the activity of soil microorganisms, including that of nitrogen-fixing root nodules, making more nutrients available for plants. Some native plant seeds need scarring by fire to germinate. All of these things contribute to a rejuvenated prairie or savanna—one with taller, more robust plants, more flowers and more seed production. Visit a prairie in midsummer after a spring burn. People seeing one for the first time are always astonished at the beauty and vigor of the plants, despite having been burned to the ground only a few months before.

Oak-hickory woodlands benefit from prescribed burns in three ways: fire thins tree stands which makes conditions more favorable for oaks, helps control invasive species like honeysuckles and Garlic Mustard, and stimulates regeneration of herbaceous understory plants.

Prescribed burns, however, can be dangerous and need to be carefully planned and conducted. They need well-placed fire breaks, certain weather conditions, good equipment and sufficient help. An excellent publication explaining the basics is Wayne Pauly's *How to Manage Small Prairie Fires* (see Resources for Readers at the end of this chapter.) I suggest getting experienced professional help to conduct your first few burns. You might be able to hire staff at native plant nurseries or organizations like Pheasants Forever. Nature centers or fire departments may also have trained people to help.

Mowing

Where burns are not permitted, mowing is an excellent alternative. We could not burn at our suburban home and instead mowed regularly, with good results. You can use a mulching mower or flail to chop the debris into fine particles so it can be left in place to break down further. Otherwise, remove the clippings and litter so the soil surface is exposed to the sun, as if it were burned. Tom and Nancy Small have come up with a clever use for this litter. They make small bundles of the stems and place them as edging along the border of their plantings. Doing this, they say, ensures the survival of the eggs and pupae of butterflies and other beneficial insects that have overwintered on or in the stems. The debris can also be shredded or put in a compost pile.

Burning or Mowing Schedule—Think of the Birds

Prairies. The timing of burns or mowing can affect birds and wildlife, as well as plants. To avoid harming nesting birds, it's best to act very early in spring before nesting occurs. In Wisconsin, spring prairie burns are usually done in April for this reason, but in more southerly locations February or March may be better.

Summer and fall burns or mowing will remove seeds and cover for birds and wildlife until the following year's growth. On the other hand, in large prairie restorations, a fall burn has been shown to benefit some of the prairie specialists. Northern Harriers and Upland Sandpipers have better nesting success in fall-burned fields than in spring-burned fields, presumably because the fall burns allow more cover to develop by the nesting season and help protect them from predators. Burns any time of year can affect vulnerable insects, including butterflies.

On-going studies investigate how the timing of burns affects prairie plants. (I know of no studies of the effects of mowing at different times of year, but they may be similar.) Scientists believe spring burns tend to favor warm-season prairie grasses but harm unwanted cool-season European grasses and woody species. Fall burns tend to favor forbs (wildflowers) and cool-season grasses, while winter burns tend to favor both warm- and cool-season grasses. (Note: some cool-season grasses are native.)

This complexity of results suggests that the best approach is to vary your burning or mowing schedule. Evelyn Howell of the University of Wisconsin Department of Landscape Architecture recommends burning or mowing prairie plantings two years in every five. "The season of the burn should also vary," she says, "with two out of three burns occurring in the spring and the remaining burn in late fall (late October/November)." She also suggests that mowing could replace a burn every three to five years to simulate the grazing of bison and other animals that once lived on the prairies. "One way to design a schedule," advises Howell, "is to set up a five-year cycle in which two of the five years are randomly designated for a burn and one for a mowing." More frequent burning or mowing, she adds, may be needed in case of pest species or aggressive native species. It is also wise to burn only a third to a fifth of a prairie every year to preserve insects and their eggs and pupae.

Woodlands. Burn woodlands in late October to early April to avoid the prime spring nesting season. In the southern Midwest where wildflowers emerge as early as March, don't burn in March and April. Illinois experts advise against burning more than half of a woodland in any one year.

Pruning Woody Plants

Trees

Leaves capture the sun's energy and create compounds that nourish and sustain trees. Pruning removes the wood on which leaves grow and should be avoided if possible. Pruning should be limited to dangerous, weakly attached branches and the correction of structural problems. Remember, leafless stubs provide perches for birds, and dead wood attracts woodpeckers searching for insects and nest sites.

If you do prune a branch, let it heal naturally. Don't apply sealants after pruning. New research has shown that sealants trap moisture and retard healing. Trees heal themselves by forming callus tissue around and over their wounds; they need oxygen to start this process. Only if oak trees are injured during the growing season is wound treatment advised.

The most important thing to remember when pruning is to cut off the branch just above its collar, a swollen area at its base near the trunk. For examples, see the excellent pictures in the U.S. Forest Service's "How to Prune Trees" (Resources for Readers at the end of this chapter).

Shrubs

It is vital to prune most deciduous shrubs regularly if you want them to produce abundant berries, nuts and seeds. Flowering and fruiting in most shrubs occur primarily on young branches. Older unpruned shrubs have many unproductive branches.

If you have large overgrown deciduous shrubs, you can revitalize them by cutting back the old branches. Old branches of Red-osier Dogwood, for example, are easy to recognize by their dull colors, which contrast sharply with the bright red of young branches in late winter. The rule of thumb is to cut about one-third of the stems of a healthy shrub each year. Be sure to cut off the entire stem at its base near the ground to retain the natural form of the plant.

For a mass of overgrown deciduous shrubs, consider cutting small sections at a time, allowing the old growth to provide food and cover while the cut section grows back. If looks aren't important, you can cut most shrubs down to stumps and they will grow back bushier and more fruitful than ever.

While most deciduous shrubs benefit from pruning, some, especially large-scale specimen shrubs like Pagoda Dogwood, may never require it.

Juniper shrubs, the only native evergreen shrub in the Midwest except for the rare Canada Yew, should not be pruned if you want them to grow to full size. However, both junipers and yews can be pruned by heading back—cutting a few inches off the tips of branches. Do this in early spring, and again in midsummer if needed. As an alternative, some experts suggest pruning the longest branches back to a side branch, but be careful not to cut back to a branch without any needles because it will remain bare.

When to Prune

Deciduous woody plants should be pruned when they are dormant. Prune other times of year only in the case of storm damage or if a branch is likely to fall or cause harm.

The best time to prune trees and shrubs is in late winter or early spring just before the buds swell and open. The wounds will heal quickly in the weeks ahead when the plant is actively growing. Some trees may "bleed" since sap is rising at this time. This is healthy and prevents the invasion of disease-causing organisms.

"Pruning" or "Editing" Herbaceous Plants

You can "prune" some of your wildflowers, too, although it is not necessary for the well-being of your garden. For example, some wildflowers grow leggy or flop on the edges of a path. To avoid this, you can pinch back the growing tips or even cut them back by about one-third early in the season. This will produce shorter, fuller plants with more blossoms. Stop trimming them about two months before the plants blossom so you don't remove any buds that would become flowers.

In addition, you can "edit" your garden, if you'd like. In the clay soil of my front yard suburban prairie, for instance, Compass Plant spread very well—too well for the small area.

So each year, I "edited"—cut out some of the numerous tall flowering stalks, especially those close to the front of the garden. When the plants weren't as deep-rooted as Compass Plant, I replanted them elsewhere in my garden or gave them to friends.

You may want to do some editing to ensure the survival of species in your wildflower garden. Wildflowers that are common in the early stages of a planting may be crowded out by "climax" species—those typical of well-established natural areas. One of these is the Yellow or Gray-headed Coneflower, one of my favorite prairie wildflowers. I made sure it survived in my suburban garden by pulling out nearby plants that were crowding it.

Creating Openings

Most of us do not have bison, prairie dogs, groundhogs and other animals that once wallowed, burrowed or otherwise created openings in natural areas. In prairies these openings were suitable sites for self-seeding, short-lived species like Black-eyed Susans to germinate and grow. To retain these species, it's a good idea to clear small openings in your prairie garden to simulate animal activities.

It may also be helpful to create openings in the leaf litter of woodland gardens. Woodland plants are often spread by ants and other animals. But some plants require openings in the litter for their seeds to germinate and begin growth. Jim Steffen, conservation ecologist at the Chicago Botanic Garden, suggests raking the leaves from woodlands every other year. Oak leaves, in particular, tend to remain on the ground longer than the leaves of maples and other trees. This is because the oaks withdraw nutrients from their leaves before dropping them, making the leaves less palatable to decomposers, like soil fungi and bacteria. If you decide to rake your leaves, I suggest doing so in only part of your woodland, since leaf litter harbors insects needed by ground-feeding woodland birds. Leaf litter is also essential for enriching your woodland soil.

Insects

Most of us come from traditional gardening backgrounds, and our first instinct is to get rid of all the insects we see nibbling on the leaves and stems of our garden plants. But combating insects with chemicals will harm the birds, butterflies and beneficial insects we want to attract.

Studies show that less than one percent of garden insects are pests. Many insects are vital to the well-being of native plant areas because of their roles in pollinating flowers and preying on harmful insects. Dragonflies, for example, are important predators of mosquitos. Caterpillars devouring the leaves of some of your plants may metamorphose into beautiful butterflies and moths. And at least one insect is essential for spreading wildflower seeds. At the University of Wisconsin Arboretum, trilliums introduced into the restored woodlands were not spreading as they normally do in natural conditions. Eventually it was discovered that the woodlands did not have the ants which feed on an appendage of trillium seeds and disperse the seeds as they do so.

Many birds time their spring migration to coincide with the emergence of leaf-eating caterpillars on oaks. Although the caterpillars are abundant during migration, the oak leaves develop tannins after the first few weeks of spring, making their leaves inedible, and the caterpillars soon diminish in number without human intervention.

Some people are concerned about tent caterpillars. True, their cobwebby "tents" look unsightly, but leave them alone and you may get a chance to see the secretive Black-billed or Yellow-billed Cuckoo in your yard. Cuckoos are voracious eaters of caterpillars and are among the few birds that eat hairy ones like tent caterpillars.

It is a myth that tall vegetation harbors more mosquitoes than lawns. Mosquitoes breed in shallow puddles or depressions wherever they occur. Native habitat gardens, except for wetland and water gardens, actually discourage pools of standing water, because native plants typically have longer roots that can more quickly soak up water than the short roots of lawn grasses. Mosquitoes require a few days of standing water to complete their life cycle, so if rain or snowmelt is absorbed more quickly, mosquitoes will not have a chance to breed.

Ponds and wetlands restored with native vegetation provide habitat for many natural enemies of mosquitoes, including frogs, fish and some birds and insects. Dragonflies find cover and perching sites from which to hawk for mosquitoes and other insects in wetland vegetation. According to a study cited in *Audubon* (November–December 1996), the mosquito population was actually reduced by 90% in a restored wetland in Essex County, Massachusetts. In New Jersey, the cost of mosquito insecticide applications in wetlands was reduced by over 97% by eliminating stagnant breeding waters and managing for mosquito predators like dragonflies, damselflies, water striders, predacious diving beetles and topminnows.

Other natural ways to reduce mosquito populations include putting up bird houses for insect-eating birds like Purple Martins, Tree Swallows and Prothonotary Warblers. Consider adding a bat house, too—bats eat thousands of insects, including mosquitoes.

Since mosquitoes breed in standing water, be sure to remove anything that holds water—old pails, tires, swimming pool covers, kids' toys. Clean out clogged rain gutters and change the water in birdbaths every few days.

Fertilizers

Native plant gardens do not need fertilizers. In prairies, weeds are favored by rich soils. Native prairie plants, in contrast, are well adapted to survive poor soils and harsh conditions. There is also the danger of overfertilizing, which kills microorganisms in the soil that are important for plant health and growth. Any native plant that is well suited to its site, planted properly and cared for during its first year should thrive without any fertilizers, other than compost.

There is also evidence that fertilizers increase insect damage to shrubs, despite a long-held belief that well-fertilized, vigorously growing trees and shrubs are better able to resist such damage. A review of the evidence by biologist D. A. Herms in the journal *Environmental Entomology* (31:6, 2002) found that the use of fertilizers, particularly nitrogen fertilizers, increases the susceptibility of woody plants to damage by wood-boring and piercing/sucking insects. The extra nitrogen in the plant tissues spurs the growth and reproduction of insects. At the same time, the plants themselves put most of their energy into growth and reduce their production of compounds that defend against insect damage. The insects that increased in fertilized woody plants include aphids, adelgids, scales, plant bugs, lace bugs, spider mites, caterpillars, sawflies, leaf beetles, leafminers and the white pine weevil.

Mulching

If your soil needs enhancement, mulching is much better than using fertilizers. Mulching with compost, especially well-aged manure compost, will restore most soils in a few years. On hilly sites, where rains tend to wash away compost, shredded wood chips work better than mulch. Spring is the best time to mulch, since the mulch will slowly incorporate into the soil through the growing season.

Woodland and shrubland gardens will particularly benefit from an annual mulching. Prairie and savanna gardens, however, do not need mulching. They do best when their above-ground plant material is removed annually or every few years, through mowing or controlled burns.

Replacement Planting

Inevitably, in the natural sequence of events, some of your native plants will die out; sometimes simply because they are short lived, other times because they do not match the conditions in your yard well enough. In either case, replant as soon as possible to avoid invasion by weeds and erosion.

Seasonal Maintenance

Spring

1. Remove weeds, especially unwanted tree and shrub seedlings, while they are small and easy to pull out.
2. Mow, burn or cut herbaceous plants to the ground in prairie, savanna and rain gardens, approximately two years out of every five. Some people do this annually for aesthetic reasons—especially in front yards—but two out of every five years will be sufficient. If you don't burn your garden, rake off the material and compost it or bundle and use it for edging.
3. Prune shrubs very early in spring before the buds are out; add branches to your brush pile.
4. Mulch trees and shrubs as needed in late spring after the soil has warmed, especially if poor soils need improvement in woodland or shrubland gardens.
5. Plant replacements if needed.
6. If you do not have a fence or edging material at the border between your garden and lawn (if you have one), you can create a neat edge by digging a narrow slit with a spade around the periphery of your garden.

Summer

1. Weed once a month after the first two years.
2. Pinch back or "edit" herbaceous plants, as desired.

Fall

1. Weed one last time before winter, as the soil is usually moist and the plants are easy to pull. This is the best time to remove large invasive shrubs and apply herbicide to their stumps.
2. Let the dormant plants stand through the winter to supply seeds, berries and shelter for birds. Cut back any herbaceous plants that you think are messy. (Prescribed

burns are sometimes conducted in fall.)

3. Protect the lower trunks of young shrubs and trees from herbivores by wrapping or fencing. See chapter 22 for more information.
4. Clean and sharpen gardening tools.
5. Create an opening in your prairie, woodland or other gardens to provide a place where seeds can germinate and grow.

Winter

1. Fill bird feeders, if desired, to supplement the fruits, nuts and seeds provided by the plants in your habitat garden.
2. Build a brush pile near your feeders to provide cover and protection from predators.
3. Add a heated birdbath, if desired.
4. Then sit back and enjoy the birds!

RESOURCES FOR READERS

Identification Guides for Seedlings

Although these two publications offer guidelines for prairie seedlings, many of the species are commonly used in any type of garden featuring native wildflowers and grasses.

Jackson, Laura, and Lora Dittmer, 1997. *Prairie Seedlings Illustrated: An Identification Guide.* Vol. 1. Cedar Falls: University of Northern Iowa. Prairie Seedlings Illustrated, Department of Biology, University of Northern Iowa, Cedar Falls, IA 60614. Illustrations of 20 common grasses and forbs.

Morgan, J. P., Douglas R. Collicutt and Jacqueline D. Thompson, 1995. *Restoring Canada's Native Prairies: A Practical Manual.* Prairie Habitats, Box 1, Argyle, Manitoba, R0C 0B0. Photographs of 119 northern prairie seedlings.

Prescribed Burns

Pauly, Wayne R. 1989. *How to Manage Small Prairie Fires.* Madison, WI: Dane County Park Commission. Available from several native plant nurseries, including Prairie Moon Nursery, 31837 Bur Oak Lane, Winona, MN 55987; phone: 866-417-8156; www.prairiemoon.com/

Pruning

"How to Prune Trees." 1995. Details of how, when and why at the USDA Forest Service Northeastern Area;
http://www.na.fs.fed.us/spfo/pubs/howtos/ht_prune/prun001.htm

CHAPTER 20
SUPPLEMENTAL HOUSING

If your trees and snags haven't developed natural cavities, you can improve bird habitat by providing supplemental housing for cavity-nesting birds. As urban sprawl encroaches on the countryside and tidy, flawless landscaping traditions eliminate old trees, fewer and fewer natural cavities are available for birds. And to make matters worse, nonnative House Sparrows and starlings compete with our native birds for existing cavities.

The number and kinds of nest boxes to put up in your yard will depend a great deal on the kinds of birds in your neighborhood, the habitats you've created in your yard and the size of the birds' territories. Most birds defend territories during nesting time. The size of territories vary from many square miles for some birds of prey to less than an acre for robins and Red-winged Blackbirds. Some species, like Purple Martins and Great Blue Herons, are colonial nesters who defend only a small area around their nests. See the chart listing the breeding territory size of some common birds in chapter 5.

Birds are territorial because they protect the food sources and nest sites they need. These needs differ among species. Most species drive away their own kind because they compete for the same things, but will tolerate birds of other species whose requirements are different. Thus, while you may not be able to attract two pairs of nesting robins in your yard, you could well have one nesting pair each of House Wrens, nuthatches, chickadees, and bluebirds, along with the robins. We had a bonanza last year in our two-acre yard—a pair each of nesting bluebirds, robins, Tree Swallows and to my greatest surprise, Great Crested Flycatchers, plus several nesting pairs of wrens.

The key to attracting a variety of cavity-nesting species is to provide nest boxes of different dimensions suitable to each species likely to nest in your yard. Seventeen species of midwestern birds commonly use nest boxes, dimensions for which are given on the following pages. Also see "Special Housing for Purple Martins" in this chapter.

Generally, for yards of one acre or less, it is useless to erect more than one box for each species, except for wrens and Tree Swallows. Tree Swallows will accept neighbors of their own species as close as 30 feet, so several boxes can be erected on a relatively small property. Wrens like to have many nesting options. The male wren arrives before the female in spring and will construct up to seven or more nests in boxes and natural cavities. He'll show all these off to the female, who will eventually accept only one as a nesting site. Because of this behavioral idiosyncrasy, a yard with several wren boxes is particularly enticing to a pair of these charming birds.

photo: Bluebird fledgling

BASIC NEST BOX DIMENSIONS

Birds are versatile and have nested in cavities and on ledges of all shapes and sizes since time immemorial. So it is not surprisingly that, for any given species, there are a number of suitable nest box and shelf designs of various dimensions. The following are the general dimensions for basic nest boxes and shelves for various species, based on information provided by Cornell Lab of Ornithology and the North Prairie Wildlife Research Center. The sizes given are length x width x height.

Basic nest box size for songbirds (flycatchers, swallows, titmice, chickadees, nuthatches, wrens, and bluebirds)
= approximately 4" x 4.5" x 11"

Basic nest box for kestrels & screech owls
= approximately 8" x 9" x 16"

Basic nest box for mergansers, wood ducks and kestrels
= approximately 10" x 12" x 24"

Basic nest box for flickers
= approximately 5" x 7" x 24"

Both the Cornell Lab of Ornithology and the North Prairie Wildlife Research Center have construction plans for nest boxes and shelves on their websites. In addition to box and shelf plans for the bird species listed on the following pages, they also have a design for a Prothonotary Warbler nest box made from milk cartons and a Mourning Dove nest basket, plus several designs for predator guards.

Avoid using herbicides and pesticides in your yard when you put out boxes. These substances are harmful to birds and also are likely to decrease or even eliminate insects that are the primary source of food for nestlings.

The Basic Nest Box Design

The nest box on page 296 illustrates the important features that every box should have, whether you build it yourself or buy it. Although this is a standard design, you can make or buy a variety of other suitable styles that incorporate these features. The basic design shown here can be used for many different species of birds by changing the dimensions. Here are the important features to look for in a good nest box:

Materials. Wood is the best choice for a nest box, since wood is durable, insulates well, yet breathes. It is also the material of natural cavities. Cedar and redwood are long-lasting even when left unpainted, but pine and plywood can also be used. Avoid pressure-treated wood, which contains toxic compounds. Try to use lumber that is certified (FSC or Smart Wood Certified Forestry) from a

HOLE SIZE & NESTING HABITAT FOR NEST BOXES*

Species	Entrance Hole Size	Nesting Habitat	Box Height (ft.) Above Ground
Eastern Bluebird	1-3/8" x 2-1/4" vertical oval	Open, with scattered trees (savanna); see chapter 10 for details	4–6'
Black-capped & Carolina Chickadee	1-1/8" diameter	Woodlands & wooded yards with 40–60% sun; 1" of wood shavings can be added to box	5–15'
Wood Duck	4" wide, 3" high	Wooded wetlands or marshes or small ponds; place boxes in deciduous trees within 100' of water, 600' apart	6–30'
Northern Flicker	2-1/2" diameter, facing SE direction	Woodland edge or savanna-like habitat; fill box with wood chips or shavings	6–30'
Great Crested Flycatcher	1-3/4" diameter	Deciduous or mixed deciduous/conifer forests, orchards; on post or tree at forest edge	3–20'
American Kestrel	3" diameter	Open with some trees; place boxes on isolated trees in fields, on trees at woodland edge or on farm buildings	10–30'
Purple Martin	2-1/8" diameter	Open fields, wetlands or water bodies; see "Special Housing for Purple Martins" for more details	12–15'
Hooded Merganser	3" high, 4" wide; horizontal oval	Quiet shallow water bodies in or near the edge of deciduous woods; add 3" wood shavings & inside ladder for young	6–25'
Red-breasted Nuthatch	1-1/4" diameter	Mixed coniferous-deciduous forests, farms, parks; put wood shavings in box	5–15'
White-breasted Nuthatch	1-3/8" diameter	Deciduous woodlands, mature forests and edges, often near water; place wood shavings in box	5–20'
Eastern Screech-Owl	3" diameter, facing north	Forests & woodlands, parks, under a tree limb; add 2–3" wood shavings	10–30'

Species	Entrance Hole Size	Nesting Habitat	Box Height (ft.) Above Ground
Tree Swallow	1-3/8" diameter, facing east	Open areas near water or wetlands; on post near tree or fence, 30–100' apart	5–15'
Tufted Titmouse	1-1/4" diameter	Deciduous forests or forest edges; woodland clearings, along rivers; 1 box/8 acres	5–15'
Prothonotary Warbler	1-1/4" diameter	Lowlands subject to flooding; box should be over or near water	2–12'
House Wren	1-1/4" diameter	Variety: woodland edge, shrubland, parks, gardens; close to trees or tall shrubs	5–10'
Carolina Wren	1-1/2" diameter	Brushy or open forests, shrubland, parks, gardens; close to trees or tall shrubs	5–10'

*Based largely on information provided by the Cornell Lab of Ornithology and the North American Bluebird Society.

Northern Flicker female at a tree cavity.

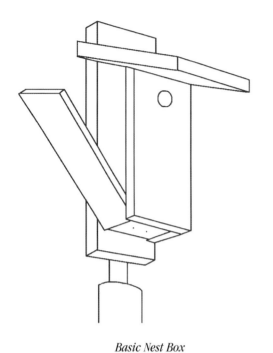

Basic Nest Box

well-managed forest. Walls should be at least 3/4-inch thick. This helps to keep the box warm in cool weather and cool in hot weather. The latter is most important for birds that prefer nest boxes in sunny locations. Use galvanized screws, nails and hinges to resist rust and to hold boxes together tightly as they age. Painting or staining is not needed, but if done, use light colors to minimize the internal heat and paint only the outside of the box. One of the main exceptions to using wood is Purple Martin nest boxes, which are often made of aluminum to minimize weight. Some bluebird houses are made of PVC pipe with wooden roofs.

Roof. The roof should be sloped and extended on front and sides to protect from predators and rain. The back of the roof should fit into a slot in the backboard of the box to prevent water from entering.

Ventilation. Without ventilation, nest boxes can be ovens for birds. Ventilation can be provided either by 1/4-inch holes just below the roof and above the entrance to avoid drafts or by gaps between the roof and sides of the box. These vents can be plugged or covered in winter to keep the box warm for roosting birds.

Accessibility. Easy access is needed to monitor and clean boxes. A hinged side or front opening that can be closed securely will do the job.

Floor. The floor should be recessed and have drainage holes to prevent the nest from getting wet.

Walls. The interior walls should be rough or grooved to assist the birds in exiting the box.

Entrance hole. The entrance hole should be the correct size for the desired species. (See "Hole Size and Nesting Habitat for Nesting Boxes" on pages 294–295.) It should be positioned away from prevailing wind and rain. Don't attach a perch outside the entrance; the birds don't need it and predators might use it.

Backboard. A back that extends a few inches beyond the top, bottom and sides makes a convenient place to nail the box.

Predator guard. A predator guard should be placed below boxes mounted on posts and, if possible, on trees. Such guards prevent cats, raccoons and others predators from attacking nest box birds. Guards can be in the form of baffles or cylinders (stovepipe or galvanized or PVC tubing). Construction plans for several kinds of predator guards can be found on the website of the Cornell Lab of Ornithology.

Hanging Your Nest Box

Nest boxes on posts are generally safe for birds if predator guards are placed below the box. Boxes with extended backboards can easily be nailed to posts. Avoid placing a nest box near trees or fences from which predators can jump to reach the box.

It's also best to avoid hanging boxes on trees or fences where predator guards are more difficult to attach. The rough bark of trees and wooden fences make easy climbing surfaces for cats, raccoons, snakes and other predators. Some experts suggest that birds are cautious about using boxes in trees due to the likelihood of predators. If you do choose to hang a box in a tree, be sure not to use nails, which can harm the tree by creating openings for fungus and insect attacks. Instead, loop galvanized wire around the vent holes or around holes drilled into the backboard. Then attach a bungee cord or slip the wire through a piece of old rubber hose before looping around the tree, just above a branch so the box can't slide down.

Wherever you decide to hang your nest box, make sure there is an open flight path to its entrance. Birds like to perch a short distance from their nest site to check for danger before taking a direct path to reach it.

Nesting Shelves

A nesting shelf is, basically, an open nest box—a roof, back and bottom with narrow sides or no sides at all. Common birds that may use nesting shelves are robins and Barn Swallows. Occasionally, phoebes and Mourning Doves may also use one.

The basic nest shelf has a floor about 7-by-7 inches, a slightly larger roof about 8-by-8 inches, and a height of about 10 to 13 inches. You can find construction plans for a nesting shelf on the website of the North Prairie Wildlife Research Center. Mount the shelf under the overhanging eaves of your house, shed or barn or beneath a vine-covered arbor.

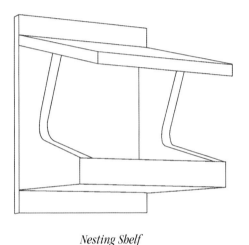

Nesting Shelf

Barn Swallows, more common in open rural areas than in urban areas, will also use shelves without roofs, placed under eaves for weather protection. Similarly, they'll nest on the ledge of a two-by-four board attached horizontally to the side of a building.

To further aid robins, phoebes, Barn Swallows, and other birds that use mud in making their nests, provide a nearby mud puddle. This can be as simple as a shallow hole kept wet or a garbage can lid filled with muddy clay.

When to Mount Your Nest Box or Shelf

Mount your nest boxes well before the nesting season, by late February or early March for most of the Midwest. Because ice and snow are likely to be on the ground during those months, I put up boxes in the early fall. Another advantage of putting the boxes up in fall is that, with the leaves still on the trees, you will be able to determine how much sunlight the boxes will get, an important factor for some birds like chickadees. In addition, the boxes may be used as roosting boxes during the winter (see chapter 15). In any case, the boxes will weather over winter and become more acceptable to birds.

Don't be discouraged if the birds don't use your nest boxes the first year. Sometimes it takes several seasons for them to find a box. We've found that use varies from year to year. Birds might use a box one year, not the next, but again the following year.

Providing Nest Materials

You can welcome birds to your yard not only with nest boxes but also with nesting materials. These materials will attract birds that make their own nests, as well as those that use nest boxes. Birds must search for thousands of twigs, blades of grass, plant down or other natural fibers to build a single nest. Such material can be especially hard to find in super-tidy yards. Put nest material in visible, accessible spots in your yard, and you will save birds a great deal of time and energy.

For example, you can put bits of yarn, string, or hair in an empty suet feeder or wire container and hang it up in a conspicuous spot. I was delighted one year when chickadees used some of my own hair that I had placed in a suet feeder to construct their nest. Strands of yarn or string put out for birds should be no longer than eight inches—longer ones have been known to entangle or strangle birds. You can also put out small piles of twigs. Don't put any materials in the nest boxes themselves, however, since the birds may think the boxes are already occupied.

You can also grow plants in your habitat garden which provide nesting material for birds. American Goldfinches, House Finches and vireos use narrow strips of grape vines and milkweed bark to weave their nests. Eastern Bluebirds, American Goldfinches, vireos and wrens find pine needles suitable for nesting. Baltimore Orioles have been known to collect dogbane fibers and the filaments on dandelion seeds for nesting material. (Although I'm not encouraging you to grow dandelions, you now can postpone digging them up without feeling guilty. Goldfinches also will eat dandelion seeds.) All habitat gardens are sure to include grasses, lichens and mosses that birds commonly collect for their nests.

Monitoring and Maintaining Your Boxes

Monitor your nest boxes regularly, once you begin to see activity around them. Approach slowly and sing or whistle quietly to warn the birds inside before opening the box. Monitor only on calm, warm days to prevent chilling the eggs or nestlings. It's best to monitor in the afternoon because most females lay their eggs in the morning and are absent from their nests later in the day. Avoid monitoring during incubation and when the young are close to fledging; you might cause them to leave the nest prematurely.

If you find House Sparrows or starlings are nesting in your boxes, remove the nests immediately. These two species are nonnative birds that aggressively compete with our native birds for boxes and cavities. Neither they nor their nests are protected by law and can be destroyed. Remove any dead birds you find within a nest box.

You can provide scientists with valuable information about your nests through the Birdhouse NestWatch, a citizen-science project of the Cornell Lab of Ornithology. As a participant, you gather and submit information on the number of eggs and young in your nest boxes. This information becomes part of a nationwide database, which tracks bird populations across the country. It's a rewarding way to enjoy your nesting birds and to contribute to scientific research at the same time.

Nest materials are usually removed at the end of the breeding season, but new research suggests that this is not always best. Boxes containing old nest material are preferred by birds, mice or squirrels for roosting in the winter. However, if a box is soiled with fecal matter, experts recommend removing the nest and cleaning the box with a solution of 1 part bleach to 10 parts water.

SPECIAL HOUSING FOR PURPLE MARTINS

Purple Martins are the only cavity-nesters that will nest in colonies. Their graceful flight and lively gregarious ways make them one of our most loved birds. The Native Americans were the first to put out gourds to entice them to nest near their villages, perhaps, as early reports suggest, to chase crows from cornfields and vultures from meat hung out to dry.

Before people put up artificial housing for them, Purple Martins used natural cavities in dead trees, giant saguaro cactus, or cliffs. Western martins still use such natural sites, nesting singly or in loose colonies. They also nest in birdhouses. In contrast, almost all Purple Martins in eastern North America nest in communal birdhouses and gourds.

According to the North American Breeding Bird Survey, an annual avian monitoring program, Purple Martin populations have been declining, especially since 1983. The exact causes are unknown but may be related to a decrease in natural cavities and suitable habitat, or competition for nest sites from nonnative European Starlings and House Sparrows.

More than one million people put up housing for Purple Martins but few folks are able to attract them. Once martins do nest at a site, they will return year after year as long as the habitat remains the same. Here are few tips for attracting those first Purple Martins.

Location. The most important requirement is to place the nest box in a suitable spot. Purple Martins need space so they can swoop down to their nest boxes with long gliding flights.

A box should be located in an open area with no trees taller than the birdhouse for at least 40 feet, preferably 60 feet. Put the house on a pole about 12–20 feet high. The box should also be located about 30–100 feet away from buildings. Purple Martins seem to associate humans with safety from predators and like to be relatively close to our houses.

Scientists think Purple Martins originally inhabited broad open river valleys. Erecting a box near or in similar large open areas like wetlands or lakes attracts martins. Such habitats provide the space they need to catch insects on the wing, which make up their entire diet.

Color. White seems to attract Purple Martins best, perhaps because it reflects the sun and keeps the box cooler.

Size. Many construction plans and some manufactured houses have incorrect dimensions, which will make it more difficult to attract Purple Martins. The minimum size for the floor of the box is 6" x 6", but a deeper box, 8" x 12", is even better because it offers more protection from predators and bad weather and allows more room for the nestlings. Round entrance holes can be between 1-3/4" and 2-1/4" wide and should be placed about 1-1/2" above the floor. Starling-resistant entrances are 3" wide and 1-3/16" high and should be placed no higher than 1/2" from the floor.

Construction. Due to their position high on poles, Purple Martin houses are particularly vulnerable to harsh weather conditions and must have adequate insulation, ventilation and drainage.

Keeping Other Species Out. This is essential, since Purple Martins won't nest in any box already occupied, even in part, by other species. Keep the box closed to exclude other birds until the martins arrive in the spring. You should be able to raise and lower the box so it can be monitored regularly, even daily, if needed. Purple Martins tolerate humans and won't be scared off by this disturbance.

Nonnative birds like European Starlings and House Sparrows are not protected by law. You can control them by removing nests, eggs and birds. Trap them and use starling-resistant entrances. Also, plug the compartments that aren't being used by the martins. Native birds, including wrens, bluebirds and swallows are protected by law and should not be harmed. The best approach to control them is to put up suitable housing in nearby locations.

Predator Control. As with all birdhouses, put predator guards on the pole. Raccoons, snakes and squirrels can easily climb both metal and wooden poles; cats can climb wooden poles, too. To deter avian predators like owls, crows and hawks provide deep nesting compartments. These allow martins to nest farther from the entrance hole out of predators' reach. Use owl guards, even with deep compartments. Buy or make them from hardware cloth to form a protective cage on the outside of the box, which you can remove when you monitor the martin house.

Playing the Martins' Dawn Song. Once you have the perfect box in the perfect place with all the essential amenities, try this final enticement. Play a recording of the birds' dawn song. You may be able to draw pioneering Purple Martins to start a colony in the birdhouse.

It's certainly worth the effort to encourage these beautiful glossy blue-black birds to nest again in numbers in the Midwest. With luck, we may be able to stem the decline in their populations.

Purple Martins at nest box (female at left).

Resources for Readers

Books and Pamphlets

"Homes for Birds." 1991. U.S. Fish and Wildlife Service, Department of the Interior. http://library.fws.gov/Bird_Publications/house.html

Stokes, Donald, and Lillian Stokes. 1990. *The Complete Birdhouse Book.* Boston: Little, Brown.

Stokes, Donald, Lillian Stokes and Justin Brown. 1997. *Stokes Purple Martin Book.* Boston: Little, Brown.

Wolinski, Richard A. 1994. *Enjoying Purple Martins More.* Marietta, OH: Bird Watcher's Digest Press.

Organization

Purple Martin Conservation Association, 301 Peninsula Drive, Erie, PA 16505; phone: 814-833-7656; www.purplemartin.org/

Websites

Cornell Lab of Ornithology. For information on building, placing and monitoring birdhouses, see the downloads at NestWatch: http://nestwatch.org/

Northern Prairie Wildlife Research Center. For information on birdhouses, shelves and more, see www.npwrc.usgs.gov/resource/tools/ndblinds/ndblinds.htm

Wood Duck Society. For information on wood duck houses, see http://www.woodducksociety.com/

Chapter 21
SUPPLEMENTAL FEEDING

photo: Elderberries

Your bird habitat garden is the best way to provide for the year-round needs of birds once it is landscaped with a variety of native plants offering food, cover, nesting sites and water. But you may choose to supplement the natural foods in your garden with a few feeders. Feeders bring birds up close where you can see them from the comfort of your home and for the entertainment of the whole family.

Costs and Benefits of Feeders

Although feeders can be fun for us, how do they affect birds? Biologists Margaret Brittingham and Stanley Temple of the University of Wisconsin found that feeders help chickadees to survive in very harsh winters. Furthermore, they found that chickadees accustomed to feeders were able to switch back readily to feeding in the wild and had not become dependent on feeders. (Their studies are described in more detail in chapter 15.)

Besides helping resident birds like chickadees survive extremely harsh winters, feeders may also have helped some southern birds extend their ranges northward. The House Finch, Northern Cardinal, Mourning Dove, Red-bellied Woodpecker and Tufted Titmouse are moving north, some ornithologists think, because of the increased availability of food at feeders during winter.

Feeders clearly make it easier for birds to find food. The serving sizes are also larger—a big nutritious sunflower seed is often bigger than the seeds of many wildflowers, and a chunk of suet is likely to be bigger than an insect egg in the bark of a tree. "Feeders may also reduce the risk of predation," says Stephen Kress of the National Audubon Society, "since feeder birds spend less time foraging and have more time to watch for predators."

Nonetheless, Kress and other experts acknowledge some downsides to feeders. Perhaps one of the greatest is crowding at feeders, which makes birds more vulnerable to contagious diseases. Birds are also more likely to injure themselves by flying into windows. In addition, house cats and the occasional dog are common predators at feeders.

Myths about Feeding

It is not true that birds will delay migration if feeders are available. Birds get their cue for migration from the photo-period, or length of day. As the days get shorter in fall, their urge to migrate south increases and healthy birds will soon be on their way. Feeder food can actually help by providing the extra fat they need for migration. Birds that stay at feeders are either abnormal or too weak to migrate.

Another myth is that feeders increase the populations of birds that harm other nesting birds. Some of the birds of concern are Blue Jays, which prey on the nestlings of other species; Brown-headed Cowbirds, parasitic birds that lay their eggs in the nests of other birds; and House Sparrows, which compete for nesting sites with native birds. These three species, however, are declining in the Midwest according to North American Breeding Bird Surveys conducted between 1966 and 2004. In contrast, many of our favorite feeder birds, like Hairy Woodpeckers, White-breasted and Red-breasted Nuthatches and Tufted Titmice are increasingly abundant. As woodland species, they may owe their greater numbers to the regrowth of woodlands and decline of farms in some areas of the country.

Menu Selections: Types of Bird Food

Not long ago, people fed birds simply by throwing out a few leftover crumbs. But today there is a phenomenal variety of bird seed and bird seed mixes from which to choose. Different species of birds are attracted to different kinds of seeds, according to beak size and shape and nutritional needs.

Among all the available bird foods, black-oil sunflower seed is the favorite among the greatest variety of birds, especially in the Midwest. It has a high meat-to-shell ratio and high oil content, making it more nutritious than the larger gray-striped sunflower seed. The black-oil sunflower seed also has a softer husk, making it easier for birds with smaller bills (like sparrows, juncos and goldfinches) to crack open. Birds enjoy hulled seeds which are often packaged as "no mess" since no empty husks pile up below feeders. The black-oil sunflower seed should be the staple at your bird feeding station. You can add it to almost any type feeder or scatter it on the ground.

Northern Cardinals and a few other birds like safflower seed. I replace sunflower seed with safflower seed when Brown-headed Cowbirds show up at my feeders in spring, since safflower seed doesn't appeal to cowbirds. I don't want to encourage this parasitic bird to stay in the vicinity when other birds begin

FEEDER FOOD PREFERENCES OF COMMON FEEDER BIRDS

Sunflower Seeds
  Blackbirds, Cardinals, Chickadees, Doves, Finches, Grosbeaks, Indigo Buntings, Jays, Juncos, Nuthatches, Siskins, Sparrows, Titmice, Woodpeckers

Safflower Seeds
  Cardinals, Chickadees, Finches, Grosbeaks, Nuthatches, Titmice

Cracked Corn
  Blackbirds, Jays, Juncos, Sparrows, Doves

Millet
  Blackbirds, Doves, Finches, Juncos, Sparrows

Niger (sometimes spelled Nijer) or Thistle Seed
  Finches, Indigo Buntings

Peanuts
  Chickadees, Jays, Nuthatches, Titmice, Woodpeckers

Suet
  Chickadees, Jays, Nuthatches, Titmice, Woodpeckers, Orioles

Sugar Water
  Hummingbirds, Orioles

Catbird

nesting. Once cowbirds migrate in fall, I switch back to sunflower seed. Squirrels and European Starlings and House Sparrows don't like safflower seed either.

Cracked corn is popular with ground-feeding birds, but it is prone to rotting. To prevent this, be sure to keep the corn off the ground on low feeding tables or place it in hopper feeders. Also, avoid fine cracked corn, which can turn mushy. Coarse cracked corn and whole corn are hard for smaller-beaked birds like sparrows and goldfinches to eat, but are favorites of jays, doves and pheasants.

Millet comes in two colors, white and red, and is the best seed to attract ground-feeding birds. Most birds prefer white millet.

Niger (sometimes spelled nijer and also referred to as thistle seed) is particularly attractive to small finches like goldfinches, siskins and redpolls. Since it's quite expensive, it is usually offered in tube feeders with tiny portals so the seed isn't wasted. Don't confuse niger with the wild (although not usually native) thistles that grow here. Niger seed is actually of African origin.

Peanuts, either cracked or whole, are popular with many birds, but I've found cracked peanuts are prone to clumping together and becoming water-logged. Most birds that like suet also like peanut butter.

Seed mixes attract a variety of birds and are best offered at low feeding tables. When placed in higher hopper feeders, a great deal is thrown onto the ground by birds that only want one type of seed. A good mix for the Midwest is black oil sunflower seed, cracked corn and white millet. Avoid mixes with milo seed, which is popular with western birds but not with our midwestern birds. Check any bird seed mixes that you buy since milo is a common filler seed in inexpensive mixes and is a waste of money. Other fillers that go uneaten are wheat and oats.

Suet is a preferred food of chickadees, nuthatches, titmice, woodpeckers and other insect-eating birds. If you buy it at the meat counter of your local grocery store, use it only in winter, since it will become rancid and unhealthy for birds during warmer seasons of the year. It can also damage their feathers, causing them to lose their waterproofing. Many people prefer the widely available suet blocks, which can be used year-round. In summer you can make your own suet-like bird puddings with peanut butter, cornmeal and vegetable shortening.

Sugar water dispensers, used mainly to attract hummingbirds, are discussed in chapter 8.

Household leftovers will attract birds, some of which relish dried pumpkin, melon and squash seeds even more than sunflower seeds. Because of their hard seed coats, you'll first need to chop or grind them up for smaller birds. Birds eat bits of stale breads and baked goods, but be sure they are not moldy. Stop putting them out if you find they attract starlings, House Sparrows, rats or raccoons.

Other "human" foods can also attract birds that don't usually visit feeders. Softened raisins and other dried fruit will tempt robins, thrushes and bluebirds to visit. Orange halves bring in orioles, especially in spring. Grape jelly is very appealing to both orioles and catbirds.

As you can see, most of the foods I have named appeal to a variety of birds. Although the greatest variety of birds like black oil sunflower seeds, most will also eat other offerings. Your yard birds may have some distinct preferences, so experiment to see what they like best.

Red-breasted nuthatch

Setting the Table—Types of Feeders

Seed feeders come in three main styles—hopper feeders, tray or table feeders and tube feeders. Hopper feeders are commonly mounted on posts or hung from trees, decks and poles. They are excellent for the larger birds like cardinals, grosbeaks and jays. Sunflower or safflower seed are good choices for hopper feeders.

Tray or table feeders are usually placed low to the ground and are particularly welcomed by ground-feeding birds. The best seed choices for these feeders are the favorites of ground-feeding birds like millet and cracked corn. Mixes will attract a wider variety of birds and can also be offered on trays. We use an old screen mounted on a platform a few inches above the ground as a tray feeder. Rain or melting snow will drain right through so the seeds are less likely to become moldy. Similar feeders are commercially available.

Tube feeders come with tiny portals for thistle seed or with larger portals for sunflower or safflower seed. They are most popular with finches, titmice and chickadees. Fine mesh bags make good thistle feeders.

Heavy wire cages or plastic mesh bags (like the bags onions come in) dispense suet; wire mesh tube feeders dispense whole or cracked peanuts. Peanut butter puddings can be tucked into large pine cones or into holes drilled in a short log.

Stewardship of Your Feeding Station

The three main problems for birds using feeding stations are disease, collisions with windows and cats. Cleanliness of your feeders and feeding area is of utmost importance to keep your birds healthy. To spare birds from flying into windows, put netting over your windows and place feeders within a few feet of your house. Keep cats indoors. Follow the tips in chapter 20 to keep the birds alive, safe and healthy.

Add a brush pile or shrubbery near your feeders to provide a hiding place from neighbors' cats and other predators, but place it several feet from feeders, so it does not become a hiding place for predators waiting to ambush birds.

Then, fill up your feeders, sit back in the warmth of your home and get ready to enjoy some great birding right beyond your windows. You may also want to participate in Project FeederWatch, a winter-long survey of birds visiting feeders, which is operated by the Cornell Lab of Ornithology, as mentioned in chapter 15. I've participated in Project FeederWatch for a number of years and enjoy comparing my yard surveys from year to year and finding out what birds are visiting other yards.

This information helps scientists track the movements of winter bird populations, as well as long-term trends in abundance and distribution.

Resources for Readers

Books

Barker, Margaret, and Jack Griggs. 2000. *The Feeder Watcher's Guide to Bird Feeding.* New York: Harper Resource.

Dennis, John. 1994. *A Complete Guide to Bird Feeding.* New York: Knopf.

Dunn, Erica H., and Diane L. Tessaglia-Hymes. 1999. *Birds at Your Feeder.* New York: W. W. Norton.

Stokes, Donald, and Lillian Stokes. 1987. *The Bird Feeder Book.* Boston: Little, Brown.

Websites

Cornell Lab of Ornithology. "About Birds & Bird Feeding." http://birds.cornell.edu/pfw/AboutBirdsandFeeding/abtbirds_index.html

National Audubon Society. "Seed and Feeder Selection Guide." http://marketplace.audubon.org/sites/default/files/documents/seed_and_feeder_selection_guide_2010.pdf

National Bird-Feeding Society. http://www.birdfeeding.org/

Dickcissel on thistle

CHAPTER 22
PROBLEMS IN
BIRD HABITAT GARDENS

> *Just as a deer herd lives in mortal fear*
> *of its wolves, so does a mountain live in*
> *mortal fear of deer.*
>
> —Aldo Leopold, *A Sand County Almanac*

> *Feral and free-ranging domestic cats are exotic species to*
> *North America. Exotic species are recognized as one of the*
> *most widespread and serious threats to the integrity of native*
> *wildlife populations and natural ecosystems."*
>
> —Policy Statement on Feral and Free-ranging Domestic Cats, approved by the
> Wildlife Society, March 2001; adopted by the Wisconsin Society for Ornithology, July 2001

Your bird habitat garden will bring you many pleasurable moments as you watch birds sing, bathe, feed, court, nest and raise young amid the blossoms and beauty of native landscaping. Occasionally, however, problems may arise. This chapter discusses these problems and offers solutions on how you can deal with them.

Problems with Herbivores
Ob, Deer

White-tailed Deer are, by far, the greatest threat among herbivores to bird habitat gardens in the Midwest, whether well-established remnant habitats or newly planted restorations, particularly woodlands. Not only do deer browse on the woody plants, they also chomp on wildflowers and rub their antlers on soft-barked trees and shrubs.

Left uncontrolled, deer can wipe out virtually all vegetation except large trees, grasses and ferns, eliminating even the saplings needed to replace the trees as they age and die. This reduction in vegetation brings about a devastating loss of cover, nesting sites, fruits and seeds for birds. In addition, the decline in the abundance and variety of plants results in fewer insects and other animals that depend on the lost plant species for their well-being—fewer insects for insect-eating birds and fewer small mammals for birds of prey.

A number of studies have documented the detrimental effects of high populations of deer on birds. The declines of Ovenbirds in Maryland, a variety of understory birds in New York, and all bird groups in Pennsylvania have been correlated with an overabundance of deer. At the National

photo: Grassbopper

Zoo's Conservation and Research Center in Virginia, biologist William McShea monitored the precipitous decline of Kentucky Warblers, a songbird that nests and hunts for insects in low foliage, like raspberry and blackberry patches. After deer hunting was stopped at the center in 1979, the deer herd burgeoned and wiped out much of the low foliage preferred by the warblers, and the Kentucky Warbler disappeared from four of five habitat zones.

In 1994 biologist David deCalesta of the U.S. Forest Service was one of the first to conduct a controlled study of the effect of deer on birds. Using enclosures with different deer densities in forest areas in Pennsylvania, he found that the level of vegetation most affected by high densities of deer was the middle canopy—the height of saplings and shrubs was greatly reduced. Although the deer also ate plenty of wildflowers on the ground level, grasses and ferns increased in their place. As a result, although the plant mix changed, the density of the ground cover remained the same.

Not surprisingly, the birds of the midlevels of the forest suffered most from overgrazing by deer. The Eastern Wood Pewee, Indigo Bunting, Least Flycatcher and Yellow-billed Cuckoo were the midlevel birds first to decline as deer numbers rose to 39 per square mile. One upper canopy bird, the Cerulean Warbler, and the cavity-nesting Pileated Woodpecker also dropped in abundance at this deer density. When deer rose to even higher levels, 68 deer per square mile, the numbers of American Robins and Eastern Phoebes fell.

In 2000, William McShea at the National Zoo did a controlled study following his observations on the decline of the Kentucky Warbler. For nine years, he and his colleague John Rappole monitored birds inside and outside areas fenced to exclude deer. In the fenced areas, both the density and diversity of the understory woody shrubs increased significantly and so did the abundance and diversity of birds.

Of the 25 most common birds monitored in the study, 15 increased in number, especially those preferring the low and mid levels of forest, responding to the increased vegetation at those levels following deer exclusion. The birds that increased in number were migratory birds, a number of which are of management concern and included the following: Hooded Warbler, Ovenbird, Worm-eating Warbler, Gray Catbird, Eastern Towhee, Veery, Wood Thrush, Indigo Bunting, Red-eyed Vireo, American Redstart, Acadian Flycatcher, Cerulean Warbler, Great Crested Flycatcher, Scarlet Tanager and Brown-headed Cowbird. Several resident birds decreased, such as the Carolina Wren, but they were species with stable or increasing populations, not normally of management concern.

In addition to eating vegetation that woodland birds need, deer have been documented eating eggs and nestlings out of bird nests located in shrubs.

What You Can Do: Solutions for Gardeners

Some immediate solutions for the gardener are repellents, fencing and landscaping with deer-resistant plants.

Repellents. Repellents have mixed results. Homemade remedies include painting egg-based mixes on vulnerable plants and hanging bags of human hair near plants. Some people hang strong-smelling soaps, such as Coast or Dove, near plants or shred and sprinkle them around the plants. Many commercial repellents are available. Trial and error will show what works for you. A volunteer at the Wehr Nature Center in Milwaukee County tried using Fels Naptha soap, but the deer ate it. Her egg-mix does the trick, until it washes off with the rain (see the sidebar, next page).

Fencing. The most popular type of deer fencing is black polypropylene mesh netting that is nearly invisible. Since deer are champion jumpers, fencing needs to be at least six or seven feet high and should slope away from the garden. For small areas, you can drape the netting over the plants or place it over stakes around the plants to be protected.

Electric fencing is the most reliable way to keep deer out of your yard. Install a single strand of the bait-and-shock type four feet above the ground and attach bait (peanut butter or salt) every few yards to attract the deer, whose noses are shocked when they attempt to eat the bait.

Landscaping. Many experts suggest planting species less favored by deer, but I have looked at lists of such plants and found conflicting advice. Deer in my yard eat Nannyberry Viburnum and Downy Arrowwood Viburnum, which some publications list as deer-resistant. On the other hand, deer rarely eat my Virginia Bluebells, which some lists include as particularly vulnerable. In the end, no plant is deer-proof. If the population of deer is high enough, hungry deer will eat virtually everything. Also, I suspect that deer populations and even individuals have their preferences.

A few deer delights and dislikes are well established. The first woody plants to be lost to deer are usually White Cedar and Canada Yew. Deer favorites among herbaceous plants include, unfortunately, some of our most beautiful and beloved wildflowers, particularly orchids and plants in the lily family, like trilliums and Solomon's seals. Indeed, researchers have found that the number, height and/or proportion of flowering stems of wildflowers in the orchid and lily families are directly related to deer densities. (This finding has led some to suggest using these vegetation measures to guide deer management goals, just as ranchers look at the condition of their pasture grasses to determine if it's time to move the cattle.)

Deer do not like White Snakeroot, a woodland wildflower toxic to deer, and the unpalatable Spicebush. Nor do they like ferns. Some heavily grazed forests, in fact, have only ferns in the understory and are called fern parks. They can be attractive, but they support relatively few birds and other wildlife. In addition, the ferns interfere with the germination and growth of trees, jeopardizing the long-term survival of the forest.

Lorrie Otto, a midwestern champion of natural landscaping, had to deal with a deer-ravaged yard before local deer control was implemented. In an article in the Wild Ones journal,

DEER-B-GONE & RABBITS TOO

Keep a dozen eggs at room temperature or in a warm garage for two to three weeks. The older they are, the better. Then fill a three-gallon pail nearly full of water. Add the eggs, 1/3 cup Tabasco sauce, and 1/3 cup Murphy's oil soap or other natural oil soap. It's important to add the water first to avoid excess foam. Mix well. The oil helps the mixture adhere to plants. Use a small cup to splash the mixture on and around the plants. After a hard rain, you'll have to reapply the mixture.

A volunteer naturalist at the Wehr Nature Center combined several similar recipes to come up with this winner. She was amazed and gratified to see a deer standing in the middle of her prairie garden and walk away without munching a single plant, apparently due to the repellent smell. (Fortunately, humans can't detect any odor.) Should the deer decide to nibble the plants anyway, the hot sauce makes them unpalatable!

DEER OR RABBIT— WHO'S THE CULPRIT?

Both deer and rabbits browse on twigs, but which are the culprits in your yard?

The tips of the damaged twigs hold the telltale evidence. Rabbits have sharp incisors in both their upper and lower jaws and nip off twigs cleanly, at a 45-degree angle. Deer have incisors only in their lower jaw and as a result, the twigs they browse have ragged tips.

Cottontail Rabbit

she wrote about selecting plants unattractive to deer to landscape the edges of a new path in her suburban Milwaukee yard. She chose violets because even if they lose their blossoms to deer, they can reproduce through self-pollinating flowers at their base. Her other selections included strawberries because they can spread by runners; Virginia Waterleaf for the vigor of its luxuriant green leaves even if deer nibble off its flowers; Mayapple, which is poisonous; and Wild Ginger, Nodding Onion, Blue-eyed Grass and ferns, all of which, she said, "fail the deer-taste test."

Find out about deer tastes in your own area by checking with experts at your local university extension, nature center, Wild Ones chapter or native plant society. Unless deer are so abundant that they are starving, selective landscaping will probably help you create a sustainable habitat garden for birds.

Long-term solution. Above all, support efforts to bring the deer populations under control. At the time of this writing, the only effective long-term remedy for controlling deer populations is through hunting or sharp-shooting. Although some animal lovers oppose these measures, it is important to note that, in essence, hunters are fulfilling the role of wolves, the natural predators of deer. Wolves are found only in the northern reaches of the Upper Midwest, and it is unlikely that they will ever be able to coexist with humans in more populated areas.

Native vegetation has rebounded where wolves do occur and keep deer numbers in check. As noted in the studies, this increase in vegetation should also bring back more birds. Wolf specialist Adrian Wydeven says, "Studies in Wisconsin show that the middle of wolf pack areas has a richer variety of wildflowers than the edge of wolf territories. Studies in Yellowstone show increased regeneration of aspen and willow after wolf reintroduction in areas that had been over-browsed by elk."

Culling deer benefits us as well as birds, animals and plants. Every year thousands of deer-car collisions in the Midwest injure and kill people, kill deer and cause millions of dollars of damage to cars. Lyme disease, carried by the deer tick, and Chronic Wasting Disease have also been on the rise as deer populations grow.

The goal of deer control is to reduce their numbers to levels that available acreage can support. Birds, trilliums and other plants and animals would have a better chance of surviving in our yards, parks and natural areas.

Other Herbivores

Rabbits are a great threat to plants, especially in spring and early summer. They are very fond of tender seedlings and leafy greens, but their preferences change from year to year. The best defense is a three-foot wire-mesh fence around sites with young plants. Experts Steven Carroll and Steven Salt, authors of *Ecology for Gardeners*, insist that you must install the fencing one foot underground as well. We never needed to do this, perhaps because our soil is hard to dig.

I have also put a wire protector around a single plant, such as a newly planted aster, which the rabbits would devour. Other rabbit deterrents are the same smelly substances used to repel deer—rotten egg batters applied to plants or highly perfumed substances, like grated soaps or baby powder, sprinkled around the plants.

Rabbits, mice and voles can be a problem in winter, when they gnaw on the bark at the base of young trees and shrubs. Generally they work under cover of mulch or snow. Be sure to keep mulch three or four inches away from the base of trees. The trunks of young woody plants should be protected with tree shelters or wrapping material for a year or two until they are less susceptible to damage.

Rabbits often eat the tips of twigs. If the damage becomes significant, protect the shrubs with wire fencing.

Another creative solution enlists the help of hawks. Several Wisconsin homeowners with young trees have erected T-shaped perches at different levels among the trees, and they regularly see Red-tailed Hawks and American Kestrels on the perches, scanning for rodents.

Predators: Exotic & Native

The Exotic Domestic Cat

The domestic cat, *Felix catus*, is not native to North America. It arrived here with the first colonists. It is a descendant of the wild cat of Africa and southwestern Asia, *Felix silvestris,* and retains both the appearance and behavior of its ancestors. The cat was first domesticated around 2000 BC by the Egyptians, who worshiped it as a goddess. Gradually, the cat was introduced around the world.

Extensive studies of predation by cats, over four continents and spanning half a century, confirms that domestic cats hunt and kill birds and other small animals. Lots of them.

We owned several cats when our sons were growing up. Occasionally, our cats brought home their hunting trophies—mostly shrews that they had caught. One of our sons saw our cat Blacky kill a robin, and Blacky was already declawed! When we realized that our cats could kill the very birds that we hoped to attract to our yard, we started to keep them indoors. Two studies carried out in Michigan and Wisconsin highlight the problem.

The Wisconsin study, completed in the early 1990s, was initiated by biologists with the U.S. Department of Agriculture and the Wisconsin Department of Natural Resources who wanted to determine the cause of the low reproductive success and high mortality of grassland birds. The government was spending millions of dollars to encourage farmers to set aside acreage and improve habitat for grassland birds to little avail. Could free-ranging cats be to blame? Stanley Temple, professor of wildlife ecology at the University of Wisconsin, and his colleague John Coleman conducted the study. After four years of research they came away shocked at the numbers of native birds and small mammals they estimated that cats killed.

Cats kill millions of birds yearly.

"Cats may be a major threat to some bird populations," says Temple, "especially ground-nesting birds living near farms." He believes cats may be contributing to the decline of midwestern grassland birds. "Western Meadowlarks are particularly hard-hit by cats and are declining in Wisconsin at an annual rate of 8 percent," he says.

To monitor cat predation for the study, 30 farm cats were radio collared. From the data collected, along with that of other studies, the researchers estimate that the 1.4 to 2 million free-ranging rural cats in Wisconsin kill between 8 and 217 million birds each year, with the most reasonable estimate being 39 million birds. It is important to note that the figure does not include predation by urban cats.

The Michigan study, conducted in 2000 by biologist Christopher Lepczyk and his colleagues Angela Mertig and Jianguo Liu, focused on three Breeding Bird Survey (BBS) routes along a continuum from rural to suburban to urban areas. The researchers asked cat owners to report the number and kinds of birds their outdoor cats killed. As shown in the table, cat owners identified 23 species of birds or groups of birds (some owners could not identify specific species). They represent 12.5% of the 184 species of breeding birds reported on the routes, two of which are of special concern in Michigan—the Eastern Bluebird and the Ruby-throated Hummingbird. Aside from these two species, most of the birds feed on the ground or in low brush.

From the data they collected, the researchers estimate that along the three BBS routes, which totaled 73 miles, 800 to 3,100 cats killed between 16,000 and 47,000 birds during the 22 week breeding season. "Our results, even taken conservatively," say Lepczyk and his colleagues, "indicate that free-ranging cats are killing a large number and wide range of bird species." Furthermore, they point out, "Our study illustrates how important private landowners are in influencing the ecosystem around them."

The number of small native mammals killed by cats is even higher than the number of birds. The Wisconsin study found that small mammals, like shrews, mice and voles, made up about 70% of cat kills; birds constituted about 20%, while a mix of other animals made up the remaining 10%. Some people believe that the killing of certain animals by cats is beneficial. But many of these animals, like mice and shrews, are important food sources for hawks and owls and other native predators.

What You Can Do

In almost all circumstances, cats should be kept indoors. The only possible exception is on farms, where free-ranging cats should be spayed or neutered to control their numbers. Well-fed, neutered females will stay close to the farm buildings where they help the farmer by killing rodents. Even better, farmers should consider using pest-proofing and environmentally safe rodent control methods—not rodenticides, which harm birds of prey, such as hawks and owls, that eat the poisoned rodents.

Keep your cat indoors; you will save the lives of countless birds and other native animals. Bells and declawing are not effective measures. And don't count on the fact that your cat is well fed. The hunting instinct in cats is independent of hunger.

Not only is keeping cats indoors better for birds, it's also better for cats. Free-roaming cats face many hazards. They can get by hit by cars, stolen, trapped, abused, poisoned and attacked by dogs or other animals. They can contract fatal diseases like feline distemper, rabies and viruses. According to the Humane Society of the United States, outdoor cats live an average of less than five years, whereas indoor cats often live to seventeen years or more. In view of all the hazards, the Humane Society of the United States and the American Humane Association support keeping cats indoors.

The American Bird Conservancy operates a program called *Cats Indoors! The Campaign for Safer Birds and Cats*. It also offers many useful tips on how to make your outdoor cat a happy indoor cat, how to prevent damage to furniture without declawing your cat and how to deal with stray cats.

Be sure to support laws in your local communities prohibiting free-roaming cats. Such laws greatly benefit birds. Duluth, Minnesota, for example, approved a cat-leash ordinance in 2000. Before the ordinance, the highest number of Northern Cardinals on the Duluth Christmas Bird Count was 6, with an average of about 2. Afterward, the numbers were significantly higher, ranging from 15 to 20 birds.

Native Predators

Raccoons, opossums and skunks can prey on birds' eggs and nestlings. In many cities and suburbs, these animals are far more abundant than they would be in natural conditions because they have easy access to food in garbage cans and dumps. The best solution is to use predator guards on posts supporting nest boxes. Also, keep a tight lid on your garbage can or store it in the garage.

Hawks and owls are often attracted by songbirds at backyard bird feeders. Consider it a privilege to watch these beautiful birds of prey when they visit, as the National Bird-Feeding Society suggests. Like all predators, these birds of prey play an important role in removing weak, sick and old birds.

It is rare even for ornithologists to see a hawk or owl capture a songbird. A study by the Cornell Lab of Ornithology found that only 10% of winter bird feeders lost birds to hawks or owls and of those, generally only one incident occurred at any one feeder. Overall, researchers concluded, raptor predation at feeders is a minor problem, compared with the many birds lost to cats and window collisions.

The most common hawks at feeders are Cooper's and Sharp-shinned. Sometimes, especially in the northern Midwest, Northern Goshawks, largest of the accipiters (the main bird-feeding hawks), stop for a visit—a spectacular sight in any yard. Paul and Susan Damon of Saint Paul, Minnesota, whose landscaping is featured in chapter 4, were excited by a few rare sightings of this impressive hawk in their yard.

Window Collisions

Many millions of birds are killed each year by flying into windows, according to Daniel Klem of Muhlenberg College in Pennsylvania, who has been studying the phenomenon for many years. Other than habitat destruction, he says, the only other comparable human-associated cause of bird mortality is the domestic cat. Birds crash into windows because they cannot distinguish between their real natural habitat and that reflected in a window. Tragically, 50% of window collisions result in the death of the bird.

Anything that breaks up or reduces window reflections will save the lives of birds. The best technique is to install netting—such as black polypropylene 3/4-inch mesh, which is nearly invisible—about six inches from the window so that birds will not hit the hard surface. You can attach a rigid frame with shelf brackets to hold the netting in place. It takes some effort to put up this protection, but those who have done so are pleased with the results and report no bird fatalities.

Screens on the outside of windows, which were once common, are also very effective. Like the netting, they break up the reflections and cushion any bird that might try to fly through.

New products include framed screening that attaches to a window with suction cups and easy-to-apply film that reduces reflections and allows good visibility from inside. Both of these products are available from the Wisconsin Humane Society website (see Resources for Readers at the end of this chapter).

A simpler but less effective solution is to attach streamers of ribbon or colorful tapes to the window, which will blow in the wind and break the reflection. I've attached them four inches apart to both the bottom and top of the window, allowing some slack so they won't blow completely to the side on very windy days. Stained glass designs or dividers also break up window reflections. Closing drapes or drawing blinds may also help; white ones reduce reflections.

Owl and hawk decals or silhouettes pasted on the window don't work unless most of the window is covered. Silhouettes attached with suction cups are somewhat more effective because they move in the wind.

Locating bird feeders close to the windows helps reduce collisions—the closer the better, according to Klem's studies. Feeders placed about 3 feet from the window were safest for the birds. Despite a few collisions, there were no fatalities. As the distance of feeders from the windows increased, so did fatalities. The increases were moderate at distances of about 6 to 13 feet but jumped dramatically when distances increased to 16 and 32 feet. Researchers recorded a total of 73 bird fatalities over the 12 weeks of the study.

Drilling and Drumming by Woodpeckers

In spring and fall, woodpeckers are apt to drill holes in the siding of houses or drum on metal rain gutters. They drum to attract mates or declare territory, and they drill, it is thought, to dig out insects burrowing in the wood or to create nesting and roosting cavities. The woodpeckers known to drill and drum on houses are the Downy Woodpecker, Hairy Woodpecker, Northern Flicker, Red-bellied Woodpecker and Pileated Woodpecker. The Downy Woodpecker seems to be the most common culprit.

It is important to deal with the problem quickly before the woodpecker gets attached to the site. An effective technique is to cover the site where the woodpecker is drilling. Tack a large plastic drop cloth or garbage bag over the area, with the bottom left free to blow in the wind. It prevents the woodpecker from getting a grip on the site and scares the bird away when it blows. Another method is to stretch netting at least six inches from the site so the woodpecker can't reach it.

A scare tactic might work. It involves tacking six-foot mylar streamers, available at party supply stores, ten inches apart at the top of the site. As they blow in the wind, they may frighten off woodpeckers. You can also spray the birds with a hose whenever you catch them in the act.

Problems with woodpeckers can usually be resolved with these techniques. Preserve dead trees in your yard to provide natural drilling and drumming sites for woodpeckers. The birds will be less likely to use your house as a substitute.

Remember that woodpeckers are protected by federal and state laws. It is illegal to shoot or harm them.

Bird Diseases and Deaths

When birds concentrate at your feeders, there is risk of disease spreading among them. Mosquitos breeding in stagnant water in birdbaths and other containers can also be agents of disease. Six common diseases can infect the birds in your yard.

Finches disease, also called **mycoplasmal conjunctivitis**, causes finches to have red, swollen, crusty or runny eyes. Their eyes can even become swollen shut, blinding the birds. While some infected birds recover, others die of starvation, exposure or predation. House finches were first to exhibit this disease, but recently it has spread to goldfinches. If you would like to help monitor this disease, visit the Cornell website listed in Resources for Readers at the end of this chapter.

Salmonellosis is caused by Salmonella bacteria and is spread when birds ingest food or water contaminated with feces. Sick birds are often thin, lethargic and easy to approach.

Avian pox is caused by a virus and is spread by contact with an infected bird or with contaminated surfaces, food or water. The more common form causes warts on the featherless parts of a bird's body, such as bill, legs or feet. The other form causes difficulty in breathing and eating.

Aspergillosis, spread by damp, moldy bird food or waste seed below feeders, causes bronchitis and pneumonia. Birds appear thin and have difficulty breathing and walking.

Trichomoniasis is caused by a protozoan often present in the mouth secretions of healthy birds, like pigeons, that carry the disease. Infected birds contaminate birdbaths, exposing other birds. Birds having difficulty closing their beaks may be suffering from this disease.

West Nile Virus is spread by mosquitos and can cause encephalitis—an inflammation of the brain and meningitis—the swelling of brain and spinal cord tissue. The virus can affect humans as well as birds.

What You Can Do

To avoid the occurrence of these diseases among your yard visitors, clean your feeders carefully every few weeks. Immerse them in a solution of one part bleach to nine parts water to disinfect. Dry the feeders thoroughly before refilling, so the seed doesn't become damp and moldy. Hummingbird feeders need to be cleaned frequently—every few days, especially in hot weather.

In addition, clean regularly below your feeders to prevent moldy waste seed from spreading disease. Such waste seed also attracts rodents. To reduce this problem, consider using no-mess seed which is already hulled and leaves little debris below the feeders. If possible, move your feeders to new locations periodically so that bird droppings and any hard-to-remove seed debris can compost in place and grass below the feeder can revive.

Be sure to keep bird seed in clean, dry metal trash cans or other containers. Mice sometimes chew through plastic trash cans.

To avoid West Nile Virus, eliminate items that collect water in which mosquitos can breed—clogged rain gutters, old tires, pots. Turn over wheelbarrels, pails and kids' toys when they are not in use or drill drain holes in them. Keep swimming pools clean and chlorinated.

Put minnows or mosquito-eating fish in ponds that don't attract frogs. And be sure to clean and change the water in birdbaths every three or four days.

Orphaned or Injured Birds

Most baby birds that people find are not orphaned or abandoned. If the bird has feathers, it is likely to be a fledgling that has left its nest but is still too young to fly and forage on its own. It's not unusual for fledglings to be on the ground at this time, and their parents will continue to feed them. Experts advise leaving the birds where you find them and keeping cats and dogs indoors.

A featherless or down-covered bird should be placed back into its nest if you can locate it. Be sure your hands are warm for the bird's sake and because its parents may throw out what they perceive as a cold object. If you don't know where the nest is or it is too high to reach, place the bird in a tree or bush close to where you found it. Call a rehabilitator if a parent bird doesn't show up within half a day.

An injured bird should be covered with a towel to calm it and then placed gently in a box lined with soft material. Call a wildlife rehabilitator immediately. If a bird has flown into a window and shows no sign of injury, put it in a box in a warm place. Stunned birds will often recover and be able to fly away after a few hours.

If you have trouble finding a local rehabilitator, check with your state wildlife agency or contact the International Wildlife Rehabilitation Council (see Resources for Readers at the end of this chapter).

Feeder Pests
Squirrels

Squirrels are considered the number one pest at feeders. The easiest way to deal with the problem is to use baffles that prevent squirrels from accessing feeders. Many kinds are available for different feeders. A baffle should be placed below a pole-mounted feeder. A tilting baffle at least 18 inches wide can keep squirrels off hanging feeders. Homemade baffles can be constructed with soda bottles, old records, plastic bowls or stovepipes. Other ideas include hanging feeders from three or four feet of fishing line, rather than wire or rope. To protect feeders hung on horizontal lines, place light-weight plastic tubing around the line on each side of the feeder. Squirrels will tumble when they try to walk across the tubing.

Some people like to set up a feeder specifically for squirrels in an isolated corner of their yard. This may help, but could also increase the number of squirrels attracted to your yard, defeating your purpose. Do not live trap squirrels and drop them off in remote areas, since it is difficult for any animal to survive and establish a territory in a new location.

Although squirrels can be troublesome, I enjoy these agile and clever little

The Red Squirrel is an entertaining animal—or a pest. Put up a separate feeding station if you enjoy its antics.

mammals. When I was in France, I had only a passing glimpse of one of their rare native squirrels and apparently residents seldom see them. In *Guide to Animal Tracking and Behavior*, Donald and Lillian Stokes tell of a French guest at their home who was thrilled to see a Gray Squirrel at their feeder and raced off to get his camera to take a photo.

Gray Squirrels were once rare in our country, too. By the early 1900s, squirrel populations had plummeted as land was cleared for farms and lumber. There was actually concern that our Gray Squirrels might become extinct. But throughout the last century, as farming and lumbering decreased, woodlands grew and the Gray Squirrel had a comeback. Most of us would never want to be without these engaging animals.

Other Mammals

Raccoons, bears, deer and moose sometimes become pests at feeders. You may have to fence your feeders to keep them away. It may also help to take down feeders for a few weeks. In Wisconsin and some other states, feeders that attract deer are illegal because they concentrate deer and could spread Chronic Wasting Disease.

If these pests raid your feeders at night, your best bet is to empty them or take them in before dark, and put them back out the next morning.

Undesirable Birds

Pigeons can overrun a feeder and make a mess with their droppings. Native birds like grackles, cowbirds and crows can also become nuisances. To discourage these large birds, use feeders with small perches designed for small birds and avoid basin or tray-type feeders on which larger birds can get a footing.

Cowbirds are parasitic birds that lay their nests in other birds' nests. When they show up at my feeders in spring, I switch from sunflower seed to safflower seed, which cowbirds don't like (nor do my squirrels). It works well in keeping cowbirds away and sometimes also checks the pesty grackle and blackbird crowd.

Raccoons are natural predators of birds and nests.

Resources for Readers

The Exotic Domestic Cat

American Bird Conservancy. "Cats Indoors." www.abcbirds.org/cats/

Coleman, John S., Stanley A. Temple and Scott R. Craven. 1997. "Cats and Wildlife: A Conservation Dilemma." University of Wisconsin–Extension and U.S. Department of Agriculture. http://wildlife.wisc.edu/extension/catfly3.htm

Harrison, Kit, and George H. Harrison. 1998. *Bird Watching for Cats.* Minocqua, WI: Willow Creek Press.

White-tailed Deer

National Audubon Society. "Public Menace." http://audubonmagazine.org/incite/incite0507.html

Squirrels

Adler, Bill. 1996. *Outwitting Squirrels.* Chicago: Review Press.

Window Collisions

American Bird Conservancy. "Windows: A Human Hazard for Birds." http://www.birdconservationalliance.org/campaigns/collisions/window_paper.pdf

FLAP, Fatal Light Awareness Program. http://www.flap.org/

National Audubon Society. "Minimizing Window Collisions." http://audubon.org/bird/at_home/SafeWindows.html

Wisconsin Humane Society. "Preventing Home Collisions." http://www.wihumane.org/wildlife/wings/homecollisions.aspx

Wildlife Rehabilitators

International Wildlife Rehabilitation Council. PO Box 8187, San Jose, CA 95155; phone: 408-271-2685; http://theiwrc.org/

Finch Disease

Cornell Lab of Ornithology. "House Finch Disease Survey." http://birds.cornell.edu/hofi/index.html

Problems with Woodpeckers

Cornell Lab of Ornithology. "Woodpeckers: Damage, Prevention and Control." http://birds.cornell.edu/wp_about/

CONCLUSION
THE PROMISE OF BIRDSCAPING

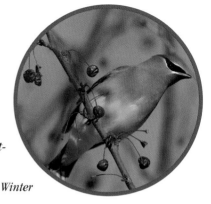

Nature is entertainment—the greatest show on earth.

—Bernd Heinrich, *Ravens in Winter*

As we work to transform our yards and welcome birds and other wildlife to share our lives, we have front-row tickets for an incredible show unfolding around us. We see birds, butterflies and blossoms as an everyday experience, not a vacation-only event. We're entertained by the antics of birds and other wildlife, moved by their beauty, intrigued by their remarkable behavior.

We're also likely to consider their habitat beyond our property boundaries. As we transplant a beebalm to feed hummingbirds, we may stop to wonder where other beebalms grow to nourish the rest of their clan. When we dig up our lawns to create havens for migratory birds, we can't help but think about how their fellow migrants fare outside our yards. When we seed in a prairie patch to feed finches and sparrows, we're likely to be mindful of the rarity of the original prairies in which they once flourished.

This awareness can lead us beyond our garden gates to work for the protection and restoration of bird habitat on a larger scale—in our neighborhoods, our local schoolyards, our communities, our states, even our country. We can strive to protect our last green spaces wherever they remain. And we can work to restore them to their best potential as wildlife habitat, enlarging them where we can to create habitat for those birds and animals that need larger landscapes and connecting them to reduce fragmentation and to create corridors for better reproduction, seasonal movement and seed dispersal.

Many of the gardeners whose yards have been featured in this book are doing just that.

Pat Brust in Wisconsin has been an officer on both the local and national levels for the organization Wild Ones: Native Plant, Natural Landscapes, for over a dozen years, encouraging members to improve habitat on their properties. She is the president of a Milwaukee chapter. She also volunteers for invasive weed control work days in Milwaukee County parks and has "adopted" one of them, and along with another volunteer, provides regular invasive weed monitoring and control.

Kitty and Kevin Clasing in Iowa educate and inspire many visitors who tour their yard each year. "Our goal," they write, "is to teach people, especially children, that wildlife is very important in life and must be encouraged so that future generations will know the joy and serenity of a beautiful and wildlife friendly habitat." Kitty also gives talks on landscaping for wildlife to various clubs, organizations and schools.

Photo: Cedar Waxwing

Similarly, Kim and John Vollmer in Illinois "want to provide a beautiful island of natural habitat welcoming life in a sea of sterile, boring home landscapes," and are dedicated to sharing information on native landscaping with others, especially young people. To that end, Kim has established a prairie garden at the school where she teaches in Clinton, Wisconsin. The couple also share plants and seeds from their yard with neighbors and friends interested in starting their own native habitat gardens.

Tom and Nancy Small in Michigan are a dynamic duo, devoting virtually all of their retirement hours to habitat restoration, in their yard, nearby parks and natural areas. Working with the Southwest Michigan Land Conservancy, they harvest, clean and germinate seeds of local ecotypes and help plant in the conservancy's preserves. They participate in plant rescues and take care of the plants until they can find good homes for them, ideally in protected areas. They pot up the native plants that volunteer or clone in their yard and have given away thousands to Wild Ones members, friends, neighbors, passersby, delivery people—"whoever will take them, along with some information about the value of native plants," they explain. They also use many of their plants in their projects, one of which is a streambank restoration along an urban creek that runs from their neighborhood to the downtown area. And when they're not working hands-on with native plants, they give educational presentations and write articles and pamphlets, including a "Guide to Natural Landscaping" distributed by the city of Kalamazoo.

Mary and James Norton in Iowa have received awards from the Trees Forever Buffer Initiative Program, as well as National Wildlife Federation, for work done on their land at Prairie Hills Farm, and harvest seed from their land for other prairie restorations in their area. Mary, a former teacher, received many awards for her outstanding environmental education work at an elementary school in Iowa, including the Iowa Wildlife Federation Environmental Educator of the Year Award, the Environmental Protection Agency Teacher of the Year Award, and the Sierra Club Educator Award, among others. Later, she developed a school-grounds prairie restoration project and became a consultant for similar projects across the Midwest. She went on to teach environmental education courses at the college level and coordinated an after-school nature club for children through the University of Iowa.

Susan Damon in Minnesota considers herself a missionary for replacing lawns with native plants. She says, "I think monoculture lawns are passé. Lawns are unnatural monocultures, and they are boring. Compare that to a native plant garden that brings your yard to life." To illustrate the point, she talks about neighbors to whom she gave a Wild Golden Glow (Green-headed Coneflower) plant, which soon attracted the first-ever goldfinches to their yard. Susan and her husband Paul promote landscaping for wildlife by hosting frequent tours of their yard. In addition, Paul, who has a degree in landscape architecture, has designed gardens for his family and given personalized landscape plans as door prizes for church fund raisers. Susan helps coordinate her neighborhood's "Buckthorn Busts."

Christine McCullough of Ohio is alarmed that the impenetrable jungle of honeysuckle beneath the woodland trees has wiped out the beautiful wildflowers she enjoyed as a child. She also tells of a neighbor's daughter who loved "those red birds" in her yard. To Christine's dismay, neither the neighbor nor her daughter could identify the Northern Cardinal, Ohio's official state bird! To help remedy the problem, she serves as president of the Greater Cincinnati chapter of Wild Ones: Native

Butterfly/Hummingbird garden at Lakota Early Childhood Center in West Chester, Ohio.

Plants, Natural Landscapes, trying to spread the word about the importance of preserving our native landscapes and wildlife. In addition, she coordinated the planting of a butterfly/hummingbird garden and an alphabet garden, using as many native plants as possible, at the Lakota Early Childhood Center in West Chester. Now she's busy working on the ecological restoration of a small wooded area on the center's grounds. Chris hopes that the children will grow up with "a sense of place."

Elizabeth Mueller in Indiana has been the moving force behind her town becoming the first Community Wildlife Habitat in the Midwest to be certified by the National Wildlife Federation. More than 150 of her friends, neighbors and other residents in Zionsville now have certified habitats. Her widespread influence is due, in part, to her "Habitat Happenings" column for the Zionsville newspaper. She also gives tours and presentations in her naturally landscaped yard. The Community Wildlife Habitat certification has given Zionsville favorable publicity, bringing many visitors and tourists. Other communities, like Bloomington, Indiana, are starting to follow suit, suggesting that Elizabeth's influence may be extending beyond the borders of Zionsville.

Birdscaping can entice more of us to join in such efforts. By working together and expanding the scope of habitat restorations, at home and beyond, we will help preserve the diversity of birds around us. The personal gain is the fun and joy of birding wherever we are. We'll also ensure that birds, those astonishingly complicated and beautiful winged creatures, will continue to bring pleasure to our children, grandchildren and generations to come.

Birding Organizations & Websites

State Birding Organizations

The Audubon Society of Missouri. Contact: Bonnie Heidy, 501 Parkade, Columbia, MO 65202; http://mobirds.org/

Illinois Ornithological Society. PO Box 931, Lake Forest, IL 60045; www.illinoisbirds.org/

Indiana Audubon Society. Contact: Vic Riemenschneider, IAS Membership Chair, 20451 Brick Road, South Bend, IN 46637; www.indianaaudubon.org/

Iowa Ornithologist's Union. Contact: Tammy Hertzel, 1432 East State Street, Mason City, IA 50401; www.iowabirds.org/

Michigan Field Ornithologists and Bird Banders. Contact: Brenda Keith, 5716 East S Ave.,Vicksburg, MI 49097; http://amazilia.net/MFOBB/

The Minnesota Ornithologists' Union. J.F. Bell Museum of Natural History, University of Minnesota, 10 Church Street S.E., Minneapolis, MN 55455-0104; http://moumn.org/

Ohio Ornithological Society. PO Box 14051, Columbus, OH 43214; http://www.ohiobirds.org/

Wisconsin Society for Ornithology. Contact: Christine Reel, WSO Treasurer; 2022 Sherryl Lane, Waukesha, WI 53188-3142; http://wsobirds.org/

National Organizations

American Bird Conservancy. PO Box 249, The Plains, VA 20198; phone: 540-253-5780; www.abcbirds.org/

The American Ornithologists' Union. Suite 402, 1313 Dolley Madison Blvd., McLean, VA 22101; www.aou.org/

National Audubon Society. 700 Broadway, New York, NY 10003; phone 212-979-3000; www.audubon.org/ (Be sure to see their "Audubon At Home" program.)

Birding Websites

http://www.allaboutbirds.org/
Cornell Lab of Ornithology's All About Birds: bird identification, location, conservation, reporting.

http://ebird.org/
A checklist for reporting bird sightings.

http://eNature.com/
Information about birds and other wildlife, as well as plants in the U.S.: field
guides, games and more.

Native Plant & Habitat Enhancement Organizations

Lady Bird Johnson Wildflower Center. 4801 La Crosse Avenue, Austin, TX
78739; phone: 512-292-4100; www.wildflower.org/ (Has regional "Factpacks")

National Wildlife Federation. 11100 Wildlife Center Drive, Reston, VA 20190;
phone: 800-822-9919; www.nwf.org/

Native Plant Societies
Chapter and meeting information given when available.

Illinois
Grand Prairie Friends-Prairie Grove Volunteers. PO Box 36,
Urbana, Il 61803; http://grandprairiefriends.org/

Illinois Native Plant Society. Forest Glen Preserve,
20301 E. 900 North Road, Westville, IL 61883; http://www.ill-inps.org/

Indiana
Indiana Native Plant and Wildflower Society. Contact: Karen Hartlep,
107 S. Pennsylvania St., Suite 100, Indianapolis, IN 46204;
phone: 317-253-6164; www.inpaws.org/
Chapters: West Central, South Central, Central, East Central

Iowa
Iowa Prairie Network. PO Box 572, Nevada, IA 50201;
www.iowaprairienetwork.org/

Michigan
Michigan Botanical Club. Contact: Pamela Laureto, phone: (res) 616-454-4328;
(off) 616-234-3896; www.michbotclub.org/
Chapters:
Ann Arbor Northwest; meeting locations vary.
Huron Valley; meets at Matthaei Botanical Gardens.
Red Cedar; meets at Michigan State University, East Lansing.
Southeastern; meets at the Royal Oak Senior/Community Center in Royal Oak.
Southwestern; meets at the Oshtemo Branch, Kalamazoo Library, Kalamazoo.
White Pine; meets at Grand Valley State University, Allendale.

Minnesota

Minnesota Native Plant Society. 250 Bio. Sci. Center, University of Minnesota, 1445 Gortner Avenue, St. Paul, MN 55108; http://mnnps.org/

Missouri

Center for Plant Conservation. PO Box 299, St. Louis, MO 63166; phone: 314-577-9450; http://www.centerforplantconservation.org/

Missouri Native Plant Society. PO Box 20073, St. Louis, MO 63144; http://missourinativeplantsociety.org/
Chapters: Hawthorn (Columbia); Kansas City; Osage Plains (Clinton); St. Louis.

Ohio

Cincinnati Wild Flower Preservation Society. Contact: Robert Bergstein, 3425 Lyleburn Pl., Cincinnati, OH 42520; http://cincywildflower.org/
Meeting locations vary.

Native Plant Society of Northeastern Ohio. Contact: Judy Barnhart, 10761 Pekin Road, Newbury, OH 44065; phone: 440-286-9504; http://nativeplantsocietyneohio.org/

Ohio Native Plant Society. 6 Louise Drive, Chagrin Falls, OH 44022; phone: 440-338-6622; http://dir.gardenweb.com/directory/onps1/

Wisconsin

Botanical Club of Wisconsin. Contact: Mariquita Sheehan, Chequamegon-Nicolet NF, PO Box 1809, Eagle River, WI 54521; phone 715-479-2827; https://sites.google.com/site/botanicalclubofwisconsin/
Chapters: LaCrosse, Madison, Milwaukee, and Stevens Point.

The Prairie Enthusiasts. Contact: Renae Mitchell, PO Box 1148, Madison, WI 53701; phone: 608-577-0584; http://www.theprairieenthusiasts.org/
10 Chapters in IL, MN and WI

Society for Ecological Restoration International. 285 W. 18th Street, Suite 1, Tucson, AZ 85701; phone: 520-622-5485; fax: 520-622-5491; www.ser.org/
Regional Chapter in OH.

University of Wisconsin–Madison Arboretum. 1207 Seminole Highway, Madison, WI 53711; phone: 608-263-7888; http://uwarboretum.org/

Wild Ones: Native Plants, Natural Landscapes. PO Box 1274, Appleton, WI 54912; phone: 877-394-9453; www.wildones.org/ *Chapters are located in the areas given below.*

Illinois

Greater DuPage; meets in Naperville and Glen Ellyn.

Illinois Prairie; meets in the Bloomington-Normal area.

Lake-to-Prairie; meeting locations vary.

Macomb; call 309-836-6231.

Northern Kane County; meeting locations vary.

North Park; meets at the North Park Nature Center, Chicago.

Rock River Valley; meets at Burpee Museum of Natural History, Rockford.

Indiana

Gibson Woods; meets at the Gibson Woods Nature Center, Hammond.

Michigan

Ann Arbor; meeting locations vary in Ann Arbor.

Calhoun County; meets at the Calhoun Intermediate School District Bldg., Marshall.

Central Upper Peninsula; meets at Bay de Noc Community College.

Flint River; meets at Mott Community College.

Houghton-Hancock; call 906-482-0446.

Kalamazoo Area; meets at First United Methodist Church, Kalamazoo.

Mid-Mitten; meets at Chippewa Nature Center, Midland.

North Oakland; meets in Clarkston.

Oakland; meets at Old Oakland Township Parks/Police Bldg., Oakland Township.

Red Cedar; meets at the MSU campus.

River City–Grand Rapids Area; meeting locations vary.

Southeast Michigan; meets in Warren.

Minnesota

Arrowhead; meeting locations vary.

Brainerd; meeting locations vary.

Northfield Prairie Partners; meeting locations vary.

St. Cloud; meets at Heritage Nature Center.

St. Croix Oak Savanna; meeting locations vary.

Twin Cities; meets at Nokomis Community Center, Minneapolis.

Missouri

Mid-Missouri; meeting locations vary.

St. Louis; meeting locations vary.

Ohio

Akron Chapter; meets in area.

Greater Cincinnati; meeting locations vary.

Columbus; meets at Inniswood Metropolitan Park, Westerville.

Oak Openings; meets in Sylvania.

Wisconsin

Central Wisconsin; meets at Portage County Extension Building, Stevens Point.

Door County Chapter; meeting locations vary.

Fox Valley Area Chapter; meets in Appleton or Oshkosh.

Green Bay; most meetings at Green Bay Botanical Garden.

Kettle Moraine; meeting locations vary.

Madison; meeting locations vary.

Menomonee River Area; meets at Valley View School, Menomonee Falls.

Milwaukee North; meets at Urban Ecology Center, Milwaukee.

Milwaukee Southwest-Wehr; meets at Wehr Nature Center, Franklin.

Root River Area; meets at Riverbend Nature Center, Racine.

Wolf River; meets in Shawano area.

Websites

Natural Resources Conservation Service. United States Department of Agriculture. See their Backyard Conservation website:
http://www.nrcs.usda.gov/wps/portal/nrcs/detail/national/newsroom
/features/?&cid=nrcs143_023574

Missouri Department of Conservation.
See their Grow Native! website: http://www.grownative.org/

Midwestern Native Plant Nurseries & Consultants

In the Midwest, we are fortunate to have a growing number of native plant nurseries. For the convenience of readers, a few in each state are listed below. No endorsement nor discrimination of specific vendors is intended or implied. Sources for more complete lists of native plant nurseries are also given when available.

Midwest

Applied Ecological Services, Inc. Nurseries/Offices in IL, MN, WI. Headquarters: 17921 Smith Road, Brodhead, WI 53520; phone: 608-897-8641; www.appliedeco.com/

J.F. New Native Plant Nursery. Nurseries/Offices in IL, IN, MI, OH and WI (Prairie Ridge Nursery). Headquarters: 128 Sunset Dr., Walkerton, IN 46574; phone: 574-586-2412; www.jfnewnursery.com/

Illinois

Bluestem Prairie Nursery. 13197 E. 13th Street, Hillsboro, IL 62049; phone: 217-532-6344; e-mail: bluestemnursery@yahoo.com

Genesis Nursery, Inc. 23200 Hurd Rd., Tampico, IL 61283; phone: 815-438-2220.

Midwest Wildflowers. Box 64, Rockton, IL 61072; phone: 815-642-7040.

The Natural Garden, Inc. 38W443 Highway 64, St. Charles, IL 60175; phone: 630-584-0150; www.thenaturalgardeninc.com/

See listing of native plant nurseries at the website of the Grand Prairie Friends: http://grandprairiefriends.org/nurseries.html

Indiana

Edge of the Prairie Wildflowers. 1641 Oak Hill Road, Crawfordsville, IN 47933; phone: 765-362-0915.

Heartland Restoration Services. 14921 Hand Road, Fort Wayne, IN 46818; phone: 260-489-8511; www.earthsourceinc.net/heartland.html

Indiana Department of Natural Resources. Division of Forestry, 402 West Washington Street, Room W296, Indianapolis, IN 46204-2739; phone: 317-232-4105; www.in.gov/dnr/forestry/

Munchkin Nursery & Gardens LLC. 323 Woodside Drive, N.W., Depauw, IN 47115; phone: 812-633-4858; www.munchkinnursery.com/

Also see "Landscaping with Plants Native to Indiana" at http://www.naturalheritageofindiana.org/participate/INPAWS2.pdf

Iowa

Allendan Seed Company. 1966 175th Ln., Winterset, IA 50273; phone: 515-462-1241; http://allendanseed.com/

Integrated Roadside Vegetation Management Plan. Iowa Department of Transportation. Contact: Kirk Henderson, University of Northern Iowa, Cedar Falls, IA; phone: 319-273-2813; e-mail: kirk.henderson@uni.edu

Ion Exchange: Native Seed & Plant Nursery. 1878 Old Mission Drive, Harpers Ferry, IA; 52146; phone: 800-291-2143; www.ionxchange.com/

Carl and Linda Kurtz. 1562 Binford Ave., St. Anthony, IA 50239; phone: 641-477-8364; e-mail: cpkurtz@netins.net

Reeves Wildflower Nursery. 28431 200th St., Harper, IA 52231; phone: 888-411-9767; e-mail: RayReeves@lisco.com/

Also see Iowa and Local Ecotype Seed Dealers and Land Stewardship Providers at the Iowa Prairie Network's website:
www.iowaprairienetwork.org
Integrated Roadside Vegetation Plan, Ion Exchange & Kurtz's were recommended by Mary Norton.

Michigan

Michigan Wildflower Farm. 11770 Cutler Rd., Portland, MI 48875; phone: 517-647-6010; http://michiganwildflowerfarm.com/

The Native Plant Nursery. PO Box 7841, Ann Arbor, MI 48107; phone: 734-667-3260; www.nativeplant.com/

Sandhill Farm. 11250 10 Mile Rd., Rockford, MI 49341; phone: 616-691-8214; e-mail: cherylt@iserv.net

Wetlands Nursery. 13428 Caberfae Hwy., Wellston, MI 49689; phone: 231-848-4202; http://WetlandsNursery.com/

WILDTYPE Native Plants. 900 N. Every Rd., Mason, MI 48854; phone: 517-244-1140; www.wildtypeplants.com/

Also see Nursery Contact Information, available on the Michigan Native Plant Producers Association's website: http://mnppa.org/
The Native Plant Nursery & WILDTYPE Native Plants were recommended by Nancy & Tom Small.

Minnesota

EnergyScapes, Inc. 1708 Selby Ave., St. Paul, MN 55104; phone: 612-821-9797; http://www.energyscapes.com/

Landscape Alternatives. 25316 St. Croix Trail, Shafer, MN 55074; phone: 651-257-4460; www.landscapealternatives.com/

Morning Sky Greenery. 44804 E. Highway 28, Morris, MN 56267; phone: 320-795-6234; http://www.morningskygreenery.com/

Prairie Moon Nursery. 31837 Bur Oak Lane, Winona, MN 55987; phone: 866-417-8156; www.prairiemoon.com/

Out Back Nursery. 15280 110th Street South; Hastings, MN 55033; phone: 651-438-2771; www.outbacknursery.com/

Also see Native Plant Suppliers in Minnesota, available on the website of the Minnesota Native Plant Society at http://www.dnr.state.mn.us/gardens/nativeplants/suppliers.html *Landscape Alternatives & Outback Nursery were recommended by Susan Damon.*

Missouri

Easyliving Wildflowers. PO Box 522, Willow Springs, MO 65793; phone: 417-469-2611; www.easywildflowers.com/

Flick Seed Company. PO Box 128, Kingsville, MO 64061; phone: 866-328-0494; www.seedguys.com/

Hamilton Seeds and Wildflowers. 16786 Brown Rd., Elk Creek, MO 65464; phone: 417-967-2190; www.hamiltonseed.com/

Missouri Wildflowers Nursery. 9814 Pleasant Hill Rd., Jefferson City, MO 65109; phone: 573-496-3492; www.mowildflowers.net/

Pure Air Native Seed Co. 24882 Prairie Grove Trail, Novinger, MO 63559; phone: 660-488-6849; http://www.pureairseed.com/

Also see Buyer's Guide at the website of Grow Native, a joint program of the Missouri Department of Conservation and Missouri Department of Agriculture, at www.grownative.org/

Ohio

Baker's Tree Nursery. 13895 Garfield Road, Salem, OH 44460; phone: 330-537-3903.

Companion Plants. 7247 North Coolville Ridge Rd., Athens, OH 45701; phone: 740-592-4643; www.companionplants.com/

Envirotech Consultants, Inc. 5380 TWP 143 NE, Somerset, OH 43783; phone: 740-743-1669; www.envirotechcon.com/

Land Reformers. 35703 Loop Road, Rutland, OH 45775; phone: 740-742-3478.

Ohio River Grass. 220 Wenner Street, Cincinnati, OH 45226; phone: 513-871-1158.

Land Reformers & Ohio River Grass were recommended by Christine McCullough.

Wisconsin

Agrecol Corporation. 2918 Agriculture Drive, Madison, WI 53718; phone: 608-226-2544; www.agrecol.com/

Dragonfly Gardens. 491 State Hwy. 46, Amery, WI 54001; phone: 715-268-7660; www.dragonflygardens.net/

Prairie Nursery. PO Box 306, Westfield, WI 53964; phone: 800-476-9453; www.prairienursery.com/

Prairie Seed Source. PO Box 83, North Lake, WI 53064; http://prairiebob.com/

Reeseville Ridge Nursery. 512 South Main Street, Reeseville, WI 53579; phone: 920-927-3291; http://reesevilleridgenursery.com/

Also see Native Plant Nurseries and Restoration Consultants in Wisconsin, available through the Wisconsin Department of Natural Resources, Endangered Resources Bureau; phone: 608-266-2621; http://dnr.wi.gov/org/land/er/plants/nurseries.htm Prairie Nursery was recommended by Pat Brust.

Trumpet vine is a favorite of hummingbirds.

INDEX

Barn Swallow stretch

Meeuse, Bastiaan, 103
Melampy, Michael N., 6
Mertig, Angela, 312
Meyer, Gretchen A., 5
Mills, G. Scott, 4, 22
misters, 227–228
Moretti, Anne and Patrick, 225, 228
Morris, Sean, 103
Morrison, Gordon, 3, 6 9
Morton Arboretum, 23, 143–144
mowing, 285–286
Mueller, Elizabeth and Steve, 36–37, 70, 72, 322, 336
Muir, John, 141–142, 146, 150, 152
mulch, mulching, 94, 289
Murray, Molly, 5, 160
Mutel, Cornelis F., 124

National Audubon Society, 62, 323
National Wildlife Federation, 76, 81–82, 324
National Zoo, 308
native range, definition, 17
Natural Resources Conservation Service, 66, 183
Nature Conservancy, The, 21, 78, 86, 248
neighbors, 75–77
nest box, books, 301
    dimensions, 293–294
    designs, 296–297, 299–300
North American Breeding Bird Survey, 155, 205, 303
Northington, David, 84
Norton, Mary and James, 40–41, 321, 336
Nowak, David, 336

Olin, Chauncy C., 141
openings, 288
Otto, Lorrie, 80, 309

Packard, Stephen, 78, 124
Parrish, Jeffrey D., 196
Pate, Nathan and Janet, 48, 179, 221, 228, 233, 305, 321, 336
Pauly, Wayne, 285
pesticides, 64, 66, 90, 108, 199, 293
Piaskowski, Vicki, 26, 193, 196
plants, (see also invasive plants; plant lists & tables; vegetation)
    herbaceous species, 90–92
    naming (nomenclature), xii–xiv
    native, definition, 14
    naturalized, 14
    planting, 90–93
    selecting, 77–79
    thorny, 64, 67
    woody species, 92–93
plant lists & tables
    bluebird, 147
    butterfly, 123
    clay soil, 122
    conifers, 257
    ferns, 275
    goldfinch, 45
    grasses, 136–137, 278
    hummingbird, 45, 110–113
    invasive, 28–29
    migratory bird, 200–202
    ponds, 236–237, 240–242
    prairie, 130–136, 138
    rain garden, 184–190
    rushes, 137, 279
    savanna plants, 130–136, 145, 147–148
    sedges, 137, 279
    shrubs, 210–211, 258–261
    trees, deciduous, 252–255
    vines, 263
    wetland, 184–190
    wildflowers, 130–135, 267–275
    winter, 222
    woodland, 159, 165–172

Ploch, Mandy, 179–180, 233, 234, 239, 336
ponds, 229–233
Powdermill Nature Reserve, 24
Powers, Randy, 88, 110
predators, native, 313
Project FeederWatch, 221, 305
pruning, 286–287, 291

rabbits, 310–311
Rappaport, Bret, 75
Raven, Peter H., x
rock piles, 69
rodenticides, 64, 66, 313
roosting box, 150, 215
Rosenberg, Ken, 193
Rosenzweig, Michael, 62, 83
Ross, Laurel M, 78

Salt, Steven, 311
sand, 64–65
Sands, Mike, 177, 225, 239
Sauer, Leslie J. 155, 235
Schlitz Audubon Center, 69
Schmidt, Kenneth, 23
Schmidt, Rusty, 182
Schneck, Marcus, 23
seeds, 20
septic fields, mounds, 118
Shaw, Daniel, 182
Skutch, Alexander, 102, 215
Small, Nancy and Tom, 32, 182, 230, 336
Smith, Albert, 5
snags, 68–69
soil, 71–72, 89–90, 120, 158–159
space, for birds, 71
squirrels, 316–317, 319
Steele, Eliza, 115
Steffen, Jim, 159, 160, 288
Stein, Sara, 205, 229
sun/shade, 72
Swink, Floyd, xiii, 248

ABOUT THE AUTHOR

Mariette Nowak was the director of the Wehr Nature Center of the Milwaukee County Parks system (Wisconsin) for eighteen years. Now retired, she is active with the organization Wild Ones: Native Plants, Natural Landscapes and is a board member of the Lakeland Audubon Society. She is also involved in the Walworth County Land Conservancy and the Walworth County Park Committee.

Mariette lives in East Troy, Wisconsin, with her husband Dave, and can be found out in her garden as soon as the frost is out of the ground. She is also the author of *Eve's Rib*.

Swainson's Thrush

Photo Credits

All photographs © copyright 2007 the photographers listed below.

Jack R. Bartholmai: Bird photographs on front cover, back cover, i, ii, 1, 2, 8, 9, 14, 19, 26, 34, 38, 43, 47, 50, 53, 56, 59, 60, 61, 64, 68, 76, 96, 98, 107, 109, 114, 115, 117, 118, 139, 145, 146, 149, 155, 158, 161, 164, 166, 173, 174, 177, 178, 193, 194, 195, 198, 199, 201, 205, 206, 213, 217, 219, 225, 226, 237, 245, 246, 251, 256, 279, 280, 282, 283, 292, 295, 300, 304, 306, 320, 333, 336

Robert Cashman: 78, 169

Kitty L. Clasing: 40, 123, 144, 181, 188, 228, 241, 305, 317

Susan Damon: iii, iv, 15, 30, 31, 45, 46, 48, 58 (bottom r), 83, 84, 91, 93, 96 (top), 112, 124, 190, 302, 307

EyeWire: 318

Flying Fish Graphics: 69, 126
Also: color map and garden illustrations

Brian F. Jorg: front cover bottom, 61 (top), 74, 139 (top r), 160, 162, 173 (top, bottom r)

Joanne Kline: 22

Christine McCullough: 52, 163, 171, 322

Elizabeth Mueller: 37 (both), 38 (top)

James & Mary Norton: 41 (both), 58 (bottom l)

David J. Nowak: xii, 29, 43 (bottom), 44, 55, 57, 58 (top), 71, 81, 88, 101, 106, 121, 128, 139 (top l), 141, 142, 154, 172, 197, 204, 230, 232, 234, 239, 244, 248, 249, 266, 281, 284, 310, 312, 335

Mariette Nowak: 3, 11, 13, 18, 23, 102, 207, 211, 214, 224, 262, 265, 331

Nathan Pate: 50, 51, 54 (both)

Mandy Ploch: 179

Tom Small: 42

Kim L. Vollmer: front cover large, 17, 20, 32, 34 (top), 35 (all), 97, 137, 178 (bottom l)